MEDICINE BEFORE SCIENCE

This book offers an introduction to the history of university-trained physicians from the Middle Ages to the eighteenth-century Enlightenment. These were the elite, in reputation and rewards, and they were successful. Yet we can form little idea of their clinical effectiveness, and to modern eyes their theory and practice often seem bizarre. But the historical evidence is that they were judged on other criteria, and the argument of this book is that these physicians helped to construct the expectations of society – and met them accordingly.

The main focus is on the European Latin tradition of medicine, reconstructed from ancient sources and relying heavily on natural philosophy for its explanatory power. This philosophy collapsed in the 'scientific revolution', and left the learned and rational doctor in crisis. The book concludes with an examination of how this crisis was met – or avoided – in different parts of Europe during the Enlightenment. Historiographically, the book is directed at how the technical content of traditional medicine can inform its social functions.

ROGER FRENCH was Lecturer in the Department of History and Philosophy of Science, University of Cambridge, and a Fellow of Clare Hall. He taught in the universities of Leicester, Aberdeen and Cambridge, and for twenty years was Director of the Wellcome Unit for the History of Medicine at Cambridge. His publications include *William Harvey's Natural Philosophy* (1994), *Ancient Natural History* (1994) and *Gentile da Foligno and Scholasticism* (2001).

D0217379

MEDICINE BEFORE SCIENCE

The Rational and Learned Doctor from the Middle Ages to the Enlightenment

ROGER FRENCH

CAMBRIDGE
UNIVERSITY PRESS

PUBLISHED BY THE PRESS SYNDICATE OF THE UNIVERSITY OF CAMBRIDGE
The Pitt Building, Trumpington Street, Cambridge CB2 1RP, United Kingdom

CAMBRIDGE UNIVERSITY PRESS
The Edinburgh Building, Cambridge, CB2 2RU, UK
40 West 20th Street, New York, NY 10011-4211, USA
477 Williamstown Road, Port Melbourne, VIC 3207, Australia
Ruiz de Alarcón 13, 28014 Madrid, Spain
Dock House, The Waterfront, Cape Town 8001, South Africa

http://www.cambridge.org

First published 2003

Printed in the United Kingdom at the University Press, Cambridge

Typeface Adobe Garamond 11/12.5 pt   System LaTeX 2ε [TB]

A catalogue record for this book is available from the British Library

ISBN 0 521 80977 0 hardback
ISBN 0 521 00761 5 paperback

Contents

The publisher wishes to acknowledge the valuable assistance given by Dr Cornelius O'Boyle in preparing this book for publication, following the death of Dr Roger French in May 2002.

Introduction

This book presents an argument rather than a narrative survey. The premiss of the argument is that from the high Middle Ages onwards, physicians built up their trade into an elaborate professional stucture, endowed it with an even more elaborate theory, and contrived to present it with great authority. Some physicians became rich, others famous and powerful, as teachers and practitioners. Great households retained physicians as part of the 'family' and towns sought out university-trained physicians for contract-based employment.[1]

Many physicians were, then, *successful*. We have no way of measuring their clinical success, for that would be to ask modern questions and expect modern answers from inappropriate historical material. Moreover, our instinct is to believe that old medicine was less effective than our own, which is so conspicuously scientific. Indeed, from a modern viewpoint pre-scientific medicine can look ridiculous in its theory and bizarre and disgusting in its remedies. How, then, did physicians in the past meet the expectations of their society, and so succeed?[2]

The argument of this book is that they did so partly by helping to create those expectations, which were accordingly easier to satisfy. The fully trained university doctor had two main methods of cultivating his image as a capable medical man, his reason and his learning. These two characteristics will often be capitalised in this book to show that they are technical terms in a historical sense. The Learned and Rational Doctor was

[1] See for example Michael R. McVaugh, *Medicine before the Plague. Practitioners and their Patients in the Crown of Aragon 1285–1345*, Cambridge (Cambridge University Press), 1993; and Luis García-Ballester's introduction to Luis García-Ballester, Roger French, Jon Arrizabalaga and Andrew Cunningham, eds., *Practical Medicine from Salerno to the Black Death*, Cambridge (Cambridge University Press), 1994.

[2] As Nancy Siraisi observes, a doctor's 'success' in the Middle Ages consisted of prolixity of authorship, fame and senior teaching positions. Success in attracting students into the *studium* was a financial benefit to the town, and on this basis, for example, Taddeo Alderotti received privileges from the civic authorities in Bologna. See Siraisi's 'Medical scholasticism and the historian' and 'Two models of medical culture, Pietro d'Abano and Taddeo Alderotti', in Nancy Siraisi, *Medicine and the Italian Universities 1250–1600*, Leiden (Brill), 2001, pp. 140–56 and 79–99, respectively.

'learned' in a sense that we do not now recognise as valid in any medical or practical sense, for it was largely a question of acquiring the knowledge of the ancients. He was 'rational' not in a sense of reaching the truth, but in the simpler sense of using arguments, which were largely dialectical and philosophical, also of ancient origin and not necessarily valid to us.[3]

Whatever we think about the validity of these attributes of the university-trained physician, or of his clinical practice, we should note that it took about as long to train a doctor in the high Middle Ages as it does now. He therefore had a great deal of knowledge and many modes of handling it, which he could use in persuading an audience that he was an effective practitioner. He used it primarily in constructing a story about his kind of practitioner, a Good Story (also sometimes capitalised here) that he could tell his patients, his pupils, the powerful and the legislators about the effectiveness of his medicine and about his right to practise it.

We need not suppose that such a physician was always coldly cynical about telling the Story and developing his image. Professional attitudes – and medical ethics – tended to develop along lines that had the *effect* of benefiting the profession, but this was not always recognised by the individual: properly professional or ethical ways of behaving are rarely absorbed as part of a rationalist training.

Although not a narrative survey, this account of medicine before it became scientific is based on a chronology that runs from the high Middle Ages to the Enlightenment. There are a number of reasons that make this a self-contained story to tell. One of them is that although much of the medicine in this period was based on ancient doctrines, there is a much greater cultural link between us and the Middle Ages than between the Middle Ages and antiquity. Indeed, much of the development of medicine in the period was due to the slow and difficult business of recovering and trying to understand ancient medicine; while between us and the men who did this there was no cultural hiatus, no second 'Dark Age'. This means that although a good deal is said here about ancient medicine, it is not as a background or early history of the topic, but as the material out of which later physicians constructed their own medicine. That is, the attempt has

---

[3] It also needs to be said that 'rational' is not used here to mean the opposite of 'superstitious', for superstition is simply someone else's belief. If that belief includes gods or demons that cause disease, then it is rational to do what is necessary to placate them. 'Rational' is also sometimes used to mean 'natural' (as with Greek ideas about the causation of disease) as opposed to 'supernatural' (as in Egypt). No such opposition is implied here. See James Longrigg, 'Medicine in the classical world', in Irvine Loudon, ed., *Western Medicine. An Illustrated History*, Oxford (Oxford University Press), 1997, pp. 25–39. See also Longrigg's *Greek Rational Medicine. Philosophy and Medicine from Alcmaeon to the Alexandrians*, London (Routledge), 1993.

been made to look at ancient medicine through the eyes of the medieval doctors, or at least to emphasise what they found important in it.

A word should be said too about the *terminus ad quem* of this account of medical history. Some historians would argue that 'science' began in the seventeenth century and others that it was a product of the nineteenth; the reasons for choosing the Enlightenment, a deliberately vague term, are given below. A related question asks when medicine itself became scientific. A possible, although rather extreme answer is 'not until the last years of the nineteenth century' when the science of bacteriology gave medicine a demonstrable power of curing certain infectious diseases. Certainly this power of medicine gave the doctor a new authority, and one that he used in examining the nature of the history of medicine: it was his subject, after all, he was the master of it, and it seemed natural that he should know best how it came to arrive at its present state. This has been the prevailing historiography in the history of medicine as a discipline until comparatively recently, and it is still present in a virulent form in the sub-discipline of retrospective diagnoses. This book is an attempt to abandon the present-centredness of much of medical history, which is why the story ends in the eighteenth century.

Indeed, it is equally arguable that some features of science were present in medical research in the eighteenth century. The medical experiment, recognised as part of the ancient medical tradition by anatomists in the sixteenth century, was central to the generation of new medical knowledge in the seventeenth century, and was adopted by the natural philosophers of the time.[4] By the eighteenth century, systematic experimentation (largely on animals), statistical methods and clinical trials were recognised procedures for the validation of medical knowledge.

But a good story is defined not by its boundaries, but by its content. The story of this book is about the relationship of medicine to natural philosophy – *Aristotelian* natural philosophy. Aristotelian natural philosophy was known to and used extensively by Galen, the Greek physician to Marcus Aurelius and Commodus in Rome, and formed the basis of university natural philosophy from the early years of the thirteenth century in Oxford and from the middle of the century in Paris.[5] It retained its

---

[4] On the medical experiment see Roger French, *William Harvey's Natural Philosophy*, Cambridge (Cambridge University Press), 1994, esp. ch. 10.

[5] The Parisian statutes can be found in H. Denifle and E. Chatelain, eds., *Chartularium Universitatis Parisiensis*, 4 vols., Paris, 1889–97. Student notes of natural philosophy lectures can be found in a number of manuscripts of the Aristotelian *corpus vetustius*, which were annotated in an English hand in Oxford. See especially London, British Library, MS Royal 12 G II.

place as the university man's means of understanding the natural world until the seventeenth century in Protestant countries, and longer in some Catholic countries. The Learned and Rational Physician had based his Good Story almost wholly on traditional natural philosophy. Philosophy was the basis of the theory of medicine. It supplied the doctor with a series of unassailable axioms about how the natural world and the body worked. It offered a method of extending these principles down to the particulars of medicine and its practice. The logic employed in natural philosophy not only demonstrated the solidity of these principles but provided the doctor with a means of convincing other people that the philosophical doctor's philosophical medicine was the best possible. When and where traditional natural philosophy collapsed under the attack of the new philosophers the Learned and Rational Doctor was at a crisis.

The ways in which doctors reacted to this crisis combine to form the thread that links together the narratives of this book. It is a thread by which we may link the internal details of the physicians' scheme of things – the concern of traditional intellectual history – to the social uses (as well as therapeutic applications) of that knowledge. Historiographically, then, this is not an 'internal' history of medical 'ideas' nor can it claim to be an 'external' history of the profession; rather, it attempts to show that we can read the technical detail of medical literature and 'listen' for the effect that it would have had on the intended audience. However subtle the arguments of the rational doctor and however detailed his learning, we must not slip into the error of believing that both were sterile, for every word could have an effect on his listeners or readers, generally an effect that reflected well on the doctor.

Medical history has its traditional heroes, from Vesalius to Harvey and Boerhaave, and although these too are linked by the thread, it is not the intention here to retell well-known accounts of such men. There are other figures who perhaps better illustrate the theme of this book because they were less heroic and more ordinary or more typical of some group. In what follows we shall proceed partly by figures who are examples and we shall look at them in a little more detail than would be usual in a survey of this size.[6] This approach means too that the *modus tractandi* here is not

---

[6] This book is aimed at a readership of 'senior students' and is not therefore a narrow research monograph. I have, however, included a 'research' component in reading the texts of the men I have chosen as examples. Critics will doubtless point out that these are not important examples. But 'important' here is an attribute of traditional evolutionary history, and carries little meaning in the kind of story I am trying to tell.

a magisterial survey of the secondary literature, most of which has been concerned with medical progress. Such men as are used for examples here have often been ignored because of a perceived lack of a 'contribution' to the development of medicine, and tend nowadays to be left to the obscurity of their Latin treatises.

Indeed, an alternative way of presenting the argument of this book is that it deals with the *Latin tradition* of European medicine. Everyone agreed that the Father of Medicine was the Greek Hippocrates, but Greek was a language essentially lost to Western Europe after the fall of Rome. A Latin tradition might have started with the Greek Galen, who taught in imperial Rome and became physician to the emperor at a time when educated Romans increasingly learned Greek; or a few years earlier with Celsus, who wrote in a widely admired style of Latin. But the bulk of Galen's work was not recovered until the high Middle Ages and Celsus was unknown until the early fifteenth century. It was from a Latin translation of Hippocrates and Galen that the Western doctors put together their medical tradition and it was the Latin tradition that came to an end in the Enlightenment with the collapse of traditional natural philosophy and Galenic theory and the replacement of Latin as a medium of education with the vernaculars.

Looked at in this way continuities are as important as novelties. When publishers of the early sixteenth century printed huge commentaries that had been written two centuries before, they were making a very sizeable investment which could be recouped only in the market which fed the enduring programme of the schools. The same can be said of Galenic texts published a century after Harvey had convinced some doctors that Galenic theory was untenable. Even the editions of Hippocrates and Galen by Littré and Kühn in the nineteenth century indicate that classical learning was still a worthwhile attribute for the gentlemanly (and pre-germ-theory) doctor. The forces of conservatism were considerable and varied from place to place and in different groups of doctors.

It is a rash historian who attempts to cover as wide a chronological period as this, where many specialists have spent careers on parts of it. Inevitably this book contains shortcomings. As Goldsmith says in introducing *The Vicar of Wakefield*, 'There are an hundred faults in this thing, and an hundred things might be said to prove them beauties'. But he proceeds robustly, 'But it is needless'. To adapt his defence, a book may claim to tell an interesting if imperfect story, 'or it may be very dull without a single absurdity'. Goldsmith is not wholly without relevance here, for he had been, among many other things, a student at the famous medical school at Edinburgh, with which this book effectively ends. It was a school on which he bestowed no lustre whatever; and of his brief excursion into medical practice his biographers note only that he once prescribed a medicine of such horrific strength that the apothecary refused to make it up. Here is an allegory of the lost authority of the doctor.

PART I

Sources

CHAPTER I

Hippocrates and the philosophers

MEDICAL WISDOM

When the medieval doctor looked into the past for the beginnings of his own profession, what he found was the figure of Hippocrates, the Father of Medicine in the medical tradition from the Middle Ages to the Enlightenment. Modern scholarship has not revealed much about the historical Hippocrates or which of the 'Hippocratic' works were written by him,[1] but the medieval doctor felt more secure in his knowledge. The Hippocratic works gave him a number of things. There was technical advice in a practical subject, which told him what to do and what to expect. For instance, the *corpus* includes works that explain how to reduce dislocations and how to bandage wounds.[2] The Hippocratic works were also valuable because they *were* Hippocratic, that is, ancient and authoritative in an age that revered antiquity. These first two chapters are not directly concerned with the first of these aspects of antiquity, the technical content of Greek medicine and philosophy. They are not, that is, a background to or an early history of a professional activity developed during the Middle Ages and beyond. Rather, they present an image of the medieval and later perception of antiquity, a construction (however false in our historical terms) within the

---

[1] Hippocrates was mentioned by Aristotle and Plato who says (*Protagoras* 311b) that he taught medicine for a fee. In the *Phaedrus* (270a) the Platonic Socrates argues that rhetoric is like medicine, for they define the nature of the soul and the body respectively; Hippocrates 'the Asclepiad' is credited with the declaration that the body can be understood only as a whole. Biographies of Hippocrates were written by Soranus and Suidas. Tradition has it that he was born in 460 BC. Most of the works attributed to Hippocrates were written between 430 and 330 BC, and some later. See G. E. R. Lloyd, ed., *Hippocratic Writings*, Harmondsworth (Pelican Classics), 1978, p. 9 and W. H. S. Jones' general introduction in vol. I of the Loeb Library series (see note 2 below). For a recent account of the historical Hippocrates and the *corpus*, see Jacques Jouanna, *Hippocrates*, trans. M. B. DeBevoise, Baltimore (The Johns Hopkins University Press), 1999 (first published as *Hippocrate* in 1992).

[2] The Greek text of the Hippocratic works, with an English translation by W. H. S. Jones and E. T. Withington, may be found conveniently in the Loeb Library series: *Hippocrates* (vols. I–IV), London (Heinemann) and Cambridge, Mass. (Harvard University Press), 1962–8.

Latin tradition and on which the later Western doctors based their actions.
It is not a story of beginnings but of resources.

What the medieval doctor found in Hippocrates was primarily medical
wisdom. This was the first kind of medical learning used by the Rational and
Learned Doctor in the West; we shall meet the other forms below. It went
hand in hand with a useful knowledge of what natural things were good
for this or that disease, or part of the body. Hippocratic medical wisdom
was found primarily in the text called the *Aphorisms*. This had probably continued in circulation during the earlier Middle Ages, and was certainly translated into Latin as the Eastern Empire tried to regain control of
Italy.[3]

The medical wisdom of the *Aphorisms* is of a particular kind. It is im-
parted with great confidence and authority and appears to be the distillation of long experience by a retentive and perceptive mind. Indeed, the first
aphorism of them all declares that the art of medicine requires much time
to acquire and that, in comparison, life is short. It was generally agreed later
on in the West that such had been the clarity of Hippocrates' mind that
he had achieved this medical wisdom without the aid of other arts such
as dialectic and philosophy, which had not then been invented and which
later came to be such a prerequisite of learning medicine. In our terms this
air of original authority of the Hippocratic writings may well be because
they include some of the earliest written medical material.[4] No doubt they
reflect an earlier oral tradition, but there were no earlier books to be used as
an authority or as a basis of discussion, which became important features of
the later Western tradition. Possibly the Hippocratic *corpus* is a collection
of early Greek medical writings made and named by a librarian, possibly in Alexandria; possibly the collection is itself the remains of a medical
library.[5] At all events, literate doctors from the middle of the fifth century
were discussing the nature of medicine and using rhetoric to persuade their
readers of the superiority of their own medicine in a competitive situation.
Public lectures could also be used,[6] but 'it is clear that they felt that the

---

[3] See A. Beccaria, *I Codici di Medicina del Periodo Presalernitano*, Rome (Storia e Letteratura), 1956,
esp. p. 6.

[4] On literacy, see I. M. Lonie, 'Literacy and the development of Hippocratic medicine', in *Formes de
Pensée dans la Collection Hippocratique. Actes du IV ͤ Colloque International Hippocratique (Lausanne
21–26 Septembre 1981)*, ed. F. Lasserre and P. Mudry, Geneva (Librarie Droz), 1983, 145–61. The first
prose book in medicine seems to date from the middle of the sixth century, and the doctors were the
first to create a distinct body of technical literature.

[5] As suggested by Jones in the Loeb Library series, vol. 1.

[6] For example, the Hippocratic *Nature of Man* opens with a reference to public debates on medical
topics, from which a victor emerged. The context is whether 'man' could be reduced to the few
elements of the philosophers or the few humours of some physicians. (Loeb Library series, vol. 4.)

written word offered the possibility of a wider audience, and an enhanced authority'.[7]

Medical aphorisms, as wisdom, share features with other forms of expression. Like proverbs and the words of oracles, they speak with their own authority without supporting reasons and are open to the implication that this authority depends on either long experience or some kind of revealed knowledge. It can be argued that transmitting knowledge in this way is characteristic of pre-literate societies. Oral transmission in a complex business like farming has to be precise and not subject to accumulated errors. *Structured* oral expression helps here: the verse of Homer was famously committed to memory, and terse and expressive proverbs and aphorisms are memorable and useful. Pliny in imperial Rome reports some agricultural aphorisms of this kind. One of them was to have pruned the vines before the first cuckoo is heard (leave it too late and the vines bleed alarmingly. Pliny says that the farmer who *did* leave it too late might be embarrassed by his neighbours making jeering cuckoo noises at him).[8] Proverbs also often have a rhymed structure to give them memorability. 'Sell in May and go away' used to be a stock-market proverb reminding the broker of the slack summer season. 'Oak before ash and we'll have a splash; ash before oak and we'll have a soak' is a rustic proverb of prediction based on the bursting of the buds. (It is also an English joke, because the rain will come anyway.)

PREDICTION

Thus an important feature of proverbs, aphorisms and oracles is that many of them are predictive. 'When sleep puts an end to delirium, it is a good sign' is a predictive aphorism. The third aphorism of the collection is both paradoxical and predictive when it says (at first sight) that good health in athletes is dangerous because it can only change for the worse. In medical terms prediction was very important. The doctor gained a good reputation by being able to predict the outcome of a case, and he avoided a bad one by refusing to take on a case where the patient was clearly going to die. The Hippocratic *corpus* contains a text devoted to medical prediction, *Prognosis*. The Greek author was quite explicit about the benefits to one's reputation from correct prognosis, but the medieval version read by aspiring doctors down to the sixteenth century was much more so. It opens directly by

---

[7] See John Vallance, 'Doctors in the library: the strange tale of Apollonius the bookworm and other stories', in Roy MacLeod, ed., *The Library of Alexandria. Centre of Learning in the Ancient World*, London and New York (I. B. Tauris), 2000, pp. 95–113, at p. 99.

[8] *Historia Naturalis* XVIII. 66.

advising the doctor who wants 'glory' and 'lots of friends' to be careful in prognosis.[9] These are important words, for we are looking at the figure of Hippocrates through the eyes of later Western doctors as they tried to recover ancient medicine. The Greek text does not have these words. Possibly they were introduced into the text when it was paraphrased in Arabic or when the Arabic was translated into Latin.[10] At all events they provided authoritative justification for medieval doctors to seek monetary rewards from their practice of medicine. It was a message reinforced by *Decorum*, where the rewards of proper 'ethical' behaviour are said to include glory.[11]

Prognosis goes on to explain that medical 'foresight' is more than predicting an outcome and includes giving an account also of the patient's present symptoms and those that he has suffered in the past. It is very helpful, the text says, if the doctor can describe past symptoms that the patient himself has forgotten about or not mentioned to the doctor. It was all good advertising for the doctor's skills, and *Prognosis* is quite clear that the purpose is to impress the patient. An impressed patient trusts his doctor, gives himself more readily into his hands, and obeys him.[12]

In other words, the doctor has persuaded the patient that he knows about the kind of thing the patient is suffering from and can guide him through it: he has told the patient what in this book we shall call the Good Story.

Prognosis then dwells on the uncertainty of the outcome in acute cases. Perhaps the patient has delayed too long before calling the doctor. Perhaps the disease is severe, and the patient will not last the day. It was vitally important to foresee death because in predicting it, the text says, the doctor will escape blame. For this purpose there follows the famous *facies Hippocratica*, the appearance of the face of a dying person, with its sunken eyes and sharp nose. As with the *Aphorisms*, the descriptions in *Prognosis* are brief pieces of medical wisdom, seeming to derive from long experience.

---

[9] *Omnis qui medicine artis studio seu gloriam seu delectibilem amicorum consequi desiderat copiam: adeo prudentum regulis rationem suam muniat. Videtur mihi ut sit ex melioribus rebus ut medicus utatur previsione.* See the *Articella*, Venice, 1483, f. 47r.

[10] They are not included in the new translations from the Greek by Cornarius and Copus. See *Hippocratis Coi Medicorum longe Principis, Opera quae ad nos extant Omnia*, trans. I. Cornarius, Basel, 1557, p. 617; *Hippocratis Coi Medicorum Omnium longe Principis, Opera*, Basel (Cratander), 1526, p. 355. On the Arabic paraphrase, see C. O'Boyle, *The Art of Medicine. Medical Teaching at the University of Paris, 1250–1400*, Leiden (Brill), 1998, p. 90.

[11] See also V. Nutton, 'Beyond the Hippocratic Oath', in *Doctors and Ethics: The Earlier Historical Setting of Professional Ethics*, ed. A. Wear, J. Geyer-Kordesch and R. French, Amsterdam (Rodopi), 1993, pp. 10–37.

[12] *[E]st dignus ut de eo credatur quod est potens scire res egrorum ita ut illud provocet infirmos: vel sit fiducia ad confidendum: et committendum se in manibus medici. Articella*, Venice (H. Liechtenstein), 1483, f. 47r.

Like oracles, medical aphorisms and prognostic advice were often expressed in terse and even obscure language. Ambiguity in an oracle left room for interpretation after the prediction had or had not come true, without destroying the credibility of oracles in general. The practising doctor had to be more direct, but generally left himself some room for manoeuvre after the event. What was important in this case, and in the terse language, was *interpretation*. Sometimes an aphorism omits a verb, or uses a pronoun in place of a noun, so that we are left to guess who 'he' is. Medical teachers found that aphorisms had to be explained, all the more so when they had to be translated out of old-fashioned Greek into Latin.

But the most important form of interpretation that aphorisms seemed to need was the giving of reasons behind the situation so curtly described. How do winds from the south make people deaf? Why do acute diseases come to a crisis in fourteen days? Why was it that those whose bowels were loose in youth became constipated in age? Every age that followed the Hippocratic period had its own preferred reasons for the truth of the aphorisms (and explaining an aphorism was part of medical graduation down to the eighteenth century). In an important sense aphorisms were not *rational* statements, but declarations of medical wisdom. They were not of course irrational in our sense, but were conspicuously without *arguments*.[13] The rational doctor, in the sense we are using in this book, supplied his own arguments to the aphorisms to show why they were true or what must have been in the mind of Hippocrates when he wrote them. We shall see below that the most important of the rational interpreters of Hippocrates was Galen, the Greek doctor in imperial Rome.

GROUPS OF DOCTORS

In these ways, medical knowledge – wisdom – could be used directly to treat a patient and less directly to enhance the reputation of the doctor. It is often remarked that there was no system of licensing doctors in the ancient world, and therefore the doctor's reputation and that of his teacher were very important.[14] There was competition in the medical marketplace. If, like Hippocrates, the Greek doctor taught medicine for money, then potentially at least, he competed with other teachers to attract pupils. Naturally, a

---

[13] Lloyd calls the *Aphorisms* one of the 'scrapbooks or notebooks' of the Hippocratic collection. Lloyd, *Hippocratic Writings*, p. 11.

[14] The reputation of his school was also important for an aspiring city physician; Alexandria came to be important in this respect. See O. Temkin, *Hippocrates in a World of Pagans and Christians*, Baltimore and London (The Johns Hopkins University Press), 1991, p. 20.

good reputation always helped. Practice among fee-paying patients held out greater rewards and some Greek doctors became very rich, whether as physicians to the rich and powerful or to the Greek city-states.[15] Democedes of Croton earned over thirty times as much as the average skilled worker.[16] Such men were clearly successful, and when Democedes moved from Aegina to Athens his salary increased, no doubt in line with his reputation. But not all doctors agreed on what kind of business they were in, how patients should be treated or how reputations should be maintained. There is abundant evidence that Greek doctors belonged to different 'schools', whether schools of thought, cliques or confraternities, and articulated their differences.

One particular aspect of this is especially important as we unravel the process by which medieval doctors tried to reconstruct and emulate the medicine of the ancients. Like-minded members of a group naturally believe that their common beliefs and practices are superior to those of a rival group, particularly if the groups are competing in a calling such as medicine. It can easily follow that a rival group's success can be seen as being achieved by dubious means. In the case of medicine it would equally have followed that their medicine, being of the 'wrong' kind, was incapable of being practised ethically, because it damaged the patient.

In fact, the Hippocratic collection of texts contains some that deal with the ethics of medical practice and teaching. There are two ways of reading such texts. The traditional internal reading of the texts rests on the (not unreasonable) assumption that there are some general or absolute ethics in the relationship between people. In Renaissance editions of the Hippocratic *corpus*, the ethical works were often placed first, as though they formed an introduction setting out the moral basis of the practice of medicine.[17] But it is also possible to read these texts 'externally' by considering who they were directed at and what they were designed to achieve. Let us take as a first example the text called *Precepts*.[18] It is addressed to the 'brothers' of a 'family of physicians', that is, to a self-defined group. Part of the motivation of the group was altruistic, for 'where there is love of man, there is also love of the art',[19] but it would not be unduly cynical to guess that the physician also loved his fee. The author advises against negotiating the fee when first meeting the patient, for worry about providing it and the

---

[15] Public physicians were chosen by a panel of laymen.   [16] Lloyd, *Hippocratic Writings*, p. 19.

[17] See, for example, Cratander's edition. A similar sequence was maintained into the eighteenth century, the end of the period considered in this book. See, for example, *Magnus Hippocrates Cous Prosperi Martiani Medici Romani Notationibus Explicatus*, Padua, 1719. The ethical works drew the attention of medieval doctors at a comparatively late date. They were not discussed by Parisian masters, for example, until about 1400, and they appear in the *Articella* only in the late and printed versions.

[18] Loeb Library series, vol. I, p. 312.   [19] *Ibid.*, p. 318.

possible departure of the physician will make him worse: better to press for the fee when the patient has recovered. Indeed, forgoing the fee from a poor patient is recommended for 'brothers of the art' because the gain in reputation will be greater than the financial reward. Although a personal choice, the brothers of the same fraternity would have gained from such a reputation.

The most important of the ethical works is the *Oath*.[20] It has been treated as an expression of high ethical ideals, on a level that gives it a timeless validity, and for this reason has often been revived. It was an oath sworn by a new doctor at graduation down to the time when medicine became scientific.[21] But it is also clearly the product of a group of doctors with a particular kind of medicine, one that was atypical of ancient medicine in general.[22] It is in fact a document of entry. The candidate or new recruit who swore the oath was agreeing to a set of rules that governed the group he was joining. The rules of such a group are its *ethics*, and while some of the rules may well be designed to benefit others outside the group, the effect of the ethical rules of a group is the survival of the group. The individual, after all, joins the group to enjoy the privileges it can secure by being an organised group; this may entail some sacrifice, but collaboration with fellow-workers generally brings benefits. The long-term beneficiary of such ethics is the group itself.[23]

The medical man who swore the Hippocratic *Oath* did so by appeal to Apollo and Aesculapius, so probably he was joining a fraternity that was partly religious; perhaps the members believed that medicine was originally a gift from the gods. He swore to treat his teacher as a father and to teach his teacher's sons as he would his own. This seems to reflect a father-to-son type of education, and the new doctor was entering an arrangement where the ethics of family responsibility were added to those of religion. He swore to teach other incomers, provided that they followed the rules, that is, became

---

[20] See L. Edelstein, *Ancient Medicine*, Baltimore (The Johns Hopkins University Press), 1967, which includes earlier papers, especially that of 1943 on the *Oath*.

[21] Thus the *Oath* is a 'deathless gem' for Jacques Jouanna: 'The birth of Western medical art', in M. D. Grmek, ed., *Western Medical Thought from Antiquity to the Middle Ages*, trans. A. Shugaar, Cambridge, Mass. and London (Harvard University Press), 1998, pp. 22–71, at p. 63.

[22] Edelstein argues that the *Oath* is Pythagorean in origin; Darrel W. Amundsen, *Medicine, Society and Faith in the Ancient and Medieval Worlds*, Baltimore and London (The Johns Hopkins University Press), 1996, p. 41 points out that it was little known in the ancient world before the coming of Christianity.

[23] Again, this is not to deny personal or corporate altruism, but what is prominent in the historical records is the physicians' advice to each other on how to maintain a reputation. 'Many, if not most, of the ethical principles expressed in the medical literature were motivated by the physician's concern for his reputation': see Amundsen, *Medicine, Society and Faith*, p. 35.

members of the family. He also swore not to give to patients substances that could be used by them to commit suicide or procure abortions. Was this a lofty expression of eternal ethical values? Some historians have treated it as such, but we have to remember that there have been times and places when suicide, abortion and even infanticide have been acceptable and thus not ethically problematic. Suicide in particular was rarely censured in the ancient world.[24] Whatever the intention of the author of the *Oath*, we can see that the external effect of these prohibitions might have been to enhance the reputation of the group of doctors who swore to obey them. An abortion might leave an aggrieved father, denied his legal right to his child. The family of a suicide victim might feel the tragedy had been avoidable. These were the people who might, or might not, call in medical help again, and the doctors needed a fixed code of behaviour. Some doctors were itinerant: they needed guidance on the properties and diseases of different locations (supplied in the text *Airs, Waters and Places*),[25] and they needed to leave behind a good image so that the itinerant doctors who followed them would also benefit from the high esteem in which Hippocratic doctors were generally held.

The converse of ethics seen in this light is the Greek doctor's need to recognise hopeless cases, so that he could avoid them.[26] This looks timelessly *un*ethical to us, but it meant that the doctor could avoid being linked to failure, that is, death. Greek prognosis was not only a matter of predicting an outcome; it also involved diagnosis in the sense of persuading the patient that the doctor knew about the condition itself. In describing the symptoms to the patient, perhaps symptoms that the patient had forgotten to mention, the doctor could make a display of his technical knowledge that would impress the patient and family. This knowledge was valuable. Indeed, it was a stock-in-trade that the doctor used in two ways: to treat his patients and to maintain the reputation of the group to which he belonged. Some groups were aware of this to the extent of keeping their medical knowledge secret. The father-to-son education of the *Oath* and the strict rules about who could be taught imply that medical knowledge was a family secret. The Hippocratic text called *Law* suggests that medicine was originally a gift of the gods and that knowledge of it had to be protected from the profane. A

---

[24] Amundsen, *Medicine, Society and Faith*, p. 38.   [25] See Lloyd, *Hippocratic Writings*, p. 15.

[26] See *The Art*, in vol. 2 of the Loeb edition of *Hippocrates*, ed. W. H. S. Jones, London (Heineman), 1923, pp. 185–217, chs. 3 and 8. This is another polemical text, against an unknown critic. The identification of hopeless cases was an important characteristic of the author's kind of medicine, and his refusal to tackle them was an important criticism. In Cratander's edition of the Hippocratic *corpus*, *The Art* stands in first place, as if defining what Hippocratic medicine was.

number of the ethical works carry the message 'holy things should be given only to holy men'. Professional secrecy, the refusal to take on hopeless cases and the management of prognosis for professional gain were all devices to enhance the reputation of the doctors and to form the expectations of the public.

We can usefully glance at another of the Hippocratic ethical works, *Decorum*.[27] This sets out what is decent for the good doctor to do. He must, for example, dress modestly and not be too elegant or conspicuous. It was an article of ethics that came to be copied in the Renaissance in a fairly uncomplicated way, simply on the authority of Hippocrates. Later doctors may have seen the utility of modesty for creating an image or reputation, but we must for once go beyond later perceptions of the Hippocratics to the circumstances of the Greek text. It soon becomes clear on reading *Decorum* that it is a partisan document. The tract is aimed against another group of medical men, who profess and practise another kind of medicine. Necessarily the two groups had different ethics in the sense in which we are using the term. To our author the other group seemed obviously not ethical or 'decorous'. From his attacks on this other group we can learn a little about its characteristics. That the members of the group wore 'ostentatious' clothing means most likely that they dressed with studied elegance. From other complaints by our author we can conclude that they also had great powers of persuasion. Perhaps this was evident in the public disputations that the Greeks used to arrange in order to judge between speakers. At all events, this is the nub of the matter: the two groups were in competition. *Decorum* says that the other doctors appealed especially to the young, which might imply that pupils were being poached by the other group. They are sophists, says *Decorum*, giving them the no doubt gratuitous image of claiming to be able to teach anything for a fee (and so teaching nothing properly).

PHILOSOPHY

So far we have seen some of the uses to which medical *wisdom* could be put, particularly the authoritative and experiential wisdom of aphorisms. We can distinguish this from the technical medical *knowledge*, perhaps of divine origin, that was a stock-in-trade. Both were kinds of medical learning that characterised our Learned Doctor, and both were used by later European

---

[27] O. Temkin dates the text to the first century AD: *Hippocrates in a World of Pagans and Christians*, Baltimore and London (The Johns Hopkins University Press), 1991, p. 25.

doctors in trying to re-establish ancient medicine. But our Learned Doctor
was also Rational in the sense indicated above, and he drew this too from
the ancient world. The use of *argument* in medicine in the high Middle
Ages was taken directly or indirectly from Aristotle, a circumstance we
examine next. For the medical man, Aristotle's style of argument was most
interesting in the context of natural philosophy, and the theory of medicine
was to become almost wholly Aristotelian in its principles.

But the situation was very different for the early Greek doctor. Returning
to *Decorum*, it finally becomes clear that the enemy were doctors who based
their medicine on natural philosophy. They invoked grand principles of
change, common to the macrocosm and microcosm; they denied the role
of the gods; they held that all physical change was wholly natural and intelligible; and they claimed that the number of principles or causes of change
were few. This was all very different from the medicine of texts such as
Decorum and *Ancient Medicine* and other works ascribed to Hippocrates.
We have seen that the *Aphorisms* and *Prognosis* do not deal with physical
causes at all and are implicitly based on the accumulation of human experience. The author of *Ancient Medicine* likewise accepted the superiority of
long experience over a few imagined physical causes, and asserted that far
from being godless, medicine had originally been born with divine help.
'Ancient' medicine was primarily dietetic and had begun with a study of
the diet of the ill and grew, indeed was still growing, with the accumulated
experience of the difficult business of how different foods affected different
people. The art indeed was long, life was short and judgement difficult. In
contrast, the physical principles of the new philosophy were of but recent
origin. It is absurd, says the author of *Ancient Medicine*, to explain medicine
and indeed the whole world on the basis of the four elementary qualities,
the Hot, Cold, Dry and Wet. These were the few physical principles of
the philosophers, the active powers that governed the four elements, Earth,
Air, Fire and Water.[28] For the author of *Ancient Medicine* the world was a
much more complex place. It was the many and subtle qualities of foods,
like the bitter, salt and acid, which affected the body for good or evil; the
elementary qualities were not causal, for a fever patient may feel hot but
shiver with cold; a cold bath makes the patient glow with heat on being
dried; frostbite is like a burn and only becomes apparent when the patient
is warm again. In a complex world, medical experience was everything, for

---

[28] *Regimen* I for example is a philosophical-medical text that, having announced the general principle
that to be an effective doctor one must know the basic components of the body, bases the body and
soul of man on two elements, fire and water, which between them supply the four qualities (Loeb
Library series, vol. 4, p. 230).

foods, patients and circumstances varied, and medicine was still being en-
riched by accumulated experience. Wisdom gained over time could not be
replaced by the simplistic qualities of the philosophers or the false precision
implied by their use of numbers.[29]

In traditional historiography, Greek medicine of the Asclepiad kind was
'rational' in a modernist sense, in considering the natural world and the
case history of the patient, eschewing divine causes.[30] It may be that writing
historia as in medical case histories, the Hippocratic physician was 'rational'
in this sense, but it should be emphasised again that in this book rationalism is to do with arguments, not with naturalness. Nevertheless, despite
the antagonism between 'old medicine' and the new philosophy, some conflation was possible between 'nature' and 'reason' in medicine, and in late
antiquity medicine and philosophy soon came to be regarded as sisters:
philosophia et medicina duae sorores sunt, said the Alexandrians, attributing
the doctrine to Aristotle.[31]

When medieval and later physicians tried to emulate Greek medicine
they thus had two rather different models within the medical literature.
The 'in-family' method of education treated medicine as a lifetime art that
depended on accumulated experience and may have had divine origins. It
was a valuable commercial asset and was often treated as secret, to be revealed
only to the properly initiated. We may suppose that in these circumstances
the composition of medical knowledge varied according to the 'school' or
'family' concerned.

On the other hand, the philosophical doctors made a virtue of the open-
ness of their teaching (causing their opponents to make sour remarks about
their verbosity). The reason for this may have been that the early Greek natural philosophers often constructed their theories with an agenda in mind.
A not uncommon aim was to enable man to reach a stability of mind. This
could be done by accepting that all the difficulties of life were in some sense
inevitable and had to be accepted. Certainly all were natural, and if one
understood the laws of nature then it was easier to bear the misfortunes of

---

[29] *Ancient Medicine*, in vol. 1 of the Loeb edition of *Hippocrates*, ed. Jones, pp. 1–64, chs. 1–2, 14, 16–17
and 20.

[30] Jouanna, *Hippocrates*, especially p. 56 and ch. 8.

[31] The Aristotelian locus was probably in *De Sensu et Sensato*, where Aristotle says that the natural
culmination of natural philosophy would be the study of man and his health. See Cornelius O'Boyle,
'Discussions of the nature of medicine at the university of Paris, ca. 1300', in John van Engen, ed.,
Learning Institutionalized. Teaching in the Medieval University, Notre Dame, Indiana (University
of Notre Dame Press), 2000, pp. 197–227. That medicine was the philosophy of the body and
philosophy the medicine of the soul was a doctrine eagerly taken up by the later rational and learned
doctor, as we shall see. See also Temkin, *Hippocrates*, p. 8, who derives the opinion from Aristotle's
observation that the philosopher finishes where the philosopher begins.

life. An important freedom that this aim helped to foster was freedom from fear of the gods. Some philosophers held that there were no gods, others that the gods were incapable of interfering with human and natural affairs. It was not Zeus who threw thunderbolts, said the philosophers, but a hot vapour arising from the earth, or the clouds exploding, or something of that sort. Ordinary Greeks worried about suffering from wilful gods not only in life but perpetually after death in some kind of quasi-material afterlife. The philosophers told them not to worry: death was so complete and final and *nothing* could happen afterwards.

Not all Greek philosophers argued in this kind of way. It was the young Socrates who despaired of finding satisfactory answers to physical and natural questions and turned instead to human matters. His pupil, Plato, followed him, but also wrote two works of great interest to later doctors and natural philosophers. One of them was the *Republic*, which explained the workings of an ideal city-state. The state in fact worked rather like the human body, with a threefold hierarchy. Controlling the city were the philosopher guardians, who alone had the wisdom to govern; its counterpart in the body was the rational soul, drawn down from the heavens into the head and possessing at least the rudiments of true knowledge. Below the head was the heart, the seat of the vital soul, the source of motion. Its place in the city was taken by the army, brave and vigorous but needing the direction of the guardians. In the lowest place in the body was the liver and its nutritive faculty, corresponding to the workers and kitchens of the city.

Plato described this body in the second text, the *Timaeus*, which contains an account or a parable of the creation of the world by a deity, the demiurge. Like the *Aphorisms* of Hippocrates, this text and the commentary on it by Calcidius were remembered in the West after the fall of Rome. No doubt this was because the Christian church could sympathise with the doctrine of a soul with divine origins that returned to its celestial home after the death of the body. And the *Timaeus*, unlike the works of Aristotle, dealt with a creator god, as did the Old Testament. To all appearance, Plato had been struggling to reach a Christian truth, hampered principally by being unable to receive revealed knowledge. The doctrine of a wise and creative deity was taken up by Galen, as we shall see, and this gave it double authority with the later Christian doctors of the West. Because the body was the microcosm of the world at large, the doctor found it to be of advantage to have specialist knowledge of both, of nature as a whole. 'Nature' was *physis*, which covered the natural world and Aristotle's nature-of-a-thing (as explained later). The doctor full of natural knowledge became in the Latin tradition a *physicus*, which could mean 'natural philosopher' or 'medical man' and which ultimately gave rise to the term 'physician'.[32]

DEMOCRITUS *PHYSICUS*

When the medical man of the Middle Ages and Renaissance looked back at the beginnings of his subject he also saw a literature that has been treated as problematic by historians of the classical period. This includes letters attributed to Hippocrates in early medieval medical collections, and the story of Democritus the Philosopher. This too was a story of 'medicine meets philosophy', and it was remembered down to the time when traditional natural philosophy met its crisis in the seventeenth century. It concerns Democritus the natural philosopher, who preferred to spend his time in a retreat in the woods dissecting animals rather than live in his native city. His fellow citizens thought him mad and called in the great Hippocrates to examine him. Hippocrates duly came, interviewed Democritus, and declared him saner than the citizens. Not only that but, as if to symbolise the close relationship between medicine and philosophy, Democritus showed Hippocrates that he had discovered the physical cause of madness in animals. Democritus *physicus* was a philosopher with a great reputation, the details of whose philosophy could not easily be found by the men of later centuries. This was not inconvenient if, for example, an alternative to Aristotle had to be found. Democritus was even more ancient than Aristotle and the hints he left as to the nature of the world could be readily adapted to some later system. 'Democritean philosophy' in later ages only sometimes meant 'atomic' and often referred to the pragmatic sylvan dissector.

ARISTOTLE AND NATURAL PHILOSOPHY

As with the case of Hippocrates, it is not the intention of this chapter to give a chronological or analytical account of a historical figure and his works. Rather we need to know what it was that the medieval and later doctors chose to pick upon as they sought to reconstruct the medicine and philosophy of the ancient world.

We can conveniently begin with those philosophers whom Aristotle sometimes calls his predecessors. There are two cautions to be observed

---

[32] We shall see in later chapters that it became convenient to use *physica* for 'philosophy' where the latter term had pejorative connotations. See also, J. Bylebyl, 'The medical meaning of *physica*', *Osiris*, 2nd series, 6 (1990), 16–41.

here. First, Aristotle often began his physical treatises with a refutation of other men's theories on the topic under discussion. This was partly a dialectical exercise, giving greater credibility to his own doctrines by the destruction of others. This meant that it was to Aristotle's advantage to make it appear as if earlier philosophers were engaged in the same kind of exercise as he was himself, but not so successfully. It would have been of no use to refute popular fables or the poets, and Aristotle occasionally points to the very different nature of these other forms of Greek thought.[33] But we have only fragments of the works of the early philosophers and cannot tell what their agenda was; before Socrates it seems unlikely that there was a 'succession' of philosophers with any common programme.

Second, the physical works of Aristotle were first explored in the later West, like the medical works, partly in the form of Arabic paraphrases. The process of abbreviation was selective, and certain kinds of materials were left out.[34] Occasionally pieces of additional matter were added, as we saw at the beginning of *Prognosis*. This meant that, at first, later Western scholars did not have a very good idea of what Aristotle had written. For our purposes this does not matter. We are not concerned with any process of transmission of the text of Aristotle in which the criterion of success was a faithful delivery of an accurate text, but with what later doctors made of Aristotle's texts, in whatever form they existed.

We saw that the Hippocratically 'decorous' doctors, who found rivals in philosophically inclined medical men, objected strongly to the doctrine that the fundamental principles of the world were the four elements and their paired qualities (each element had two qualities so that water, for instance, was Cold and Wet). This was a doctrine much developed by Aristotle, and it may be that the encounters described in *Decorum* (which is difficult to date) took place after Aristotle's time. To understand Aristotle's undertaking, however, it is necessary to glance back at his 'predecessors'.

It is well known that the 'pre-Socratic' philosophers were interested in questions of nature and the physical world, and we saw above that they wanted to keep the gods out of their answers to their questions. As we have seen, traditionally it was the young Socrates who despaired of finding answers to natural questions and turned instead to questions dealing with men. There was a true succession, of master and pupil, between Socrates and Plato, and Plato and Aristotle. Aristotle, the son of a doctor, returned to an enquiry into nature. He agreed that the gods had no place in the motions

---

[33] *Meteorologica* 357a24–28.
[34] See Roger French, 'Teaching meteorology in thirteenth-century Oxford. The Arabic paraphrase', *Physis*, 36 (1999), n.s., fasc. 1, 99–129.

and changes of the physical world, but held that earlier philosophers had been too 'materialist' in asserting that the natures of things arose from the characteristics of the matter of which they were composed. The necessity involved in this seemed too rigid to Aristotle, who wanted to put *purpose* into the world. He could not accept the rational and creative demiurge who, Plato had taught, created the world, and Aristotle made 'nature' a local principle of action. Every natural thing, and especially those living, had its own nature and purpose, that of achieving the full potentiality of its form.[35]

First, we must note some of Aristotle's circumstances. He taught in his own school, the *Lyceum*. He and his colleagues taught a wide range of subjects, of which we have space here only for those concerned with the natural world. The cycle of lectures seems to have been repeated often and the content modified, no doubt after discussion. Probably no fully edited and polished lectures were produced, for Aristotle's text is sometimes loosely organised and even appears as notes. But those on the natural world are an organic whole. Aristotle began with the fundamental principles of natural change, or 'motion' in the text called the *Physics*. He then went on to explain how these principles operated in increasingly physical circumstances. He developed his doctrines of the structure of the world and of the actions of the four elements and their qualities in his text *On the Heavens and the Earth*, and in his work *On Meteorology*. As the cycle progressed, Aristotle often recalls the 'original undertaking' – nothing less than an explanation of the natural world – and refers backwards and forwards to other topics in the series.[36]

The cycle took him through more and more elaborate forms of natural action, including those of animals. As we have seen, these were the natural objects that best exemplified his general doctrine of the nature-of-the-thing, and it is important from our point of view to note some details of Aristotle's procedure. First, he placed much more emphasis than Plato did on the role of the senses in generating knowledge (Plato held that the senses distracted the soul from uncovering the reality of its ideas). Aristotle liked empirical knowledge. In the *Lyceum* they kept written accounts of the winners of the games, maps and itineraries, and accounts of the constitutions of different city-states.[37] With animals Aristotle adopted what we might call a 'historical' approach. For the Greeks, a *historia* was a report on an event

---

[35] See Roger French, *Ancient Natural History. Histories of Nature*, London (Routledge), 1994, ch. 1.
[36] See, for example, the *Meteorologica* 339a8 and 390b21.
[37] *The Oxford Classical Dictionary*, ed. Simon Hornblower and Anthony Spawforth, 3rd edn, Oxford (Oxford University Press), 1996, p. 166.

given by a man who had done his best to visit and interview those with first-hand knowledge of it. The report was factual and modest in language, very different from other forms of Greek literature. Aristotle adopted it for philosophy. He and his colleagues sought *historiae* about animals from people professionally involved with them. That on elephants (and the amount they drink, in Macedonian measures) seems to have come from India. Aristotle's *History of Animals* is a selection of these reports, written in 'historical' language, while the *Parts of Animals* presents generalisations, first principles and conclusions about causes. These books contain a famous passage in which Aristotle, having dissected many animals, praises the knowledge to be gained from the inside of animals, however disgusting these are at first sight. It is natural knowledge, worthy of a philosopher, he says, because it is more certain than that of distant things like the heavens.

This empirical side of Aristotle's method led him to promise a work on plants to match those on animals, and to deal with the most complex of all natural motions, that of the human soul. He declared that the natural end to the cycle of teaching, from the simplest to the most complex of motions, was a study of man. In addition to the soul, he meant medicine. The maxim 'Where the philosopher finishes the physician begins', which was adopted so eagerly in the Middle Ages, is Aristotelian. But Aristotle did not teach medicine. It was, after all, a productive art. Aristotle knew that doctors traded in a marketplace and sold health, or at least treatment, for money. The philosopher's business was to teach people to handle knowledge, not how to make and sell things. He taught those who had the leisure to come and hear him and he gave them a liberal education. Indeed, the term 'liberal arts', so important in the Middle Ages, had its origins in Greece, and in both it meant studies suitable for the 'free' man. Liberal studies owed something of their status to the fact that in comparison to the productive arts they were quite useless: only the man with free time and ability could acquire them.

REASONING

We have now glanced at Hippocratic medical wisdom and seen how it could be used to win over patients and perhaps pupils, and to defend its practitioners from the rivalry of 'sophistical' philosopher-physicians. The other great characteristic of the Rational and Learned Doctor whose historical career we are inspecting was his rationality, that is, his use of arguments. They were very largely Aristotelian. We need to explore this a little to see what kind of arguments were used in philosophy.

Plato often strengthened his own position by allowing others to talk themselves into an untenable position. Since this is a characteristic of the dialogue format, we can broadly call it dialectical. Aristotle used a form of it in rejecting the views of his predecessors, but of course they were dead and could not reply in the manner of the circle round Socrates. But Aristotle in addition used, indeed almost invented, logic. In a sense this too was an observational business, observing, naming and classifying the ways in which people argued. It was also a theoretical business, which did not need Socratic conversation. A basic form was the syllogism, which the medievals seized on with such enthusiasm. Syllogisms came in many forms and could be inductive or deductive. Inductive syllogisms relied on repeated instances of the characteristics of a group, and a famous example is the link between rumination in animals and the possession of horns. Discover that the cow is a ruminant and it becomes known that it has horns. It is of course philosophically imperfect, for a perfect inductive syllogism would involve observation of *all* ruminants and *all* cows (the medievals found a way around this obstacle).

There is a good sense in which Aristotle was doing this kind of exercise in the *Parts of Animals*. He was looking for correlations between parts and behaviour of animals, for example between diet, dentition and the number of stomachs. Such features could remain constantly linked in different groups of animals, as repeated observation – the *historiae* – showed. The point about the linkage of these features was that they were co-ordinated for the benefit of the animal. This was not a *rational* or conscious plan of a creative demiurge, but was the product of the nature-of-the-animal striving to achieve its full expression during the development of the animal. It was of course a *purposeful* action, and, as we have seen, Aristotle had wanted to put purpose back into nature.

So Aristotle was using logic in looking at animals and making inductions. But there was also a deeper sense in which his natural philosophy involved logic. His insistence on the purpose of nature led him to what he considered the most valid form of knowledge. We can recall that he criticised earlier philosophers for ascribing the features of natural things to the matter from which they were made. This was a very partial explanation in Aristotle's view. Certainly, matter had irreducible characteristics which Aristotle called the 'material cause' of an object. But it also had shape or Form, and Aristotle systematised the position by adding to the Material and Formal cause the Efficient, generally the agent that brought it into being: a table might be made of wood, have a flat top and a number of legs, and be made by a carpenter. By far and away the most important of the four causes listed by

Aristotle was the last one, the Final. This was the *purpose* of the object, whether man-made or natural. Aristotle argued that full knowledge of a thing came from an awareness of what it was *for*, whether it was a tooth, a horn or a stomach.

In the more strictly logical works Aristotle worked at a related theme. The practical limitations of induction meant that it could not produce philosophically certain knowledge. Aristotle also wanted to produce *de*ductive knowledge, from first principles to observed instances. This he called 'demonstrative', knowledge that a thing could not be otherwise. It related to Final Causes, knowledge of which was the best path to knowledge of a thing. To the medievals Aristotle's texts on logic, such as the *Posterior Analytics*, looked like a programme that could generate proper knowledge of the natural world that was displayed in the physical works.

The attractions of logic were great. Knowledge of syllogisms could prove an opponent wrong or prove that he had framed his premises badly. This touched on rhetoric and public speaking, whether political or medical, which we perhaps saw in the case of *Decorum*. To produce demonstrative knowledge of the physical world in an irrefutable way with an elaborate apparatus of learning was a huge asset to the medical man, who could argue that the human body was the most important part of the physical world and that Aristotle had said it was the natural end-point of all natural philosophy. When he finally obtained Aristotle's philosophical and logical works, the Learned Doctor also became Rational.

ANATOMY

We have seen from the different works that Hippocratic medicine was a distillation of long experience, partly based on knowledge revealed by the gods, somewhat oracular in its aphorisms and prognosis, and largely concerned with diet. Such anatomy as it contained was incidental rather than fundamental. For Aristotle, on the other hand, anatomy *was* fundamental, for true knowledge of the parts of animals was gained through a knowledge of their function, which their shape indicated. The organs could not be otherwise in order to perform their function. We saw that Aristotle made dissections and vivisections to study form and function. But Aristotle's interest was philosophical, not medical. His subjects were animals, not men. The inside of the human body remained for him, as he said, one of the most unknown of all things.[38]

---

[38] *Historia Animalium* 494b21–24.

Yet Aristotle's treatment of animals was immensely important for later rationalising doctors. They adopted it for the human body and it became a major part of their argument about the superiority of rational and learned medicine. We can call it anatomical rationality. But this adoption was not a straightforward business. It meant claiming to know the inside of the human body, and we shall see that this led ultimately to human dissection, which in turn meant the overturning of ancient and widespread taboos about mutilating the dead body. Many societies, including that of ancient Greece,[39] believed in a quasi-material afterlife, and the real punishment of judicial mutilation – lopping noses or the hands of criminals – was the fear of eternal disfigurement. Somehow European doctors overcame these taboos, practised human dissection and animal vivisection, and brought Aristotle's philosophical anatomy into their medicine.

They might never have done so had it not been for certain events in Alexandria, a few years after Aristotle's death. We have already met Alexandria in the third and fourth centuries BC where, probably, librarians were arranging early Greek medical works under the name of Hippocrates, thus causing immense trouble for later scholars. But in another quarter of town something much more sinister was going on, at least according to a persistent rumour. This story said that two Greek doctors, Herophilus (c. 330–260 BC) and Erasistratus (c. 315–240 BC), had not only broken the taboo against mutilating the body, but were performing *vivisections* on human beings.

Historians have thrown doubt on whether in fact these men were in Alexandria at the same time,[40] but of course what is important from our point of view is that later European doctors believed the story and that belief affected their actions. The context of their belief included some pieces of circumstantial evidence in favour of the rumour. The first is that Aristotle's view of the philosophical utility of dissection and vivisection may well have been known, together with his view that medicine followed naturally upon natural philosophy. Medical men would have seen that knowledge of internal human form and function would improve medicine, and the rumour asserts that Herophilus and Erasistratus were indeed inflicting great pain upon their subjects for the greater benefit of later generations. Second, it was believed that the vivisectionists' subjects were condemned criminals who had forfeited their right to live, which seemed to be some justification

---

[39] See H. Von Staden, *Herophilus. The Art of Medicine in Early Alexandria*, Cambridge (Cambridge University Press), 1989, p. 141.

[40] For a discussion on this point see Von Staden, *Herophilus*, p. 37; see also Vallance, 'Doctors in the library', p. 97.

for the manner of their death. Moreover, the rumour added that the exercise was carried out at the wishes of the ruling Ptolemy, a patron of learning.[41] Third, Greek philosophers did not put much faith in an afterlife. Plato held that the important thing was the soul, which returned to the heavens at death, leaving its prison, the wholly corporeal body, on earth. Aristotle held that the most active part of the soul was indestructible, and the way in which he said the body and soul interacted in life could hardly be extended to a quasi-material afterlife. The Stoics and atomists said that death was absolute. In none of these cases was what happened to the body after death important. If our two Greek doctors were learned in philosophy, as seems likely, then they probably did not think they were inflicting eternal punishments on their subjects.

There are also some circumstances which suggest that the rumour was not true. These are also of interest to us for if they kept a false rumour alive they equally helped to form people's beliefs and actions. The first is that in form the rumour resembles the late-antique paradoxes. These constituted a genre of literature that presented stories of marvellous things and events. It may have grown out of the very sober Greek *historiae* which, as we have seen, were reports, as original as possible, on important things and events. Important events were interesting, and so were marvellous events, and so perhaps the form of the *historia* was extended to cover 'paradoxes'.

Alexander the Great enters the story here. Not only did he found the city of Alexandria in Egypt (in 331 B C) and several other cities of the same name in territories he conquered, but he took with him surveyors to assess the resources of these territories, and learned men to send home accounts of things done and found. Perhaps in being retold, these accounts became exaggerated, emphasising both the glory and abilities of Alexander as a general and conqueror, and the strangeness and richness of the distant countries now under Macedonian control. These stories were part of the 'Alexander literature' that survived through the Middle Ages. Impossibly strange races of men and animals found, for example, on medieval world maps derive from such forms of paradoxology that originated either from the Alexander literature or from the similar circumstances of Roman military expansion and found in Pliny.

---

[41] Ptolemy Soter reigned from 323 BC to 283 BC and Ptolemy Philadelphus from 283 to 246. The latter thought that it would be possible to build a universal library, containing all the books in the world; and he tried to acquire Aristotle's library. See Luciano Canfora, *The Vanished Library*, London (Vintage), 1991, p. 20. For a criticism of Canfora and a discussion of the destruction of the library in Alexandria, see Robert Barnes, 'Cloistered bookworms in the chicken coop of the muses: the ancient library of Alexandria', in MacLeod, ed., *The Library of Alexandria*, pp. 61–77, at p. 74.

Alexander was in essence sending home ready-made *historiae*. Some of them were concerned with animals. It was generally believed, after the event, that Alexander had sent specimens of animals back to his old tutor, Aristotle. This has been discounted by modern historians because it looks like a story constructed round the relationship between the greatest philosopher and the greatest general of ancient times. But as we have seen, there was certainly a Macedonian source for Aristotle's knowledge of elephants and there seems no reason to doubt that when Aristotle and his colleagues in the *Lyceum* set out to solicit *historiae* they could make use of Alexander's lines of communication.

Late classical and medieval interest in stories about cannibals and the dismemberment of one's parents was similar to the interest shown in the Alexandrian rumour about two Greek doctors vivisecting prisoners.[42] It was an unforgettable paradox, doctors killing rather than curing; the great cruelty, set against the benefit to future generations; the royal sanction that partly absolved the doctors, and the criminality of the victims who as condemned men were judicially dead before they reached the hands of the vivisectors, who thereby received a further degree of absolution. These issues also made the topic a useful one in rhetoric, which may be another reason for its survival.

The story reached the Middle Ages in a number of ways. It was given by the Roman medical writer Celsus in the first century AD who remarked on the advantages of vivisection for medical progress, but repudiated it for its cruelty. Celsus' work was not recovered until late in the Middle Ages, but he quickly became a model of medical Latinity. The story was retold by the Christian writer Tertullian in about AD 200. Tertullian condemned vivisection in strong language, possibly to illustrate the greater barbarity of pagans compared to Christians; but his source was a medical man, Soranus.[43] Galen (a contemporary of Tertullian's in Rome), who was in favour of vivisecting animals and, if he got the chance, of dissecting dead human bodies, reported directly that Herophilus dissected people.[44]

An important aspect of the affair of the Alexandrine rumour was that the people who heard it and repeated it recognised as an arguable opinion the idea that the body *could* be investigated physically, that its parts and actions could be understood rationally. While there is nothing to suggest this in the experiential, partly divine and largely dietetic medicine of the Hippocratic texts we have looked at, it forms the underlying assumption

[42] John Block Friedman, *The Monstrous Races in Medieval Art and Thought*, Cambridge, Mass. (Harvard University Press), 1981, p. 10, quoting Pliny.
[43] Von Staden, *Herophilus*, p. 142.   [44] In *De Uteri Dissectione*: Von Staden, *Herophilus*, p. 143.

in Aristotle's works on animals. Aristotle's procedure was one of generating knowledge, from *historiae* and dissection to physical correspondences and causes: it was a method that could be developed. Likewise in the Alexandrine rumour the prize, benefit to future generations, clearly depended on new knowledge being produced from vivisectional procedures. Indeed, the two Greek doctors may have discovered something quite unexpected, the central nervous system.

CONTROLLING CENTRES

The Greek notion of the superiority of thought over intractable matter is a commonplace of histories of philosophy. In the case of the human body it was associated with the belief that there must be a special entity that gave life to and directed the body. At different times different philosophers held that there were souls or spirits providing the body with one or more of the features of life. The terms *psyche*, *pneuma* and *thymos* were variously used to denote something that gave physical life, mental life and even life after death. Sometimes they represented a respired spirit, drawn from the life-giving air; often there were two or more of these principles in the body. Aristotle used *psyche* for 'soul' and held that it interacted with the body by a quasi-material *pneuma* (which was innate, not respired).

The philosophers also placed these principles in different parts of the body. There was a tradition that linked the life-giving breath to the heart, which was connected to the rest of the body by its ramifying system of vessels. The notion that somehow air reached the heart remained characteristic of Greek and medieval medicine. Aristotle placed all faculties of the *psyche* in the heart, grouping them into three, the faculties of simple vitality, shared with plants; sentience and motion, common to all animals; and rationality, possessed by man alone. Plato had three separate souls, each broadly similar to Aristotle's categories of faculty, but located in the liver, heart and head respectively. This drew on another tradition, which recognised the importance of the brain as a controlling centre of the body. Those who worked with animals must have known about the vulnerability of the brain, and philosophers as early as Alcmaeon had placed the soul in the brain.

What seems to have happened in Alexandria was that vivisection not only confirmed that the brain was the seat of many soul-faculties, but that the effects of these faculties reached the body by means of the nerves. The Greeks had no word for nerve and used *neuron*, 'fibre' in a specialised way, just as the Romans came to use *nervus*. Nerves are not large or obvious structures in the dissected body, and communication within the body was taken to be effected by the blood vessels. But nerves would be very obvious in the living body, where disturbance of the motor nerves would cause muscular spasms or convulsions, and paralysis when cut through. Stimulating or cutting nerves close to their origin in the brain or spinal cord reveals their distribution as these effects are seen in different parts of the body.

It would be a guess to say that Herophilus was trying to resolve the philosophers' difference on the seat of the soul by vivisection. But we know something of his work on anatomy which shows him to have been particularly interested in the brain and nerves. He distinguished between motor and sensory nerves and gave a formal enumeration to the cranial nerves. The presumption would be that he was at first an Aristotelian, for to be a philosopher in Alexandria almost meant to be an Aristotelian.[45] But Aristotle was in our terms conspicuously ignorant of nerves, believing that the function of the brain was to cool the heart. Aristotle was also ignorant of muscle as the organ of motion, and talked instead of the connate *pneuma* as moving the body. With the ever-present possibility of confusion with the term *neuron* it cannot be quite certain that Herophilus recognised fibrous muscle in the modern sense. Perhaps he shared an earlier Greek view that animal motion was performed by the fibrous structures at the joints. He certainly held that the nerves worked by transmitting a humour or spirit of some kind, a belief from an older Greek tradition.[46]

We know that Herophilus was taught by Praxagoras of Cos and we know the name of one of his own pupils.[47] That is, there was almost certainly a school around him, whether or not connected with the Museum in Alexandria. It seems likely that what was first discovered accidentally, as in vivisection, was then taught systematically in a manner appropriate to the classroom. Classrooms are important groupings of people, with their own rules and 'ethics' as outlined above, and we shall frequently meet such groupings later in this book. It is notable that Celsus hints that there was a standard list of things to be looked for in performing a vivisection, a formal rote of observables systematised for a class. These are the position, shape, colour, size, arrangement, hardness, softness, smoothness, relation, processes and depressions of each organ, and whether one organ was inserted

---

[45] Von Staden, *Herophilus*, pp. 39, 97.
[46] See also Friedrich Solmsen, 'Greek philosophy and the discovery of the nerves', *Museum Helveticum*, 18 (1961), 150–97.
[47] Von Staden, *Herophilus*, p. 41.

into another.[48] 'Arrangement' is *ordo*, which might be disposition of, for example, serial structures such as the vertebrae, or the sequence of organs revealed in the process of dissection. Celsus says that the advantage of following this sequence of observations was that the doctor would be able to locate pain in his patient and that when he saw interior parts in accidental wounds he would know whether they were in a morbid or natural condition; that is, by making comparisons with vivisected parts. Celsus' account not only hints at formal teaching in a group with shared technical knowledge and procedures, but also at the opposition the group encountered from outside, from those who believed that not much could be learned from dissection or vivisection. We shall look at these outsiders in the next chapter, and here we can note that, as in the case of the dietetic Hippocratic doctors and the philosopher-physicians, an encounter between two different groups often reveals interesting things about the nature of the groups.

Finally, we should note that the library itself at Alexandria gave status to medicine. Medical texts were treated as literature and the first commentaries on Hippocrates were written in Alexandria. Doctors talked to scholars and librarians and wondered, for example, how Hippocrates' use of terms differed from that of Homer. The Ptolemies continued to patronise learning after the time of Herophilus and saw libraries as desirable. Galen, in the second century AD, tells the story of ships arriving in Alexandria being obliged to surrender any books they were carrying so that the library could be enlarged; the owners had to be content with a copy. In commenting on Hippocrates the Alexandrian scholars were effectively placing him at the head of a tradition which suddenly acquired the dignity of age. The Alexandrian doctors argued for their medicine as a rational activity, and so effective was their rhetoric and intellectualism that the historian Polybius complained that they were called on by people who were not even ill.[49]

CONCLUSION

This chapter has presented some of the features of Greek medicine and natural philosophy known to the men of the Middle Ages and Renaissance. They were in fact building up their own tradition of medicine by choosing their heroes and doctrines. They were of course ignorant of what only

---

[48] *[P]ositum, colorem, figuram, magnitudinem, ordinem, duritiem, millitiem, levorem, contactum, processus deinde singulorum et recessus, et sive quid inseritur alteri.* See the Loeb Library edition: *Celsus de Medicina with an English Translation by W. G. Spencer*, vol. 1, London (Heinemann) and Cambridge, Mass. (Harvard University Press), 1971, p. 14.

[49] Vallance, 'Doctors in the library', p. 104.

modern scholarship – and there has been a mass of it – has revealed, and it must again be emphasised here that this chapter is not a history of Greek medicine in a chronological and inclusive sense. Medieval doctors knew of Herophilus and Erasistratus by reputation only, but it was a potent one. They knew Aristotle at first partly in incomplete versions of his works that had passed through perhaps three languages. The more oracular Hippocratic writings needed constant interpretation. We shall see in later chapters that it took centuries to recover Galen's works. And while this was going on, the doctor of medieval and post-medieval times was building up an image of the origin and lineage of doctors to which he felt he belonged. In this tradition the work of the Alexandrians was very important. The fact that physical structures, the nerves, confirmed the old notion that the brain was a controlling centre of the body, gave them enormous importance in the study of the origin and distribution of the causes of motion and sensitivity. Part of the Learned and Rational Doctor's rationality was now an *anatomical* rationality.

CHAPTER 2

Galen

INTRODUCTION

Galen was, in the words of a number of Renaissance title-pages, the 'Prince of Physicians, second only to Hippocrates'.[1] For those who founded and followed the Latin medical tradition of the West, what was the relationship between the Father of Medicine and the great Galen, physician to emperors? What did medieval and Renaissance man find in Galen as he found medical wisdom in Hippocrates? The answer in brief is that he found rationality and learning in a richer measure and partly of a new kind. Galen was a potent image of the Learned and Rational Doctor who had a Good Story to tell to his patients.

We can best demonstrate this by following Galen's life. Galen wrote voluminously and often very personally, quite unlike the impersonal *historia*-like reports, case-histories and aphorisms of the Hippocratic writings. It was partly a question of time and place: Galen was born in about A D 129, some five hundred years after the earlier of the Hippocratic works had been written. His home town was Pergamon, an important Hellenistic city, but the political centre of his world was imperial Rome where, he decided, his medical career was to be. Galen was the son of a prosperous architect called Nikon and as a young man had received an extensive education in philosophy. He seems to have had a particular interest in problems of proof, or demonstration. But Galen's father, guided by a dream (we might call it non-medical prognostication) sent his sixteen-year-old son to learn medicine. Galen's particular interest was anatomy, and he pursued the famous teachers of the time – particularly Numesianus the anatomist – at Smyrna, Corinth and Alexandria, where a human skeleton was on show. However, it appears he was not given much opportunity to dissect human

---

[1] See, for example, the address by Fabius Paulinus to the Venetian College of Physicians in the first volume of the Giunta edition of Galen of 1625: *Galeni Opera ex nona Iuntarum Editione*, Venice (Giunta) 1625.

bodies. Galen returned to Pergamon where, at the age of thirty, he was appointed physician to the gladiators. It is worth noting that although temples to Asclepius were being built in Galen's time he does not discuss the kind of medicine associated with them; for us the doctors or priests of the temples did not form a group of practitioners comparable to the followers of the sects, discussed below.

MEDICAL COMPETITION IN ROME

Galen arrived in Rome in 162, the year after Marcus Aurelius became emperor. It was a city full of tensions for someone in Galen's position. Certainly, this city at the centre of the world, with some 1 million inhabitants, held great opportunities – but also many dangers. First, there were cultural difficulties. Galen in language and training was Greek, but was seeking a career at the centre of the Roman Empire. Romans were ambivalent about Greeks. On the one hand, as the empire absorbed Hellenistic towns like Pergamon, educated Romans began to admire the language and culture of Greece. Some Romans came to think of Greek as their primary means of expression, even though they had never, perhaps, left Italy.[2] On the other hand, the self-image of other Romans, perhaps sharpened by this Hellenisation, was that of a sturdy and self-reliant agricultural and military race, full of grave moral virtues. They distrusted Greeks as overly loquacious, full of theory, smooth and untrustworthy. Galen said that the view such Romans took of the subtleties and *minutiae* of Greek philosophy was that it was as useful as drilling holes in millet seeds.[3] Greek medicine seemed particularly suspicious, for there was nothing like its elaborate theory in Roman medicine, which was practical at the veterinary level. Nothing was worse to Romans of the old school than smooth Greek doctors with a plausible line in patter, with unpleasant remedies like letting blood. There was no more licensing of doctors in Rome than there was in Greece, and patriotic authors like Pliny were inclined to believe that Greek doctors were deliberately killing Romans close to the centre of imperial power.[4] There were many immigrant doctors in Rome, almost all of them Greek, and Galen faced stern competition. Professional rivalry was another source of tension and at times Galen feared for his life.[5]

---

[2] An example is Aelian, born in Galen's lifetime. See Roger French, *Ancient Natural History: Histories of Nature*, London (Routledge), 1994, p. 262.

[3] See Vivian Nutton, ed., *Galen on Prognosis*, Berlin (Corpus Medicorum Graecorum), 1979, p. 74.

[4] See, for example, the beginning of Book XXIX of Pliny's *Natural History*.

[5] Nutton, *Galen on Prognosis*, p. 93.

Yet Galen triumphed, becoming physician to the young Commodus, son of Marcus Aurelius. He may, of course, have been simply the best doctor in Rome, but as has already been observed, there are no historical criteria on which we can judge clinical effectiveness. We have to rely on hints as to the strategies employed by doctors to become successful in professional, social and monetary terms, and Galen left many such hints. We shall consider these later on in the categories already established, rationality and learning. First we need to know a little more about the nature of medicine in Rome.

MEDICAL GROUPS

Again it is useful to look at medical groupings. It is clear from Galen's writings that some practitioners in Rome adopted the name and the beliefs of a great teacher. Galen was soon at loggerheads with the followers of Erasistratus, whose view on the contents and pathology of the blood vessels differed from Galen's. It was an enduring group, to judge by the fact that Erasistratus had died roughly four centuries earlier. Galen also distinguishes as a kind those doctors who owed their success to being obsequious to the rich. Galen (not unusually) uses sneering language, but what he seems to be referring to was the formal relationship between patron and client. The patron was generally a rich and powerful figure who supported and often ate meals with a number of clients. The patron gained status from the number of his clients, whom he protected. The clients were in turn supporters of the patron, sometimes in a political sense; if they were doctors, their services were available to the patron and they were essentially retained by him. This was in some ways an ideal mode of medical practice, and one which doctors afterwards also sought. Client doctors must have felt even more protected since in Rome no action at law could be prosecuted between patron and client. The client–patron relationship effectively removed the practitioners from the competition in the medical marketplace; Galen does not say whether they had special beliefs or practices, which doctors in the marketplace were so often strident about.

GALEN AND THE DEMIURGE: RATIONALITY OF THE BODY

Galen reports fully on the medical sects of imperial Rome. These competed with each other and with him, and form the context in which his strategies for advancing his career were played out. The sects were not ancient. They seem to have arisen from an increasing use of philosophy in medicine. We have glanced at the anatagonism felt by some Hippocratic doctors for the new and logical philosophical medicine, expressed in texts which are difficult to date. We are on firmer ground with the two vivisectors, Herophilus and Erasistratus. Herophilus at least seems to have been mindful of Aristotle's natural philosophy and the group of pupils and followers around him formed a 'school'[6] that concerned itself with 'logical medicine', by which we should probably understand the production of knowledge about the body by reasoning, from a few first physical principles.

It has been convincingly argued[7] that in reaction to this, from about 225 to 50 BC, there developed a group of doctors who emphasised the empirical side of medicine – the long experience and accumulated wisdom that we met in *Ancient Medicine*. By this time the Hippocratic *corpus* had been collected together and the new empiricists found support for their views in the empirical works of the collection, particularly those, such as *Ancient Medicine*, that were rhetorical in defence of empiricism.[8] In doing so they were inventing a medical tradition for themselves and choosing Hippocrates as its founder. Not everyone at the time thought of Hippocrates as the Father of Medicine, and the new empirics were the first to write commentaries on the empirical Hippocratic works.[9] That is, experience was now not only a question of personal observation, but the experience of others, which could be read in books. This was a question of *historia*, which we met in the previous chapter, and knowledge gained from books came to have a privileged status.[10]

Naturally the rationalist physician reacted in turn and became more rationalist. Their opponents called them 'dogmatists' and in the first centuries BC and AD two new forms of rationalist medicine appeared. One was that of Asclepiades, who drew on atomism for his natural philosophy and supplied the material for the sect known to Galen as the Methodists. The second was the Pneumatist sect, which drew on humoral theory and Stoic logic, and which also practised in Galen's Rome. Thus, in Rome, Galen faced four sects – the Empiricists, Rationalists, Pneumatists and Methodists. He regarded himself as separate from them, for his philosophical training told him that both empiricism and rationalism were valuable in their own way; and at the same time he used some doctrines that had found favour with the Pneumatists. He regarded himself as a follower of Hippocrates,

---

[6] 'Herophilus and his house' was a near-contemporary expression. See Wesley D. Smith, *The Hippocratic Tradition*, Ithaca and London (Cornell University Press), 1979, p. 194.

[7] Ibid., p. 178.   [8] Ibid., p. 209.

[9] See also John Vallance, 'Doctors in the library: the strange tale of Apollonius the bookworm and other stories', in Roy MacLeod, ed., *The Library of Alexandria. Centre of Learning in the Ancient World*, London and New York (I. B. Tauris), 2000, pp. 95–113, at p. 105.

[10] Vallance, 'Doctors in the library', p. 107.

and as his battles with his opponents in Rome moved him further towards a rationalist position he claimed Hippocrates as the first Rationalist, with an excellent knowledge of anatomy. It seems to be generally true in the history of medicine that those authors who are defending a position against attack, or setting up a new one, are given to constructing a history or lineage for it, preferably with a revered Father. Thus, while Herophilus and Erasistratus did not recognise rival schools,[11] and Erasistratus apparently ignored Hippocrates, in the competitive situation in Rome both Empiricists and the rationalising Galen (ultimately thought of as the arch-Rationalist) could choose Hippocrates as the Father of their different systems.

The main opposition was between the Rationalists and the Empiricists. Importantly for our story a central issue between them was anatomy. The Empiricists refused to make the assumption that the body was intelligible: if it were, they said, then men would understand it and agree about it, while in fact the Rationalists disagree greatly, and philosophers cure no one. Celsus' account of the dispute between the two sects recalls the defence of dietetic medicine against the invasion of philosophical principles, which we met in chapter 1. But now the issues were enormously inflated by the human vivisections attributed to Herophilus and Erasistratus.[12] The Empiricists dwelt on the cruelty of vivisection and the paradox that it should be done by doctors, whose calling was the preservation of health. Not only cruel, they said, but useless: the colour and physical characteristics (listed formally at vivisection) of the parts change so much in a dying man that nothing can be inferred from them. Moreover, penetration of the diaphragm or chest kills a man instantly and so the heart and lungs can never be seen in their living condition.

The Rationalist position was that, in principle, medicine would be im-proved by the knowledge provided by dissection and vivisection. A large part of this claim was that future generations would benefit. As the other arm of the paradox about present cruelty it was, of course, hypothetical. The vivisectors and the Rationalists who followed them were philosophers and held that the body *was* intelligible and that knowledge about it was valuable in itself. Moreover, this knowledge included that of the nervous system and could be demonstrated dramatically: there were many situations in which this knowledge could be used professionally, quite apart from the future.

---

[11] Nor did Meno, a student of Aristotle's, discuss sects in his history of medicine. Smith, *The Hippocratic Tradition*, p. 182.

[12] *Celsus De Medicina*, trans. W. G. Spencer, 3 vols., Cambridge, Mass. (Harvard University Press, Loeb Library series), 1935–8, vol. 1, p. 22.

GALEN'S DEMONSTRATIONS

Galen's early interest in anatomy was surely inspired by the story of Herophilus and Erasistratus. 'Anatomy' was not, of course, simple morphology but in a philosophical way included function.

Galen would have been aware of the Aristotelian doctrine that knowledge of a part is primarily what the part is for, its action or use. Moreover, he believed that the body had been put together by a deity very like the demiurge of Plato, who created the world of the *Timaeus*. Unlike Aristotle's 'nature', this was a creator god who put the body together *rationally*, using reason to do the best possible job with the materials available. In dissection Galen was looking for anatomical rationality and his prime example was how the body was controlled by the brain, spinal cord and nerves.

The link with Herophilus and Erasistratus was fairly direct. Their work had been revived and examined by the anatomist Marinus, who dissected apes. One of Galen's earliest works was an abstract of Marinus' *Anatomy*.[13] With this background Galen made an important discovery. He cites three cases in which the patient, undergoing surgery in the neck, became wholly or partially dumb. Perhaps Galen was there at the operation or came to know of it quickly, for he says that everyone was surprised, because the larynx and windpipe were undamaged. But to Galen it looked like loss of nervous control. The implication is that the cases prompted him to do experiments in which he discovered that the voice is controlled by the 'recurrent' laryngeal nerve, which arises in the brain, loops round a blood vessel in the thorax and rises again to the organs of speech in the throat.[14]

When he made this discovery, early in his first spell in Rome, or even while still in Pergamon, Galen had a sophisticated knowledge of the mechanics of respiration, which we may guess had been a topic of interest to Herophilus and his followers. Certainly Galen's teacher Pelops understood the function of the diaphragm, and Galen came to see the action of the intercostal muscles.[15]

---

[13] Smith, *The Hippocratic Tradition*, pp. 65, 74.

[14] Galen's description is partly in *De Locis Affectis*. The standard edition is that by C. G. Kühn, *Galeni Opera Omnia*, 22 vols., Leipzig (C. Knobloch), 1821–33; vol. VIII, p. 53. There is an English translation by Rudolph E. Siegel, *Galen on the Affected Parts*, Basel (S. Karger), 1976; see pp. 36–7. It is an implication because while Galen pointedly claims the discovery of the nerve as his own, he presents the three cases as examples of the nerve's operation, not as circumstances of its discovery, which he does not give. Perhaps he glosses over this in order to present himself as knowledgeable about the nerve when explaining the matter to the puzzled observers.

[15] Smith, *The Hippocratic Tradition*, p. 85.

Galen made great use of his knowledge of the nervous control of respiration and the voice. In the summer of 163, a year after arriving in Rome for the first time, Galen was asked by Flavius Boethus (whom we shall meet again) to perform vivisections to demonstrate his opinions.[16] The performance was from the start a public display, designed to convince. Boethus had assembled a crowd of Stoics, Aristotelians, other philosophers and medical men, with whom Galen disputed. Here would have been discussed the issues between the different kinds of philosophers. Very likely the Aristotelians believed that the voice came from the heart, which they preferred to think of, with Aristotle, as the controlling centre of the body. If they had heard about nerves, they would probably have argued that they arose in the heart, as did Aristotelians in the Middle Ages and Renaissance, citing Aristotle's description of fibrous structures within the heart.[17] The vivisections then formed a sort of physical argument to demonstrate the cranial origin of the nerves, and hence voice, and prove Galen right. On Galen's advice Boethus had arranged for a supply of pigs and young goats, rather than apes. Perhaps apes would have made a better spectacle because (as Galen said) they resemble man, but pigs have louder voices. Clearly Galen intended to stage-manage the demonstration carefully.

But it nearly went wrong. It was arranged that Galen, the doctor, would demonstrate the structure (of the nerves and larynx) while the philosopher Alexander of Damascus would guide the crowd to the conclusions. Alexander was Boethus' tutor and it was probably expected that, like other Aristotelians in Rome, he would support Galen. But Alexander was also familiar with Plato's philosophy, in which the senses were held to be a distraction from the soul's search for truth within itself. Perhaps for this reason Alexander began prematurely by asking whether they all agreed that they would accept the evidence of the senses. Merely to raise the question was to throw doubt on the essence of Galen's demonstration, and he angrily walked out. The debate continued and Alexander was silenced. A bigger demonstration was arranged and over several days Galen demonstrated the nervous control of the actions of muscles in respiration and production of the voice. It must have been a convincing moment when Galen silenced the

[16] Nutton, *Galen on Prognosis*, p. 95.
[17] See, for example, Pietro d'Abano, *Conciliator Controversiarum, quae inter Philosophos et Medicos Versantur*, Venice (Giunta), 1565, f. 62v. Pietro in the early fourteenth century could find support for the idea in the truncated paraphrase of Galen's *De Usu Partium* that circulated widely under the title *De Juvamentis Membrorum*. See Roger French, 'De Juvamentis Membrorum and the reception of Galenic physiological anatomy', *Isis*, 70 (1979) 96–109.

squealing pig, as he had promised, by compressing its recurrent laryngeal nerve. He was demonstrating, that is, not only that he had knowledge of how the body worked, but that he had control of it. It was a demonstration of rationalism and Galen was the Rational Doctor: the body was capable of being understood and responded to intervention.[18]

It is worthwhile spending a little more time on the recurrent laryngeal nerve because it illustrates a number of other features of Galen's rationalism. The three surgical cases he describes are in the text *On Affected Places*, which deals with signs and causes of disease. It is partly anti-empirical in tone and Galen makes a great deal of the fact that in diseases involving the nerves the causes often occur in places that an Empiricist would not expect. The point of the three surgical cases was not only that the practitioner did not know of the nerve, but that he was puzzled that the non-functioning organ was not damaged. Galen also recalls the case of a man who had lost all feeling, but not motion, from three fingers. His own doctor applied various remedies to the fingers, to no avail. When he was called in, Galen discovered that the patient had damaged his neck in a fall from his carriage, and Galen's knowledge of anatomy told him that the cause of the complaint was located at the cervical origin of the nerves serving the fingers. In a similar case a blow to the back paralysed the intercostal muscles and the legs so that the patient could not walk or talk. Galen again stopped the (rather empirical) applications of remedies to the larynx and legs and treated the inflammation of the spine.

The recurrent laryngeal nerve also receives attention in Galen's work *On the Use of the Parts*. This too is a rationalist text, in emphasising that the body is intelligible because it was created by a rational divinity, the demiurge (Galen uses the term interchangeably with 'nature', *physis*). The rational anatomist can understand, and must admire, the reasoning of the demiurge: Galen has many passages of natural theology. A good example is the question Galen has to answer: why does the recurrent nerve run down to the thorax and then back up to the larynx?[19] Galen's answer is in several parts. First, he believed that all motor nerves enter their destination muscle at its head, that is, the end opposite to the motion it produces – Galen supposed that some form of traction was exerted by the nerve itself.

---

[18] The story is given in the text called *De Praecognitione* in the 1625 edition of the collected works: *Galeni Librorum Quarta Classis*, Venice (Giunta), 1625, p. 216 (the pagination is false, 215 following 224).

[19] Galen, *De Usu Partium Corporis Humani*, Kühn, vol. III, p. 570. There is an English translation by M. T. May, *Galen on the Usefulness of the Parts of the Body*, 2 vols., Ithaca (Cornell University Press), 1968, p. 362.

This meant that the muscles closing the larynx were obliged to be innervated from below. But, of course, nerves begin in the brain, and so nature in constructing the body sent the recurrent nerve down into the thorax, bent it round a blood vessel and directed it straight to the larynx. Galen believed that this once more defeated the Aristotelians (for if the heart were indeed the origin of the nerves, they could reach the larynx in a straight line).

More to the point in this text is that the arrangement shows that the rationality of the demiurge consists partly in overcoming the difficulties of matter. Galen held that sensory nerves had to be soft for functional reasons, but that some, like that to the mouth of the stomach, where hunger is felt, had to reach across long distances from the brain. This made them vulnerable to damage from motion, and nature consequently reinforced them at intervals with ganglia. The blood vessel round which the recurrent nerve turned not only acted in this way but also behaved as a *glossocomion*, a device in which a capstan on a single shaft pulls different parts of an object in different directions. Fractures of the bones of the leg were reduced with such a device. Thus the traction exerted by the recurrent nerve was reversed in direction.

In this case, nature's rationality is close to human not only in being intelligible to man, but in resembling human rationality in machines. Galen inflates the natural theology of the situation.

I want you now to pay me closer attention than you would if you were being initiated into the mysteries of Eleusis or Samothrace or some other sacred rite and were wholly absorbed in the acts and works of the hierophants. You should consider that this mystery is in no way inferior to those and no less able to show forth the wisdom, foresight and power of the Creator of animals, and in particular you should realize that I was the very first to discover this mystery which I now practise... fix your mind now on holier things, make yourself a listener worthy of what is to be said, and follow closely my discourse as it explains the wonderful mysteries of Nature.[20]

GALEN'S GOOD STORY: PROGNOSIS

Boethus arranged Galen's demonstration by vivisection in order to promote him. He was in fact one of a small circle of friends who were of considerable assistance to Galen when he first arrived in Rome. This part of the story of Galen's life in Rome begins with Eudemus, an Aristotelian philosopher

---

[20] May, *Usefulness of the Parts*, p. 367.

who had once been Galen's teacher.[21] Eudemus accordingly thought that philosophy was more important to Galen than medicine, but it was natural that he should call in Galen when he felt ill; perhaps knowing of Nikon's dream for Galen's future helped. When Galen arrived, he told his patient that he had a quartan fever – a fever with crises at four-day intervals. Galen continued his treatment during Eudemus' fever, inspecting his urine from time to time. He was, that is, making predictions about the outcome of the fever, both from correctly identifying it and from the appearance of the urine. Galen was proved correct, for Eudemus recovered.

During the illness, two important things happened. First, Eudemus was visited by Boethus, who had heard about Galen's skill in 'anatomy' and was anxious to set up the vivisectional demonstrations.[22] Like Eudemus, Boethus was an Aristotelian; moreover, as he had been a consul, he was a person of importance. He was accompanied by Sergius Paulus (shortly to become a prefect) who having talked to Boethus was also keen on seeing the demonstrations. Galen adds to this list the uncle of the emperor Lucius and another Aristotelian, Severus. When at the end of the case Galen's prediction was shown to be true, his reputation in the higher social and intellectual circles was enhanced. The second event was that, while still ill, Eudemus demanded an explanation for Galen's prognosis. He was after all an Aristotelian and would only have been satisfied with a philosophically rigorous reply, which in Aristotelian terms would have been the discovery of natural causes. Galen's explanation rested easily on Aristotelian natural philosophy. He explained that fever was a localised excess of the elementary quality heat, which reached the heart and was disseminated through the arteries. Eudemus would have known, of course, of the four elements and their qualities and could make connections with the special medical knowledge being expounded by Galen. Galen explained the periodicity of the crises by describing how the body 'concocted' the corrupt humour at the root of the trouble, making it, if possible, less damaging and then ejecting it. This was the effort of 'nature' within the body, explained Galen, and again Eudemus would have found connections with the Aristotelian doctrine of the nature-of-the-thing, although Galen's medical interpretation owed something also to Hippocrates. Galen also took Eudemus' pulse and explained that he was testing the ability of the faculty of the soul that

---

[21] Nutton, *Galen on Prognosis*, pp. 75, 83.

[22] Galen begins the *De Anatomicis Administrationibus* with a brief autobiographical section, and calls Boethus a keen anatomist (Kühn, *Galeni Opera Omnia*, vol. 11, p. 215). There is an English translation (somewhat cavalier in parts) by Charles Singer: *Galen on Anatomical Procedures*, London (Oxford University Press), 1956, p. 1.

resided in the heart to expel the concocted humour at the end of the given period, that is, at a crisis. If nature were strong, the patient survived; if the disease were stronger, the patient died.

In other words, Galen was full of the doctor's sickroom patter, in this case appropriate to an Aristotelian philosopher. The patient in fact already possessed some knowledge of the medical principle of the expulsion of morbid matter, and asked particularly what Galen meant by 'nature' and 'concoction'. In both cases, in fact, Galen had drawn his doctrine from Hippocrates, and since in a sense his whole medical programme was to find Aristotelian rationality under Hippocratic medical wisdom, he was in a position to explain Eudemus' quartan on the very fundamentals of the Aristotelian world picture. He was, in short, telling Eudemus the Good Story of the Rational and Learned Doctor: I am the doctor, I have specialist knowledge of what it is you are suffering from, I can predict the outcome because of my knowledge and medical first principles, and I can trace your very symptoms back to the axiomatic first principles of the natural world. Eudemus had asked for all the details, and he got them. He said (it is, of course, Galen reporting) that he followed Galen's arguments better than those of other doctors, and that he admired Galen's logic.[23] Galen made sure he told his Good Story to men of position and understanding: it is striking that he had no interest in the very young as patients.[24] He needed patients he could talk to.

In fact, Galen had not realised when he went to Rome that the doctors there did not prognosticate. Galen thought of himself as a Hippocratic and was aware of the advantages of it expressed in the Hippocratic text *Prognosis*. Galen thought that the reason the Roman doctors did not prognosticate was that they 'toadied to the rich' – he means the patron–client relationship, discussed above. Secure in that position, says Galen with Hippocratic disapproval, they dress in an ostentatious way and attract many pupils by claiming that medicine can be taught quickly. Galen adds significantly that being followed by a large number of pupils increased the influence of such doctors in the city. Nor did the followers of Erasistratus prognosticate, and when one of them, Martianus, heard Galen's prediction in Eudemus' case, he said it was like divination from the flight of birds or horoscopes.

Galen was in a difficult position. His reputation among doctors was not enhanced by prognostication. Is it your own idea, they asked him, or do you

---

[23] Nutton, *Galen on Prognosis*, p. 87.
[24] See Danielle Gourevitch, 'The paths of knowledge: medicine in the Roman world', in M. D. Grmek, ed., *Western Medical Thought from Antiquity to the Middle Ages*, trans. A. Shugaar, Cambridge, Mass. and London (Harvard University Press), 1998, pp. 104–138, at p. 135.

follow some master? Rather than being thought a sorcerer, Galen at first kept his attachment to Hippocrates a secret. He was teased by Martianus, who had found a denial of prognostication in the second book of the Hippocratic *Prorrhetics*. It's spurious, said Galen. Moreover, to make predictions about the emperor was a capital offence; and the medical marketplace in Rome was dangerously competitive.

Eudemus took Galen's aside and explained that things in Rome were not as they were back home in Pergamon, for in 'our own' country the doctors did not have the vices of the metropolis.[25] Most of Galen's enemies in Rome, added Eudemus, were also from provincial cities and often poor or ignorant; they wanted to make money quickly and to return home as soon as possible. They were accordingly savage in their fight for success, and Eudemus warned Galen to beware of plots to poison him, recalling the death of a young doctor and his two servants some ten years earlier. Galen was clearly worried and wanted to go home; but there was trouble too in Pergamon and Galen decided to remain and face his problems.

He did so by insisting on the Hippocratic nature of his medicine. He not only made prognosis acceptable but successfully promoted the letting of blood, which he took to be fundamental to Hippocratic medicine. There could perhaps be no more striking example of the power of a doctor to use his learning and reasoning to promote his own kind of practice and his own career. Galen was in an almost murderously competitive situation. The other doctors in Rome did not practise venesection and their patients were unused to it. Imagine that you are a Roman citizen, sturdy, grave and stoical, but with a pain in your side. It gets worse, and you finally agree to the calling of a doctor who, you suspect, will be Greek. It is Galen. He carries a sharp knife and wants to make a hole in your arm. Not a prick, but a hole large enough for *lots* of blood to come out. Do you let him do it? The answer for many Romans was often enough 'yes'. What powers of persuasion did Galen have? The opponents of venesection, after all, had a good case.[26] It was a nuisance to have to open the blood vessel, and to make sure that it was a vein and not an artery, which would be dangerous. Some patients died from fear even before the vessel had been cut while others fainted during the operation and never recovered. In others it was difficult or impossible to stop the bleeding, and in those where it could be controlled, how was the doctor to know how much blood to take? Moreover, the Erasistrateans,

[25] Nutton, *Galen on Prognosis*, p. 93.
[26] Galen himself lists the apparent disadvantages of venesection. See Peter Brain, *Galen on Bloodletting. A Study of the Origins, Development and Validity of his Opinions, with a Translation of the Three Works*, Cambridge (Cambridge University Press), 1986, p. 18.

Galen's enemies who held that the arteries contained not blood but *pnuema*, argued that removing blood from a vein would cause the pathological entry of *pneuma* from the arteries, with disastrous results.

Galen may have had an uphill struggle to make his case, but in such cases he was a mountaineer. He demonstrated in experiments with ligatures that the arteries do contain blood and that no Erasistratean pathology would occur. He quoted passages from Hippocrates to give authority for letting blood. He cited medical cases known to himself and his opponents.[27] In one of them he was present with the Erasistrateans who agreed that the patient had a dangerous plethora of blood. Their method of reducing it was starvation, for it was generally admitted that blood was produced from food. Galen asserted that this was far too slow and that many patients had been killed by Erasistratus and his followers. The patient in the case had a spontaneous nosebleed and recovered. Galen seized his chance and proclaimed that this was nature's own venesection and that physicians could do no better than follow nature. It was a useful tactic, for he was in a position again to employ the whole of the philosophy of nature in explaining an actual medical case.[28]

Another strategy Galen used was the public disputation. 'At that time the custom had somehow sprung up of speaking in public each day on any questions that were put forward', recalled Galen.[29] This was a Roman continuation of the Hellenistic habit of giving public lectures for the benefit of the citizens, but they had now become debates, perhaps at a recognised meeting place of doctors, that could be used to challenge opponents.[30] Preceding the dispute Galen was about to recount was the case of spontaneous nosebleed, in which Galen had argued with the Erasistrateans. 'While they were saying this, however, a certain Teuthras, a fellow citizen and schoolfellow of mine – he was exceedingly frank in his ways – said: "You will never influence these men; they are too stupid to remember the patients who were killed by Erasistratus."' For a moment Teuthras was centre stage. He rolled off a list of all the patients he said had been killed, made a rude gesture with his hand and dragged Galen away from the meeting.[31] The following

---

[27] Multiple consultation was usual. See Nutton, *Galen on Prognosis*, p. 160.

[28] The patient was female and had suffered a suppression of menstruation, nature's routine evacuation of blood. Galen describes how she leapt from her bed and rushed shrieking outside before the nosebleed, which removed all symptoms. Galen leads rhetorically to this climax and reflects sententiously on the doctor following nature. Brain, *Galen on Bloodletting*, p. 40.

[29] Ibid., p. 41.

[30] Nutton, *Galen on Prognosis*, p. 187. At Ephesus there were formal contests between doctors, with a list of winners displayed publicly.

[31] Brain, *Galen on Bloodletting*, p. 41.

day Teuthras went to the public meeting with the works of Erasistratus, hoping to provoke a dispute with the older doctors, but they refused to engage with someone so young. But by chance or design (perhaps Galen had planted Teuthras in the audience) at a later meeting 'someone' raised the question of whether Erasistratus was right in not letting blood. Galen was fully prepared with a speech, which he and Teuthras had arranged to be written down from Galen's dictation. Galen claimed that as a result of his speech and the leaking of the dictated text all the Erasistrateans changed their minds and adopted venesection.

The written word was another useful means of persuading people. Teuthras wanted Galen's words dictated because he was shortly going on a journey and presumably had a use for them in connection with it. Boethus sent experts in shorthand to capture what Galen said when demonstrating the nervous and muscular control of respiration in the living animal.[32] Galen himself wrote voluminously, promoting his own doctrines, rejecting those of others and defending the memory of what he had written or done long before, and he continued to write during the rest of his career. The troubles in Pergamon came to an end just as Boethus was making moves to recommend Galen to the emperor (Galen had just cured Boethus' wife of a watery swelling) and Galen lost no time in slipping hastily home, eager to avoid the dangers of Rome and anxious in case the emperor should prevent him from leaving. But when the imperial call came three years later he had to return. Galen records that he was recommended to the emperor Lucius on the basis of his philosophy as well as medicine – in our terms as a Rational Doctor – but Lucius died and was succeeded by Marcus Aurelius. Famously the Stoic emperor, Marcus Aurelius was probably sympathetic to the place given to 'nature' by the philosophers, and to Galen's basing medicine on natural principles. Galen impressed the emperor with his skill at prognosis and analysis of the imperial pulse. Galen's recruitment to the palace may have been part of the preparation for the German wars, but Galen did not want to go to war. He knew that in wartime more opportunities arose for human dissection than in Rome, but that was not enticement enough. He asked to stay in Rome and look after Commodus, son of Marcus Aurelius. He lived close to Commodus in the palace partly for his own safety. Galen wrote many works during the German wars. One of them was *On Crises*[33] which, Galen said, makes the theory of prognosis available to anyone trained in geometry and dialectic – that is, our Rational Doctor.

[32] Nutton, *Galen on Prognosis*, p. 104. Galen recounts a similar story at the beginning of the *Anatomical Procedures*, which he says grew out of the notes given to Boethus.
[33] Nutton, *Galen on Prognosis*, p. 121.

Others were *Critical Days* and *The Difference of Fevers*: all were designed to show that the theory of medical prediction comes out of Hippocrates.

RATIONALISING HIPPOCRATES

Galen held throughout his life that proper medicine was Hippocratic, and devoted his later years to commentaries on the Hippocratic works. His purpose was to interpret Hippocrates and show why Hippocrates had been right. It was partly that some of the Hippocratic works were 500–600 years old and needed to be rendered into modern Greek. But much more it was that the pithy words of works such as *Aphorisms* and *Prognosis* abounded in wisdom but did not engage in argument or learning, in the sense we are using in this book. Galen saw his principal duty to be to explain Hippocrates by pointing out the reasons and learning that must underlie the medical wisdom of Hippocrates: Hippocrates needs interpretation, said Galen.[34] A good and simple example is the pearl of wisdom from *Breaths*: 'Opposites cure opposites'. In the Middle Ages this became known as the Law of Hippocrates and was used axiomatically as the premiss of syllogisms. This was because of the interpretation put on it by Galen, who assumed that 'opposites' were the opposing elementary qualities of Aristotelian natural philosophy. Indeed, Galen attributed the four-element theory itself to Hippocrates.[35] This gave Galen and subsequent doctors the whole range of peripatetic doctrines and arguments to construct a rational Hippocrates.

In fact Galen the phlebotomist and prognosticator was reconstructing Hippocrates in his own image. Hippocrates gave him ancient authority: Galen knew that the common people admired physicians who knew their history, believing that it gave these doctors an added knowledge of the theory of medicine.[36] Historical medical learning was, in other words, useful in the medical marketplace. Hippocrates was also called on to fight Galen's battles. When Galen disagreed with Martialius, an Erasistratean and anatomist, Hippocrates in Galen's eyes became a great anatomist; he must have known all about anatomy, Galen reasoned, but did not express it because it was kept as a secret in the family.[37] One of the main purposes of Galen's vivisections was to demonstrate that the controlling centre of the body was in the brain and not the heart as Aristotle had said. There were works in the Hippocratic *corpus* that seemed to support this, and Galen

[34] See Smith, *The Hippocratic Tradition*, p. 72.
[35] In *The Elements according to Hippocrates*. See Smith, *The Hippocratic Tradition*, p. 88.
[36] Smith, *The Hippocratic Tradition*, p. 163.   [37] Ibid., pp. 78–9, 105.

knew too that Plato had located the highest soul in the brain. This meant to Galen that Plato was a follower of Hippocrates, and he wrote *On the Opinions of Plato and Hippocrates* – dedicated to Boethus – to demonstrate it. He adapted the work 'to serve as the philosophical prolegomenon of his system generally'.[38] It is notable too that Galen dedicated the first book of his great anatomical text *On the Use of the Parts* to Boethus. Both works were begun early in Galen's first period in Rome and the dedications look like a tactic to secure the patronage of an important man. Here was another 'external' use of technical knowledge.

Perhaps the clearest example of Galen's rationalisation of Hippocrates was his treatment of the aphorisms. We have already noticed that these are condensed pieces of medical wisdom, sometimes brief to the point of obscurity but with a confident authority that seemed to be the product of long experience. They always seemed to need a little explanation and every subsequent generation of doctors interpreted them in its own way, indicating what they surely had meant in antiquity in terms accessible to the contemporary world. Let us look at how Galen treats the first aphorism of them all, which famously begins with remarks on the shortness of life and the length of the art of medicine. It then adds a little on the doctor, the patient and external circumstances. Galen opens his commentary by saying that whether this is a single aphorism or several, all commentators are agreed that it is like a proemium to the whole work. This indicates two important things to us. First, that the *Aphorisms* had already attracted commentary. Second, it shows that Galen (and by implication the earlier commentators) were seeking an *argument* through the 'work' as a whole. It is the purpose of introductory material to set out the rationality of what follows and Galen was clearly examining the first aphorism in this light. But as we have seen, the *Aphorisms* is not rational in this way, and Galen, although always ready to find the arguments behind the aphorisms, doubted whether Hippocrates had intended the first aphorism as an introduction.[39]

Galen's resolution of this doubt begins as soon as he has expressed the above in a couple of sentences. Let us analyse the words of the aphorism, he says, to discover what Hippocrates' intention was. To see what Galen does, we can start with the aphorism itself. Its economy of language is partly achieved by omitting verbs, which adds to its oracular nature.

---

[38] Ibid., p. 99.
[39] Lists of things, like aphorisms or case-histories, can always be added to, particularly when in the possession of a 'school' of physicians, but readers often sought threads of rationality running through them.

Life short, art long, opportunity fleeting, experience deceptive, judgement difficult.
It is necessary for him to make appropriate himself, the patient, the assistants and
the circumstances.

When we have supplied the verbs and guessed, as Galen guessed, that
'him' is the doctor, it is still a rather obscure expression of wisdom. Any
explanation that Galen made would necessarily draw on his own experience
and reading, and since his purpose was to make the aphorism clear to his
contemporaries he had to express himself in terms that they too would
understand. The art is long, explains Galen, because the time in which
the doctor has to do individual things seems short. What may have been
in Galen's mind, but what could not have been in Hippocrates', was the
Aristotelian doctrine that particulars of experience build up over time to
form more general statements, by induction.[40] When Galen now says that
two things are needed to bring any art to actual practice – namely, experience
and reason – he is clearly thinking of the Rationalist–Empiricist dichotomy
of the Rome of his time. We have seen that this did not have a long
history and would have been unknown to 'Hippocrates'. Galen makes the
'deceptive experience' of the aphorism the business of the Empiricists and
the 'difficult judgement' a Rationalist affair; and it is reason that judges
the thing to be proved. He rejects those who asserted that it was a difficult
experiential judgement. Galen's discussion is a *philosophical* one, drawing
on issues that had been important to him throughout his educated life
and which derive partly from Aristotle's distinction between observed and
theoretical knowledge. Galen concludes his analysis of the first part of the
first aphorism with the unambiguous statement that Hippocrates, in all the
aphorisms, was a Rationalist.[41]

A major tool of Galen's for expounding Hippocrates was that as a
Rationalist Hippocrates *must have known* the physical principles behind
the appearances. The fourteenth aphorism says

Those who are growing have much innate heat and therefore need much food. If
they do not get it, the body wastes. Old men have little heat and accordingly need
little nourishment, and much of it destroys the heat of the food. For this reason
too fevers are not so acute in old men, for their bodies are cold.

This somewhat homely piece of medical wisdom called out to Galen for rational explanation. Without preliminaries he returned to his own book on

---

[40] *Artem longam: quia tempus in quo particulariter est operandum strictum videtur atque parvum: quam
siquis velit capere longis exercitiis et longo usu capi est necesse. Articella*, Venice, 1483, f. 9r.
[41] Following the translation of Leoniceno in the 1625 Giunta, who uses 'dogmatic'.

complexions and its theoretical discussions. Complexion was fundamental to Galenic medicine, for it was a mixture of the elementary qualities which determined how the parts of the body worked and reacted to external things. Bad complexion was illness, and evacuation of offending humours and their elementary qualities was a central technique of practical medicine. But how much was 'much' innate heat? How does one measure a quality? In *De Complexionibus* Galen rehearsed the arguments of doctors who had discussed whether infants or youths were hotter. This involved the distinction between *more* heat and 'sharper' or 'stronger' heat.[42] Galen begins his dialectical treatment by saying that sometimes the word 'hot' is applied to the quality, while at other times it is the name of a hot body, particularly in old writings. There is then more heat in a larger hot body than in a smaller. If two vessels of different sizes are filled with warm water, the larger vessel contains more heat. The underlying problem was Aristotle's assertion that quality and quantity are separate categories and that qualities cannot be quantified.

Galen also rationalised Hippocratic prognosis. Here Galen was in a difficult situation. It seems to have been some sort of prediction from the pulse that secured his appointment to the emperor, but as we have seen, it was a dangerous business making predictions about the emperor. While Galen had successfully promoted his own techniques of prognostication, it was another matter when he had to explain the words of Hippocrates, as he did in his commentary on *Prognosis*, written late in life. The problem was partly that Hippocrates talked less precisely than Galen would have wished about foretelling the future. Like the *Aphorisms*, the Hippocratic text on prognosis is not a reasoned argument but a description of signs that bode ill or well. This was uncomfortably close to the soothsayers' practice of seeking signs in entrails or the flight of birds, particularly since both practices were based on a knowledge of what was normal, in order to identify the abnormal. No doubt Galen remembered being called a soothsayer when he first made a prognostication in Rome. He now urgently needed to rationalise Hippocratic prognosis to distance it from soothsaying.

Part of ancient soothsaying was predicting what was going to happen by the will of the gods, which was not at all a philosophical thing to do. We have seen that many Greek philosophers wanted to keep the gods out of nature, and although Galen believed in a creative demiurge, he held that it was above all a *rational* creator. Prognosis too had to be rational. But Hippocrates had used words that seemed to allow for forms of prediction

---

[42] *Articella* (1483), f. 12r: *abundantius and acutior et fortior.*

other than the rational, and Galen had to deal with this. The problem was perhaps a common one in the Greek and Latin tradition and even those that followed. We use the term 'divination' for seeing the future or other difficult things, as if by appeal to the gods. 'Providence' is some principle that guides us into the future, perhaps the Deity, although literally it is 'seeing before', seeing something before it happens.

Galen was faced with similar problems when interpreting Hippocrates. This is no place for a discussion of Greek etymology, but we must look briefly at Galen's commentary, for it was an important text in the Latin tradition of Western medicine. Indeed, the Latin tradition characteristically takes on a life of its own, raising matters not in the conversation between Galen and Hippocrates. While Galen had recognised the political and philosophical dangers of predicting the future, these became largely religious problems in the Middle Ages. Predicting the future seemed to deny man's free will and usurp the authority of God.[43] But medically prognostication was very important. We have already seen that the medieval version of the Hippocratic text emphasised the utility of prognosis in enhancing the reputation of the practitioner, and perhaps no other text is quite so blunt about marketplace strategy. The predicting doctor is 'nobler than divine prophets', says the medieval text.[44]

Galen begins by saying that originally Hippocrates had not used the word for prediction that appeared in the text Galen was commenting on. He believed that Hippocrates the rationalist had used, or at least *meant* 'prognosis' rather than a simpler and non-rational term that meant 'seeing into the future' – *previsio* in the Latin – as used by the poets Homer and Euripides.[45] It was clearly an important matter for Galen, who invokes Solon and the usage of the rhetors to explain *previsio*. He also mentions philosophers who talk of *previsio* as the beneficial governance of the world by a creator – our 'providence'. Galen can accept this usage of the term, for his demiurge was rational: *previsio*, he says, is a name that is derived from a thing that is reasoned about before it comes into being.[46] What he could not accept was foresight in a world governed only by chance. Prognosis, then, was rational *previsio* that rested on the natures of things and the signs they gave. It was an ordered body of knowledge, a *scientia*; it rationally prepared the doctor for what was to come, and generated in the patient a trust which made the doctor's task easier. He had to defend this *scientia* against other doctors who thought the job of the physician

---

[43] See Roger French, 'Astrology in medical practice', in García-Ballester et al. (1994), pp. 30–59.
[44] *Articella* (1483), f. 47r.   [45] *Articella* (1483), f. 47r–v.
[46] *Manifestus est ergo quod nomen derivatur a re que ratiocinatur ante esse suum. Articella* (1483), f. 47v.

was to maintain and restore health and that trying to look into the future was divination. These seem to have been doctors who also had commented on Hippocrates, and Galen has to deal with the troublesome Hippocratic opinion that there was something divine in acute diseases.[47]

Galen was well aware of the power of prognosis to impress. He tells the story of meeting the philosopher Glaucon, who taxed Galen with making prognoses that were closer to soothsaying than medicine.[48] To test Galen's medicine, Glaucon led him to the sickroom of a patient whom Galen had not previously visited. Galen snatched a glance at the patient's excreta as they were being carried away, and he stole another at the medicine containers near the bed; Glaucon did not notice these glances and when Galen made the correct prognosis after taking the pulse was astonished that so much could be told from the pulse alone. The patient, moreover, was a doctor himself, and said little to Galen. From the nature of the discharge and from the hyssop in water and honey, Galen concluded that the patient-doctor thought himself to be suffering from pleurisy: Galen guided the patient's hand to where he knew it would hurt when the patient took a deep breath or coughed. So Galen had in an intelligent and rather sly manner used adventitious information and the patient's own professional knowledge to produce a result that startled Glaucon and the patient into admiration. Galen was gratified but remained silent: the moral of the story, he tells the reader, is to use cleverly such pieces of luck as come your way in order to gain a great reputation.

CREATION AND OMNIPOTENCE

We have seen, then, that the whole purpose of Galen's treatment of Hippocrates was to supply the physical reasons that lay behind the great man's medical wisdom. Galen took little on trust, and we can recall that one of his earliest philosophical interests was in demonstration, the rational proof of argument. Nature was also rational: Galen uses *physis* and *demiurgos*, which both emerged in the Latin tradition as *natura*. As we have seen, the demiurge was Platonic and rationally and with foresight created the world and the human body. Galen's admiration for the demiurge reaches a

---

[47] Some translators made these Hippocratic commentators Empirics and Methodists and so reconstructed Galen's circumstances in Rome: for example, Laurentius Laurentianus in the 1625 Giunta edition. Note that Galen's comment is much longer here than in the *Articella* (which includes a long quotation from Hunain).

[48] Galen reports Glaucon as using the word *mantike*, which came into the Latin as *divinatio*. Kühn, *Galeni Opera Omnia*, vol. VIII, p. 362 (*De Locis Affectis*).

level of natural theology in *De Usu Partium* and the essence of his wonder is the rationality with which the demiurge handled matter. Teeth had to be hard, but the hardest substances were brittle and would not serve; sensory nerves had to be soft, which made them liable to damage when extended over long distances (such as those to the stomach), so the demiurge took special steps to protect them: the demiurge took all things into consideration and achieved the best possible compromise.

It was the demiurge's foresight that made the eyelashes remain the same length, for if they were shorter they would not serve their purpose of protecting the eyes and if they were longer they would be cumbersome and impede vision. What was it that kept the eyelashes at a certain length (while the remaining hair on the head grew continuously)? Galen argues that the demiurge endowed them with the necessary feeling. It is not the case, he continues, that the eyelashes live in fear of the creator, subject to his direct order: is this the way that Moses argues? Galen here is on the edge of another world. He lived until almost the end of the second Christian century and knew of the Christians and perhaps more about the Jews. But he could have no sympathy with the doctrine of omnipotence. The intractibility and pre-existence of matter was fundamental to most Greek philosophy, inherent in the doctrines of Plato and Aristotle, and absolutely basic to Galen's view of the demiurge. Creation *ex nihilo* by a Creator who could, if he wished, make water dry, was profoundly unphilosophical to Galen.[49] To accept such a Creator on the basis of faith rather than reasoned demonstration was as bad. Yet ultimately and slowly the Christian Middle Ages, a wholly different climate and one in which the highest truth was undemonstrated revealed knowledge, adopted Galen's medicine.

CELSUS AND PLINY

To complete this account of the ancient sources employed by the later Latin tradition of medicine, we should take note of two authors, Pliny and Celsus. Both were Roman and wrote in Latin, not Greek. They lived over a century before Galen and so we have to jump back in time a little, but they lead the narrative a little more naturally than Galen into the Middle Ages.

We have seen that Celsus reported the story of Alexandrian vivisection: it was part of his *De Medicina*, sometimes called a medical encyclopaedia and

---

[49] It is not decent, said Galen, to observe laws not properly demonstrated by reason 'as in the school of Moses and Christ'. Kühn, *Galeni Opera Omnia*, vol. VIII, p. 579. See also May's translation, p. 533.

thought to be part of a bigger collection of works on the other arts.[50] Pliny
refers to Celsus, who is, then, one of the comparatively few Latin writers
that Pliny uses. But Celsus' medicine is not the traditional simple Roman
affair that heads of households often knew, but draws heavily from Greek
sources. Indeed, his proemium is partly a history of medicine, which begins
with the Greeks. It is here that he discusses Alexandrian vivisection and the
medical sects of the time. Scholars in the past have wondered whether or
not Celsus' book is an adaptation of a Greek original, and whether he was
an active practitioner; but these are not questions that need detain us, for
what is important in this story is that his text is a model of Latinity that
could be put to a particular use when it was finally rediscovered.

Pliny is quite different. The Latin of the *Historia Naturalis* is often terse
and compressed as he tries to cover his multitude of facts. Like Celsus he
depends primarily on Greek sources, but sometimes resents it. His objective
was to do what no Greek had ever done – to report fully on the natural
world and its contents. Part of that world was medicine and it is here that
his dislike of Greeks is most pronounced. He knew that early and worthy
Latin writers had expressed the Roman ideal of a sturdy race full of *gravitas*
and not afraid of hard work, with a simple medicine to match. But the
new Greek doctors had *theory*: it was overly sophisticated, persuasive but
unreliable. Modern urban degeneracy of the Romans gave them diseases
which opened the way for plausible Greeks to establish their medicine at
the very heart of the empire: Pliny even suspected that Greek doctors were
secretly killing important Roman citizens who were their patients. Greek
doctors were greedy, said Pliny, and there was no remedy at law if treatment
went wrong.[51]

Unlike the text of Celsus, that of Pliny was known in the Middle Ages
and abstracts were made of it; one was a collection of medical remedies, the
Medicina Plinii.[52] The number of times the *Historia Naturalis* was printed
suggests that it was a very popular work and Pliny's criticism of doctors
may well have shaped later attacks on doctors, which we will meet below.

[50] *Celsus De Medicina*, vol. i, p. vii. Celsus may have been born in 25 BC.
[51] See Vivian Nutton, 'The perils of patriotism: Pliny and Roman medicine', in Roger French and Frank Greenaway, *Science in the Early Roman Empire: Pliny the Elder, his Sources and Influence*, London (Croom Helm), 1986, pp. 30–58.
[52] See Roger French, 'Pliny and Renaissance medicine', in French and Greenaway, *Science in the Early Roman Empire*, pp. 252–81. On Pliny in his time, see also Mary Beagon, *Roman Nature. The Thought of Pliny the Elder*, Oxford (Clarendon Press), 1992. The recent *Pliny the Elder on Science and Technology*, by John F. Healy, Oxford (Oxford University Press), 1999 unfortunately omits medicine (and is a rather whiggish account); a different view is offered in my *Ancient Natural History: Histories of Nature*, London (Routledge), 1994.

CONCLUSION

It is perhaps necessary to say again that these two chapters have not attempted to be a chronological history of Greek medicine, but rather to outline the sources from which the Latin medical tradition grew. But neither
has it been an attempt to register the translations and commentaries by
which the Latin tradition excavated the mine of ancient medicine. Such a
story would certainly be possible, but it would not necessarily help very
much. The date of a translation, theoretically making a text 'available', says
nothing about who read it or when, and these two chapters cover material
that was clearly part of the formed Latin tradition.

PART II

The Latin tradition

CHAPTER 3

Medieval schools

INTRODUCTION

The Latin medical tradition was a long time in forming. Medicine remained Greek with Galen, and might have become Latin with Celsus, but the loss of the Western Empire a little over two centuries after Galen's death meant the end of any elaborate form of Roman medicine.[1] All of Celsus and most of Galen remained unknown until the Middle Ages. Learned and rational medicine survived in a Greek form in the Eastern Empire, which lasted a thousand years longer than the Western. The Eastern Empire tried to recover the Western by establishing exarchates, for example in Italy, and it seems to have been in such places that some Greek medical works were translated into Latin.[2] There were two main centres of teaching in the east, Constantinople and Alexandria; there was an Alexandrian medical tradition in the Salerno area in the sixth and seventh centuries, and it is known that the Abbey of Montecassino received a copy of the *Aphorisms* as a gift in the tenth century. In the mid-twelfth century there were schools in Salerno favoured by Jews; there were Greek monasteries in the area; and the political and economic growth of Salerno also favoured its cultural development.[3] But in the seventh century Alexandria was taken over for a

[1] Further south and east it was a different matter. St Augustine used Hippocratic medicine in discussing astrology (which he was tempted with but wanted to deny). He was a friend of the medical man Vindicianus, who may have informed him about Hippocratic medicine. See O. Temkin, *Hippocrates in a World of Pagans and Christians*, Baltimore and London (The Johns Hopkins University Press), 1991, pp. 132–6. In general, philosophy and medicine were useful in 'Christian anthropology' and the Christians recognised that these disciplines supplied many things of which they were ignorant. Bishop Nemesius' *Nature of Man* was an anthropology and was paraphrased into Latin by Archbishop Alfanus of Salerno when the medical school there was growing in reputation.
[2] See Loren C. MacKinney, *Early Medieval Medicine with special reference to France and Chartres*, Baltimore (The Johns Hopkins University Press), 1937. See also David C. Lindberg, 'The transmission of Greek and Arabic learning to the West', in his *Science in the Middle Ages*, Chicago (University of Chicago Press), 1978, pp. 52–90. The pre-Salernitan *summa* (see below) seems to have originated in such translations of the fifth to seventh centuries.
[3] See Patricia Skinner, *Health and Medicine in Early Medieval Southern Italy*, Leiden (Brill), 1997, pp. 128, 130–3, 140.

brief period by the Persians and then by the Islamic Arabs, who very rapidly swept through North Africa, up through Spain (beginning in 711) and into Occitania. Greek remained a working language in Arabic Alexandria, and some translations were made directly from Greek to Arabic.[4] The Arabs also encountered the Greek-speaking cultures of the Eastern Mediterranean, whose mathematics, medicine and philosophy they began to admire and translate.

When the Western Christians became strong enough to begin to push the Arabs back to the south they thus had on either side of them two different cultures. The Arabs were alien in language and religion, but had some interesting ideas on astrology and the Greek material they had absorbed. The Christians of the Eastern Empire regarded the Westerners as barbarians who had usurped the position of the old emperor and who spoke a graceless Latin in place of Greek, the old language of culture. Eastern Christianity also differed, being centred on the emperor and not on the bishop of Rome. But these were chronic rather than acute antagonisms and the West had much time to interact with the two cultures as it became slowly more prosperous and powerful.

EARLY SCHOOLS

The institutional arrangements of medical teaching become an important part of our story. Traditionally there were 'schools' of medicine in the ancient world, such as that at Cnidus and another at Cos, associated directly with the name of Hippocrates. The same thing may be said of 'schools' of philosophy, with Plato and the Academy and Aristotle and the Lyceum. These were schools in the sense that they centred on a famous teacher, who may even have owned the physical building or its library.[5] After the death of the famous teacher it was still possible to recognise academics or peripatetics by their doctrines: they constituted a school of thought, like the Erasistrateans in Rome. We do not know how formal the instruction was in such places, although as we have seen it is possible to recognise a cycle in Aristotle's teaching in the Lyceum.

However, in the Eastern Empire there is good evidence of formal instruction, and vestiges of a detailed curriculum of studies are plain.[6] The works

[4] See M. Ullmann, *Islamic Medicine*, Edinburgh (Edinburgh University Press), 1978, p. 8. There was no communication between Alexandria and Byzantium after 642.

[5] See W. Jaeger, *Aristotle. Fundamentals of the History of his Development*, 2nd edn, London (Oxford University Press), 1962, p. 315.

[6] See A. Z. Iskandar, 'An attempted reconstruction of the late Alexandrian medical curriculum', *Medical History*, 20 (1976) 235–58.

of Galen were important here. As we have seen, Galen wrote diffusely and at great length, often refining his works over the years and maintaining disputes with opponents: he had no school and his writings were unsuitable for a fixed-term curriculum. By the year 500 Galen's works had been compressed to the 'Twenty Books', a canon that was studied in Alexandria and Ravenna.[7] The Alexandrian curriculum was designed to allow a partial medical education for those who could not continue for very long at the school, and there must have been, as in all formal schools, pressure on the teacher to select what was important and teach it in a short time. The full course was based on theory and began with the 'naturals' – the elements, complexions, humours, faculties and so on – which related the body to the world at large.

The first work to be studied in the Alexandrian curriculum was Galen's *De Sectis*, together with a commentary on it by John of Alexandria, who is thought to have lived in the first half of the seventh century. This may have been a standard commentary, for another form of it is known and attributed to Agnellus of Ravenna.[8] *De Sectis* was a good introductory text for it set out the different ways of doing medicine that Galen had met in Rome. But while Galen had considerable sympathy with the methods of sensory observation used in Empirical medicine, the commentary by John moves firmly in the direction of the Rationalists. This was perhaps a natural tendency on the part of a classroom teacher. His business was with words, not sensory perception. The constraints of time not only ruled this out – for the art was long and life was short – but favoured a medicine that could be drawn out of first principles, which could be introduced quickly. John's commentary shares a feature of later medieval commentaries, namely that in discussing Galen's medicine it makes the circumstances of Galen's medicine those of John and his medicine. Galen's enemies were still there, as were the sects. John repeats the vivisection rumour – naturally, Herophilus and Erasistratus were Rationalists – and even discusses in the present tense those who vivisected animals in his day.

John's commentary contains a doctrine which became central to the medicine of the Middle Ages and later, an item of faith of the Learned and

[7] See Vivian Nutton, 'God, Galen and the depaganization of ancient medicine', in Peter Biller and Joseph Ziegler, eds., *Religion and Medicine in the Middle Ages*, The University of York (York Medieval Press), 2001, pp. 17–32, p. 25. See also Iskandar, 'Alexandrian medical curriculum'. Ravenna was the capital of the exarchate from 568 to 752: see Danielle Jacquart, 'Medical scholasticism', in M. D. Grmek, ed., *Western Medical Thought from Antiquity to the Middle Ages*, trans. A. Shugaar, Cambridge, Mass. and London (Harvard University Press), 1998, p. 200.

[8] See C. D. Pritchett, ed., *Iohannis Alexandrini Commentarium in Librum de Sectis Galeni*, Leiden (Brill), 1982; Agnellus of Ravenna, *Lectures on Galen's De Sectis*, Buffalo, N.Y. (Department of Classics, State University of New York at Buffalo), 1981.

Rational Doctor in the Latin tradition of medicine. It was that medicine and philosophy are sisters, *philosophia et medicine duae sorores sunt*.[9] Related to it was the doctrine that 'medicine is the philosophy of the body and philosophy the medicine of the soul', which also had an Alexandrian origin and was used by Agnellus of Ravenna.[10]

The schools of the Eastern Empire and the commentary on *De Sectis* are important because they helped shape later medicine, and not just by encouraging a rationalist approach, the rationalism of the Rational and Learned Doctor.[11] The constraints of the classroom led to special ways of presenting and handling knowledge: learning and rationality were changed by the schools. Philosophy too was taught in schools, and since medieval medicine became highly philosophical, we can glance at some features of the classroom. Aristotle's philosophy in particular was taught with the help of a classroom device called the *accessus ad auctores*, literally a means of access to the authors, or how to understand them.[12] The essence of the technique was that the teacher took his class through a routine set of questions when introducing a new text. The questions asked about the title of the work, its correct attribution to the author, the author's intentions in writing, the mode of exposition he employed, and the part of philosophy to which it belonged. The answers to these questions added to the pupil's understanding of the text, whatever its technical content, which would be explained in a commentary. Treating all texts in a similar way gave a degree of uniformity to the curriculum and helped the teacher to cover a large number of texts in a comparatively short time.

The commentary was another classroom device. We have seen that Galen wrote commentaries on the *Aphorisms* and *Prognosis*, with the aim of defending his interpretation of Hippocrates' old medicine. But Galen had written freely, for an educated public; by contrast, commentaries used for teaching in the classroom were highly structured and, as in the *accessus* (which they often included), routine questions were repeatedly asked. John

---

9   See Cornelius O'Boyle, 'Discussions of the nature of medicine at the university of Paris, ca. 1300', in John van Engen, ed., *Learning Institutionalized. Teaching in the Medieval University*, Notre Dame, Indiana (University of Notre Dame Press), 2000, pp. 197–227.

10 See O. Temkin, *Galenism. Rise and Decline of a Medical Philosophy*, Ithaca, N.Y., and London (Cornell University Press), 1973.

11 'Medicine and philosophy are sisters', said John, in passing on a piece of Alexandrian wisdom to those who would read his book (such as Pietro d'Abano in the late Middle Ages). See O'Boyle, 'Discussions of the nature of medicine'.

12 See E. A. Quain, 'The medieval accessus ad auctores', *Traditio*, 3 (1945) 215–64. For medical examples of the *accessus* see also O. Temkin, 'Studies in late Alexandrian medicine. 1: Alexandrian commentaries on Galen's *De Sectis ad Introducendos*,' *Bulletin of the History of Medicine*, 3 (1935) 405–30.

of Alexandria's commentary on *De Sectis* shows some of these features. We have already seen that of the kinds of medicine discussed in this text the rational kind was best suited to the classroom. Certainly John as a professional teacher would not have been sympathetic to the Methodists' opinion that medicine was essentially simple and could be learned in a short time. John thought and taught that medicine was difficult, rational and needed time to be learned. He readily went back to Herophilus and Erasistratus as the first Rationalists and argued that, except for its cruelty, human vivisection was the best way of learning about the body. We can recall that when Celsus had discussed the same matter he listed a number of things that could be better seen in the opened living body than in a dead dissected one. John of Alexandria does something similar, telling his pupils that there are six things to be observed in an anatomical investigation into the body: for each organ, consider its position, shape, size, composition, number and connections. As a rote of questions to be asked of the organs in turn, this list is related to the *accessus* to the authors, and indeed we might call it an *accessus ad corpus*, an access or introduction to the body.[13] Clearly a classroom device in inspiration, it became surprisingly widespread among later anatomists, who used it to structure their texts. The point for us again is that the circumstances of the classroom changed rationality and learning, producing a sort of anatomical rationality, or at least an accepted structure of knowledge.

While classroom teaching generated such devices as abbreviations of texts, the *accessus*, and particular structures of commentary, outside the classroom scholars had the opportunity to treat texts differently. We are concerned here primarily with the Arabs, who made determined efforts to find and translate technical material from the Greek. Prime among them was Hunain ibn Ishaq (c. 808–73), who worked directly from the Greek, but who was sometimes forced to use the intermediary Syriac or to make re-translations where the task had been poorly done. The intention was to render the Greek as precisely as possible. It was then the business of other scholars to make the medicine so uncovered suitable for the classroom, or to weld it together in great synthetic reference works. Much of medieval Western medicine came out of the Arabic and the formation of the Latin tradition was a question of attempting to reconcile material from Arabic and from Greek sources.

[13] See Roger French, 'A note on the anatomical accessus of the middle ages', *Medical History*, 23 (1979) 461–8.

EARLY TEXTS

The way texts were handled thus depended on what they were used for. Medicine in the early Middle Ages was taught by individual masters, each of whom had a favourite selection of texts. But they were not canonised or necessarily agreed upon by different masters, and the pupils of one master were expected to learn from the collected exemplar of their master. The more important a text seemed to be, the more it was rearranged, excerpted, added to and dismembered. The florilegia and textual fragments of the earlier period give no clear historical picture of the use of texts, but some generalisations are possible. The first is that there is a striking absence of theoretical material. There is almost no anatomy; prognosis is reduced to lists of signs or divination; the action of the humours is described in the simplest way; and pathology is descriptive rather than causal. Pharmacy and *materia medica* are prominent.[14] This is medical learning of a kind, of course, and perhaps similar in broad outline to that of many other cultures; but it was quite different from the medical learning of the Arabs and the Byzantines. Possibly theory was offensive to Christian clerks who must have been responsible for copying many of the manuscripts, and probably it was some 'Christian filter' of this kind that removed a reference to the divinity of the cosmos from Galen's *De Victus Ratione*.[15] Such an action is consistent with a view that a book is respected for its practical utility, not for the integrity of the words of an author. Indeed, authors' names were often lost as the material was reworked. Lists of remedies constituted a large category of these early medical texts, and such things lent themselves naturally to rearrangement.

A survey of manuscripts of the earlier part of the Middle Ages shows clusters of them round the topics of herbs and the names of Galen and Hippocrates.[16] But this is a statistical grouping, rather like the 'pre-Salernitan *summa*' which includes frequently occurring texts.[17] But among all this the Hippocratic *Aphorisms* stands out as an early Latin translation firmly associated with the name of Hippocrates: we still have manuscripts

---

[14] See Faith Wallis, 'Signs and senses: diagnosis and prognosis in early medieval pulse and urine texts', in Peregrine Horden and Emilie Savage-Smith, eds., *The Year 1000. Medical Practice at the end of the first Millennium* [*Social History of Medicine*, 13, 2000], pp. 265–78, at p. 266.

[15] See Faith Wallis, 'The experience of the book: manuscripts, texts and the role of epistomology in early medieval medicine', in Don Bates, ed., *Knowledge and the Scholarly Medical Traditions*, Cambridge (Cambridge University Press), 1995, pp. 101–26.

[16] Wallis, 'The experience of the book', p. 104.

[17] See A. Beccaria, *I Codici di Medicina del periodo Presalernitano*, Rome (Edizioni di Storia e Letteratura), 1956.

of the Carolingian age,[18] and we shall see later the importance of this text for the Rational and Learned Doctor.

The economic recovery of the West was associated with the growth of towns and of trade, conditions that made possible schools and cultural interchange. This is also the background to the customary story of the first of the great translators from the Arabic, and one of the fathers of the Latin tradition of medicine, Constantine the African (who died in 1087). According to this story, Constantine, an Arabic merchant from Muslim North Africa, arrived in the Bay of Salerno in southern Italy. His command of Latin was no more perhaps than his trading required, but he was surprised to learn that the Latins had no medical books on prognostication from urine. Ultimately he settled at the monastery of Montecassino and devoted himself to translating into Latin the medical works that the Arabs had taken from the Greeks, and the big Arabic compendia.[19] Chief amongst them was the *Pantegni* of Haly Abbas, which begins with a discussion of medical theory.[20] Western doctors began to see that medicine could be very theoretical, and if we can date the beginning of the Latin medical tradition to Constantine, doctors soon saw the advantages of a medicine that, in our terms, was rational. While Constantine's material came from what is now Tunisia, later translators at Montecassino, such as Desiderius and Alfanus (archbishop of Salerno),[21] made a concerted effort to find Greek texts in southern Italy (where there were Greek-speaking areas, sometimes known as *magna Graecia*).[22]

TO WHAT PART OF PHILOSOPHY DOES IT BELONG?

Cathedrals had had schools since Carolingian times, but in the new and prosperous towns, schools expanded in their intake and subject matter. Often their popularity depended on a single teacher, a 'hero' who could attract pupils from all over Europe. In the 'Renaissance' of the twelfth century professional teachers gave attention to the whole range of human

---

[18] See MacKinney, *Early Medieval Medicine*, p. 98.

[19] In fact the library at Montecassino did contain at least one manuscript containing a tract on prognostication from urine. See Wallis, 'Signs and senses', p. 269.

[20] See Jacquart, 'Medical scholasticism', p. 204.

[21] See Paul O. Kristeller, 'Batholomaeus, Musandinus and Maurus of Salerno and other early commentators of the *Articella*, with a tentative list of texts and manuscripts', *Italia medioevale e umanistica*, 19 (1976) 57–87. See also Cornelius O'Boyle, *The Art of Medicine. Medical Teaching at the University of Paris 1250–1400*, Leiden (Brill), 1998, pp. 88, 94.

[22] See also Danielle Jacquart, 'The influence of Arabic medicine in the medieval West', in *Encyclopedia of the History of Arabic Science*, vol. 3, London (Routledge), 1996, pp. 963–84, which contains a useful chronological table.

knowledge. This was all 'philosophy', often defined as knowledge of God and His works. The purpose of philosophy was to lead the good life, perfecting the soul as far as was possible on earth.[23] Teachers argued that philosophy became necessary because knowledge and the ability to hold it had been lost at the Fall.[24] It was no longer possible to know God directly or read His word in the Bible with full understanding. It could be read literally for a surface meaning or spiritually for its deeper and often allegorical meaning, but a training in the arts was necessary for both (said the teachers).

Some urgency was felt in all this, for before the Second Coming Christian society, so the schoolmen argued, should be stable and extended as far as possible; the means of doing so was the recovery of prelapsarian knowledge according to the divisions of 'philosophy'.[25] Even the old pagan philosophers were useful because of the detail in their work, which had proceeded some way along the path to true Christian knowledge. But too much attention to the detail of natural philosophy, for example, seemed to churchmen to be 'curiosity', a sin that drew the observer away from revealed knowledge.[26] Nevertheless, in the twelfth century there was an optimism that one could learn more about God from the elements of the physical world and from man's body.

Medicine was in a difficult position here. The doctor who knew about the natural world and the human body demonstrated that he was an expert and had medically useful knowledge.[27] Undoubtedly doctors used their natural knowledge as a form of advertising, and a number of their patients recognised this. But Christians objected to the global and naturalistic explanations of disease,[28] which was part of the dangerous tendency of doctors to attribute power and autonomy to nature, thereby detracting from God's omnipotence. They also objected to the doctors' discussion about the soul, which, like nature, had been a topic in Greek philosophy

---

[23] See, for example, Hugh of St Victor's account of philosophy: Bro. Charles Henry Buttimer, ed., *Hugonis de Sancto Victore Didascalicon. De Studio Legendi*, Washington, DC (The Catholic University of America Press), 1939 (Hugh's preface).

[24] See, for example, B. Smalley, *The Study of the Bible in the Middle Ages*, 3rd edn, Oxford (Clarendon Press), 1984, p. 26; G. R. Evans, *The Language and Logic of the Bible*, Cambridge (Cambridge University Press), 1984, p. 1.

[25] See R. W. Southern, *Scholastic Humanism and the Unification of Europe*, vol. 1 *Foundations*, Oxford (Blackwell), 1995.

[26] See, for example, Vincent of Beauvais (Vincentius Burgundus), *Bibliotheca Mundi Speculum Quadruplex, Naturale, Doctrinale, Morale, Historiale*, 4 vols., Douai, 1624: *Doctrinale*, I, 26, p. 23.

[27] Words derived from the Greek word for nature, *physis*, generally hovered in meaning between 'nature' (as in Aristotle's *Physics*) and 'medicine' (as in our 'physician'). See Brian Lawn, *The Rise and Decline of the Scholastic 'Quaestio Disputata'*, Leiden (Brill), 1993. See also J. Bylebyl, 'The medical meaning of *physica*', *Osiris*, 2nd series, 6 (1990) 16–41.

[28] See Wallis, 'The experience of the book', p. 119. See also Wallis, 'Signs and senses', p. 266.

and was inappropriate for the Christian tradition. Philosophy indeed was a major part of the problem. The church had need of philosophy only to defend and promote itself and was traditionally cautious lest its disciples be led astray by the words of the philosophers. Medical men began to find an interesting philosophy in the new medical works coming out of the Arabic, and the grammarian at Chartres, William of Conches (c. 1085–aft. 1154), for example, was familiar with the *Pantegni*, the medical reference work translated by Constantine the African.[29] William treated the story of the creation of Eve from Adam's rib in a *literal*, or physical way (rather than spiritual), an attitude that brought down on his head from the church the severe rebuke that he thought like a heretic or, as bad, a philosopher.[30]

'Global and naturalistic explanations of disease' were also clearly part of the doctors' patter, the story they told to their patients. For John of Salisbury (c. 1115–80) a *physicus* was a man who, giving too much authority to nature and not enough to God, studied natural signs about the future, that is, medical prognostication. Probably this now included uroscopy, which Constantine had been surprised to find lacking among the Latins, but which thereafter became the symbol of the doctor. As Daniel of Morley found with astrology, forecasting the future was theologically dangerous.[31] John too disliked medical talk about the soul, the body and its growth, death and resurrection, and the causes and cures of diseases. The soul was central, for it was here that the Christian doctrine of human immortality, derived from the scriptures and the Fathers, came face to face with Greek philosophical teaching, including the nature of, and details of reproduction of animals and plants. As for the causes and cures of disease, John objected in particular to talk of 'complexion', the mixture of elementary qualities in the body, which played such an important part in medical theory. Indeed, to the *physicus* the whole action of the upper world, where first principles

---

[29] The major influence was on William's *Dragmaticon* (about 1144–9), but also on the earlier *Philosophia*. It resulted in William's rather odd corpuscular theory of the four elements. See Italo Ronca, 'The influence of the *Pantegni* on William of Conches' *Dragmaticon*', in Charles Burnett and Danielle Jacquart, eds., *Constantine the African and 'Alī Ibn Al-'Abbās Al-Magūsī: The Pantegni and Related Texts*, Leiden and New York (Brill), 1994, pp. 266–85. On the economic background see B. Stock, 'Science, technology and economic progress in the early middle ages', in Lindberg, *Science in the Middle Ages*, pp. 1–51.

[30] His critic was William of St Thierry, who compared William of Conches with the condemned Abelard (who had also used the *Pantegni*) and the Albigensian heretics; these were the first major clashes between the church and revived ancient philosophy. See J. P. Migne, ed., *Patrologiae Cursus Completus*, (Latin series), 221 vols., Paris, 1866–; vol. 180, cols. 333–40.

[31] Daniel's text is given by K. Sudhoff, 'Daniels von Morley Liber de Naturis Inferiororum et Superiorum', *Archiv für Geschichte der Naturwissenschaften und der Technik*, 8 (1918) 1–40. See John of Salisbury, *Polycraticus*, in Migne, *Patrologiae Cursus Completus*, vol. 199, pp. 415–75 (Book II), at p. 475.

lay, upon the lower was a 'complexioning', a physical action where the theologian saw only the hand of God. When John complained of the doctors' claim to be able to control disease, neutrality and health he is using three categories which are discussed in the Galenic text, the *Tegni*, which became important in medieval medical education.

John's disapproval of doctors was shared by a significant figure. This was Alfred of Shareshill. He is significant because he was one of the first to translate and comment on the physical works of Aristotle, which transformed the philosophy of the late twelfth century. We shall look at this below and here we must complete our glance at twelfth-century perceptions of medicine and doctors. Alfred, as a translator of philosophy, called himself a philosopher, using the word *physicus* in one of its senses. He distanced himself from the medical men, who were mere 'mercenary treaters of disease'.[32] Alfred shared the suspicions of the theologians that the medical men were too inclined to make nature an autonomous principle. He argued forcibly, for example, that what moved the heart was not nature, but the soul.[33] Part of his scorn for doctors was that they (unlike the 'philosophers') were still using pre-Aristotelian philosophy: *plebei medicine professores*, he calls them in his commentary on Aristotle's *Metheora*.[34]

It was not only Alfred who thought doctors mercenary. Churchmen saw that while *medicine* was praiseworthy (for Christ had been a healer) *doctors* were often greedy and deceitful. Even teaching medicine for money could be seen as sinful. The various church decrees forbidding the religious to take up medicine were designed to prevent a loss of recruitment into theology as able men were attracted to the monetary rewards of medical practice. Not only that, but medicine could be seen as a mere manual trade, a productive art that ranked well below the 'liberal arts', which were intellectual and had no physical end-product. The 'division of the sciences' literature ranked theology as the highest study with medicine below even law, another productive and lucrative art.

The fact that the twelfth-century doctor could be attacked on the moral grounds that he sold health for a fee reminds us that he was in a medical marketplace. Attacked for excessive naturalism, for claiming to know the future, for being mercenary and for being intellectually vulgar, the doctor

---

[32] See Carl Sigmund Barach, ed., *Excerpta e libro Alfredi Anglici de Motu Cordis item Costa-ben-Lucae de Differentia Animae et Spiritus*, Innsbruck, 1878, p. 94.

[33] Alfred's book on the motion of the heart, *De Motu Cordis*, dates from about 1200 and thus falls neatly between the twelfth-century philosophers of nature and the use of the new Aristotle in the universities.

[34] See Alfred of Sareshal, *Commentary on the Metheora of Aristotle*, ed. James K. Otte, Leiden and New York (Brill), 1987, p. 42.

was obliged to develop a line of patter, a Good Story, to convince his patients that they were in the hands of a capable man. 'When I hear them they seem to me to be able to raise the dead, thinking they are as good as Aesculapius', said John of Salisbury.[35] He added significantly that he was unable to give faith to the doctors – to believe their stories – because they disagreed so much. Practitioners of an art who disagree about its principles or practice bring the art into disrepute and when doctors disagree the patient is disillusioned. But, as we shall see shortly, the doctors soon found themselves with new weapons, including collaboration and agreement, in their attempts to persuade.

INCORPORATION

An important feature of the growth of towns in the West was the appearance of corporations. The voluntary association of people with common interests was a way of promoting those interests. Guilds were corporations and were formed by people making and selling things or people who traded abroad. Guilds had a major voice in the running of towns, which were themselves corporations. The biggest corporation, albeit of a special kind, was the church. In some places the cathedral schools, under the guidance of the bishop's chancellor, grew enormously, often under a charismatic or 'heroic' teacher. Aristotle's logic was a popular subject, for with it came the power to argue convincingly and secure a career, perhaps in the court of a potentate. But in the later twelfth century an important change took place. Some schools were so big that they had a number of masters and in some places the masters realised that they could do better by collaborating rather than competing. In short, they formed a guild of teachers; those in Paris called theirs a *consortium*.[36]

A guild was a legal person: it could sue and be sued, it could hold land, write its own statutes, elect its own officers, including those who represented it to other important corporations of persons, and possess a common seal. The only external condition was that its business had to be a genuine and lawful activity.[37] This has an important corollary for us. The first schools taught the liberal arts, but soon the teachers of medicine also formed masters' guilds. The essential thing about them both

---

[35] C. C. I. Webb, ed., *Ioannis Saresberiensis Episcopi Carnotensis Policrati sive de nugis curialium et vestigiis philosophorum*, 2 vols., Oxford (Clarendon Press), 1909; vol. I, p. 167.

[36] See H. Denifle, O. P., *Chartularium Universitatis Parisiensis*, vol. I, Paris, 1889.

[37] The principle was established by Innocent IV (d. 1254). See Antony Black, *Guilds and Civil Society in European Political Thought from the Twelfth Century to the Present*, London (Methuen), 1984, p. 20.

was that it was the masters of the guild who decided what their business was. The *consortia* of teachers drew up curricula, decided who the founders and heroes of their subject were, and canonised the texts they chose. No one outside a guild of medical men had the authority to say what medicine was; and when princes uttered decrees about medical training or licensing, it seems always to have been done on the advice of a panel of doctors. Finally, a guild of teaching masters taught their pupils to a level where they became masters themselves: in doing this the guilds controlled the size of the group, that is, the number of teaching and practising doctors. Part of the attraction of university-trained doctors was that they were not ten-a-penny. Control of the monopoly of the practice of internal medicine was made possible by this control of numbers entering the profession, and it was made possible too by the fact that inception and the licence now constituted a medical *qualification* in some nearly modern sense.

THE RATIONALITY OF THE DOCTOR

Half the story of the learned and rational doctor is how he acquired his rationality. At the root of it all was the syllogism, invented, or at least codified, by Aristotle. Up to the middle of the twelfth century the medieval scholar had only the 'old logic' of Aristotle, consisting mainly of his *Categories* and *Interpretation*.[38] *Interpretation* is concerned with logical propositions. *Categories* deals with the terms used in syllogisms and they are grouped under a number of heads: substance, quantity, quality, relation, place, time, position, state, action and passion.[39] For future reference there are two things we need to note about this list. The first is that quantity and quality are different categories. In strict Aristotelian terms a quality had no characteristics of quantity; but in medical theory a quality of, say, a medicine was the means by which it had its effect, and it became desirable for Galen and much more for the medieval doctors to give some numerical assessment of the activity or power of the medicine. The quantification of qualities was a major medieval undertaking. Second, the categories represent a list of attributes that could be sought in a variety of circumstances, especially when Aristotelian logic became well known. It is argued below

---

[38] For an introduction to the question of logic see Norman Kretzmann, Anthony Kenny and Jan Pinborg, *The Cambridge History of Later Medieval Philosophy*, Cambridge (Cambridge University Press), 1990, Introduction, p. 5.

[39] See D. P. Henry, 'Predicables and categories', in *The Cambridge History of Later Medieval Philosophy*, pp. 128–42, at p. 129.

that they could be sought in relation to the human body, in both textual and physical anatomies.[40]

In the second half of the twelfth century, thanks largely to the translations of James of Venice, the 'new logic' became available. This made logic much more powerful, and we can see the attractions for the teacher and student of the whole collection, called the *Organon*, the 'tool' or 'instrument' of argument. The heroic teacher attracted students looking for careers in which the presentation of facts and the arguing of cases were important. Aristotle's *Sophistical Refutations* (*De Sophisticis Elenchis*), for example, was one of the most important texts of the new logic and it taught the debater how to recognise apparent refutations of his arguments that were in fact based on fallacies (sophistical syllogisms).[41] Finding these in one's opponent's argument and avoiding them in one's own was a recipe for success in the man of affairs.

Another important text in the new logic was the *Topica*.[42] Aristotle said that its purpose was to enable the reader to argue properly about any problem from generally accepted opinions. Again, in a career outside the university it was 'probable opinions' that a diplomat or agent of a potentate was most likely to encounter. The arguments used were correctly syllogistic in form, which gave the arguer the extra authority of Aristotle's theoretical discussion of the syllogism in the *Prior Analytics*. The other book on 'analytic' – Aristotle's term for logic – was the *Posterior Analytics*. This held out the offer of certainty in knowledge: knowledge that could be demonstrated to be true. Commentators have wondered how far this text offers a programme for dealing with the natural world, of which Aristotle gave an account in the *libri naturales*, from the general principles of natural motion up through the earth and heavens to texts such as the *History of Animals*. Could Greek *historia* become demonstrable knowledge? The medieval doctors thought it could. Already in the possession of the *Posterior Analytics*, when the physical works began to be translated in the late twelfth century, scholars saw a huge opportunity to gain fully philosophical knowledge of the natural world. The rationality of the learned doctor, developing over the thirteenth century, interpreted the natural world and the human body in a certain way. Logic was more than words, meanings and syllogisms:

---

[40] See French, 'Anatomical accessus', p. 464.

[41] '. . . arguments that appear to be refutations but are really fallacies', *De Sophisticis Elenchis*, 164a20, and see the Introduction to E. S. Forster and D. J. Furley, *Aristotle On Sophistical Refutations, On Coming-to-be and Passing-Away, On the Cosmos*, Cambridge, Mass. (Harvard University Press), 1992 (i.e., the third volume of the Loeb Library series of Aristotle), pp. 2, 11.

[42] We shall see below that it was these two texts, the *Topics* and the *Sophistical Refutations*, that Bacon complained of doctors using too much.

the world itself acted in a logical way. It had, after all, been created with divine rationality, and it came to be accepted that God had put it together in an Aristotelian way. Logic was physical, in a sense we find it difficult to recapture.[43] Thus there were many facets of the authority that the Rational and Learned Doctor used to introduce his subject into the new incorporated schools.

SALERNO AND THE *ARTICELLA*

Tradition attributes great age to the medical 'school' of Salerno, but this has not been supported by recent scholarship.[44] It is not clear how formal this school was in the twelfth century, but Salerno was clearly known as a good place to go to learn medicine; perhaps there was an assemblage of medical teachers there who had begun to collaborate rather than compete as heroes.[45] Salerno is not far from Montecassino, where Constantine the African made his translations from the Arabic, and again tradition gave these an important role in medical education in Salerno. It has even been suggested that Arabic institutions of learning were models for European teaching guilds, but the matter has not been resolved.[46]

One circumstance that suggests a degree of formality about the school of Salerno was the appearance of a textbook. Textbooks imply a settled curriculum, agreed among the teaching masters. In practice the textbook acted like the statutes of a guild, defining what medicine was. If the Latin tradition in medicine can be said to have begun with Constantine's translations, then it was canonised with the fully developed textbook, known generically as the *Articella*. This 'small art' of medicine was quite different from the individual selections of texts of the heroic medical teachers. There, practical

---

[43] See Roger French, *Canonical Medicine. Gentile da Foligno and Scholasticism*, Leiden (Brill), 2001, pp. 111–24.

[44] See Kristeller, 'Bartholomaeus'. For a summary view see also Kristeller's 'Philosophy and medicine in medieval and renaissance Italy', in Stuart F. Spicker, ed., *Organism, Medicine and Metaphysics*, Dordrecht (Reidel), 1978, pp. 29–40. See the scholarly summary in Luis García-Ballester's introduction to *Practical Medicine from Salerno to the Black Death*, eds. Luis García-Ballester, Roger French, Jon Arrizabalaga and Andrew Cunningham, Cambridge (Cambridge University Press), 1994. Many universities have myths of very early origins in order to secure the authority of age. Many humanists ignored such myths because they were stories of the early Middle Ages, not the classical period. See Walter Rüegg, 'Themes', in Walter Rüegg, general ed., *A History of the University in Europe. Volume I Universities in the Middle Ages*, ed. Hilde de Ridder-Symoens, Cambridge (Cambridge University Press), 1992, pp. 3–34, at p. 7.

[45] Medicine at Salerno seems to have been vocational: see Danielle Jacquart, ' "Theorica" et "practica" dans l'enseignment de la médecine à Salerne au xiiᵉ siècle', in her *La Science médicale Occidentale entre deux Renaissances*, Aldershot (Variorum), 1997, item VII.

[46] See G. Makdisi, *The Rise of Colleges*, Edinburgh University Press, 1981; and his 'The scholastic method in medieval education: an enquiry into its origins in law and theology', *Speculum*, 49 (1974) 640–61.

utility had been of the essence and authors' names had little weight. Here, as befitted a canonical collection, it was important to know which of the founding fathers of medicine had written the texts. Although in its early form the *Articella* was not very theoretical, it was a highly structured collection of knowledge about what medicine was and instructions about what to do. Most of those instructions related to prognosis, including uroscopy, which brings us back to Constantine's surprise that before him the Latins did not prognosticate in this way.

In its first form the *Articella* was known simply as 'The Art of Medicine', *Ars Medicine*, and it is arguable that the collection was formed round a nucleus of the Hippocratic *Aphorisms*. We have already seen that this particular collection of medical wisdom was important to Galen and that it was translated early in the Middle Ages into Latin (but the *Ars Medicine* version was another translation). We also saw that many of the aphorisms are prognostic and one of the purposes of the *Ars Medicine* was to enable the medieval doctor to judge when a case was going to turn out well or not. Indeed, the next most important component of the *Ars Medicine* was the Hippocratic *Prognosis*, which is almost a manual for detecting hopeless cases. The medieval form of *Prognosis* opens with much more emphasis than the original Greek on the glory to be obtained from correct prognosis, and when students in the philosophy course read about 'the most glorious Hippocrates' it was a reference to this.[47] The *Ars Medicine* also corrected the earlier Latin ignorance of uroscopy by including a short tract by the Byzantine Theophilus. This was matched by an incomplete tract on prognostication from the pulse attributed to a Philaretus (about whom little is known). In short, almost the whole early collection of texts was prognostic in intent. Clearly, medieval doctors were aware of the rewards of good prognostication. A successful outcome of a case enhanced the practitioner's reputation and a prediction of death avoided damaging it.

The only theoretical component of the *Ars Medicine* was the *Isagoge* of Joannitius, which always came in first place.[48] This is a very short tract of a hundred sentences setting out the principal headings of the theory of medicine, mostly Galenic. It is so terse that it could not be used in any fundamental way to explain the medical wisdom of the Hippocratic texts, but it introduced the Salernitans to a philosophy of nature that could be used

[47] See London, British Library, Royal 12 G II, f. 358v: [*ipocratis*] *gloriosissimi quia inter omnes loquentes de medicina prognostica laudis debetur ypocrati*. Also Royal 12 G V, f. 221v; London, British Library, Harleian 3487, f. 202v and Durham Cathedral, C III 17, f. 381r.
[48] On the *Isagoge* see Danielle Jacquart, 'A l'aube de la renaissance médicale des xie–xiie siècles: "l'Isagoge Johannitii" et son traducteur', in her *La Science médicale Occidentale entre deux Renaissances*, Aldershot (Variorum), 1997, item I.

in conjunction with medical wisdom. We have already seen that twelfth-century physicians could talk grandly about nature as a principle and about the action of the upper world on the lower, but here at hand was an emerging philosophy – that of Aristotle – that looked more systematic, inclusive and convincing. The Salernitans and medical teachers in other schools explored this possibility in two main ways. First, they sought to understand Hippocratic medical wisdom better by adding Galen's commentaries to the textbook. In this way the *Ars Medicine* became the *Ars Commentata*, and much bigger. Between themselves physicians often referred to medicine simply as 'the art' in reference to the first aphorism, and sometimes as 'the art of Hippocrates'; *Articella* is a comparatively late Italian vernacular term meaning 'little art'. As the *Ars Commentata* developed it increasingly took on the form of a Galenic rationalising explanation of Hippocratic medical wisdom, and a big new addition to the collection was the *Tegni*, thought to have been written by Galen in old age as a summary of medical principles. In some sense the heart of medieval medical education was explaining the *Aphorisms* on the basis of the *Tegni*.

It has also been argued that northern France was also a likely place for the new medicine to have developed. The *Ars Medicine* was being glossed there in the twelfth century in the biblical manner; and the schools there were familiar with the new Greek–Latin translations of Aristotle's physical works. Masters at Chartres were also commenting on the texts of the *Articella* at the time of John of Salisbury (d. 1180) and it has been argued that the *Articella* could have had a French origin.[49] With these schools were associated scholars such as Hugh of St Victor, John of Salisbury and Bernard Sylvestris; Norman political power linked the area with southern Italy, a natural place for translations from the Greek; and scholars such as William of Conches at Chartres were familiar with the *Pantegni*.[50]

ARISTOTLE AND THE LATIN TRADITION

The second way in which the Salernitans explored the opportunities of the new rationalism was by using Aristotle's physical works directly. In the

[49] For a summary of the literature see Francis Newton, 'Constantine the African and Montecassino: new elements and the text of the Isagoge', in Burnett and Jacquart, *Constantine the African*, pp. 16–47, at p. 17.
[50] See O'Boyle, *The Art of Medicine*, p. 99; Marie Thérèse D'Alverny, 'Translations and translators', in *Renaissance and Renewal in the Twelfth Century*, ed. Robert L. Benson and Giles Constable, Cambridge, Mass. (Harvard University Press), 1982, pp. 421–62.

1160s, when in other parts of Europe Aristotle was known principally as a logician, the Salernitans were reading his physical works to give rationalist explanations to medical wisdom.[51] This was an important change, and we need to look a little at its context. Indeed, the first use and then the canonisation of Aristotle's physical works was a defining moment in the intellectual history of the West. We need to note a few points about it. First, the importance of the Aristotelian works in an internal and external sense has encouraged historians to treat them as if they had a career of their own, and we often read that the works 'arrived' or occurred in the West as a 'legacy'. But this was not the case and what in fact happened is important for the argument of this book. There was a contemporary parallel with astrology, an exciting art of prognostication that could be found in Arabic sources. When they came to know this, would-be astrologers went and sought out the texts, which was sometimes an arduous business. What was new about Arabic astrology was that it predicted the future with certainty and mathematical precision: it was not only exciting but commercially valuable.[52] A second parallel was law. Part of the urban renewal was a new interest in Roman Law, which was different from the customary law that stretched over much of Europe. It had been the law of Rome, and some thought that Rome again ought to be a seat of the law. It had been, too, the law of emperors and was therefore of interest to the Holy Roman Emperor, who claimed the power of the Caesars. The emperor had become 'holy' with the aid of the pope, and the pope became more powerful with the aid of the emperor; but it was never an easy alliance, and it was important to have authority when negotiating claims to political power. The great works on Roman Law were found as a result of a deliberate search for them, and they were found – perhaps it was not a coincidence – in about 1070 in the monastery of Montecassino, where Constantine had translated the *Pantegni*.

Indeed, books were now important in a new way. Authority lay in books, as it did in the Bible. The bible of the doctors was first the *Pantegni* and then the huge *Canon* of Avicenna, translated by Gerard of Cremona (c. 1114–87) in Toledo, at the boundary of Muslim and Christian Spain. The bible of the lawyers was the *Digest* of Justinian, before the discovery of which, law, like medicine, had been a question of fragmentary ancient texts and abridgements set in a matrix of contemporary knowledge, but containing

---

[51] See D'Alverny, 'Translations and translators'.
[52] See for example Roger French, 'Foretelling the future. Arabic astrology and English medicine in the late twelfth century', *Isis*, 87 (1996) 453–80.

nothing reflective that could be described as theory.[53] The importance of
the new law texts was such that the earliest groups of scholars which we
can recognise as having been in some sense incorporated were the legists of
Bologna.[54]

To many historians the central event of the early history of Western
medicine was the 'reception' of texts, particularly Greek. This is a view
partly conditioned by the concerns of the classical scholar, for whom texts
are classical and canonical. But medical texts, like those of law and astrology, did not arrive: they were fetched. Accounts of the transmission of
texts do not normally give much attention to the motives of the translators but some of the circumstances are suggestive.[55] First, the translations
were often supported by men who we can assume had some interest in
the result. The model is the translation of religious materials. Robert of
Chester (fl. 1141–50) was asked by Peter of Cluny to translate the Koran;
Mark of Toledo (fl. 1191–1216) was supported by the archbishop of Toledo
while he translated Islamic materials for use in the archbishop's campaign
against the Muslims.[56] Michael Scot, the early translator of Aristotle, was
also supported by the archbishop. Rulers had a need for educated men
and sometimes, like Roger, Frederick II and Manfred (all kings of Sicily),
funded translations. When Western translators such as Michael Scot and
Alfred of Shareshill worked from Arabic with the help of Jewish translators,
it was often possible because the Jews too had a need for the texts of astronomy, medicine and other technical subjects. Where we do not hear about
patronage, as in the case of Daniel of Morley[57] and Alfred of Shareshill, it
seems that the translators spent a great deal of money and time (perhaps
at the risk of their careers) travelling to centres of translation. In addition
to religious materials, astrology and medicine are conspicuous in the translations of the eleventh and twelfth centuries. Both were valuable forms of
knowledge, even in a commercial sense, and both were concerned with the
important business of prognostication.[58]

[53] See Stephan Kuttner, 'The revival of jurisprudence', in Benson and Constable, eds., *Renaissance and Renewal in the Twelfth Century*, pp. 299–323.

[54] Law students began forming nations in Bologna at the end of the twelfth century, and Bologna is generally regarded as the oldest university. Rüegg, 'Themes', p. 6.

[55] A standard source for 'transmission' is the detailed account given by D. C. Lindberg, 'The trans-mission of Greek and Arabic learning to the West', in D. C. Lindberg, *Science in the Middle Ages*, Chicago (University of Chicago Press), 1978, pp. 52–90.

[56] Lindberg, 'Transmission', p. 66.

[57] On Daniel, see also R. W. Hunt, 'English learning in the late twelfth century', in R. W. Southern, ed., *Essays in Medieval History*, London and New York (Macmillan), 1968, pp. 106–28.

[58] Astronomy, long esteemed by historians of science as the model 'science' of the Middle Ages, can also be seen as the theoretical basis of the practice of astrology. See French, 'Foretelling the future'.

THE UNIVERSITIES

The discovery and use of Aristotle's physical works is a story that has to be told in conjunction with that of the universities. These *studia* play a central role in the story of the Rational and Learned Doctor, for they secured for his subject the autonomy of the guild; they provided him with the intellectual component of his trade; and they were the institutional arena in which he secured the professional standing he needed for it. There were two main models on which European universities were founded. In the south, particularly in Italy, the schools in which medicine was taught were associations of students, set up for the mutual protection and promotion of young men coming into a strange town.[59] They elected their teachers and established the rules, at least at first. They wanted a practical training, and read arts and medicine together. The Bolognese schools of medicine appeared in about 1260 but the lawyers did not recognise it as a proper university until 1316.[60] The first known medical degree was in 1268.[61] In Montpellier there had been unincorporated schools of medicine as early as 1135 (separate from the earlier schools of law). Again, the pope took control (1220) with statutes that gave the masters authority; what seems to have happened was that the college of doctors was absorbed into the student university. Montpellier, like the universities of Spain and Portugal, was mixed, with the students electing their rector.[62]

The northern model, of which Paris was the exemplar, was less vocational. It grew out of the cathedral school, and the chancellor long claimed the right to control it. It was essentially an incorporation of masters, and we have seen that the Parisian masters called it their *consortium*. We also noticed the popularity of logic in the schools of the twelfth century, and now, thinking of Paris at the beginning of the thirteenth century, this was taught with grammar and rhetoric, all useful skills of communication for a later career. This *trivium* was taught early in the arts course (and so became known

---

[59] In Bologna in 1230–40 the two universities, transmontane and cismontane, were clearly distinct. The masters were often Bolognese and readily swore not to go elsewhere; the rectors, elected by students, did not. Control was secular until the pope took charge, for example by asserting in 1219 that the archdeacon of Bologna should award the licence. Law students in Bologna were generally adults and often high in social scale. See Jacques Verger, 'Patterns', in Ridder-Symoens, *Universities in the Middle Ages*, pp. 35–68, at p. 49.

[60] Verger, 'Patterns', p. 50.

[61] See Nancy Siraisi, 'The faculty of medicine', in Ridder-Symoens, *Universities in the Middle Ages*, pp. 360–86, at p. 368.

[62] Verger, 'Patterns', pp. 39, 52; Siraisi, 'The faculty of medicine', p. 367. There were new medical statutes in 1239, when Henry of Winchester flourished there: he wrote the earliest known medical text, a commentary on the *Isagoge*.

pejoratively as 'trivial') and was followed by the four mathematical arts that completed the seven liberal arts: the *quadrivium* of astronomy, arithmetic, geometry and music. Comparatively few students went from the arts course to the higher faculties, and the greater number of masters of arts gave them much political power within the *consortium*.

This pattern of teaching was greatly changed when the physical works of Aristotle began to circulate.[63] The masters began to teach natural philosophy, generally known simply as 'philosophy' unless there was need to distinguish it from Aristotle's 'moral philosophy'. But the church was ambivalent about philosophy. The principal problem was that Aristotle, keeping the divine out of nature, had said that the world was eternal, not created. As with the case of William of Conches, Aristotle could lead one into 'curiosity' or a literal reading of the natural world. In Paris there was an outbreak of heresy that could be attributed to reading too much Aristotle, and the general feeling was that Aristotle wrote too much about creation (the natural world) and not enough about the Creator. Consequently, reading the physical works was prohibited in Paris in 1210 and again in 1215. On the other hand, there was a heresy of a different kind in Languedoc which the church thought could be suppressed by using the physical works, and the masters of Toulouse wrote to other schools, urging masters to come and defend the faith, with the added freedom of reading Aristotle.

The Cathar heretics in and around Albi and Toulouse argued that the world was so obviously an evil place that it must have been created by an evil God, whom the good God had created but could not control. The Catholics were horrified and insisted that God was the omnipotent and good Creator, who had, however, given his created angels free will to choose good or evil. The heretics retorted that in that case God as omniscient must have known that one of his angels would choose evil. When the arguments from the scriptures ran out, the discussion turned to causes and effects. Intended to demonstrate the relation between Creator, angels and evil, this argument was taken from philosophy. The Dominicans, the order of friars formed with the sole intention of destroying the heresy, at once found that the physical works of Aristotle could be used to demonstrate that the natural world was in fact a *good* place. It was good in the realisation of potential, in the fulfilment of *purpose* that Aristotle saw in the expression of the nature-of-the-thing, and which the Catholics saw as the purpose of the Creator.[64]

---

[63] See also Gordon Leff, 'The trivium and the three philosophies', in Ridder-Symeons, *Universities in the Middle Ages*, pp. 307–36.

[64] See Roger French and Andrew Cunningham, *Before Science. The Invention of the Friars' Natural Philosophy*, Aldershot (Scolar Press), 1996.

When the church had crushed most of the heresy with a military crusade and burned most of the heretics, the Dominicans, for the purpose of
re-education, set up schools of natural philosophy to train the brothers. It
was Aristotelian and Christian together and the pinnacle of its expression
was Aquinas' *Summa Theologica*. In other words, their theology was philosophical, and where it was taught it needed a philosophical arts course, just
as the older theology needed the seven liberal arts. Toulouse became a full
studium generale that taught not only (as we have seen) Aristotelian natural philosophy but also Galenic medicine. The Dominicans spread over
Europe, wherever heresy was suspected and wherever they could recruit.
This made university towns a natural target, and the Dominicans with the
help of the pope secured dominance in the teaching of theology, with the
results for philosophy that we noted above. There is some suggestion that
when dialectical natural philosophy reached Italian medicine, it was by the
mediation of the friars.[65]

The different circumstances of Oxford meant that the masters and students there too were free to read Aristotle, which they seem to have done
since Alfred of Shareshill made his translations in the last years of the
twelfth century. We know of teachers such as Adam of Buckfield who
made extensive commentaries on the physical works, and traditionally it
was the English Oxonian Roger Bacon who in the 1240s took philosophy to Paris when the prohibitions had ceased to be effective. It was the
English Nation in Paris that set up the first statute that related to the reading of the physical works, and very soon (in the middle of the thirteenth
century) a very complete set of decrees was in force, setting out how the
physical works were to be read. It was partly a political matter, for the masters of arts were in dispute with the friars, the theologians and sometimes
with the pope. They took to philosophy as their own, and in the second
half of the arts course made knowledge of it a condition of becoming a
master.

This much has been necessary to explain how Aristotle's rationality became available to the medical man, our Rational and Learned Doctor.
While in the Italian universities natural philosophy came to the arts-and-
medicine course rather later than in the north,[66] Aristotle came to dominate the medieval university, and Aquinas' great theological work shows

---

[65] It was not only the Dominicans who used Aristotle, for the Franciscans of Santiago de Compostella
in north-west Spain were using all the *libri naturales* of Aristotle by 1222. See Luis García-Ballester,
'The construction of a new form of learning and practising medicine in medieval Europe', *Science
in Context*, 8 (1995) 75–112, at p. 85.

[66] See Nancy Siraisi, *Taddeo Alderotti and his Pupils. Two Generations of Italian Medical Learning*,
Princeton (Princeton University Press), 1981, pp. 10, 147.

how even central Christian dogma could be seen through Aristotelian eyes.
By means of philosophy too the doctor, so often seen as avaricious and
duplicitous, could make the lowly and manual craft of medicine part of
a properly instituted *studium generale*. Indeed, in the north, he made it a
higher faculty, along with law and theology. We shall look at the Medical
Faculty in the next chapter, and must end this one with a glance at how
medicine related to philosophy when the latter was being taught in its new
statutory form.

Let us return briefly to Oxford. Adam of Buckfield had completed his
commentaries on the physical works of Aristotle by the 1240s, while they
were still banned and under investigation in Paris[67] and before the Oxford
medical faculty flourished. His purpose was to lay out the intellectual morphology of the text so that students could find their way in it.[68] He does
not mention medicine where we might expect it, for example in commenting on the text *On the Difference between the Soul and the Spirit*, which
discusses matters of interest to both medical men and philosophers.[69] In
contrast, two or three decades later, the Oxford masters had agreed a common gloss on the physical works, also called the *libri naturales*, a term that
seems to have given rise to the philosophy teachers' name for themselves, the
naturales. This common gloss contains more reference to medicine than we
might expect, and would have furnished the medical man with a powerful
argument for regarding medicine as a subject proper for a *studium generale*.
The central textual basis for this argument is in the Aristotelian text *On
Perception and the Perceived (De Sensu et Sensato)* where Aristotle says that
the philosopher should acquaint himself with the first principles of health
and disease, because these occur only in living things. That is, Aristotle
has now reached the point in the cycle of teaching at the Lyceum where
the general physical principles have been set out and explained in circumstances of increasing complexity to the point where life itself became the
centre of attention. The Parisian statutes of 1252 set out the *libri naturales*

---

[67] In 1231 Gregory IX set up a committee to inspect the physical works of Aristotle, preserve what was
useful to the faith and reject what was offensive. See Denifle, *Chartularium Universitatis Parisiensis*,
vol. I, p. 143.

[68] Strictly, he was an *expositor* rather than a commentator, who would have resolved problems with the
text, pointed out parallel passages elsewhere, and so on.

[69] *De Differentia Spiritus et Anime*. See E. J. French, 'Adam of Buckfield and the Early Universities',
PhD thesis, University of London, 1998, pp. 131–43. This text is the only one on the *corpus vetustius*
known not to be by Aristotle. The *corpus vetustius*, the 'older' collection of Aristotle's physical works,
is a textbook in the sense of carrying the texts specified by statutes in Paris and Oxford for the
completion of the arts course together with much space for the reception of students' notes. It dates
from the second half of the thirteenth century. It was, that is, a textbook in the same way as the
Articella was the textbook of medicine.

in approximately the same sequence, and the Oxford gloss followed it too.

This opinion of Aristotle became codified as 'where the philosopher finishes, the physician begins'.[70] This aphorism was picked up by Isidore,[71] and was exactly what thirteenth-century doctors wanted everyone to think. It suited their purpose too that Aristotle had not descended to teaching the manual craft of medicine but had declared that its principles were philosophical. Moreover, they believed that Aristotle had written a book on the principles of medicine, which had been lost.[72] The essence of this relationship between philosophy and medicine was *subalternation*, another Aristotelian doctrine. A subalternated discipline drew its first principles from another discipline and did not set them up itself.[73] Medicine, said the medievals, was subalternated to philosophy and the principles it drew from it had to be treated as unassailable axioms. The medical man could not question them and should not try to. *Medical* principles, they said in Oxford, were 'proximal'.[74] The medical man could thus argue that, yes, the physician begins where the philosopher finishes in going further than the philosopher. This meant that philosophy was fundamental and had to be learned first, but for that reason was also more basic, while medicine in going further could be seen as a higher discipline.

This reflects what happened in institutional terms when finally, in the fourteenth century,[75] medicine was represented in its own faculty and as a higher discipline in Oxford. Subalternation also crossed disciplinary boundaries in terms of text. The Oxford teachers said that the chain of subalternation was that Aristotle's work on the soul, *De Anima*, was fundamental to *De Sensu et Sensato* which in turn was fundamental to the first work in

[70] *quia ubi naturales terminant ibi incipiunt medici ut dicitur in libro de sensu et sensato*, as the Oxford masters said. Durham Cathedral, C III 17, f. 382r.

[71] Faye Getz, *Medicine in the English Middle Ages*, Princeton (Princeton University Press), 1998, p. 48. The aphorism was used by philosophers such as Albertus Magnus at a time in the thirteenth century when not all doctors were using the *Canon* of Avicenna, and when boundaries were developing between philosophy and medicine. Like other authors, Albertus derived the opinion from the Aristotelian *De Sensu et Sensato*. See Nancy Sraisi, 'The medical learning of Albertus Magnus' in her *Medicine and the Italian Universities 1250–1600*, Leiden (Brill), 2001, pp. 11–36.

[72] '... *sua medicina quam [ad hoc] non habemus*.' London, British Library, Royal 12 G V, f. 209v and London, British Library, Harleian 3487, f. 200v. For 'His [Aristotle's] medicine' see also London, British Library, Royal 12 G II, f. 355v and Royal 12 G V, f. 209v as well as London, British Library, Harleian 3487, f. 200v.

[73] '*sicut illud quod probatum est in scienta subalternante debet supponi in scientia subalternata*.' Nuremberg, Cent. V 59, f. 221r.

[74] London, British Library, Royal 12 G III, f. 245r '[*de medicina*] *idest ad proxima principia que sunt de consilio medici, et non considerant prima principia sanitatis et egritudinis de quibus tantum considerat naturalis*.' Also Royal 12 G II, f. 382v.

[75] Getz, *Medicine in the English Middle Ages*, p. 17.

the medieval textbook of medicine, the *Isagoge* of Joannitius.[76] We have
seen that this brief tract was the only theoretical piece in the early *Articella*
and in a sense is an introduction to the whole of medieval medicine. This
was the place where (the Oxford masters thought) all the unassailable axioms of philosophy passed from one discipline and one textbook, the *corpus
vetustius*, to another discipline, another textbook, and ultimately another
incorporated group of men.[77] The chain is even longer than this, for the
Oxford masters selected a passage from the *Isagoge* where Joannitius names
three states of the body, sickness, health and neutrality. This is a doctrine
from the *Tegni* which, as we have seen, was added to the *Articella* as a
summary of medicine, and for which, the medievals believed, Joannitius
wrote the *Isagoge* as an introduction. The process of subalternation provided additional mechanisms for the Rational and Learned Doctor to trace
his practice back to the fundamentals of the world picture.

BEFORE THE FACULTIES

Medical men in Oxford took longer than those in other *studia* to set up
their faculty, and no university-educated English doctor is known from
the thirteenth century.[78] It is difficult to tell what the nature of pre-faculty
medicine was, but it was a time when the doctors were adapting their
medicine to the new circumstances. According to Roger Bacon, the doctors of the 1240s practised poor medicine because they did not read the
Arabic authors, particularly Avicenna's *Canon*. He was familiar with Paris
as well as Oxford and was speaking in general terms;[79] what he meant was
that the doctors were insufficiently learned. The *Canon*, a vast compilation from largely Galenic sources, had been translated and glossed by the
other great medieval translator, Gerard of Cremona, but spread through
the European *studia* rather slowly, no doubt because of the difficulty and
expense of copying it.[80] Bacon has praise for earlier doctors who learned

---

[76] Madrid, Escorial, F II 4, f. 181r '[*consequens est*] *scilicet in hoc libro et in quibusdam sequentibus libro
de anima subalternatis aliquo modo*'. And '[*subiaceatur*] *idest supponantur in hoc libro et in relinquis
sequentibus sicut determinata in superiori scientia*'. (See also Madrid, Escorial, III, f. 245r and II,
f. 382v).

[77] The philosophical axioms were largely the nature of the elements and their qualities, which provides
the foundations of the theory of complexion. We have seen how this was objectionable to John of
Salisbury, and now with the accessibility of the *libri naturales*, it was a much more elaborate theory.

[78] Getz, *Medicine in the English Middle Ages*, p. 17.

[79] See the *Opera hactenus Inedita Rogeri Baconi. Fasc. IX: De Retardatione Accidentium Senectutis*, ed.
A. G. Little and E. Withington, Oxford (Clarendon Press), 1928.

[80] The *Canon* was becoming known by the 1190s and was used by some philosophers and physicians
in the following century, but it was not until the fourteenth century that it was used routinely by

their medicine by experience 'which alone qualified them' and to whom, perhaps, he thought the *Canon* was not available. His criticism of contemporary doctors was not only that they ignored Arabic sources but that they enthusiastically engaged in dialectical methods.[81] He speaks of them giving themselves to 'disputations of infinite questions and useless arguments' instead of experience. He mentions the introductory topics of logic as taught in the universities and derides the 'accidental' questions and the sophistical and dialectical arguments that surely speak of a university context.[82]

So it seems that the doctors were enthusiastically becoming rational in the Aristotelian way, the attractions of the Old Logic of the previous century now enhanced with the circulation of the New. The implication of Bacon's view that experience alone used to confirm men as doctors is that they were now seeking to do so by succeeding at academic logical exercises, that is, securing some sort of institutional validation of their medical worth. Something similar happened in the early thirteenth century in Sicily, where the doctors advised the king, Frederick II, that a knowledge of logic should be a formal requirement for anyone wishing to begin a study of medicine.[83] He enacted that three years of logic were necessary and that the medical course should be five years.

The result was that those who followed these rules then practised medicine by royal assent. This took the form of a licence to practise, *licentia practicandi*, awarded after an examination by a panel including 'masters of the art'. This was the term used only for doctors educated at Salerno, another Norman kingdom and where, after all, they knew what medicine was. The decree specifies the 'genuine books of Hippocrates and Galen' which together with the three years of logic indicates the Salernitan model

---

medical men, although it was not popular for example in Montpellier. See Danielle Jacquart, 'La réception du Canon d'Avicenne: comparaison entre Montpellier et Paris aux xiiie et xive siècles', in *Histoire de l'École Médicale de Montpellier*, Actes du 110e Congrès National de Sociétés Savantes, Montpellier, 1985, pp. 69–77; and Nancy Siraisi, 'Changing concepts of the organization of medical knowledge in the Italian universities: fourteenth to sixteenth centuries', in *La Diffusione delle Scienze Islamiche nel Medio Evo Europeo*, Rome (Accademia nazionale dei Lincei), 1987, pp. 291–321.

[81] There was an earlier parallel in the increasing use of dialectic in theology: the reflective theology of the cloister became dialectical and systematic as it was used increasingly in urban situations. Law became increasingly dialectical. See Southern, *Scholastic Humanism*, and French and Cunningham, *Before Science*. esp. ch. 3.

[82] '*vulgus medicorum dat se disputationibus questionum infinitarum et argumentorum inutilium, et non vacat experientie ut oportet. Ante 30 annos non vacabant nisi experientie, que sola certificat; sed nunc per artem topicorum et elencorum multiplicant questiones accidentales infinitas, et argumenta dialectica et sophistica infinitiora, in quibus absorbentur ut semper querant et numquam inveniant veritatem. Inventio enim est per viam sensus memorie et experientie, et maxime in scientiis, quarum una est medicina.*' See Little and Withington, *Opera hactenus Inedita Rogeri Baconi*, p. 154.

[83] See, for example, Lawn, *Quaestio Disputata*, pp. 66–8; Siraisi, *Medieval and Early Renaissance Medicine*, pp. 17, 18.

of the Rational and Learned Doctor. Frederick was reasserting Norman control over Sicily, and it is at such times that the rules are changed or written down.[84]

In the new Latin Kingdom of Jerusalem, case-law was established by 1245 and specified that should a patient die after undergoing a recognised mode of treatment the doctor should be whipped round the streets, holding a urine flask symbolically in his hand, and then hanged.[85] Here was an excellent reason to be good at prognostication.

Whatever their source, the new logic and philosophy were used more systematically in the north, which remained a resource for the south in these matters down through the first half of the fourteenth century. Before the medical faculties were incorporated in the north the word 'faculty' was in use in a more general sense in the south, meaning an area of study in which it was possible to become a master. In the south, we know from John of Salisbury that, like Salerno, Montpellier was a good place to go to learn medicine, but, unlike Salerno, it became a full university, defended by the monarchs through whose hands it passed. Its medical training was probably vocational until the arrival of the new logic and philosophy.[86]

In short, philosophy and other technical material in Arabic (and increasingly in Greek) had uses as varied as the men who sought it out. Men of the church wanted to know how other cultures worked. Kings husbanded their resources of men educated in the arts course by protecting the universities. The pope effectively patronised the friars by sending them all over Europe, inserting them into faculties of theology and telling the local bishops to support them as mendicants. The doctors thought philosophy would improve their medicine and make them better doctors. They also found that it was attractive to pupils and enhanced their reputation as teachers.

THE *PANTEGNI* AND SCHOLASTIC MEDICINE

'Scholastic' as an adjective applied to medieval medicine is often used in a pejorative way,[87] indicating excessive reliance on logic and authority in place of the use of the senses. This is partly an inheritance from the Hellenists of the Renaissance, who wanted to get back to the medicine

---

[84] On Sicily in general see Donald Matthew, *The Norman Kingdom of Sicily*, Cambridge (Cambridge University Press), 1992, esp. chap. 5.

[85] See the articles by Darrel W. Amundsen in Warren T. Reich, ed., *Encyclopedia of Bioethics*, 4 vols., New York (Free Press), 1978; vol. 3.

[86] On Montpellier medicine see Louis Dulieu, *La Médecine à Montpellier*, 2 vols., Avignon (Les Presses Universelles), 1975.

[87] Cf. the rhetorical question posed by Jacquart in 'Medical scholasticism'. See also Siraisi, 'Medical scholasticism and the historian', pp. 140–56.

of the Greeks and who disliked the period in-between. They called this period the 'middle' ages, that is, intervening, and derided its technical and dialectical commentaries and analysis. This was, in short, what we are calling in this book the Latin tradition of medicine; it did not die out, as the Hellenists hoped, but continued in the schools into the seventeenth century.

Most of it took its form from the very fact that it was taught in the schools, and we shall use 'scholastic' in this more neutral sense. We have seen in this chapter some of the circumstances of the medieval schools and we shall see in the next the full expression of the move towards incorporation of medical teaching. We can conclude here with a brief look at how the constraints of classroom teaching gave shape to scholastic medicine.

We can best do so by glancing at the first major Arabic medical text to be translated into Latin, and thus one of the major sources of the Latin tradition of medicine. This was the *Pantegni* of Haly Abbas (as the Latins called him), first loosely translated by Constantine the African.[88] A second translation was made by Stephen of Antioch in the early twelfth century, both before the formalisation of the Western schools.[89] The first half of the text is a discussion of medical theory, and is often referred to by doctors of the high Middle Ages as 'Haly's *Theory*', and undoubtedly this is what was novel about the work. Haly begins by declaring that Hippocrates, the 'great' or 'most glorious',[90] was the Father of Medicine, the first to write down the art; and his works, particularly the *Aphorisms*, contained all that was needed for the recovery and maintenance of health. Yet so cryptic was Hippocrates' language, continued Haly, that the reader needed much exposition and many examples to understand it. Galen, who was second only to Hippocrates, was prolix and diffuse; and as Greek authors such as Oribasius and Paulus gave way to the Arabic writers such as Aaron and John (son of Serapion), most authors began to write works that were defective in one important respect, namely that they gave insufficient attention to the 'naturals'. These for Haly are the fundamentals of natural philosophy, the elements and their qualities and their mixtures that produce secondary

---

[88] While Constantine's translation of the *Theorica* 'more or less' corresponds to Haly's text, the *Practica* is Constantine's compilation from a range of other sources. See Burnett and Jacquart, *Constantine the African*, p. vii.

[89] Stephen called his translation 'The Royal Book', *Liber Regalis*, but it is more convenient to retain the widespread name *Pantegni*. See Lindberg, 'Transmission', p. 58. A printed version of Stephen of Antioch's translation was edited in the Renaissance by Michael de Capella: Haly Abbas, *Liber Totius Medicine Necessaria Continens*, Lyons (J. Myt), 1523.

[90] Constantine and Stephen used different terms. See Danielle Jacquart, 'Le sens donné par Constantine L'Africain à son oeuvre: les chapitres introductifs en Arabe et en Latin', in Burnett and Jacquart, *Constantine the African*, pp. 71–89, at pp. 84, 86.

bodies, some common to living things. Like the Aristotelianism that was to give the Rational and Learned Doctor a basis for his account of medicine in the fundamentals of the world picture, the *Pantegni* provided an attractive rationalism to medicine. Medieval doctors would have seen the work as an expansion of the doctrines of the *Isagoge* of Joannitius: both begin with the division of medicine into theory and practice; both list the naturals, choosing to add to the usual number of seven the ages, colours and figures of the patients and the difference between men and women.

Haly's plan, therefore, was to begin with the axioms of natural philosophy and to proceed with rigid rules of exposition in order to include all that is necessary. His method is 'division of doctrine', one of the modes of procedure that medieval doctors loved to discuss, and he breaks it down into five sub-categories. In a similar way he treats the opinions of Hippocrates and Galen as 'rules, norms and propositions' which can be treated syllogistically.[91] The whole theory of medicine, then, is to be derived from first principles in a very rationalist way, thus overcoming the faults of earlier expositions. It is a technique aimed at, if not derived from, a rationalist teacher handling words (not observation) in the classroom for students who needed a method to help them memorise all they had to learn in a short time. Haly expects that his readers will know their logic and the arts of what the Latins called the *quadrivium*: this could well be seen as offering support for treating medicine as a higher discipline, and even for Haly it must have been an ideal, for the examples he gives for the use of these arts in medicine are not very convincing: geometry for the shape of wounds, music to read the pulse and astronomy for the astrological signs for preparing remedies.[92]

What he has to say on medical deontology also relates to the classroom. From Hippocratic sources he draws the principle that the pupil must magnify the name of his teacher and spread his glory abroad. It is the father–son relationship of the *Oath*, in which newcomers, if suitable, are treated as sons and taught without payment, and where successful pupils share rewards with their teacher. In the Latin tradition of medicine we often meet cases where the pupil has a duty of faith to his master, which seems rooted in these classroom 'ethics'; it was generally extended to the teacher of all teachers, back down a line to Hippocrates and Galen. 'Good is the word of Hippocrates!', exclaimed Haly.[93] In the practice of medicine the doctor must be ethical, modest, abstemious, always reading and learning

[91] Haly, *Continens*, f. 6va.   [92] Ibid., f. 7rb–8rb.   [93] Ibid., f. 7rb.

from others and from cases – including those in hospitals. The result will be love, honour and an honest fame with men and God.

In this chapter we have seen how a medical elite arose during the formation of the Latin tradition of medicine. Other forms of practitioner are considered in this book only for the ways in which they were excluded by the elite (although historians are increasingly studying them). The central issue is that the Learned and Rational Doctor took control of, or emerged from, a series of increasingly formal schools. It has been argued that early Western medicine was partly a continuation of Methodism,[94] but the exigencies of the classroom led more teachers to Rationalism. The learned teacher gained his authority partly from texts translated from the Arabic and Greek, and when medical teachers began to agree on which were the important texts and authors, they had the authority to determine the nature of medicine. The doctors were not without their critics and much of their rationality and learning can be seen as professional patter – the Good Story – used in defence. The recovery of Galenic medicine and Aristotelian natural philosophy provided a huge boost for this. The elite doctor in the classroom saw himself in a tradition reaching back to Hippocrates and Galen and inculcated in his pupils a loyalty to the medical tradition and its fathers.

[94] See Nutton, 'God, Galen and depaganization', p. 19.

CHAPTER 4

Scholastic medicine

INTRODUCTION

The natural context of the Rational and Learned Doctor was scholastic medicine. The term 'scholastic' is taken here in a simple sense to mean that which relates to the schools. The schools were the incorporated *studia generalia*, and within them, the incorporated medical faculty. Scholastic medicine flourished most vigorously from the beginnings of the faculties in the late thirteenth century to the middle of the fourteenth century, when the Black Death arrived. In terms of personalities, it spanned the period from the *floreat* of Taddeo Alderotti to the death of Gentile da Foligno. This was the high point in the history of rational and learned doctors: their reputation was growing, their numbers were small and they were patronised by popes and monarchs.[1] Instead of breaking down the period into smaller fragments, this chapter presents the story of the scholastic doctor from entry into the *studium* to his practice of a potentially lucrative trade.[2]

BECOMING A RATIONAL AND LEARNED DOCTOR

Where to go

It was known in the twelfth century that Salerno and Montpellier were good places to go to learn how to be a doctor. Bologna, too; and in the north, the size of the city of Paris gave many opportunities for medical practice, and

---

[1] See Joseph Ziegler, *Medicine and Religion c.1300. The Case of Arnau de Vilanova*, Oxford (Clarendon Press), 1998, p. 19. It has been estimated that there were between one and six university-trained physicians for every 10,000 people in southern Europe. See Luis García-Ballester, Michael McVaugh and Augustín Rubio-Vela, *Medical Licensing and Learning in Fourteenth-Century Valencia* (*Transactions of the American Philosophical Society*, 79, part 6), Philadelphia, 1989.

[2] Medicine was not always lucrative for teachers and practitioners. The doctors who secured a retained position in a great household generally did better. See Nancy Siraisi, *Medieval and Early Renaissance Medicine. An Introduction to Knowledge and Practice*, Chicago (University of Chicago Press), 1990, p. 21.

so was attractive to medical teachers.[3] Indeed, until the middle of the fourteenth century, Bologna, Paris and Montpellier had a virtual monopoly of
the teaching of medicine.[4] Prospective medical students knew these things,
just as arts students knew of the reputations of heroic teachers of logic.[5]
By the thirteenth century Salerno was fading as the new *studia generalia*
developed, and by the early fourteenth century the language and doctrines
of its masters could look old-fashioned to a teacher in a *studium* such as
Perugia.[6] The differences between these places would have determined the
choice of a student who wanted to study medicine, and they seem to have
arisen from the mode of teaching and the nature of the organisation of
the *studium*. Although it was generally true that the masters agreed on the
nature of medicine and settled upon the *Articella* as a textbook common to
collaborating masters and their pupils, there were considerable differences
between the *studia*. The *consortium* at Paris was an association of masters,
as were those of Oxford and Cambridge, where it was also possible to
study medicine.[7] We have little evidence about early teachers in the two
English universities, perhaps simply because medicine was a minor subject
here; but it was much bigger in Paris, and there too there were no notable
commentators until the latter part of the fourteenth century. Possibly the
collaboration between the masters extended to teaching a common commentary, as happened in the treatment of natural philosophy at Oxford
and probably Cambridge.[8]

---

[3] See Cornelius O'Boyle, *The Art of Medicine. Medical Teaching at the University of Paris, 1250–1400*,
Leiden (Brill), 1998, pp. 10–16.
[4] See Danielle Jacquart, 'Medical scholasticism', in M. D. Grmek, ed., *Western Medical Thought from
Antiquity to the Middle Ages*, trans. A. Sugaar, Cambridge, Mass. and London (Harvard University
Press), pp. 197–240, at p. 210.
[5] See R. W. Southern, 'The schools of Paris and the school of Chartres', in R. L. Benson and
G. Constable, *Renaissance and Renewal in the Twelfth Century*, Oxford (Clarendon), 1982, p. 115:
there was a 'bush telegraph' for the location of good teachers, and students refer to their teachers, not
to their schools.
[6] Gentile da Foligno speaks of *antiquus ille Maurus* in his commentary on the third book of the *Canon*,
f. 147r. This is in two volumes: (i) *Tertius Can. Avic. cum amplissima Gentilis fulg. expositione. Demum
commentaria nuper addita videlicet Jacobi de Partibus super fen VI et XIII. Item Jo. Matthei de Gradi
super fen XXII quia Gentilis in eis defecit.* This volume ends at fen 9 tract 1. (ii) *Secunda pars Gentilis
super Avic. cum supplementis Jacobi de Partibus parisiensis ac Joannis Matthei de Gradi mediolanensis
ubi Gentilis vel breviter vel tacite pertransivit*, Venice (O. Scotus), 1522.
[7] See Faye Getz, *Medicine in the English Middle Ages*, Princeton (Princeton University Press), 1998.
[8] Work on the 'Oxford gloss' has hardly begun. See Charles Burnett, 'The introduction of Aristotle's
natural philosophy in Great Britain: a preliminary survey of the manuscript evidence', in *Aristotle
in Britain in the Middle Ages*, ed. John Marenbon [*Rencontres de philosophie médiévale*, 5], Turnhout,
Belgium (Brepols), c. 1996, pp. 21–50; Roger French, 'Teaching Aristotle in the medieval English
universities: *De Plantis* and the physical *glossa ordinaria*', *Physis*, 34 (1997) n.s. fasc. 1–2, 225–206. It
is not yet known whether the *Articella* contained a similar gloss.

Many of the Parisian masters were also clerics, and financial support from the church was not uncommon, for both masters and students. Technically, a teacher on a stipend could not accept fees from his students (but he often contrived to accept gifts) and perhaps advertising oneself as a heroic teacher by writing major commentaries was not appropriate. The church's attitude to doctors was traditionally ambivalent and perhaps affected the status of the medical men in Paris, Oxford and Cambridge, the only universities in the thirteenth century where the pope allowed theology to be taught. It is important to note too that the friars had secured a commanding position in the faculty of theology and the masters of arts were obliged to teach a natural philosophy that served as a preliminary to the theology of the friars.[9] This philosophy was also in an institutional and intellectual sense preliminary to medicine which, like theology, was a higher faculty.

In contrast, the Italian *studia* were originally more vocational and the students who went there to learn a productive art formed themselves into their own incorporation and again at first chose what they wanted to learn and who was to teach them. The organisation was secular rather than ecclesiastical as in the north, although the church retained the right to give the licence.[10] In the south, too, medicine was not a higher faculty but was taught alongside the arts, and graduation was in both disciplines. Some of these differences lie behind the fact that most of the commentators and medical authors of the period were Italian. Taddeo Alderotti, Dino and Tommaso del Garbo, Mondino, Pietro d'Abano, Torrigiano, Gentile da Foligno and others compiled monuments to the scholastic method which were also claims to a fame that could attract students. They wrote for their students (whom they often address directly) and for the promotion of their *studia*. They were in competition, for the collaborative enterprise between the masters of one *studium* did not extend to masters from another, and there was no feeling of a need for an ethics of collaboration across the profession. The loyalty that the master strove for in his pupils did not extend further than them. These are the new heroic teachers of scholastic medicine. And although in theory the church's licence to teach enabled the new master to teach anywhere – the *ius ubique docendi* – in practice each

---

[9] See Roger French and Andrew Cunningham, *Before Science. The Invention of the Friars' Natural Philosophy*, Aldershot (Scolar Press), 1996.

[10] In the Crown of Aragon only about 1 per cent of medical men were also clerics. See Michael McVaugh, *Medicine before the Plague. Practitioners and their Patients in the Crown of Aragon, 1286–1345*, Cambridge (Cambridge University Press), 1993, pp. 72, 75. There was a general withdrawal of clergy from medicine during the thirteenth century as the 'profession' consolidated itself in the universities and faculties. But in fourteenth-century Oxford a fifth of the known medical scholars also studied theology. Ziegler, *Medicine and Religion*, p. 8.

studium was jealous of its own privileges and recognised those of others reluctantly. It was therefore necessary to travel a considerable distance to get a medical education, often at great expense.

Control and rewards

What made this worthwhile for the prospective doctor was the financial reward of practice. Throughout the thirteenth century medical education was increasingly recognised and its practice controlled. We might properly call these changes professional, and their ultimate effect was the creation of the medical faculty within the university as a corporation with some features of autonomy. Early steps in the direction of regulating the business of medicine were by royal decree. We have already seen that Frederick II, on the advice of his doctors, imposed a period of study of logic before the student began his medicine. Even before him, in 1140, Roger II of Sicily was able to take the advice of Salernitan doctors (Salerno being within the Kingdom) and, first, lay down what a proper medical education was and, second, perpetuate a system of examination of candidates by municipal officials and established doctors. This was long before the discovery and use of the new logic and the natural philosophy of Aristotle, but in the thirteenth century these two features came to be bound up in the conception of what a proper medical education was. It is notable that control of medical practice from the top of the political ladder was exerted in newly acquired territories, such as the Kingdoms of Jerusalem and Sicily. These were initial moves and control then passed down through society ultimately to the doctors themselves. This was part of the formation of a 'profession' and it depended in the first instance on the doctors agreeing what medicine was, that is, who its heroes were and what a medical teaching curriculum looked like. Elsewhere, in the absence of an agreed medical curriculum in the Salernitan manner, similar events came later. The Kingdom of Valencia was another new territory, seized by the Christian Spanish from Islam in 1238. It was partially integrated under a single monarch along with Catalonia and Aragon as the Crown of Aragon. In 1289 Alfons III enacted that medical men could practise only after examination by the proper officers of the town and established physicians – significantly, the enactment was modelled on another for lawyers. No university training is specified, and it is clear enough that this kind of royal initiative allowed on the one hand a system of guild-licensing, and on the other an environment in which respect for university training could lead to the introduction of new criteria into local licensing.

After the Valencian decree of 1289, those who locally controlled practice in the cities and towns throughout the Crown of Aragon began to insist on the possession of a medical degree.[11] Indeed, such royal initiatives often preceded the formation of medical faculties within the *studia* and were part of the story about the establishment of scholastic medicine as a discipline located in a corporation. Royal initiatives of this kind often had to be renegotiated, perhaps with a change of monarch or as the desirability of university education became more obvious. The Aragonese King Jaume I tried in 1272 to prevent anyone practising medicine in Montpellier who had not received a degree from a university. Four years later Montpellier passed into the hands of the kings of Mallorca and before the end of the century it was a possession of the kings of France. Each change was an opportunity for royal insistence on the possession of the medical degree for practice. The argument involved the benefit not only to public health but to the fame of the *studium*.[12] The university doctors agreed, because it gave them a monopoly of practice.[13]

The medical faculty

What made moving to a university, selecting a master and paying fees worthwhile was the medical faculty. This was essentially a corporation of teaching masters who negotiated with civil and other authorities the right to a monopoly of the teaching and practice of a certain kind of medicine in exchange for a guarantee of quality. Medical faculties began to appear in the later thirteenth century; before that, the term *facultas* meant simply an area of study proper for a *studium*.[14] The difference was that the faculty now had its own rules, officers and oaths in addition to those of the *studium* as a whole. It was a professional body that took tribute from and protected those joining it. For example, the members of the Parisian faculty in the middle of the thirteenth century had to swear by the statutes of the university, its ceremonies and its power of cessation of teaching. But from 1270 to 1274

---

[11] This did not apply to licences for surgery and to those issued to Arabs and Jews. García-Ballester et al., *Medical Licensing*, p. 12.

[12] García-Ballester et al., *Medical Licensing*, p. 3.

[13] The value of a monopoly in securing quality of the product was clear to others, besides the doctors, for example to the papal legate acting in Montpellier in 1220. See Darrel W. Amundsen, 'Medical deontology and pestilential disease in the late Middle Ages', *Journal of the History of Medicine*, 32 (1977) 403–21, at p. 407. Medical teachers there had to have a licence from the bishop, after examination. See Pearl Kibre, 'The faculty of medicine at Paris, charlatanism, and unlicensed medical practices in the later middle ages', *Bulletin of the History of Medicine*, 27 (1953) 1–20, at p. 5.

[14] See Alfonso Maierù, *University Training in Medieval Europe*, trans. D. N. Pryds, Leiden (Brill), 1994, p. 76.

the faculty issued its own statutes relating to its proper business of teaching medicine: the texts to be read, the manner of examination and inception.[15] As in the case of most corporations, its privileges had to be acquired by constant effort; by 1330 the chancellor, the traditional master of the schools, was obliged to give the licence to anyone recommended by the faculty; and by 1336 the faculty was claiming the right to control the apothecaries.[16] Medicine in the northern European universities tended to follow the pattern of Paris, where it was a higher discipline that followed the study of the arts. Cambridge had a medical faculty with its own statutes by the 1270s,[17] and in Oxford the first medical graduate appeared in 1312. Oxford medicine was miniscule in comparison to the big centres abroad, and although the reading required for inception was similar to that stipulated in Paris in 1270, sometimes the statutes cover arts and medicine together, and for many medicine was simply a stage in an ultimately theological education.[18] In German-speaking countries, the medical faculties appear in the period after the Black Death.[19] In the south, where medicine was not a separate faculty, formalisation of medical teaching occurred a little earlier, the first recorded medical degree in Bologna, for example, being awarded in 1268.[20] Many faculties seem to have been consolidated by incorporation in similar ways. In Montpellier, the long-standing tradition of medical teaching was formalised in new statutes of 1309 which Arnau of Vilanova helped to draw up.[21]

An important aspect of incorporation was the promise taken by members of the group to act in concert. They used this in a political way, for example, in solving disputes by the threat of the cessation of teaching. A *studium* was a major economic resource for a town and the threat of the masters and students going elsewhere was a serious one. It is well known that in the early thirteenth century there was a migration of scholars from Paris to

[15] See O'Boyle, *The Art of Medicine*, pp. 19, 20ff.
[16] See Kibre, 'The faculty of medicine at Paris', p. 14.
[17] Damian Riehl Leader, *A History of the University of Cambridge. Volume 1 The University to 1546*, Cambridge (Cambridge University Press), 1988, p. 203. See also M. B. Hackett, *The Original Statutes of Cambridge University*, Cambridge (Cambridge University Press), 1970.
[18] See Faye Getz, 'The faculty of medicine before 1500', in J. I. Catto and Ralph Evans, eds., *The History of the University of Oxford. Volume II Late Medieval Oxford*, Oxford (Clarendon Press), 1992, pp. 373–405.
[19] See Vivian Nutton, 'Medicine at the German Universities, 1348–1500', in Roger French, Jon Arriz-abalaga, Andrew Cunningham and Luis García-Ballester, eds., *Medicine from the Black Death to the French Disease*, Aldershot (Ashgate), 1998, pp. 85–109.
[20] See Siraisi, *Medieval and Early Renaissance Medicine*, p. 60.
[21] On Montpellier in general see Luke Demaitre, 'Theory and practice in medical education at the university of Montpellier in the thirteenth and fourteenth centuries', *Journal of the History of Medicine and Allied Sciences*, 30 (1975) 103–23.

Oxford and then from Oxford to Cambridge, which helped to consolidate the schools. The migrating masters took their students with them and needed little else save books for their essential business, as their legitimacy as teachers was secured by the church, which had granted them licence to teach.

Something similar happened in the Italian *studia* in the period we are now dealing with. Medicine had a somewhat slender beginning in the Italian cities; for example, the *studium* founded in 1224 in Naples by Frederick II encountered many difficulties. Even in Padua, where medical teaching began in 1222, the process of establishing a university medical faculty was not complete until 1350.[22] Bologna was the mother of Italian *studia* in terms of medicine, and when there was a papal interdict there, teachers such as Dino del Garbo moved to Siena in about 1306–8. Here again in Siena there had been teachers of medicine in the thirteenth century and attempts were made to attract Bolognese scholars; but these were not very successful until 1321 when a new wave of Bolognese scholars arrived. Siena now made serious efforts to create a proper, incorporated *studium*, borrowing money to pay salaries, but no papal bull was forthcoming and Siena had to wait until 1357 for an imperial decree enabling it to give degrees.[23] There was likewise a migration from Bologna to Perugia in 1321, where the *studium* began to give the degree of doctor in arts and medicine.[24] Graduation was the key. Even where, as in Siena, the *studium* was to be magisterial, the pattern of graduation was Bolognese,[25] and in Padua part of the arrangement negotiated in bringing in ex-Bolognese students was that the Bolognese statutes would be followed.[26] We have seen that graduation was the characteristic act of the academic corporation and became most significant in medicine only after the consolidation of the medical faculty.[27] In Italy this coincided with the development of the professional

[22] Jacquart, 'Medical scholasticism'.
[23] H. Rashdall, *The Universities of Europe in the Middle Ages*, ed. F. M. Powicke and A. B. Emden, 3 vols., Oxford (Oxford University Press), 1936, vol. 2, p. 31. See also Peter Denley, 'Recent studies on Italian universities of the middle ages and renaissance', *History of Universities*, 1 (1981) 193–205, at p. 198.
[24] The migration was the result of a dispute between town and gown after the execution of a student. Rashdall, *Universities*, vol. 1, pp. 172, 589.
[25] Denley, 'Recent studies on Italian universities'.
[26] Rashdall, *Universities*, vol. 2, p. 16. See also Carlo Malagola, *Statuti delle Università e dei Collegi dello Studio Bolognese*, Bologna, 1888, p. 129 and Maierù, *University Training in Medieval Europe*, p. 39.
[27] On the influence of Montpellier as a model, and the nature of the examination, see Luis García-Ballester and Augustin Rubio-Vela, 'L'influence de Montpellier dans le contrôle social de la profession médicale dans le Royaume de Valence au XIVᵉ siècle', *Histoire de l'École Médicale de Montpellier*, Actes du 110ᵉ Congrès National des Sociétés Savantes, Montpellier (CTHS), 1985, pp. 19–30.

colleges; and that of Bologna, for example, was not really effective until the 1260s.[28]

Logical reason and philosophical learning

During this period changes were happening in logic and natural philosophy, the scholastic subjects so important to the Rational and Learned Doctor. Logic was, of course, fundamental to the arts course and the subjects that depended on it, like medicine. But in the late thirteenth century and the early fourteenth logic was being greatly developed in the northern universities. The dialectic with which Pietro d'Abano resolved problems between the philosophers and the physicians had been acquired in Paris, and, later, an Italian humanist such as Petrarch could express his hatred of monstrous logical constructions built by masters at Oxford.[29] Italian medical men took to them more readily, and heroically vied with each other in resolving problems set up by the ever-growing theory of medicine. A Parisian training in arts and medicine was seen as desirable by many in Italy – the lord of Padua, for example, sent twelve youths there at the suggestion of his physician (Gentile da Foligno). Part of what motivated the physicians to study logic was the belief that it applied directly to the physical world, that is, that proper, demonstrative knowledge of nature could be gained by arguing about and examining natural bodies.

In fact, it was at this point that the learning and the reason of the doctor interacted most directly. While most of medieval logic was a complex investigation of the uses of words, in some areas it approached natural philosophy. One such area was the intension and remission of forms and the associated quantification of elementary qualities, which was of great interest to the medical man. Much of this was an English business and it reached the doctors fairly quickly. Gentile da Foligno's discussion of quantification may have been influenced by Walter Burley, whose name he mentions.[30] He may even have heard Burley's quodlibet at Bologna in 1341.[31]

---

[28] Jacquart, 'Medical Scholasticism'.

[29] Francesco Petrarcha, *Invective contra Medicum*, ed. Pier Giorgio Ricci, Rome (Storia e Letteratura), 1950. Petrarch thought of English logic as a monster wielding double-edged enthymemes. See also Brian Lawn, *The Rise and Decline of the Scholastic 'Quaestio Disputata'*, Leiden (Brill), 1993, p. 107. Another Italian humanist, Niccolo Niccoli, dreaded the very names of English logicians such as Ockham and Swineshead because of the effect they had on modern logic.

[30] See Roger French, *Canonical Medicine. Gentile da Foligno and Scholasticism*, Leiden (Brill), 2001, p. 40.

[31] See Edith Dudley Sylla, 'The Oxford calculators', in Norman Kretzmann, Anthony Kenny and Jan Pinborg, eds., *The Cambridge History of Later Medieval Philosophy*, Cambridge (Cambridge University Press), 1990, pp. 540–63, at p. 555.

Gentile's pupil Tommaso del Garbo was more definitely influenced (as we shall see) by William Ockham (d. 1347/9) so there seems little doubt that the medical men were keen to make use of medieval developments of logic. Burley was also concerned with the instant of time in which a thing came into and passed out of existence (Aristotle's generation and corruption) and he necessarily turned to physics. Ockham was also interested in what kind of entities exist in the outside world and he too approached natural philosophy. Aristotle's *Topics* also deals with the real world (place, duration, number and so on) and it is in this rather physical context that Ockham discusses the theory of logical consequence. In non-logical language, this was a study of the relationship between statements and the inferences that could be drawn from them. It included 'insolubles' such as the liar paradox: a man says he is a liar. Do you believe him? Is he a liar? A third area of logic that came to share a solution with consequences was induction, the attempt to draw universal statements out of repeated particulars. Induction was always imperfect, because observed particulars were always finite and could not add up to a completely general statement.

The common solution to these problems lay in establishing a chronological distinction. The medievals made an induction as complete as possible by adding to it something like *etcetera*, meaning 'and so in all the other cases': this was the same thing as saying that the general statement was true in respect of the time in which the particulars were observed.[32] There was a special phrase for this, which seems to have been used as much in medical texts as it was in logical works. This was *ut nunc*, 'as of now', and logicians such as Ockham used it in contrast to absolute consequences.[33] 'As of now' could ease the difficulties of insolubles, and in the sense of 'the present conditions of the world'[34] it was useful in induction.[35] Imperfect inferences (as in induction) depended more on the meaning of terms than on the formal relation between them and so could be better adapted to the physical world. The concept of *ut nunc* was well known to the medical man and it was a case in point of how a logical concept could be applied to the physical body. The Galenic *Tegni* described three states of health of the body: healthy, ill and neutral. But the scholastics wanted to know if a body

---

[32] See French, *Gentile*, p. 127.

[33] See Eleonore Stump, 'Topics: their development and absorption into consequences', in Kretzmann et al., *The Cambridge History of Later Medieval Philosophy*, pp. 273–99, at p. 295. William of Sherwood used the phrase in the previous century (p. 291).

[34] E. P. Bos, 'A contribution to the history of theories of induction in the middle ages', in Klaus Jacobi, ed., *Argumentationstheorie. Scholastische Forschungen zu den logischen und semantischen Regeln korrekten Folgerns*, Leiden and New York (Brill), 1993, pp. 553–76, at p. 563.

[35] See Paul Vincent Spade, *Lies, Language and Logic in the late Middle Ages*, London (Variorum Reprints), 1988, item V, p. 119. Ockham also used the term: item I, pp. 9–10.

that had been ill but had been made healthy in the past was truly healthy. They distinguished an absolutely – or simply – healthy body from one that was healthy at this moment in time: the one was healthy *simpliciter*, the other *ut nunc*. Health, of course, was a balanced complexion, which depended on the logically axiomatic elementary qualities that the doctor was obliged to accept without question from natural philosophy: it was all a physical as well as a logical business. The terms *ut nunc* and *simpliciter* would have been known to educated doctors from the Latin translation of the commentary on the *Tegni* by Haly Abbas, a routine component of the *Ars Commentata*. Whatever the Arabic words, Haly and his translator were using familiar technical terms, and Haly distinguishes a medical *ut nunc*, the extended present moment, from the philosophical, the instant of time between past and future. He says these terms are commonly used in the arts and sciences.

The natural philosophy with which the 'new heroes' of the fourteenth century extended their reputations came mostly from the north. It has been said that natural philosophy was a latecomer to Italian medicine, perhaps introduced by Taddeo Alderotti or the friars.[36] In Oxford there is good evidence that men connected to the *studium* knew Aristotle's natural philosophy before the end of the twelfth century, and teaching it went on when it was banned in Paris in 1210 and 1215. The bans were effective until the 1240s, when it was reintroduced from Oxford.[37] After the physical works became statutory for the arts course in Paris in the 1250s the *consortium* of masters reluctantly, under pressure from the pope, admitted Thomas Aquinas to their membership. We have seen that Aquinas was a very important figure in making Aristotelian natural philosophy consistent with Christianity and it seems that he, like Pietro d'Abano later, came north for his Aristotle.

The later Latin medical tradition

The arrangements for teaching in the faculty did not entirely blot out the earlier system in which the pupil sat at the feet of an older style of heroic teacher. On entering the faculty the pupil attached himself primarily to a certain master, who had a major part in teaching him and who promoted him at graduation, that is, the master took him for examination by the

[36] See Nancy Siraisi, *Taddeo Alderotti and his Pupils: Two Generations of Italian Medical Learning*, Princeton (Princeton University Press), 1981.
[37] Tradition has it that Roger Bacon took Oxford natural philosophy to Paris, but the commentaries of Adam of Buckfield are much more likely to have been the vehicle. See E. J. French, 'Adam of Buckfield and the Early Universities', PhD thesis, University of London, 1998.

master's peers. It was, of course, central to the success of the incorporated faculty that the collaborating masters agreed on the nature of medicine, its authorities, and the texts on which they examined the candidate. In short, they knew what the medical tradition was, and they placed themselves in it.

The masters also drew their pupils into the Latin medical tradition. The teaching master strove to develop a classroom 'culture' in which his pupils had not only to understand, but to believe what he told them. His approach was to begin with the Ciceronian, rhetorical, device of making his audience well disposed and attentive.[38] There is a discernible moral loading in what some masters said to their students about medicine. Partly it was the duty of the medical man not to question the natural-philosophical axioms on which the theory of medicine rested. As we saw in the previous chapter, the rules of subalternation made it in a sense improper for a medical man to try to question these axioms. Partly, too, the correct translation of theory into practice was a 'medical path' that the good doctor could not decently leave in treating his patients.[39] The moral tone of the exhortations of some masters was consonant with the almost religious respect accorded to the ancient authorities. The ultimate aim of medical education was, by the devices of commentary and disputed question, to make the ancients so clearly understood it was as if they were in the same room, speaking.[40]

This involved difficulties. In the northern universities, the student coming into medicine had spent a statutory amount of time in the arts, particularly philosophy. In the south, the philosophy and medical courses were taken in parallel, but the student had to be familar with philosophy before being able to understand the bulk of medical theory. But we have seen that the physician took over where the philosopher finished, and philosophical authorities were different. Quite apart from subalternation, philosophy said some things about the human or animal body that differed from what the medical authorities had declared. The medical teacher had to explain

---

[38] The practice was not uncommon in the preliminary material of commentaries on natural philosophy. See London, British Library, Harleian 3487, f. 173r: *In prohemio huius libri tria facit primo ut reddat auditorem benevolum . . . secundum ut reddat docilem . . . tertio ut reddat eum attentum.* The theory of teaching was an ongoing topic of discussion among scholastic doctors and their sources. See French, *Gentile*, p. 24; also Danielle Jacquart, 'L'Enseignement de la médecine: quelques termes fundamentaux', in her *La Science médicale Occidentale entre deux Renaissances*, Aldershot (Variorum), 1997, item XII.

[39] See Roger French, 'Gentile da Foligno and the *via medicorum*', in J. D. North and J. J. Roche, eds., *The Light of Nature*, Dordrecht (Kluwer Academic Publishers), 1985, pp. 21–34.

[40] See Roger French, 'Where the philosopher finishes, the physician begins: medicine and the arts course in thirteenth-century Oxford', in Cornelius O'Boyle, Roger French and Fernando Salmon, eds., *El Aprendizaje de la Medicina en el Mundo Medieval: las Fronteras de la Ensenanza Universitaria*, Granada, 2000 (*Dynamis*, 20, 2000).

this to his arts-educated pupils, and why it was that they now had to give their assent to medical doctrines and authorities. The career of the medical teacher highlights the case, for it was common for a university master to spend some years teaching philosophy before coming to teach medicine, and comprehensively change his medical hat.

Behind these circumstances was the medical faculty as an incorporation, with its internal rules or 'ethics'. In fact the situation was radically different from that of the educators of the late twelfth century and before, who had discussed the divisions or branches of 'philosophy' regarded as the whole body of knowledge or knowledge of God-and-His-works.[41] It was the hope of such men that the damage done to human knowledge by the Fall could be repaired for Christian purposes. But Aristotle changed all this. The arrival of the new logic and the physical works seemed to provide a programme for the creation of certain knowledge about the natural world which, unless Aristotle was read in the right way, seemed to be without a creator. The new universities were peopled by specialists who promoted their own disciplines rather than working for the unity and repair of all knowledge. This had an institutional basis in the university, and when, for example, the Parisian philosophers began to grow confident of the range and power of philosophical enquiry, they brought upon themselves the theologians' condemnations of 1277.[42] The consolidation of the medical faculties at the end of the century and in the early fourteenth extended this process, effectively establishing boundaries round the discipline of medicine. The academic 'sciences' were no longer a family of philosophy centred on the creation and the created, but a concatenated chain of separate disciplines subalternated back to the study of 'being' in general, Aristotle's *Metaphysics*.

MEDICAL TEXTS

Medical learning

It was observed in the previous chapter that the rationality of the Rational and Learned Doctor was acquired from the 'new logic' of Aristotle, which

---

[41] On the divisions of philosophy see Gundissalinus, *De divisione philosophiae*, ed. Ludwig Baur [*Beiträge zur Geschichte der Philosophie des Mittelalters*, 4, gen. ed. C. Baeumker], Münster, 1906; Bro. Charles Henry Buttimer, ed., *Hugonis de Sancto Victore Didascalicon. De Studio Legendi*, Washington, DC (The Catholic University of America Press), 1939.

[42] See Denifle, *Chartularium*, vol. I, p. 543. See also Edward Grant, 'The effect of the condemnation of 1277', in Kretzmann, Kenny and Pinborg, *Cambridge History of Later Medieval Philosophy*, pp. 537–9; see also his 'Issues in natural philosophy at Paris in the late thirteenth century', *Medievalia et Humanistica*, n.s. 13 (1985) 75–94.

became available shortly before the Aristotelian physical works were translated in the late twelfth and early thirteenth centuries. The other half of this story is the doctor's learning, the technical content of his discipline. We have seen that in the new universities the *Ars medicine* version of the *Articella* was replaced by the *Ars commentata*. This remained the basic textbook of medicine down to the early sixteenth century. Sometimes the brief tracts at its beginning – the introduction by Joannitius and the little treatises on prognostication from the pulse and urine by Philaretus and Theophilus – were dropped because they seemed too preliminary for an increasingly sophisticated audience. They were often replaced by longer works on the same topics by Isaac Israeli. In fact, the Greek and Byzantine inner core of medical education was vastly supplemented by an influx of Arabic material. Isaac's treatises on diets, in general and particular, became statutory. The *Canon* of Avicenna, translated in the eleventh century by Gerard of Cremona, came slowly into use, although it was not equally popular everywhere, for example in Montpellier. Although a huge compilation, its highly systematised contents made it a useful teaching text.[43] Avicenna sets out in the same formula the anatomy, complexion, diseases and treatment of all parts of the body, from head to toe. He lists medicines appropriate for various conditions in a systematic way; he also lists diseases separately. He gives rules for making compound medicines and systematically lists the antidotes that can be so constructed. The *Canon* was effectively the medical man's bible, giving chapter and verse for each disease, bodily part or treatment. Identifying a disease for the medical man was 'capitulation', that is, finding the chapter in which Avicenna had described it. There were Arabic and Hebrew versions of the text and assiduous scholars could make textual comparisons. But there were problems. Acquiring a copy of the whole text would have been very expensive, and when the *Canon* featured in statutes it was a question of which books should be read. It is even arguable that acquiring good copies of such large and central texts may have been one of the advantages of medical masters agreeing to collaborate in the new *studia*. Moreover, to be useful in teaching, the text needed a commentary, which was hardly achieved before the Black Death. Another major text was Averroes' *Colliget*, translated in 1286 and so, in principle, available to the faculties consolidated by the early fourteenth century.

---

[43] See also Nancy Siraisi, 'Changing concepts of the organization of medical knowledge in the Italian universities: fourteenth to sixteenth centuries', in *La Diffusione delle Scienze Islamiche nel Medio Evo Europeo*, Rome (L'accademia), 1987, pp. 293–321.

The New Galen

To this assemblage of medical authorities was added another kind of medical literature that has been called the 'New Galen' of the late thirteenth century.[44] Its importance for the learning of the doctor was almost as great as the 'new logic' had been for his rationality. It arrived in the 1270s and 1280s, at a time, that is, when the universities began to allow the consolidation of medical faculties. When in 1309 Arnau of Vilanova gave advice to Pope Clement V for a new curriculum at Montpellier, it centred on the New Galen texts on complexion, crisis and simples.[45] The New Galen was a professional business, and it has been argued that it widened the doctors' intellectual world in a dramatic way.[46] The theoretical parts of the New Galen were concerned with the theory of complexion, the fundamental construct of medieval medicine. Complexion was made up of the four elementary qualities that were so basic to the peripatetic world picture. Medicines and foods had complexion. Health was a balanced complexion, illness an unbalanced complexion and therapy was a restoration of complexion. Scholastic medicine reached its height of elaboration when the theorists applied the mathematics of quantification to the qualities that made up complexion.[47] Scholastics such as Dino del Garbo and Gentile da Foligno wanted to know in mathematical terms how intension and

---

[44] See Luis García-Ballester, 'The *New Galen*: a challenge to Latin Galenism in thirteenth-century Montpellier', in Klaus-Dietrich Fischer, Diethard Nickel and Paul Potter, eds., *Text and Tradition. Studies in Ancient Medicine and its Transmission Presented to Jutta Kollesch*, Leiden (Brill), 1998, pp. 55–83.

[45] *De Complexionibus, De Malicia Complexionis Diverse, De Simplici Medicina, De Morbo et Accidenti, De Crisi et Criticis Diebus, De Ingenio Sanitatis*. It is notable that *De Iuvamentis Membrorum* and its structural – functional anatomy is not included: the rationality is still complexional. See Michael McVaugh, 'The nature and limits of medical certitude at early fourteenth-century Montpellier', *Osiris*, 2nd series, 6 (1990) [*Renaissance Medical Learning. Evolution of a Tradition*, ed. Michael R. McVaugh and Nancy G. Siraisi], pp. 62–84. See also Luis García-Ballester, 'Medical ethics in transition in the Latin medicine of the thirteenth and fourteenth centuries: new perspectives on the physician–patient relationship and the doctor's fee', in A. Wear, J. Geyer-Kordesch and R. French eds., *Doctors and Ethics: The Earlier Historical Setting of Professional Ethics*, Amsterdam (Rodopi), 1993, pp. 38–71, at p. 39. He defines the New Galen as *De Naturalibus Facultatibus, De Interioribus (De Locis Affectis), De Morbo et Accidenti, De Complexionibus, De Malicia Complexionis Diverse, De Crisi, De Creticis, De Ingenio Sanitatis, de Medicinis Simplicibus*, and various works on the pulse.

[46] McVaugh, 'Medical certitude', p. 66. See also Luis García-Ballester's introduction to Luis García-Ballester, Roger French, Jon Arrizabalaga and Andrew Cunningham, eds., *Practical Medicine from Salerno to the Black Death*, Cambridge (Cambridge University Press), 1994, p. 10.

[47] See Danielle Jacquart, 'De crisis a complexio: note sur le vocabulaire du tempérament en Latin médiévale', in her *La Science médicale Occidentale entre deux Renaissances*, Aldershot (Variorum), 1997, item VI. The scholastic doctor also quantified the qualities of medicine in determining the appropriate dose. The work of Michael McVaugh is central to this topic. See his edition of *Arnau de Vilanova Opera Medica Omnia. II Aphorismi de Gradibus*, Granada-Barcelona (University of Barcelona Press), 1975 and the fuller edition in the same series, 1992.

remission of qualities interacted and what the perfect complexion was. The language they used was that of the Merton calculators and their discussions were highly elaborate. The body itself worked by the actions of the qualities of the complexions of its parts. We can distinguish this 'complexional rationality' from a fourteenth-century anatomical rationality which was associated with a wider dissemination of Galen's *De Usu Partium*, which was based on the practice of dissection, with which, too, Galen had made his vivisectional demonstrations in Rome.[48] We take a closer look at this below. To some extent the New Galen divided medical opinion on whether the old Greek or the much more recent Arabic authors should be given priority. But everyone agreed that these authors were *authority*: these were the names that medical professionals used to justify their beliefs and actions and which non-professionals could not challenge. They were part of the language of authority that the doctor used with his patient, his pupils and the law-givers.

DIALECTIC IN ACTION

Disputations

Like other university-educated men, the doctor was rational in a dialectical way, in using Aristotle's logic and its medieval developments.[49] He was trained in this according to statutory rules that governed how often pupils and masters should dispute. In most universities masters were obliged to respond to questions, including quodlibets.[50] Bolognese doctors who were entitled to teach had to dispute once a week and make arrangements for the publication of their solution to the questions. Physicians and philosophers of standing were also obliged to dispute on or near feast days; we know that Dino del Garbo did so in Bologna and that he once disputed with Gentile da Foligno in the street.[51] We have seen how, even in the twelfth century, logic was popular in the heroic schools, and now that the *Posterior Analytics* of Aristotle seemed to supply a programme for investigating the natural world, its range and power were greatly increased. Disputations were exercises in sustaining one thesis over another by questioning its premises or logic, and an important technique was the 'distinction' where different

---

[48] For a wider discussion, see Roger French, 'Anatomical rationality', in French et al., *Medicine from the Black Death to the French Disease*, pp. 288–323.

[49] In the later thirteenth century Paris was an important influence on European logic. Pietro d'Abano, for example, had studied there. By the early fourteenth century Oxford logic impressed some Italians and depressed others.

[50] See Maierù, *University Training in Medieval Europe*, p. 131.

[51] See French, *Canonical Medicine*, pp. 45–6.

meanings could be drawn out of a single term. The result could be an exciting or noisy meeting (we have noted Bacon's complaint that doctors were too anxious to dispute). They were also public affairs and provided an external face of university rationality, whether medical or otherwise.

Dubia

The written form of disputation was the *dubium*, the disputed question. This had a rigid and complex form and some disputed questions were hugely elaborate. These two features have repelled both sixteenth-century Hellenists and humanists and some later historians, but it will serve our purposes to take a quick look at the form. A disputed question was one that arose from the study of a text and normally took the form of a question that expected a positive answer, beginning *An*...or *Utrum*... ('Whether...'). Then came a section in which all the negative arguments were brought forward. Ideally, the form of the argument was syllogistic, with both major and minor propositions being drawn from the text, from the words of another authority or from sensory experience. These arguments were then attacked and destroyed in the same way, leaving the postive answer unscathed. Along the way other small objections or 'instances' were brought up and disposed of, as if to show that all possible objections could be satisfied. Commentators such as Dino del Garbo and Gentile da Foligno in the first half of the fourteenth century commonly put the objections in the mouth of the reader, a sort of student-figure: 'But you will at once say...', *Sed statim tu dices*...

Glosses, commentaries and the new heroes

The disputed question was such an important feature of high scholastic medicine that we need to know something more of its background. Because disputed questions were matters of theory, they involved a great deal of natural philosophy, and whereas fully-blown medical disputations seem to have happened only in the incorporated faculties, in the earlier arts course they evolved as a new type of teaching. The first versions of the physical works of Aristotle were taught by means of commentary or gloss which ran parallel to the text and explained what was going on in it, and solved difficult points of language and textual variation. These were in a strong sense personal interpretations, and in Oxford, for example, we know that the gloss written on some of the physical works by their translator, Alfred of Shareshill, was in use in the early thirteenth century. Only a generation later, Oxford commentators such as Adam of Buckfield were laying much greater stress on the logical structure of the text than Alfred had done. Although Adam's commentary was also a personal interpretation, its form was dictated by the logical structure of Aristotle's text, and it could be – and was – used by other teachers across Europe. Indeed, it was an aspect of the collaborative teaching of the corporation of the masters of arts at Oxford that they adopted, for half a century or so, a common gloss to explain the physical works.

Something similar seems to have been the case with medicine. The two similar commentaries on *De Sectis* by John of Alexandria and Agnellus of Ravenna may be variants of a common commentary. The same may be true of commentaries on the *Articella*.[52] As this textbook developed, so the commentaries of Galen on the Hippocratic texts it contained were widely adopted. But, probably towards the end of the thirteenth century, there was a change in teaching methods in philosophy from commentary to disputed question.[53]

Because of the close association of philosophy with medicine, it seems likely that when the medical faculties were consolidated, they adopted the disputed question as a major technique of teaching. Disputed questions did not cover the medical texts comprehensively, but enquired very deeply into certain points. Each master could handle different points or the same points differently. It is apparent that they were in competition in doing so: medical teachers in Bologna, Perugia and Padua, for example, strove to out-perform each other in commenting on the *Canon* of Avicenna. They were, in fact, the new heroic teachers of the fourteenth century. They were partly competing for students, and when Dino del Garbo for a while taught from Turisanus' *Plusquam Commentum* as if it were his own, the size of his class rose considerably.[54] The loyalty expected by a teacher of his pupils did not extend from one *studium* to another. Even the teachers' nicknames are evidence of this: Turisanus was the *Plusquam Commentator* because he commented 'more than' anyone else.[55] Gentile was the *Speculator*

---

[52] Paul O. Kristeller, 'Bartholomaeus, Musandinus and Maurus of Salerno and other early commentators of the *Articella*, with a tentative list of texts and manuscripts', *Italia medioevale e umanistica*, 19 (1976) 57–87.

[53] See D. A. Callus, 'Introduction of Aristotelian learning to Oxford', *Proceedings of the British Academy*, (1943) 229–81. See O'Boyle, *The Art of Medicine*, pp. 201–2 for nature of early medical commentaries.

[54] See Per-Gunnar Ottosson, *Scholastic Medicine and Philosophy. A Study of Commentaries on Galen's Tegni (c. 1300–1450)*, Uppsala (Bibliopolis), 1982, p. 23.

[55] Turisanus came from Florence, studied arts in Paris sometime between 1305 and 1319 and began to teach and practise medicine there. He returned to Bologna, where he had first studied medicine under Taddeo. The *Plusquam commentum* was finished in Bologna. See also O'Boyle, *The Art of Medicine*, p. 34.

because he saw deeper into problems of theory.[56] Pietro d'Abano (1257–c. 1315) was the *Conciliator* because he solved questions disputed between philosophers and physicians.[57] In contrast, in the north, there were fewer heroic commentaries: hardly any on the *Articella* in Paris in the thirteenth and fourteenth centuries,[58] where the masters were more concerned with securing positions in important households,[59] and the silence of English commentators is commensurable with the small size of their faculties.[60]

PHYSICIANS AND PHILOSOPHERS

Differences and resolutions

Students attending or reading disputed questions were performing class-room exercises that reflected the nature of the incorporated faculties. As an example, let us take the disputations of Pietro d'Abano, which were widely read by fourteenth-century academic teachers of medicine. His book is a collection of 'differences' which were likely to occur between philosophers and physicians. It was therefore popular among those whose statutory obli-gations compelled them to constantly find new topics for disputations. For the same reason, right up to the Renaissance, scholars searched through medical works such as commentaries to pick out and list separately *dubia* and *questiones*. Pietro's *Conciliator* also provided model answers in a di-alectical manner that he may have acquired in Paris. In it Pietro is writing as a medical man who has gone beyond the point where the philosopher finished and his overall (but not explicit) purpose is to justify the form that medicine had taken in the *studia*. The 'differences' are not therefore randomly chosen, but deal first with the questions that were most funda-mental to scholastic medicine of the faculties. The first of them is 'Does the physician need the theoretical sciences?' This is followed by 'Does the physician need logic?' and the third is 'Is medicine a science?' Now, it is clear that the answer to all three is 'Yes', because a medicine that was a mere

---

[56] See, for example, the colophon of the second volume of Gentile's commentary on the third book of the *Canon*; the term was contemporary with him.

[57] Pietro translated several works from Greek to Latin and taught in Paris from before 1295 to about 1306. He was also known as The Great Lombard. The first draft of *Conciliator* was complete by 1303 and was based on his previous ten years of teaching. The final version dates from 1310 when he was teaching medicine and astrology in Padua. See O'Boyle, *The Art of Medicine*, p. 34 and Siraisi, *Medieval and Early Renaissance Medicine*, pp. 60, 81.

[58] O'Boyle, *The Art of Medicine*, p. 199.   [59] Jacquart, 'Medical scholasticism'.

[60] Indeed, medical doctors educated in England cannot be found before the fourteenth century. Getz, *Medicine in the English Middle Ages*, p. 17.

productive art (not a *scientia*) without logic, the arts or philosophy, would be taught by experience and example and hardly at all by words. But the university teacher was full of words. He wanted to show that medicine had the intellectual standing of a *scientia* and was indeed a development of the Aristotelianism of the arts course. Above all (as we shall see) he wanted to avoid creating the idea that medicine was empirical.

Art or science

At the same time the scholastic doctor wanted to claim that his medicine was effective in physical, practical terms, for otherwise the vast intellectual structures of commentaries and disputed questions would appear as book-learning only. He accordingly argued that it was the very knowledge and reason of the Rational and Learned Doctor that made his medicine effective. Pietro's were model answers because of the exhaustiveness of the method: arguments against, arguments for, definitions and distinctions, citations of authority, demonstration of the truth and removal of objections, always in that order. It was strictly logical and, more loosely, also dialectical, because the opposing arguments were ultimately shown to result in absurdity. This was the ultimate scholastic test when knowledge was to be constructed or validated.

The method had a useful flexibility. One of the strongest arguments against the physician needing the theoretical sciences was that Hippocrates had not known them. Indeed, they had not then been invented. It was commonly thought that Hippocrates had such powers of mind that he did not need the aid of the theoretical sciences; Pietro says it was as if God had created Hippocrates as infallible in order to provide man with a perfect medical tradition.[61] This tradition, although pure and divine (says Pietro), needs to be interpreted, and this is where the sciences are useful for mortals lesser than Hippocrates. In this way Pietro saw himself in a medical tradition that had ancient and almost divine origins and could be interpreted and refined by ancients and moderns. Like a number of medical men reflecting on the nature of their subject, Pietro gave it a history to explain and justify its present. It was Aristotle (says Pietro) who said that the most necessary of the arts and sciences, including medicine, were invented first. The first medical god was Aesculapius, whose sons fought in the Trojan War and who were followed by a string of heroes down to Democritus, traditionally seen

---

[61] Pietro d'Abano, *Conciliator Controversiarum, quae inter Philosophos et Medicos versantur*, Venice (Heirs of L. A. Giunta), 1565, f. 3r.

as a pupil of Hippocrates. Pietro's little history does not extend beyond Galen, whose description of the three sects Pietro adopted for his own time.

RECONSTRUCTING ANCIENT MEDICINE

Doctors and the history of medicine

We can learn a little more about the Latin tradition of medicine by noting one or two other things about how Pietro and others saw the history of medicine. It was (in ending with Galen) a Greek business that had now to be presented in a Latin form. Scholarly doctors (such as Pietro) knew and translated from Greek[62] but their audience – pupils, patients, important learned men – communicated at the formal level in Latin. Latin medical texts were a *professional* matter. They had medical gods and heroes (Aesculapius, Podalirus, Machaon) who could be cited without difficulty in a medieval Christian context. At really important places in big commentaries, Gentile and Dino address the Christian God directly in the form of a prayer, but when they needed authority for their piety it came from the pagan philosophers of old, or the much more recent Muslim writers. They do not cite biblical authority or the *Sentences*, which were the professional arena of the school theologians.

It is notable that an author such as Pietro, who saw the history of medicine ending with Galen, made considerable use of Arabic authorities. Indeed, the doctors had done much to remedy the situation that provoked Bacon's criticism. Commenting on Avicenna's *Canon* was a life's work for Gentile. After its translation in the 1280s Averroes' *Colliget* became increasingly used as an authority. Haly Abbas and Haly Ridwan remained popular. In Latin translation these authors provided much material for European medicine, but they were not part of medical history, the self-conscious Latin tradition. That tradition indeed had as its major concern the reconstruction of ancient medicine. Not only was the aim of education to be able to understand the ancients as though they were present and speaking in the same room, but the circumstances and the practice of the ancients were to be reconstructed.

Galen was the best candidate for this. He wrote widely, and often about himself. The New Galen of the early fourteenth century was thus in the first instance a literary construction brought about by a determined effort to render the old Galen into Latin in the interest of better medicine. Galen's

---

[62] Pietro says he translated the Aristotelian *Problems*. See *Conciliator*, f. 3r.

ideals and even circumstances now became medieval ideals and circumstances. An important text was Galen's small *De Sectis ad Introducendos*
which, as we have seen, was the first work in the Alexandrian curriculum and which attracted commentary early in the Middle Ages. Those
commentaries, designed by professional teachers for a formal classroom,
identified with the Rationalist Sect of Galen's Rome. The same was true of
the later Middle Ages, when the faculties had become incorporated within
the universities: teachers who had reasons to make their medicine as philosophical and logical as possible naturally selected the Rationalists as their
own predecessors.

   We can usefully return to Pietro d'Abano to look at one form of the
argument. His point of departure is *De Sectis* and he begins by dismissing
the Methodists as unskilled because they thought only in universals and
despised particulars. In contrast, the Empirics considered only particulars
and despised universals. Only one of the three sects used both in a balanced
way, and this was the Rationalist Sect, the *logici, sive rationales* (Pietro does
not use the less flattering term *dogmatici*).[63] It is apparent that Pietro is using terms of contemporary logic which almost certainly did not represent
the three sects of Galen's Rome; moreover he has, in reconstructing Galen's
circumstances, brought those into his own time too. This brings us to an
important point. Scholastic teachers identified with the Rationalists, for
reasons we have met in outline. They identified with Galen and adopted
his enemies as their own. While Galen had some sympathy for empirical
procedures within medicine, the scholastics had none. There were practitioners in their own day who lacked theory because they had not been
educated in a university or medical faculty. This did not stop them practising, for there were local means of licensing them. They were, in fact,
rivals to the university doctors in the medical marketplace, and the doctors
complained greatly that the lack of theory meant bad medicine: their own
claim to the monopoly of internal medicine was, after all, based on the
supposition that a theory-directed medicine was more effective. The major
selling-point of scholastic medicine was that it gave the *causes* of things.
From 1271 the Paris faculty argued that the lower ranks of the profession
acted randomly in their prescriptions because they did not know causes; in
the next two centuries knowledge of causes came increasingly with Arabic
medicine.[64] The New Rationalists thus invented the New Empirics. And

---

[63] *Conciliator*, f. 3r.
[64] Jacquart argues that there was no suitable word for 'cause' in medicine before this. See Danielle
Jacquart, 'The introduction of Arabic medicine into the West. The question of etiology', in her *La
Science médicale Occidentale*, item III.

circumstances were now different from Galen's Rome, for where the power of the faculty operated it could prosecute at law the unlicensed practitioner, the mere empiric.

Rationalising Hippocrates

In distancing themselves from the new empirics, the new rationalists created a problem for themselves. We have seen that they wanted to show that their medicine was effective, but they could not afford to emphasise observation and experience, which looked rather empirical, at the expense of theory. Worse, the great Hippocrates, widely revered as the Father of Medicine, was – it was generally admitted – without the arts and sciences. He was surely not, then, *empirical*? The Learned and Rational Doctors hastened to his rescue. Pietro d'Abano argued that Hippocrates could be regarded as the first rationalist because he wrote his medicine down. As we have seen, a more usual explanation was that the hugeness of Hippocrates' mind enabled him to use naturally what only later came to be codified with the aid of dialectic. Pietro argues in a similar way in explaining how Hippocrates used, without logic, the three doctrines that Galen later set out at the beginning of the *Tegni*. This could almost be the programme of medieval medicine: to explain the medical wisdom of Hippocrates, especially in the *Aphorisms*, with the dialectical apparatus set out by Galen in the *Tegni*.[65]

Another way of making Hippocrates a rationalist was to argue that although life was short and the art was long, his great mind had been able to frame valid generalisations or, in medieval terms, universals. The *Aphorisms* seemed to be not only oracular pieces of wisdom but universals which could be used as axioms. They could be used as unassailable starting points in a rationalist argument, like the philosophical principles that came into medicine by subalternation. 'Opposites cure opposites' became known as 'the law of Hippocrates' and was the fundamental and unquestionable axiom at the root of the whole theory of complexion.[66] As we have seen, medieval logic as used in medicine derived the premises of its syllogisms from earlier demonstrated knowledge, from sense observations and from the sayings of great men: Hippocrates had a rationalist role here too.

In this way aphorisms fitted neatly into the logical structure of medical writing. But the medical man's logic was not a paper or verbal exercise: words signified things, and it was things that showed logic. The very cohesiveness

---

[65] These seem to be the most heavily glossed works in the *Articella*.

[66] Pietro says it does not need proof, being logically and medically axiomatic. Like 'the whole is greater than the parts', it is a common conception of the soul. *Conciliator*, f. 6r.

and connectedness of the physical world demonstrated logical relationships between its parts. It was, of course, an Aristotelian world, but the order and design that the medieval doctors saw in it may reflect also the rationality of the Creator. Aphorisms could be treated as expressing the natures of things, and medical men found their axiomatic authority an attractive form of expression. Some authors sought related forms. Gentile da Foligno looked for 'canons' that were rules of correct procedure in medicine. He was commenting on the *Canon* of Avicenna, of course, but as he used the term it had extensions to canon law and canonical religious life.[67] Bernard of Gordon also used canons of procedure[68] and other authors, such as the Bolognese doctors, derived rules, *regule*, of procedure.

There had been a suggestive parallel in theology. As revealed knowledge the Bible was the authority, greater even than Hippocrates, whom, as Pietro d'Abano said, God had created as a foundation of the medical tradition. But the Bible was of little use in serious discussions with infidels or heretics, who did not believe that it was the word of God. The new theology of the thirteenth-century schools was accordingly sometimes expressed dialectically, when its authority was derived from reason. There were 'rules of the Christian faith' which eschewed quotation of the sacred page and moved from one proposition to another.[69] This may have owed something to the mode of procedure in geometry, but the result looked rather like an aphorism. An idea useful in conjunction with this was 'common conceptions of the soul', statements based on reason which, once grasped, could not be denied by any rational man. For Pietro d'Abano, 'the law of Hippocrates' as a common conception of the soul was axiomatic and needed no proof.

Aphorisms and new authority

Arnau of Vilanova also chose to express some of his medical wisdom in aphorisms or rules. The first of them are mostly general and relate to the nature of medicine and the doctor. They are, that is, deontological and designed to guide the doctor in good practice. But it is possible that Arnau

---

[67] French, *Canonical Medicine*, pp. 11–14 and ch. 5.

[68] Luke Demaitre, *Dr Bernard de Gordon: Professor and Practitioner*, Toronto (Pontifical Institute of Mediaeval Studies), 1980, p. 130.

[69] See, for example, the *De Arte seu Articulis Catholice Fidei* of Alain of Lille, in J. P. Migne, *Patrologiae Cursus Completus* (Latin series), Paris, 1866–, vol. 210, p. 594. It has been more recently attributed to Nicholas of Amiens: see C. H. Lohr, 'The pseudo-Aristotelian Liber de Causis', in Jill Kraye, W. F. Ryan and C. B. Schmitt, eds., *Pseudo-Aristotle in the Middle Ages: The Theology and Other Texts*, London (Warburg Institute), 1986, pp. 53–62.

had in his mind other readers in addition to his colleagues. Some of the aphorisms are rather obvious (such as 'the course of action is determined by the desired effects') and some seem designed to deflect criticism of the doctors. Arnau first reminds his readers that all good flows down to him from God and that he serves God by practising properly (we can recall that in earlier criticism doctors had been accused of elevating nature above God). He then declares that the doctor who practises for money will fail (the greed of doctors had been a byword). Further aphorisms deal with the roles of reason and experience in practice and insist on the necessity of knowing the variation between individuals and the control of regimen, that is, the Rational and Learned Doctors' preferred form of practice. It would have done their image no harm at all if these aphorisms had also been read by their patients.

Arnau also called his aphorisms 'canons', with the range of connotations implied by Gentile. They were also 'parables', *parabole*, a term which tapped into a Christian range of meaning.[70] The essence of the parable was allegory, in which a simple story of a particular happening revealed a more general truth. As in Aesop's fables, a particular dog in a manger or a fox eyeing the grapes illustrates a deeper and wider principle, the moral. In the Middle Ages there were (at least) two ways of reading the scriptures: the literal (as William of Conches read the story of the creation of Eve) and the moral, or spiritual, the inner and deeper meaning.[71] That is, the Fall had rendered man incapable of understanding the direct voice of God, which he could now best hear by way of allegory and the use of the arts and sciences. Arnau's medical parables expressly seek to reveal a spiritual meaning,[72] and the terms of his medical learning were used as religious metaphors. Arnau was perhaps unusual in the intensity of his piety,[73] and wrote directly religious works of a heterodox nature which led to his arrest.[74]

---

[70] See also Jole Agrimi, 'Aforismi, parabole, esempi. Forme di scrittura della medicina operativa: il modello di Arnaldo da Villanova', in *Le Forme della Communicazione Scientifica*, ed. Massimo Galuzzi, Gianni Micheli and Maria Teresa Monti, eds., Milan (Franco Angeli), 1998, pp. 361–92.

[71] See in general Gillian Evans, *The Language and Logic of the Bible: the Earlier Middle Ages*, Cambridge (Cambridge University Press), 1984; Beryl Smalley, *The Study of the Bible in the Middle Ages*, 3rd edn, Oxford (Clarendon Press), 1984.

[72] See *Arnaldi de Villanova Opera Medica Omnia. VI.2. Commentum in quasdam Parabolas et alias Aphorismorum Series: Aphorismi Particulares, Aphorismi de Memoria, Aphorismi Extravagantes*, ed. Juan A. Paniagua and Pedro Gil-Sotres, Barcelona (University of Barcelona), 1993.

[73] See Michael McVaugh, 'Moments of inflection: the careers of Arnau de Vilanova', in Peter Biller and Joseph Ziegler, eds., *Religion and Medicine in the Middle Ages*, The University of York (York Medieval Press), 2001, pp. 47–67.

[74] See Ziegler, *Medicine and Religion* p. 53. The medical language of men such as Arnau and his fellow Catalan Ramon Lull (d. c. 1316) incorporated parables or metaphors which reached outside medicine. Lull was interested in degrees of qualities in medicine, and argued that the moral virtues were at a mid-point of a latitude while the vices were its extremes.

In some sense, *Conciliator*, *Plusquam*, *Speculator*, Dino del Garbo and the Bolognese doctors were setting themselves up as new authorities.[75] Gentile sometimes admits that an abstruse development of a theory could have no application whatever and indeed could not exist outside the imagination. Such things were written partly for the status they conferred on the authors. That had been true also of the authorities which the new heroic writers wanted to emulate: where there were objective reports of actual medical practice, for example in case-histories, theory was almost totally forgotten, and it has been recognised that Byzantine and Arab theorists were writing for status.[76] The same is true of surgery, where the operations described were fictitious.[77] By the later thirteenth century, Italian surgeons such as Guglielmo da Saliceto were trying to bring learned medicine and surgery together; Guglielmo argued that it was possible to learn surgery from books, like learned and rational medicine. Medieval surgeons recognised that writing a surgical text as an author conferred greater respect than commenting on old texts.[78] Gentile, calling himself an *oculista*, was quite confident on the basis of his reading that he knew the best operation for couching a cataract. He had never done it and did not know whether it could be done; but it was still the best. The scholastics took their sources literally, without realising the personal motives of their authorities, and some procedures they adopted in trying to re-establish ancient medicine, such as surgical operations or dissecting the human body, were reconstructions from words only.

Thus the university doctors had a Good Story to tell their patients, pupils and employers that included the clinical effectiveness that came from true knowledge of the world, the body and its diseases. They could refer to the great authorities, which added power to their medicine in an age that revered the ancients. They claimed to be part of a grand and successful tradition of medicine. Their grasp of logic gave them the power that logic

---

[75] See Fernando Salmon, 'Technologies of authority in the medical classroom in the thirteenth and fourteenth centuries', in O'Boyle et al., *El Aprendizaje de la Medicina en el Mundo Medieval*, pp. 135–57.

[76] See Cristina Álvarez Millán, 'Graeco-Roman case histories and their influence on medieval Islamic clinical accounts', *Social History of Medicine*, 12 (1999) 19–43; and her 'Practice versus theory: tenth-century case histories from the Islamic Middle East', in Peregrine Horden and Emilie Savage-Smith, eds., *The Year 1000: Medical Practice at the end of the first Millennium* [*Social History of Medicine*, 13, 2000], pp. 265–78.

[77] See Siraisi, *Medieval and Early Renaissance Medicine*, esp. ch. 6. See also Emilie Savage-Smith, 'The practice of surgery in Islamic lands: myth and reality', in Horden and Savage-Smith, *The Year 1000*, pp. 307–21.

[78] See M. McVaugh, 'Therapeutic strategies: surgery', in Grmek, ed., *Western Medical Thought from Antiquity to the Middle Ages*, pp. 273–318.

had been supplying to the men of the schools since the twelfth century, the power to dazzle those without it and to win arguments against those less skilled in the art. They poured scorn on the new empirics, a category they had helped to invent. They contrived a professional 'ethics' that did their image no harm by being directed towards the benefit of the patient. Their ideal form of practice was to be retained in a big household and to govern the regimen of people who were not ill. Their story emphasised how individuals varied with age, sex, location and innate disposition and that skill in medicine was the correct evaluation of these things. In contrast, the empiric had a medicine for each disease: it was a 'specific' and probably secret (a *nostrum* is 'our' medicine). They were therefore well placed in sudden epidemics, when time was short and people were anxious.

DISSECTION

In one *studium*, that of Bologna, the medical student in the first half of the fourteenth century would have met something unusual: human dissection. Historians have spent much time on the origins of anatomy; mostly because it looks like an essential stage in the growth of our anatomy-based medicine. On both counts we cannot give the topic much space here, but there are issues that relate to the history of the Rational and Learned Doctor.

First, postmortem examination of corpses had been known from the thirteenth century, often in conjunction with the law and designed to reveal the cause of death. Mondino, the dissector at Bologna, made no claim that he was doing anything new, unless it was to write a book about dissection, which he justifies in a standard literary way. His dissections were for teaching purposes, no doubt so that physicians could learn what was normal (and so be in a position to recognise the pathological) and that surgeons could be safer and more effective. But he was well known to his colleagues, even in different *studia*, as the 'famous anatomist', *famosus anatomista*. The term implies that the anatomist was a specialist, pursuing his own discipline with some of the autonomy and authority of medicine as a whole. The term is parallel to *legista*, the school lawyer, which also implies professional boundaries.

Within medicine, anatomy has a special relationship with philosophy. Almost every anatomist down to early modern times gave a philosophical or theological reason for doing anatomy before he gave a medical or surgical reason. There was philosophical interest in how the body had been put together and how it worked, and justification for dissection could be found in Aristotle and Galen. Anatomy was also central to the enduring question of whether reason or sensory observation was more important in medicine, and we shall see that the sensory component enabled anatomy to survive the crisis of philosophy. But here we need to examine the reasoning involved in anatomy, for it was fundamental to the thinking of the Learned and Rational Doctor. Anatomical rationality derived from Galen. He provided a hierarchy of 'action', 'use' and 'utility' of the 'similar' and 'organic' parts, and the whole was presented in the teleological framework of the creative demiurge, who was partly Plato's deity and partly rational 'nature' who had constructed the body. Galen's experiments on blood vessels and nerves showed that the machinery of the body could be understood and partly controlled. Anatomy was functional, for, as Aristotle said, knowledge of a part is knowledge of what it is for. Galen's functional anatomy was best expressed in the text known in the Latin tradition as *De Usu Partium*, but it is not clear whether Mondino knew the full work or a translation of the truncated Arabic paraphrase that had been circulating for some time. Mondino had no suspicion that Galen had not dissected human bodies, and so in adopting a 'Galenic' practice Mondino was claiming ancient authority. The rote of observables he has in dissection is drawn from John of Alexandria's commentary of Galen's *De Sectis* and Mondino clearly saw himself as part of a learned anatomical tradition.

Medical men who gave their allegiance more to Avicenna than to Galen had another kind of anatomical rationality. The dominating thread of medical theory in the high Middle Ages was complexion, the combination of elementary qualities of the parts. Therapy sought to restore an unbalanced complexion, often by evacuation. It could be argued, for example, that it was when the complexion of the muscles was changed by an incoming complexion of the nerves that function resulted. As we saw, Avicenna routinely gives the 'anatomy' of the parts of the body before discussing them medically. As a systematiser rather than an experimenter, Avicenna's anatomy consisted partly of the locations of different complexions, a doctrine that would be greatly developed by his commentators.

GRADUATION

Having selected his school and his master, having kept his terms of residence and having heard lectures and disputed according to the statutes, the student was ready to seek the professional qualification which would allow him to practise internal medicine. This was a complex business and varied from *studium* to *studium*, but there was generally a ritual display at some point in the proceedings.

The procedure began when the master thought that his student was ready for examination by other masters.[79] This was the first examination and it was conducted in private, probably because there was a real possibility of failure.[80] It is notable that the essence of the examination was not to test the student's grasp of medicine; rather, the candidate was expected to perform the characteristic exercises of the teaching master. He was expected to find the 'points' in a portion of a text (which was generally the Galenic *Tegni*, followed by the *Aphorisms*), that is, the articulations in the logic of the author.[81] This was equivalent to the *expositio*, the first part of a formal commentary. For example, Taddeo begins his commentary on the *Aphorisms* with an exposition which, he says, is like light, without which one cannot see either colours or the *scientia* of the author.[82] A commentator would normally follow the exposition with an interpretation, and in the same way the medical candidate was expected to 'verify' the text he had just divided.[83] Because he was working with the *Aphorisms* and *Tegni*, medical 'verification' often took the form of giving the physical reasons derived from the latter that explained the appearances contained in the former (which again underscores the importance of these two texts in medieval medical education).[84] Verifying the text was to explain it, the master's privilege in a magisterial lecture, and when the candidate, finally, defended his verification against objections,[85] he had in a sense given a specimen magisterial performance (a 'masterpiece', as they said in the productive guilds).

It will be noticed that the heroic masters we have been discussing – Dino, Taddeo, Gentile – were Italian. Arnau and Bernard of Gordon

---

[79] It may have been in the form of a disputation on a topic set previously. See Jacques Verger, 'Teachers', in de Ridder-Symoens, ed., *A History of the University in Europe. Volume 1*, pp. 144–68. See also O'Boyle, *The Art of Medicine*, p. 148.

[80] There were rules for the masters' voting on the candidate in the private examination, known in the Paduan college as the *examinatio tentiva*. See Donato Gallo, 'Statuti inediti de Collegio Padovano dei dottori d'arte e medicina: una redazione quattrocentesca', *Quaderni per la storia dell'università di Padova*, 22–23 (1989–90) 59–94.

[81] Bolognese masters covered nine 'points' in their lectures; see the statutes of the university of arts and medicine, 1405: Malagola, *Statuti*, p. 254. Maierù, *University Training*, p. 50, says that the nine points covered a cycle of lectures. *Punctum* seems to have been taken over from law usage: Jacquart, 'Medical scholasticism', p. 210.

[82] Taddeo then divides the text and gives his interpretation: '*commentum dividam et sententiam ponam*'. See *Thaddei Florenti Expositiones in arduum aphorismorum Ipocratis volumen. In divinum pronosticorum Ipocratis librum. In preclarum regiminis acutorum Ipocratis opus. In subtilissimum Ioannitii Isagogarum libellum*, Venice (A. Giunta), 1527.

[83] The term appears only in medical statutes. Maierù, *University Training*, p. 58.

[84] For these texts in the statutes, see Malagola, *Statuti*, p. 437.

[85] *Et primo legere debeat pro prima lectione testum totum puncti dati libri Tegni Galieni, deinde bene dividendo, verificando et exponendo testum secundum instantiis.* Malagola, *Statuti*, pp. 438–9.

probably represented something similar in Montpellier. In contrast, in northern Europe there were no notable authors before the Black Death. At all events, this highlights a difference we must take note of. In the north, the successful student ultimately joined the consortium of masters: this was inception. This was quite a different procedure from receiving the licence to teach, which was given after an examination conducted by the bishop's chancellor, in his role as controller of the schools. In the south, the medical student received his education at the hands of the teaching masters of his *studium* but was examined and given his professional qualification by the professional college, which was not co-extensive with the teaching faculty. It contained doctors who did not teach and did not contain all those that did teach; its autonomy was emphasised by the fact that some students went for their 'degree' to another college, where perhaps it was cheaper. But in both north and south the candidate, having been successful in his private examination and having proved that he had kept his terms and had attended all the required disputations and readings, petitioned for the licence from the chancellor.[86] In Paris the bachelor again provided evidence of his terms of residence, conducted a solemn disputation and chose a master to present him to the chancellor, who duly replied with a formal sealed letter. The award of the licence involved a grand affair with the whole faculty processing before an audience of the chancellor, representatives of the other faculties and ecclesiastical, civil and visiting dignitaries.[87]

Many left their professional qualification at this stage and went off to practise, for taking the doctorate was expensive. Some entered into contracts as town physicians, and after a period returned to their university for the doctorate. Joining the ranks of the university-trained Rational and Learned Doctors – inception – was a very public occasion, in contrast to the private examination. It was a ceremony in which the learned doctors made it clear what it was to join their ranks. It often took place in a church, which, along with the church's licence, gave authority to the proceedings.[88] The new doctor was presented with gifts as signs of his new status: in Italy, a biretta and ring, taken from the altar. The biretta was the doctor's 'hat' in a physical and metaphorical sense (we have seen that philosophers and medical men could wear different 'hats' at different times in their career);

---

[86] There are varying accounts of the different stages in the process of inception and taking the licence. See Jacques Verger, 'Teachers', in de Ridder-Symoens, ed., *A History of the University in Europe. Volume 1*, pp. 144–68; Carl C Schlam, 'Graduation speeches of Gentile da Foligno', *Mediaeval Studies*, 40 (1978) 96–119; Maierù, *University Training*, pp. 58ff.

[87] O'Boyle, *The Art of Medicine*, p. 25–6.

[88] In Bologna from 1219 the licence (to teach) was given by the archdeacon of Bologna. Siraisi, *Medieval and Early Renaissance Medicine*, p. 19.

it symbolised the proximity of a man with a *scientia* to God. The ring symbolised the marriage of the man to the science. The learning of the Learned and Rational new Doctor was represented by the gift of a book; and a kiss marked the gift of eloquence: his rationality. There was a speech from the promoting master, perhaps linking eloquence with the formal disputation conducted by the candidate, or indulging in word-play with his name. Dress was important: in Paris on public occasions the medical men wore a distinctive cope over their academic robes. Here the new doctor was given a doctoral bonnet and, in return, gave hats and gloves. There followed a procession, a public statement of the characteristics of the group on display; and a feast, a traditional way of declaring community of interests and purposes.

The essential thing about medical graduation was that it impressed the candidate and the onlookers that a major event had taken place. The medieval student learned his Latin at school – perhaps indeed a grammar school[89] – and at fourteen or fifteen went to his *studium* to learn the arts. It took about five years to reach the grade of master and another five to become a doctor of medicine. These periods were constantly revised,[90] which indicates the importance put on them by the teaching masters. Whatever the precise length of study, it was an enormous commitment of resources; and it reminds us of how much knowledge the Rational and Learned Doctor had absorbed. It is significant that part of the ceremony of 'graduation' was the proof of residence and of reading for the required time: the candidate normally presented letters or a 'schedule', *cedula*, a term used for formal and written documents, like a request from a local doctor for a *consilium* from a more famous one.[91] This was not mere administration. For example, most of the candidates for medical graduation in Paris were known to have been through the Parisian arts course, but they still had to prove their terms. It was more difficult to prove this if the candidate had learned his arts in another university, and sometimes the authorities at Paris insisted on the full university seal of Oxford on the schedule of an Oxonian candidate. Proving terms of residence was a *measurable* part of the public display, the effect of which was to announce the quality of the new doctor: his qualification to practise.

---

[89] See García-Ballester's introduction to *From Salerno to the Black Death*.

[90] O'Boyle, *The Art of Medicine*, p. 20.

[91] See, for example, Lynn Thorndike, '*Consilia* and more medical works in manuscript by Gentile da Foligno', *Medical History*, 3 (1959) 8–19; Jole Agrimi and Chiara Crisciani, *Les Consilia médicaux* [*Typologie des sources du Moyen Age occidental*, 69], Turnhout, Belgium (Brepols), 1994; French, *Gentile*, p. 277.

THE MEDICAL MARKETPLACE

Other learned doctors

These were the outward signs of the incorporated faculty and they contributed largely to the public perception of the Learned and Rational
Doctor. The new doctor paid for the feast and paid sums to his master
and the university. He was buying professional support largely in the form
of the freedom to practise internal medicine. He was joining a club whose
numbers were limited by the length and expense of the training and he
probably expected his share of the market to be proportionately large.[92]
Perhaps, too, the church approved of a form of incorporation that limited
the number of practitioners, for we have seen that for a long time there had
been nervousness about medicine damaging the recruitment to theology.
The size of the club was also governed more directly, for example by assumption of control of the southern universities by the church (as we
saw in the previous chapter) and in practice restricting the *ius ubique
docendi* to Bologna and Paris.[93] Teaching masters in general controlled
the size of their own group, as in the magisterial universities in the north;
and in Bologna the college of doctors was subject to a similar *numerus
clausus* which limited its numbers, which were fixed and low.[94] Another
strategy open to the elite doctors was to extend the length and therefore
the cost and exclusivity of the university medical course, particularly when
faced with growing competition from outsiders.[95]

   The doctoral ceremonies were rites of passage that marked the end of
medical education. The classroom culture that brought the student into
the master's vision of the medical tradition often left him with a loyalty to
his *alma mater* that did not extend to other schools. Italian masters who
had taught students in one *studium* were highly critical of those who went
off to be examined by a college in another town and even more critical of
the college that poached them. *Studia* were often major sources of revenue
for their town, which was jealous of their privileges. Heroic teachers often

---

[92] Paris produced an average of perhaps five medical doctors a year. O'Boyle, *The Art of Medicine*,
   p. 65.
[93] See Rüegg, 'Themes', in de Ridder-Symoens, ed., *A History of the University in Europe. Volume I*, p. 17.
[94] Verger, 'Teachers', in de Ridder-Symoens, ed., *A History of the University in Europe. Volume I*, p. 149.
[95] The medical guilds, which largely grew up alongside the faculties and professional colleges, contained
   many non-university doctors. On the length of the course see Nancy Siraisi, 'The faculty of medicine',
   in de Ridder-Symoens, ed., *A History of the University in Europe. Volume I*, pp. 360–87; certainly by
   1405 the Bolognese statutes suggest that the medical course was now longer (p. 379); for the situation
   in Paris, see O'Boyle, *The Art of Medicine*, p. 21.

wrote for the students and the glory of their *studium*. One of the functions of heroic commentaries after all was to do more, or better, or see further, or resolve the opinions of other teachers. We have seen that Gentile da Foligno once had a difference of opinion with Dino del Garbo in the street, and held in general that the doctors in Bologna gave too much credit to Galen. Gentile taught in Perugia and found that it was not always easy to tell quite what the Bolognese doctors *were* teaching.[96]

In other words there was in the late thirteenth and early fourteenth centuries no deontological or ethical imperative to present a unified face of university medicine. Like John of Salisbury many years before, Pietro d'Abano recognised that disagreements between doctors had disastrous effects on public confidence. Particularly in relation to acute diseases and prognosis, says Pietro, the vulgar are so distrustful of doctors that they refuse to consult them even on matters of diet and regimen; even surgery was preferable, because it was open to the senses.[97] Part of Pietro's complaint is that the vulgar did not understand medical theory. The result, of course, was that they could not be impressed with it, and the doctor was deprived of a major image-making device. It was a case of the doctors over-playing their hand, for in general they strove to speak a technical language to the patient that was just above his head. An enduring example is 'blockage of the liver' where 'blockage' is *oppilatio*, a Latin term calculated to impress but not enlighten the patient.[98]

Other kinds of practitioner

The processes and rituals that led to medical inception and a licence provided a hallmark of quality for the new teacher or practitioner. It was essentially an act of a corporation with legal standing. Bishops, popes, kings[99] and emperors could also give full licences, but it was normally on the advice of a panel of fully qualified doctors. (In a later period the London College of Physicians came into existence in this way.) But the university-trained doctor was not the only kind of practitioner. Guilds older than the medical

[96] On the problems of medical communication – the numbers of books and their inaccessibility, and the consequent writing of summaries etc. – see Luke Demaitre, 'Scholasticism in compendia of practical medicine, 1250–1450', *Manuscripta*, 20 (1976) 81–95.

[97] Pietro d'Abano, *Conciliator*, f. 7r.

[98] The *Cautele Medicorum* attributed to Arnau of Vilanova, printed in *Arnaldi de Villanova medici acutissimi Opera nuperrime revisa*, Leyden (Scipio de Gabiano), 1532.

[99] Siraisi, *Medieval and Early Renaissance Medicine*, p. 18 says Peter the Ceremonious of Aragon issued licences informally to Jews in the 1340s but complaints from the profession made his successor in 1356 reinstate university study and examination as a condition of offering the licence.

faculties and including doctors could issue licences (but their consolidation seems close in time to that of the faculties).[100] Specialists could gain licences on the testimony of successful practice. Most such local licences were partial, limited for example to surgery or even a single kind of operation and often held by followers of another trade. The university doctors claimed that only their licence was complete, since it alone extended to the giving of internal medicines; and since they claimed that their own knowledge subsumed that of the various kinds of practice, they claimed control, too, over these other medical trades.[101]

There were, then, many niches in the medical marketplace. In practice the learned and rational physician tended to avoid surgery, and his control over the other branches of medicine was often nominal and limited to large towns. The surgeon or specialist in external medicine was called out when something went wrong and earned his reputation by his success and by word of mouth recommendation. In contrast the university-trained physician had some sort of reputation by virtue of his licence and training. He was not infrequently retained in a large household or had a contract with a town.[102] And as we have seen, his business was to regulate the regimen of those under his control (and visit the poor free of charge, if a city physician). He was successful, then, if nothing happened; but if it did, he had a multitude of reasons why, and why or not his treatments worked. Conversely, a magnate or a monarch who was supporting a physician had a learned man on his hands who could be put to other uses while the household remained in health. Arnau of Vilanova, physician for the second time to Jaume II of Aragon after 1300, was dispatched on a diplomatic mission to France.[103] The French king, Charles V, had at least fifteen Paris-trained physicians, and between 1250 and 1400 there were at least seventy-five Paris doctors in big households, mostly secular. Foreign potentates sent their protégés to Paris to gain a medical education before employing them as doctors.

The physician on a contract did not legally promise to cure the diseases afflicting his patients, but to be diligent in his advice and his visiting, to let blood prophylactically at the appropriate time of year and to be on

---

[100] There were thirteenth-century Italian guilds containing doctors. Florence's guild of *medici*, apothecaries and grocers was established in 1293 and was by 1315 a federation of the three autonomous trades. Siraisi, *Medieval and Early Renaissance Medicine*, p. 18.

[101] There was, for example, a case of 1322 when the Paris faculty successfully prevented a woman from practising. Siraisi, *Medieval and Early Renaissance Medicine*, p. 19.

[102] This was the case in thirteenth-century Italy and it was a conspicuous feature in later German towns. In the middle of the fourteenth century Venice employed about four *medici* and ten surgeons a year, at a time when monastic houses began to retain medical men. Siraisi, *Medieval and Early Renaissance Medicine*, pp. 18, 38.

[103] Ziegler, *Medicine and Religion*, p. 23.

hand when epidemics arrived. The success of the physician depended on his doing these things well, and we are reminded that we cannot make judgements about the *clinical* success of a physician. The expectations of the laymen who secured physicians on a contract are manifest in the terms of what the physician undertook to do in return for his retainer, and it is part of the argument of this book that the physician himself helped to create those expectations. The rational and learned physician, after all, was the expert who defined what medicine was (and consequently what its boundaries were). It was agreed, for example, that diseases could be the vengeance of God. They could equally well be the result of a persistent lax and self-indulgent lifestyle: in neither case was there an expectation that the physician alone could effect a cure.

The practice of giving long-term advice to people who could pay for it was associated with a new genre of medical literature, the regimens of health. Especially in the second half of the thirteenth century and the first half of the fourteenth, this form of medical advice had several advantages for the learned doctor. He could practise his medicine in the traditional way, centred on the individual and modified according to the individual's constitution and circumstances. The doctor knew how the body was constituted and how it varied according to age and sex (the naturals); he knew how each particular patient reacted to things that caused illness (the preternaturals); and he could give medical advice concerning diet, exercise, sleeping, sexual activity and bathing (the non-naturals). The doctor had every opportunity to explain the reasoning behind this and so construct his Good Story and the patron's expectations. The advice was generally addressed to powerful people, like that of Guido da Vigevano to the French king, Philip VI of Valois. Such 'patients' were advised to eat and take exercise in a manner that became their class: to avoid the food of the poor and to go horseriding. This was real exercise, while the activity of the lower classes was mere labour.

To address such people added to the status of the physician, just as did his writing *consilia*, and physicians such as Bernard of Gordon and Arnau of Vilanova developed the genre fully.[104] A *consilium* was a piece of medical advice on a particular case, written by a well-known doctor for a distant patient and doctor, on the receipt of the latter's request and descriptive 'schedule'. What made *consilia* interesting was that they dealt with real cases and were not merely theoretical discussions. In offering a diagnosis and suggesting a therapy, they could be used to indicate that medicine

[104] See Pedro Gil Sotres, 'The regimens of health', in Grmek, ed., *Western Medical Thought from Antiquity to the Middle Ages*, pp. 291–318.

was not merely book-learning. They also often named the patients involved and were more convincing if the patient were famous: he or she was, in a sense, a witness to the practical skill of the doctor (who took care, of course, to report mostly his successes).[105] *Consilia* were collected together and published, by the doctors involved or others, and formed an effective mode of advertising. It has been pointed out that *consilia* in the later fifteenth century existed in a different medicinal environment from those in the thirteenth and fourteenth centuries: there were new diseases, full development of the medical guilds outside the faculties, humanism and court culture. *Consilia* became formalised on the Avicenna model and rearranged according to anatomy and disease.[106]

FORENSIC MEDICINE

The success of a medical student who had completed his course and become a Rational and Learned Doctor could be called on to provide skilled testimony in areas on the edge of medicine. As a healer, he could offer evidence in cases of miraculous cures, often used as evidence in the process of canonisation.[107] For purposes of segregation he could be called on by civic authorities to detect leprosy in suspect patients.[108] If he were appointed as physician to a city, his duties would include those of the physician on a private contract, but also the obligation to report suspicious deaths and cases of wounding to the city authorities.[109] For example, the Venetians in 1281 passed a law that obliged medical practitioners to report immediately all serious cases of wounding that looked like the result of violence; the medical man was not simply an expert witness, but was an official of the court, essentially an investigating judge.[110] Taddeo Alderotti's fame was such that these obligations were lifted, but others such as Bartolomeo da Varignana,

---

[105] Jacquart, 'Medical scholasticism', p. 231, and Agrimi and Crisciani, *Les consilia médicaux*.

[106] See Nancy Siraisi, 'Avicenna and the teaching of practical medicine', pp. 63–78 in her *Medicine and the Italian Universities, 1250–1600*, Leiden (Brill), 2001.

[107] Ziegler, *Medicine and Religion*, p. 4. The point was to prove that natural cures could not have worked. See also Zeigler's 'Practitioners and saints: medical men in canonization processes in the thirteenth and fifteenth centuries', *Social History of Medicine*, 12 (1999) 191–225. Papal coroners' inquests sought cause of death from medical men; by the end of the century this was introduced also to civil law – mainly in Italy but also in Aragon and the south of France. Most of the rules for canonisation had been formalised by 1200.

[108] See Luke Demaitre, 'The relevance of futility: Jordanus de Turre (fl. 1313–35) on the treatment of leprosy', *Bulletin of the History of Medicine*, 70 (1996) 25–61.

[109] In the case of Bologna's city physician, see Siraisi, *Taddeo Alderotti and his Pupils*, p. 298.

[110] See Catherine Crawford, 'Medicine and the law', in W. F. Bynum and Roy Porter, eds., *Companion Encyclopedia of the History of Medicine*, 2 vols., London (Routledge), 1993; vol.2, pp. 1619–40, at p. 1622.

who had successfully secured an aristocratic clientele, performed autopsies and delivered medico-legal judgements to the civic authorities.[111] To know whether a death was natural – in this context pathological – or violent, the doctor conducting the postmortem had to be aware of the normal appearance of the body, and we may suppose that human dissection in teaching played a part in this.

The Rational and Learned Doctor was also an expert witness in another legal area, that relating to childbirth. In cases of paternity, adultery and so on, the lawyers wanted to know at what age a girl could become pregnant and when a boy might be a father. They needed advice on the length of pregnancy and the resemblances that might be expected between a father and his child. The doctors built up the matter of procreation into a topic, perhaps for professional use in the law courts. The development of the foetus was, after all, a matter at some distance from the ordinary practice of medicine. The doctor could not see the foetus, he could not know whether it was ill and could not treat it. It was entirely a matter of theory (but yet with practical application in treating the mother and in giving answers to the lawyers).

The medical men of the fourteenth and early fifteenth centuries had three main sources for this topic: Avicenna's chapter on the anatomy of the uterus in the *Canon*, Hippocrates' *De Natura Fetus*, and the new translation of Galen's *De Spermate* by Nicolo da Reggio.[112] On the question of the onset of puberty, Tommaso del Garbo, son of Dino and pupil of Gentile, said that in a political context a girl could be given in marriage at twelve, when she could conceive, but a man should not marry until he could generate sperm. In legal terms this meant that it was proper for a girl of fourteen to marry, while the man should be twenty-four. It is not clear what system of law Tommaso is referring to, but it is perhaps ancient, for he adds the not uncommon complaint that in the modern, lax and greedy age, we all mature more quickly.[113] On the question of the length of pregnancy, the doctors had to explain a piece of wisdom inherited from the ancients, that while the normal period was nine months, yet a seven-month and a ten-month child stood a better chance of surviving than one of eight months. The question

---

[111] Siraisi, *Taddeo Alderotti and his Pupils*, pp. 36, 47.

[112] A frequently cited contemporary authority was Giles of Rome, Egidius Romanus.

[113] See f. 40vb of *Expositio Jacobi supra Capitulum de Generatione Embrionis cum Questionibus eiusdem. Dinus supra eodem. Dinus supra librum Ypocratis de Natura Fetus*, Venice (Bonetus Locatellus for the heirs of Octavian Scot), 1518. This is a collection put together largely to supply materials for disputation in the early sixteenth century: Tommaso del Garbo's name does not appear on the title-page and the editor explains that some attribute his commentary to Dino and others to Gentile da Foligno. The commentary of Tommaso, 'son of the once very famous Dino', begins at f. 33r.

was bound up with the duration of the various stages of pregnancy, which had sometimes been put on a 'geometrical' or mathematical basis. Dino, Tommaso and Jacopo da Forlì were inclined to think that such explanations relied too much on numerology, and they agreed that the real reason was that each stage of development was controlled by one of the seven planets. The sequence began with Saturn, a planet with malign effects, and a cycle of eight months returned the unborn child to these effects at a vulnerable stage. Nine months brought the child again to Jupiter, a benign planet.

Jacopo and Tommaso liken the period of pregnancy to a crisis in a fever, so that the eight-month birth is like a crisis on the wrong day.[114] In both cases the rational doctors built in a degree of latitude in their calculations that covered most eventualities (particularly in explaining why, if the first two Hippocratic crises were on the seventh and fourteenth day, the third was on the twentieth rather than the twenty-first). A 'medical month' could be calculated from the daily or yearly motions of the sun, or the phases of the moon: the counting could be 'inclusive' or could ignore the dark period immediately before a new moon. In any case, the doctors agreed that the term of human pregnancy was more variable than that of animals,[115] and it is clear that the doctors' rationality could explain most appearances.

Also of potential legal interest was the degree of resemblance between the child and its natural parents. Here the Rational and Learned Doctors wrestled with huge problems of theory. On the one hand, Aristotle had said that the formation of the embryo was solely due to the action of the male semen on the passive matter of the female, and it became a complex problem to explain the fact that some children resembled their mothers more than their fathers. On the other hand, Galen had said that both male and female produce sperm and that the embryo develops from a mixture of both. Hippocrates was generally read as saying that the semen is derived from all parts of the body, the characteristics of which it conveyed to the embryo. In that case, wondered our doctors, was it possible that acquired characteristics were inherited? Were diseases inherited?[116] Dino argued that the force of the imagination of the mother might make an illegitimate child resemble her husband more than the natural father,[117] an argument that might appeal to a lawyer.

These texts are scholastic in a professional sense, for they represent the authority of the doctor as the master of an autonomous discipline, the face he presented to other professionals. Much of the internal development of

[114] Jacopo, f. 6va, Tommaso, f. 41vb.   [115] For example, Jacopo, f. 7ra.
[116] For example, Tommaso, ff. 19va, 20ra–b.   [117] Dino del Garbo, f. 77rb.

his discipline can at least be related to this presentation. One of the earliest of these treatises on the embryo is that by Dino, who comments on the Hippocratic *De Natura Fetus*. As we have seen, Hippocrates was famously of such profound mind that he did not need the other arts and sciences in his medicine. The work has a correspondingly simple structure. But Dino knew that Hippocrates could be made even more convincing by showing how he could be explained in Aristotelian and scholastic terms. He brings a big apparatus to bear, showing the relationship between a science and its subject and how the sciences are grouped. He introduces fragments of Aristotle's physical works to substantiate what he says; what is unusual, however, is that he treats these brief extracts *as texts to be commented on*, and writes a brief secondary exposition before returning to Hippocrates.

Finally, these texts are scholastic in a number of other ways. Sometimes they begin with 'professional piety', invoking the name of God, but only after citing authority from non-Christian medical writers and their God. They ask questions that can never be more than theoretical and arguable. One such concerned the growth of the embryo. It was clearly being nourished, but this process, *restauratio*, was held to be that by which the independent body restored the losses occasioned by activity, *resolutio*. But the foetus was not active in this way: could there be *restauratio* without prior *resolutio*?[118] One problem that passed from the theoretical realm to the practical in the Renaissance was that of how the foetus, enclosed in the uterus, urinates. Mondino offered an answer, ostensibly on anatomical grounds, but his colleagues disagreed, also citing anatomy. The matter was put to severely practical and experimental tests only as late as Berengario da Carpi, before 1521, who had acquired a nearly full-term foetus. Lastly, an apparently sensory observation that could have been of legal interest was that the *fetus in utero* (and presumably a still-born child) had red lungs, coloured by the blood in the vessels. In contrast, the lungs in a child that had breathed air after birth were white, after expansion; such things may have been important in cases of suspected infanticide.

Although there were many niches in the medical marketplace, they were not protected. The medical hierarchy was not as rigid as the university doctors would have wished. Latin literacy was not limited to doctors and medical texts were available to many educated people who could read and use them. Many were translated into the European vernaculars. In England, university training in medicine was not automatically seen as desirable and in general in the north there were many secular clergy who practised

---

[118] Jacopo, f. 13ra.

medicine.[119] From the thirteenth to the fifteenth centuries less than half of the total number of practitioners had learned their medicine in a university. These practitioners included women and Jews who, while they may have attended lectures in some universities, could not graduate.[120] Their own system of education had been on the 'closed' model, a few students round a single teacher, like early medieval European schools. They did not develop an open, collaborative type of school or the scholasticism which went with it. But they admired scholastic medicine and its success, and while some felt depressed at their own intellectual weakness, others – a disproportionate number of the Jewish population – became well read in school texts and well rewarded in terms of practice.[121] There was always pressure on the European Learned and Rational Doctor to defend and develop his kind of medicine.

[119] See Siraisi, *Medieval and Early Renaissance Medicine*, esp. ch. 1; Getz, *Medicine in the English Middle Ages*. See also Stephen R. Ell, 'The two medicines: some ecclesiastical concepts of disease and the physician in the high middle ages', *Janus*, 68 (1981) 15–25.

[120] Historians disagree about this. On the importance of Jewish physicians see Linda M. Paterson, *The World of the Troubadours. Medieval Occitan Society, c. 1100–c. 1300*, Cambridge (Cambridge University Press), 1993. See also García-Ballester et al., 'Medical licensing', esp. p. 88.

[121] See in general J. Shatzmiller, *Jews, Medicine and Medieval Society*, Berkeley (University of California Press), 1994; Luis García-Ballester, Lola Ferre and Eduard Feliu, 'Jewish appreciation of fourteenth-century scholastic medicine', *Osiris*, 2nd series, 6 (1990) 85–117; John M. Efron, *Medicine and the German Jews*, New Haven (Yale University Press), 2001.

CHAPTER 5

The weakening of the Latin tradition

INTRODUCTION

Medical scholasticism may not have died in the Black Death, but it was not quite the same afterwards. The ambitions of the early scholastics had not been realised, and it was recognised that the goal of achieving a prelapsarian state of knowledge was unobtainable.[1] The guild-like structures of various branches of knowledge discouraged interdisciplinary approaches. The technicalities of Avicenna and the New Galen did not encourge clerics to continue to engage in medicine.[2] Following the institutional separation of medical theory and practice in Paris and Bologna before the Black Death, practical medicine became more important and better rewarded, while theory was reduced simply to an introduction.[3] The ethos that led Gentile da Foligno to lofty heights of entirely impractical speculation was rejected by his pupil Tommaso de Garbo, who found his teacher too prolix. Tommaso wielded the famous razor of the Oxonian Ockham and thought it undesirable to multiply entities; in particular he had a nominalist's dislike of elaborate and numerous distinctions.[4] For example, where Gentile, calling himself an *oculista*, had a hugely elaborate theory of vision, Tommaso denied that a real *species* – a quasi-material simulacrum – moved between object and eye. Believing that shape, number and motion signified only things in the soul and could not be sensed *per se*, Tommaso seems happy to disagree even with Aristotle. Tommaso made a great deal of money from

---

[1] See R. W. Southern, *Scholastic Humanism and the Unification of Europe. Volume I Foundations*, Oxford (Blackwell), 1995, pp. 10, 52, who argues that the failure to recapture prelapsarian knowledge was felt most in natural philosophy.

[2] See Joseph Ziegler, *Medicine and Religion c. 1300. The Case of Arnau de Vilanova*, Oxford (Clarendon Press), 1998, p. 5.

[3] See Danielle Jacquart, 'Medical scholasticism', in M. D. Grmek, ed., *Western Medical Thought from Antiquity to the Middle Ages*, trans. A Sugaar, Cambridge, Mass. and London (Harvard University Press), 1998, pp. 197–240, at p. 233.

[4] See Katharine Park, *Doctors and Medicine in Early Renaissance Florence*, Princeton (Princeton University Press), 1985, p. 207.

his medicine and rose to a position of prominence in Florence: he was successful in the terms we are using, and part of his image seems to have been cultivated by keeping up with new developments in logic (which later became known as the *via moderna*).

Histories of medicine normally pass from the Middle Ages to the new departures of the Renaissance, such as human dissection and medical botany. But when looking at medicine as a prescientific activity – a story that does not have scientific medicine as its conclusion – continuities are as important as novelty. The aim was still to understand the ancients (and the Arabs) as if they were speaking in the same room. Medical theory was still a development of natural philosophy from the point where the philosopher finished. But there were now signs of the weakening of this link, which we shall follow. There was a continuity too in the fact that the new heroic teachers were small in number, and that the bulk of medical teaching, to say nothing of practice, continued in a less heroic way. The major centres were few: Paris, Bologna, Montpellier and Padua at the beginning of our period, while many new *studia*, for example in the Germanic countries, followed the model of Paris but remained comparatively small. There were some new heroic commentators such as Jacques Despars (?1380–1458) in France and the Italian Matthaeus de Gradibus (d. 1480) but their style of commentary did not differ in kind from the high scholastic.[5] Both authors commented, for example, on Book III of the *Canon* of Avicenna, and their expository analyses, *nota, distinctiones* and *dubia* were similar to those of the late thirteenth and early fourteenth centuries, and came to be printed with them.[6] Disputations remained central to medical education. There were continuities too in the production of material for use in the schools. The commentaries of Taddeo, Dino, Gentile and others were printed in a format which indicates that they were intended for school use: 'black-letter' type, generally in double columns, structured by *lemmata* from the text and

---

[5] On Jacques Despars (Jacobus de Partibus) see Danielle Jacquart, 'Le regard d'un médecin sur son temps: Jacques Despars (1380?–1458), *Bibliothèque de l'Ecole des Chartes*, 138, Paris-Geneva (Librairie Droz), 1980, pp. 35–86; and item XIV in her *La Science Médicale Occidentale entre deux Renaissances (XIIe s. – XVe s.)*, Aldershot (Variorum), 1997. For Matthaeus see M. Portal, *Histoire de l'Anatomie et de la Chirurgie*, 6 vols., Paris, 1770–3 (vol. 1).

[6] Matthaeus is sometimes called Ferrarius de Gradi. See *Tertius Can. Avic. cum amplissima Gentilis Fulgi. expositione. Demum commentaria nuper addita videlicet Jacobi de Partibus super fen vi et xiii. Item Jo. Matthei de Gradi super fen cxxii quia Gentilis in eis defecit.* The commentaries are in two volumes, the second being *Secunda pars Gentilis super tertio Avic. cum supplementis Jacobi de Partibus parisiensis ac Joannis Matthei de Gradi mediolanensis ubi Gentilis vel breviter vel tacite pertransivit*, Venice, 1522. The commentary on the *canon* of Avicenna by the Parisian master Jacques Despars (Jacobus de Partibus parisiensis) had already been printed in Venice in about 1499.

the steps of logical analysis.[7] Indeed, the cost of printing enormous works of men such as Nicholas 'the Aggregator' and Gentile must have represented a huge investment[8] that the publisher expected to recoup through steady sales in the marketplace.

Clearly, those who, in the first half of the sixteenth century, bought printed versions of works now two hundred or so years old did not see themselves as breaking with the past. What we have called in this book the Latin tradition of medicine continued in the classroom and embraced new generations of students. While we see very easily novelties in the appearance of printed books and the features of a 'rebirth' of culture such as Hellenism and Humanism, the great bulk of medical men learned their trade in the same way and from the same sources. The concept of a period of the 'middle' ages, to be followed by a new cultural start, was a later construction, built by a minority of scholars with a special agenda. We shall meet them later.

Yet there was a major discontinuity not long before the beginning of the period with which this chapter is concerned. The plague, later called the Black Death, had a huge demographic impact on Europe, with significant effects in many other aspects of life.[9] Some medical scholars, born in the next century, saw the plague as the dividing line between what was old and new.[10] So devastating was the plague that historians have looked for and found signs of collapse of public confidence in the ability of physicians to do anything at all about it.[11] Others have found no such public disillusionment.

---

[7] The Humanists and Hellenists in contrast often affected an italic type or one resembling the uncials of early Latin manuscripts, in a single column broken up into paragraphs. Printed scholastic texts came to be presented in the same way: see, for example, *Plusquam Commentum in Parvam Galeni Artem*, Venice (Heirs of L. A. Giunta), 1557.

[8] See Giovanni Mardersteig, *The Remarkable Story of a Book made in Padua in 1477. Gentile da Foligno's commentary on Avicenna printed by Petrus Maufer*, London (Nattali & Maurice), 1967: printing the commentary without the text nearly ruined the publisher, who recouped his losses by printing large volumes of law texts used in the schools. For aggregators in general see Roger French, *Canonical Medicine: Gentile da Foligno and Scholasticism*, Leiden (Brill), 2001, pp. 191–3.

[9] For a selection of plague tracts, see Karl Sudhoff, 'Pestschriften aus den ersten 150 Jahren nach der Epidemie des "schwarzen Todes" 1348', *Archiv für Geschichte der Medizin*, 4 (1911), 5 (1912), 6 (1913), 7 (1914), 8 (1915), 9 (1916), 11 (1917), 17 (1925).

[10] See Niccolo Leoniceno, *Opuscula*, Basel (A. Cratander & J. Bebellius), 1532, ff. 47v, 51v: Jacobus de Partibus is described as the 'recent' commentator on Avicenna, Gentile da Foligno is the 'old' in having lived before the plague (ff. 29v, 43r).

[11] It is argued by Nancy Siraisi, *Medieval and Early Renaissance Medicine. An Introduction to Knowledge and Practice*, Chicago and London (University of Chicago Press), p. 42, that the Black Death did not produce a lasting loss of confidence in the medical profession. See also her 'Medical reputations in humanist collective biographies', in her *Medicine and the Italian Universities, 1250–1600*, Leiden (Brill), 2001, pp. 157–83, at p. 160. On the other hand, it has been argued that the failure of scholastic medicine was clear and this provoked some kind of crisis in medical doctrine and the profession. See Jole Agrimi and Chiara Crisciani, 'Charity and aid in medieval Christian civilization', in Grmek, *Western Medical Thought*, pp. 170–96, at p. 196.

If that was so, then clearly the expectations of the public were that the doctors, if powerless, were understandably so.[12] When the Paris faculty replied to the king that the cause of the plague had been astrological, the implication was that the principle of determinism in the actions of the planets had to be applied, a necessity so professionally framed with mathematical apparatus that it deflected criticism from the doctors. It also allowed for the recognition that disease was often God's punishment, which the doctors could not avert, as we saw in the last chapter.[13] Before the plague, for example, it was widely acknowledged, even by the doctors themselves, that leprosy was incurable.[14]

Whatever the clinical failure or success of the Learned and Rational Doctor (which, as we have seen, cannot be part of this story), civil administrations ultimately came to see plague as an entity that travelled from town to town, often along trade routes, and they took practical measures to try to prevent this. From our point of view the failure of the learned physicians was to *identify* the plague, that is, to discover its proper ancient name. Only by doing this could they rapidly and completely draw it into the learned apparatus. They could not do so completely, and, insofar as medicine is a response to disease, this opened further opportunities for the civic health officials and the empirics.

As corporations, the faculties of arts and medicine (even in the face of these changes) were conservative. They had worked out a successful relationship with each other and with other aspects of life. The doctors depended intellectually on philosophy for the content of their theory and institutionally on the faculty of arts. Their understanding with society, and particularly with its law-givers, was that their philosophical medicine was the best and deserved a monopoly. Where the faculties of medicine were new or small[15] they had to struggle to implement this agreement and were under constant pressure to demonstrate the superiority of a philosophical

---

[12] Thus the criticism of the Florentine chronicler Matteo Villani (before 1368) was largely that the doctors had no *explanation* of the plague in natural-philosophical or medical terms. As Siraisi observes, 'learned explanation and systematic regimen, rather than cure . . . were and would long remain optimum therapeutic expectations'. See her *Medicine and the Italian Universities*, pp. 160, 183.

[13] The Paris faculty was also responding professionally to its patron and defender, in whose court we may suppose astrology had a bigger place than it had in the schools. See Siraisi, *Medieval and Early Renaissance Medicine*, p. 42.

[14] Lepers, tainted by the stigma of their disease, were in a sense a race apart and, with the Jews, were sometimes accused of plotting against Christendom. See Luke Demaitre, 'The relevance of futility: Jordanus de Turre (fl. 1313–35) on the treatment of leprosy', *Bulletin of the History of Medicine*, 70 (1996) 25–61.

[15] Cf. the discussion of the faculties in chapter 4.

and dialectical (i.e. Aristotelian) medicine in a natural world that was by agreement much as Aristotle had described it. After Aquinas, the church accepted that the world had been put together and worked in an Aristotelian way, and church and medicine found mutual support in each other, especially in the north, where many medical men were also beneficed clergy. The university served its patrons, its students, its town and itself. As corporations of experts who had defined medicine and philosophy in curricular and statutory terms, there was a lot to be said for keeping matters as they were; change would have been destructive in a complex set of relations. It is argued here that the doctors helped to construct the expectations of the people who experienced medical help and who were steered to approve most of the long-term advice, routine bleeding and uroscopy, charitable treatment of the poor and attendance at epidemics of their doctors.

Yet when Europe had recovered from the consequences of the Black Death matters were changing. A number of movements combined to weaken the authority that the Rational and Learned Doctor derived from his reason and learning. The Hellenists of the late fifteenth century tried to bypass the Latin tradition and hear the old authorities in their own tongue, Greek. Astrology provided a mathematical rationality that was at best indifferent to the physical reasoning of Aristotle. In Italy, ducal and other courts were cultural centres that did not directly depend on the universities. Italian 'Civic Humanism', like Hellenism, was not a creature of the incorporated faculties. There were physicians, too, outside the universities, who came to have an important influence on medicine (we shall look at Paracelsus and Cardano,[16] who were for periods rejected by the university physicians). Further into the sixteenth century the Reformation changed the way some people thought about Christianity and weakened the mutual support of the traditional areas of thought. The Latin tradition of medical scholasticism so far covered in this book corresponds broadly with what historians sometimes call the 'universal age' of medieval Europe. The term expresses the difference between 'old' and 'new' Europe. The old corresponds roughly with the old Roman Empire, while the new, to the north and east, included areas not Christianised until the first millennium; the universal age covers the period of their common history, from about 1200 to about 1380, from Innocent III to the Great Schism.[17] The latter meant loss

---

[16] See chapter 6.
[17] See Peter Moraw, 'Careers of graduates', in Walter Rüegg, general ed., *A History of the University in Europe. Volume I Universities in the Middle Ages*, ed. Hilde de Ridder-Symoens, Cambridge (Cambridge University Press), 1992, pp. 244–79, at p. 252.

of authority, and afterwards regional pressures in Europe began to threaten the unity of Christendom.

ASTROLOGY

Mathematical and predictive astrology was found by Europeans in Arabic sources at about the same time as Aristotle's physical works in the late twelfth century. There had been an older astrology concerned with matters like the astral circumstances of a birth, but the new was a highly mathematical treatment of the geometry of the planets and their effects on the sublunar world. There was a necessity in this causal relationship which made it possible to predict what would happen as the malign and benign influences of different planets waxed and waned. Much of this related to medicine. Control of parts of the body was distributed around the zodiac, allowing the construction of a celestial 'anatomy'.[18] Astrology dictated when and where to let blood or take drugs. The course and outcome – the prognosis – of acute diseases were predicted from the motion of the moon, while those of chronic diseases were predicted from the sun. Like the doctor, the astrologer had an impressive stock of theory, based (like the doctor's) on macro–microcosm relationships, which impressed the client; the astrological 'good story'.

Astrology had been linked closely in the Arabic sources[19] to medicine and even to Aristotelian natural philosophy, but when it was used in twelfth-century Europe the Aristotelianism of it meant little. Roger of Hereford, the late twelfth-century source of much English astrology, knew nothing of Aristotle's natural philosophy. The natural link with medicine remained, however, and medical men before and outside the new *studia* used it extensively. An example is William of England, who practised medicine in early thirteenth-century Marseilles and who constructed a form of prognostication combining uroscopy and astrology. The physician's display of examining the patient's urine, brought to him in a jordan carried in a wicker basket, was a show that demonstrated his skill at diagnosis and prognosis while still distant from the unseen patient. William's display was to show his skill at something even more difficult: to make astrological judgements about the urine *without seeing it*.[20]

---

[18] See Roger French, 'Foretelling the future. Arabic astrology and English medicine in the late twelfth century', *Isis*, 87 (1996) 453–480.

[19] Most important of these for Western readers is the *Introductorium in Astronomiam Albumasaris Abalachi octo continens libros partiales*, Venice (no publisher given), 1506.

[20] The text is the *De Urina non Visa*. It dates from 1219 and has not been published; it came to be taught by statute in Bologna. There are many mss., for example Cambridge, Trinity College, 0.8.31.

But when the medical men organised themselves in the new *studia* it was on the basis of their theory being derived from Aristotle's natural philosophy. This was rationality quite different from the astrological. Aristotle held that numbers (the basis of the astrologer's impressive calculations) could not reveal the essences of things. The personalities of the planets, which determined their benign or malign influences on things below the moon, were antithetical to Aristotle's world. Indeed, the capricious actions of Jupiter or Mars were precisely what the old Greek philosophers had wanted to exclude from the world, and we have seen that when Aristotle wanted to introduce purpose into the natural world, it was an aspect of nature in his rather special sense. Moreover, for Aristotle the heavenly bodies reflected perfection of a kind and were carried in their circular orbits by spheres.

Scholastic medicine was not, therefore, very astrological. Certainly, William of England's tract was taken into the curriculum in some of the Italian *studia*, but up to and including the consolidation of the faculties in the early fourteenth century, medical statutes remained committed to the *Articella*, the New Galen, and the big Arabic treatises. We have less information about what went on in the doctors' practice, of course, and certainly there was interest in astrology in princely courts, where prediction of earthly events was as important as medical prognosis. Medical advice could also be astrological, and from Pietro d'Abano to the Black Death and the French Disease at the end of the fifteenth century astrology could be used to explain medical events and to show that doctors could do little against celestial necessity. Pietro was well aware that the doctor's reputation could be enhanced by using astrological prognostication when the patient's symptoms were ambiguous.[21] Doctors at the time disputed about whether astrology was part of medicine or an adjunct to it,[22] in terms reminiscent of the philosopher/physician disputes. Indeed, it seems that these later disputes also represent a disciplinary boundary. If he crossed the boundary, the astrologising doctor had to put on another 'hat', accept other authorities and adopt a form of rationalising quite distinct from the Aristotelian. To the considerable extent to which medicine was astrological by the end of

---

[21] Differentia 168: Pietro d'Abano, *Conciliator Controversiarum, quae inter Philosophos et Medicos versantur*, Venice (Heirs of L. A. Giunta), 1565.

[22] This was the subject of a dispute in 1496 on the French Disease between Simon Pistoris, a scholastic doctor of Leipzig, and Martin Pollich of Mellerstadt, a Humanist. Pistoris argued that astrology was not a proper part of medicine, but a useful art of the doctor; Pollich changed his mind when his Italian hero, Pico, argued against astrology. See Jon Arrizabalaga, John Henderson and Roger French, *The Great Pox. The French Disease in Renaissance Europe*, New Haven and London (Yale University Press), 1997, p. 92.

the fifteenth century, it was partly divorced from its reliance on Aristotelian natural philosophy. But the doctor used astrology in the same way, for if his patients believed in astrological determinism, it was good for the doctor to be seen as skilled in its technicalities. Astrology was fashionable throughout society in the fifteenth century and the doctor responded by adopting it as part of his clinical patter; even the medical opponents of astrology (such as Jacques Despars in Paris) recognised that the physician might have to pretend to rely on it.[23] The decline in fashion of astrology began perhaps with the attack on it by Giovanni Pico della Mirandola, who contrived to make it appear scholastic in an old-fashioned way and a practice of a minority – the Jews. He argued that the astrologers had wormed their way into positions close to powerful figures by using plausible but fallacious stories of the effectiveness of their trade; in fact, exactly the same as the doctors were doing.[24] Substitute 'medicine' for 'astrology' and we have an allegory for the story of this book.

HELLENISM AND THE ANCIENTS

Another movement growing up outside the schools was an interest in things Greek. Civic teachers of Greek had been sponsored for the purposes of trade between the Italian city-states and Greek-speaking areas to the east.[25] By the fifteenth century 'Greece' was a dwindling area around Constantinople, the old capital of the Eastern Roman Empire that had long since become entirely Greek in language and character. Under pressure from the Turks, Byzantine envoys negotiated at the Council of Florence in 1439 for the military help of the Italian cities. It was not forthcoming, and the final disappearance of the Eastern Empire in 1453 was associated with a flood of Greek emigrés to Italy. The aims of these men included the setting up of a new Greek state and they made targets of the politically powerful, arguing in princely courts rather than universities.[26]

---

[23] Jacquart, 'Medical scholasticism', p. 234. Astrology was in the statutes of Bologna by 1405. See Nancy Siraisi, 'The faculty of medicine', *Universities in the Middle Ages*, ed. de Ridder-Symoens, pp. 360–87, at p. 379.

[24] Giovanni Pico della Mirandola, *Disputationes adversus Astrologiam Divinatricem*, ed. Eugenio Garin, 2 vols., Florence (Vallechi), 1946–52; vol. 1, pp. 60–3.

[25] See Deno John Geanakoplos, *Greek Scholars in Venice: Studies in the Dissemination of Greek Learning from Byzantium to Western Europe*, Cambridge, Mass. (Harvard University Press), 1962, and *Interaction of the "Sibling" Byzantine and Western Cultures in the Middle Ages and Italian Renaissance, 1300–1600*, New Haven (Yale University Press), 1976.

[26] The disputes about the French Disease in courts in Ferrara and Rome were, for example, in contrast to the 'scholastic' university disputations in Leipzig. See Arrizabalaga et al., *The Great Pox*.

The Greeks were convinced of their own cultural superiority. They had resented the Westerners as barbarians since a crusade had been diverted to Byzantium in the early thirteenth century, when a short-lived Latin kingdom had been set up there.[27] A number of Westerners agreed with the cultural claims of the Greeks and were accordingly called 'Hellenists'. As for the medical men, many recognised that the authorities of their subject had been Greek and that perhaps the medicine of the Arabs was derivative. It followed for the Hellenists that if one wanted to hear the ancients as though they were speaking in the same room, one had to 'listen' in Greek. Greek medicine was purer because it was older; it was a modern duty to learn the language of the ancient doctors. This meant that Latin became the language merely of commentators. It was, moreover, ugly, and even Western Hellenists talked of the stutterings of barbarians in contrast to the eloquence of Greek. Commentaries, disputed questions and all the apparatus that the men of the schools had used to understand the ancients could be bypassed by listening to the uninterrupted voices of the ancients in their own language.

Part of the apparent ugliness of the technical language of medicine was that it was full of neologisms, partly derived from the Arabic. The school physicians stoutly defended their Arabic sources as their professional authorities,[28] while the Hellenists indignantly accused the Arabs of stealing and distorting Greek medicine; and, as we have seen before, brief accounts of the history of medicine generally stop with Galen. The medicine of the schools was also highly dialectical, which did not add to its beauty in the ears and eyes of the Hellenists. The older Western Humanists, whose business was with literature and poetry, had also been horrified and in-timidated by the schoolmen's use of complex modes of rational argument, many of them English in origin. Hellenists, moreover, were not so tightly bound to Aristotle as the scholastics and talked a great deal more about Plato.[29]

Hellenism was not, then, the same thing as Humanism. 'Hellenist' was a contemporary term, used for example by the anatomists Berengario da

[27] The culturally important event was the attempt in 1205 by Innocent III and the new emperor, Balduinus, to encourage a migration of masters from Paris to Constantinople to 'reform' the *studium*, the seat of Greek learning. See Heinrich Denifle and Emile Chatelain, eds., *Chartularium Universitatis Parisiensis*, 4 vols., Paris, 1889–97, vol. I, p. 62.

[28] But it is notable that no new translations from the Arabic were made after the thirteenth century. Jacquart, 'Medical scholasticism', p. 215.

[29] For an introduction to these developments see the articles in Quentin Skinner and Eckhard Kessler, eds., *The Cambridge History of Renaissance Philosophy*, Cambridge (Cambridge University Press), 1988.

Carpi and Gabriele de Zerbi.[30] In this example, the context was characteristic: Greek, Arabic and Latin sources had given a number of terms for the structures of the abdominal wall, some of which in their native tongues had been synonyms, which encouraged the anatomists to look for more structures than there were. The Hellenists used the Greek term, ignored the others and had a correspondingly simpler anatomy. Scholastic medical men had used some of the devices of humanism, particularly a historical evaluation of texts, to try to reduce problems of this kind, and by the sixteenth century medicine was 'humanised' as much as a technical subject could be. Some Hellenists had a humanist education before going to a university for one of the specialised sciences.[31] One of the 'skilled Hellenists' known to Berengario was Niccolo Leoniceno (1428–1524), who was able to attack Avicenna and Pliny with such a training; Berengario himself had had a humanist training with Aldo Manuzio before learning medicine. It should be noted that the Hellenists, although having drawn the attention of historians as heralds of change, were few in number and that the bulk of even elite medical men continued as they had done for very many years.[32]

Platonism and early neo-Platonism were ways of looking at the world that differed greatly from the Aristotelianism of the schools. Much celebrated in accounts of the Renaissance, these movements touch our story insofar as they were reflected in medicine and its traditional reliance on natural philosophy. Like the newly rediscovered atomism of the ancients, it offered an alternative view of the world that threatened to cause problems for the medical man. In principle, the doctors' views were already partly informed by Galen's Platonism, and they could find Platonic support for their disputations with the philosophers when they argued that the brain and not the heart was the origin of the nerves, and that the body had been put together in a rational way by a beneficent deity.[33] Likewise the medical men

---

[30] The term they used was *periti eleni*. See Jacopo Berengario da Carpi, *Carpi Commentaria cum amplissimis additionibus super Anatomia Mundini una cum textu eiusdem in pristinum et verum nitorem redacto*, Bologna (Hieronymus de Benedictis), 1521, f. 49r; Gabriele de Zerbi, *Liber Anathomie Corporis Humani et singulorum Membrorum illius*, Venice (Octavianus Scotus), 1502, f. 7v. For a discussion of the anatomy concerned, see Roger French. 'Berengario da Carpi and the use of commentary in anatomical teaching', in Andrew Wear, Roger French and Iain Lonie, *The Medical Renaissance of the Sixteenth Century*, Cambridge (Cambridge University Press), 1985, pp. 42–74.

[31] See Paul Oskar Kristeller, 'Humanism', in *The Cambridge History of Renaissance Philosophy*, pp. 113–37.

[32] See also Vivian Nutton, 'Hellenism postponed: some aspects of Renaissance medicine', *Sudhoffs Archiv*, 81 (1997) 158–70, who remarks on the small numbers of Hellenists and the shortage of Greek texts, partly in a German context.

[33] Galen's Platonism became more apparent in his *De Placitis Hippocratis et Platonis*, which was known in a few manuscripts from the fourteenth (or even thirteenth) century. See Vivian Nutton, '*De Placitis Hippocratis et Platonis* in the Renaissance', in *Le Opere Psicologiche di Galeno*, Atti del Terzo

could find in Galen a particular mode of forming inductions from sensory observation. This became known as the 'rule of Socrates' and was a way of bringing a number of observations together to make a single statement, which was then divided at the natural articulations that had become apparent. The Hellenist Niccolo Leoniceno complained that Pliny had not used this method and was accordingly in error;[34] and in his own explanation of the famously obscure three 'doctrines' set out by Galen at the beginning of the *Tegni*, Leoniceno said that the doctrines to be used in investigating (rather than teaching) included the three 'Platonic' methods of resolution, division and definition (these had nothing to do, of course, with scholastic methods with the same titles).[35]

But most Platonism was at an entirely different level. Its advocates were generally not men of the schools – not incorporated – and lacked the institutional and intellectual barriers between the disciplines. To them, school philosophy, perhaps particularly the Averroistic Aristotelianism of Padua, was too rigid and too pagan. School medical thinking also tended towards Averroism, no doubt because of the availability of the *Colliget*. The Platonists did not accept the strict separation of philosophy and theology, as maintained by the school Aristotelians, and held that a Platonic account of the world could and should be pious in a Christian way. Plato, after all, had described a world created in a rational and beneficent way by a deity, and a soul that returned to the heavens at the death of the body, on all of which Aristotle was conspicuously silent. The search for the most ancient authors – those who authored the purest form of knowledge – focused upon the figure of Hermes Trismegistus, thought by some to be the source of Plato's wisdom.[36] To the Platonist the natural world was so obviously part of God that there was a living sympathy between its parts.[37] Marsilio Ficino (1433–99) held that earthly talismans sympathised

Colloquio Galenico Internazionale, Pavia, 10–12 settembre 1986, ed. Paola Manuli and Mario Vegetti, Naples (Bibliopolis), c. 1988, pp. 281–309.

[34] Niccolo Leoniceno, *Opuscula*, Basel (A. Cratander & J. Bebellius), 1532, ff. 2r, 3r–v, 5r, 16v. Galen had identified the first stage in the 'rule of Socrates' as a bringing together of similarities, which enabled him to find it too in the Hippocratic surgical works. It is not clear how widely this was known to medical men in the Renaissance.

[35] See Nicholas Jardine, 'Epistomology of the sciences', *The Cambridge History of Renaissance Philosophy*, pp. 685–711, at p. 705. Leoniceno's orientation was Paduan Aristotelianism: see Roger French and Jon Arrizabalaga, 'Coping with the French Disease: university practitioners' strategies and tactics in the transition from the fifteenth to the sixteenth century', in Roger French, Jon Arrizabalaga, Andrew Cunningham and Luis García-Ballester, *Medicine from the Black Death to the French Disease*, Aldershot (Ashgate), 1998, pp. 248–87, at p. 265.

[36] Ficino was commissioned by Cosimo de' Medici to translate the *corpus hermeticum*, which he completed in 1463.

[37] On Ficino see Charles H. Lohr, 'Metaphysics', *The Cambridge History of Renaissance Philosophy*, pp. 537–638, at p. 571; and Brian P. Copenhaver, 'Astrology and magic', ibid., pp. 264–300, at p. 283.

with their celestial counterparts. Important for the story of this book is that Ficino (not a scholastic, but a courtier and a leading member of the Florentine Academy) developed a notion of occult qualities. Certainly there were primary, elementary qualities of the traditional kind, and secondary qualities that followed from them, like hardness or sweetness, but he also gave attention to tertiary qualities, *qualitates occultae*. The doctrine was ultimately medical, deriving from the medieval development of the 'whole substance' action of drugs:[38] Ficino quotes Taddeo Alderotti, Arnau of Vilanova and Jacopo da Forlì, and the doctrine became important in the slow erosion of Aristotelian natural philosophy.[39]

While neo-Platonism encouraged thought on natural magic and astrology, it was not entirely sympathetic to the mathematical predictive astrology practised by doctors. When Giovanni Pico della Mirandola (1463–94) attacked judicial astrology it was because its determinism offended his conception of the nobility and freedom of man.[40] Pico, although not a man of the schools, had his medical followers and there were disputes in Italy and Germany at least on whether astrology was part of medicine.[41] In dismissing astrology Pico made it look old fashioned, impious and superstitious. Ideally, then, it was practised by other people, and as we have seen, he points to the Jews. Not only did they fail to predict the French Disease, he said, they failed to foresee their own persecution and expulsion.

THE *RES LATINA*

Distinct from the Hellenists of the fifteenth century were the Western Humanists. These were the men who studied and taught the more 'human' topics such as ancient literature and poetry; the *humanista* was, like the *legista* or *anathomista*, a specialist and he did not venture into technical subjects like medicine. Originating perhaps in northern France, 'humanism' spread to Italy: the humanist existed along with his colleagues in other disciplines early in the history of the universities and it is inaccurate to think of humanism as a Renaissance phenomenon that changed the nature

---

[38] See Linda Deer Richardson, 'The generation of disease: occult causes and disease of the total substance', in Wear et al., *Medical Renaissance*, pp. 175–94.

[39] We shall examine the medical Platonism of later years in the next chapter. There were major developments, too, arising from a new style of thinking that appeared in the late fifteenth and early sixteenth centuries and which at once offered an alternative to traditional natural philosophy and hence to the theory of medicine, Lucretian atomism and Pyrrhonian scepticism.

[40] *Disputationes adversus Astrologiam Divinatricem*, Bologna (Benedictus Hectoris), 1496.

[41] See Arrizabalaga et al., *The Great Pox*, pp. 90ff and chs. 3 and 4. It is significant that the disputes were about an epidemic that placed strains on medicine.

of university teaching and was opposed to scholasticism. Indeed, the early Humanists have been called scholastic.[42] Certainly in Italy there was some conflation of humanism with the later Hellenism, and Italian civic humanism flourished outside the universities. However, in Germany for example, humanism remained mostly a school business, despite following an Italian lead.[43]

Although the Humanists did not tackle the technical subjects such as medicine and philosophy, a number of their techniques were applicable to them. As mentioned above, they developed a historical sensitivity to their texts, thinking of them in relation to the circumstances that produced them. The same could be applied to medical texts by the men who read and taught them, and by the early sixteenth century medicine had probably absorbed as much humanism as it could take. Medical men such as Berengario da Carpi in Bologna and experts in the equally technical field of law, such as Collenuccio, who defended Pliny from Leoniceno's attack, were content to call themselves 'scholastic' in the sense of being masters of a complex discipline.[44] Only later did the Hellenists and Humanists outside the universities use 'scholastic' in a pejorative sense to mean (in the case of medicine) over-subtle and over-extensive use of logic and the practice of analysing texts by breaking them down into 'points'. Leoniceno mocked Gentile da Foligno, whom he called the 'old expositor' of Avicenna[45] (that is, before the plague), and the practice of citing *lemmata* of the text to identify where the commentary should go, so that his discussion was littered with 'there...' and 'there...', *ibi...ibi*. Leoniceno, of course, wanted the clear and unbroken voice of the Greek author to be heard without hindrance.

'Scholastic' medical men such as Berengario and Gabriele de Zerbi in Padua knew of the Hellenists and their desire to abolish all but Greek technical terms. They were the *periti eleni*, and their love of Greek was *graecitas*.[46] But the men of the schools resented the high cultural tone adopted by the

---

[42] See Southern, *Scholastic Humanism*, vol. 1, esp. ch. 1.

[43] See Lewis William Spitz, *The Religious Renaissance of the German Humanists*, Cambridge, Mass. (Harvard University Press), 1963; M. Watanabe, 'Gregor Heimburg and early humanism in Germany', in E. P. Mahoney, ed., *Philosophy and Humanism: Renaissance Essays in Honor of Paul Oskar Kristeller*, Leiden (Brill), 1976; P. Joachimsen, 'Humanism and the growth of the human mind', in Gerald Strauss, ed., *Pre-Reformation Germany*, New York (Macmillan), 1972.

[44] See Pandolfo Collenuccio, *Pliniana Defensio Pandulfi Collennuciii Pisaurensis Iuriconsulti adversus Nicolai Leoniceni Accusationem*, Ferrara (Andreas Belfortis), 1493.

[45] Leoniceno's *Opuscula* contain fragments, of which no. 22 contains a reference to Gentile the expositor of Avicenna. At f. 29v Gentile is the 'old expositor' of Avicenna ('older' at f. 43r) where the chronological division is the plague. In contrast, Jacobus de Partibus, writing in the century after the plague, was for Leoniceno one of the recent commentators (*Opuscula*, f. 47v).

[46] Leoniceno defends himself against the charge of affectation of *Graecitas* in his *Opuscula*.

Hellenists when addressing each other in the elaborate prefaces of their books. They resented their own language of exposition and commentary being described as 'stuttering' and the implication that they were rustics or barbarians. Perhaps in reaction to *graecitas* they drew attention to their own Latin culture, the 'Latin business', *Res Latina*. One of their heroes was Pliny, who had been scornful of Greek vanity, *vanitas Graecae*,[47] especially in relation to medical theory. Drawing on another Latin hero, Celsus, as a model of clear and elegant Latinity, they celebrated Western scholarship in medicine, what we are calling in this book the 'Latin tradition'.[48] It was into this tradition that the teacher of the schools worked to draw his pupils. His aim was to instil in them a faith in what they were being taught, in him and in the teachers of teachers, back to the founding fathers of medicine. This tradition *included* formal exposition, commentary and disputed questions. The considerable bulk of medieval material being printed in the early sixteenth century shows that the schools retained their appetite for the Latin way of doing things: it was the conservatism of the incorporated faculty. Authority for the Hellenists was Greek only and their histories of medicine jump from Galen to themselves. In contrast the older scholastics such as Gentile began to turn their contemporaries and immediate predecessors into authorities,[49] who became authorities, too, to the readers of the sixteenth-century editions. New authors of the late fifteenth and early sixteenth centuries also found that they could give authority to *themselves* by publishing their own works, but what they produced remained small in comparison to the printing of scholastic material.[50]

It was this faith in the Latin tradition that the scholastics saw the Hellenists as trying to destroy. Leoniceno's attack on Pliny was, after all, on a major Latin author, a classical authority from whom much medicine had been derived over the centuries.[51] Collenuccio, the lawyer who came to Pliny's defence, did not argue that Pliny had never made mistakes, but that minor crimes could be excused if the figure involved were an

---

[47] See O. Pedersen, 'Some astronomical topics in Pliny', in Roger French and Frank Greenaway, eds., *Science in the early Roman Empire: Pliny the Elder, his Sources and Influence*, London (Croom Helm), 1986, pp. 162–96, at p. 188.

[48] Celsus' writings were rediscovered in 1426 in Siena. See Nutton, 'Hellenism postponed', p. 164.

[49] See Fernando Salmon, 'Technologies of authority in the medical classroom in the thirteenth and fourteenth centuries', in Cornelius O'Boyle, Roger French and Fernando Salmon, eds., *El Aprendizaje de la Medicina en el Mundo Medieval: las Fronteras de la Enseñanza Universitaria*, Granada, 2000 [*Dynamis*, 20 (2000)] pp. 135–57.

[50] See French and Arrizabalaga, 'Coping with the French Disease', p. 269. See also Arrizabalaga, 'The death of a medieval text: the *Articella* and the early press' in French et al., *Medicine from the Black Death to the French Disease*, pp. 184–211, at p. 187.

[51] For example, a collection called the *Medicina Plinii* was published in Rome in 1509.

ornament to his society – Latin society: Leoniceno was rather unusual in combining a technical subject, medicine, with Hellenism, and he urged other Hellenists to do likewise. Collenuccio saw this as a Hellenist programme to invade scholastic topics, and argued in turn that scholastics like himself should extend their own boundaries and embrace Greek. But he knew that the separation of academic disciplines was still secure and that as a lawyer he risked censure in 'using his scythe in a foreign field', that is, one of 'eloquence' and 'letters', which were Hellenist code-words for 'Greek'.

All this left its mark on European culture and the way we look at its past. The Hellenists succeeded in the courts of the great and among the upper classes of society rather than in the schools. But ultimately, as we shall see, the schools' traditional learning was replaced and genteel education remained classical for a long time. Few of us have been untouched by the Hellenists' victories outside the schools: just when 'scholasticism' acquired a pejorative meaning, so the period of the Middle Ages became identifiable as a period between them (the classical past, mostly Greek) and us (who are trying to promote its rebirth in a 'Renaissance'). The 'middle' ages was thus defined as a period between two cultural stools, as it were. The word 'barbaric', as a classical sneer for this intermediate period, came into use even in medicine in the early sixteenth century.[52] The English term 'Middle Ages' seems to be an invention of the Enlightenment,[53] a local culmination of the movement to restore classical values begun by the Hellenists.

Faith in the medical tradition was broken in a much more radical way by Vesalius. He constitutes a topic on which much has been written, but it is not the purpose of this book to retell the stories of medical heroes. Rather, let us return to the topic with which we started. Vesalius was conspicuously successful, becoming physician to the Holy Roman Emperor.[54] His career in a sense shadows that of Galen, the man whose theory of anatomy he

---

[52] It was used of Gentile himself. See Nancy G. Siraisi, *Avicenna in Renaissance Italy. The Canon and Medical Teaching in Italian Universities after 1500*, Princeton (Princeton University Press), 1987, p. 73. But the Hellenist Leoniceno recognised Gentile's worth on the topic of compound medicines: *Opuscula*, Basel (A. Cratander & J. Bebellius), 1532, f. 29v. Gentile, he says, is the *medicus* with the greatest authority of our age.

[53] The term 'Middle Ages' seems not to occur in English before the eighteenth century (*OED*) and it seems to be the product of an Augustan assumption of identity with the classical past, leaving a period in between to be named merely by its position. 'Medieval' is first noted in the early nineteenth century in English, and worthwhile study of the period seems to have followed an encyclical of Pope Leo XIII in 1879. See Southern, *Scholastic Humanism and the Unification of Europe*, vol. I, p. 2.

[54] The *Fabrica* has been called a 'status-statement and a patronage artefact'. See Mario Biagioli, 'Scientific revolution, social bricolage, and etiquette', in Roy Porter and Milukáš Teich, *The Scientific Revolution in National Context*, Cambridge (Cambridge University Press), 1992, pp. 11–54, at p. 17.

so strongly attacked, but which directed the shape of his own work; it was partly on the merits of Galen's anatomy that he had become physician to Emperor Marcus Aurelius and his son Commodus. Perhaps the only equivalent to being an imperial retainer in Vesalius' day was being a papal one, and to earn such a position (as Arnau of Vilanova did) was the highest ambition for the Learned and Rational Doctor: he was a success.

Yet, of course, we have little information on how effective Vesalius was as a clinician. His success was that he changed the nature of anatomy and made himself highly conspicuous. In the late 1530s he guessed that Galen had never dissected a human body. This meant that the whole of Galen's anatomy was potentially wrong and the business of the anatomist was now to start at the beginning and confirm or deny Galen's descriptions. The impact of Vesalius' *De Humani Corporis Fabrica* was immeasurably increased by the impressive woodcuts, drawn and engraved by craftsmen of the highest order (who seem to have given him some trouble).[55] In the text, Vesalius attacked Galen with vigour and some venom. In order to correct Galen on as many points as possible, Vesalius was obliged to follow Galen's anatomy closely. This, together with the striking illustrations, meant that Vesalius' anatomy was largely morphological; Vesalius either agreed or was not concerned with Galen's account of function, which had been perhaps the prime object of anatomy in the philosophical tradition from Aristotle onwards.

The book divided the medical community. Those who opposed Vesalius felt that he had exhibited bad faith in attacking Galen in so bitter a way. It was breaking the faith in almost a religious sense: Vesalius was the apostate who refused to respect the teacher of all teachers. As in the case of Leoniceno's attack on Pliny, the point for many commentators was not that Galen could make mistakes (for he was human) but that he should be attacked in so wanton a way. Anatomists had already shown themselves capable of criticising Galen on the detail of his anatomy, while very properly continuing to regard him as the founder of the discipline. What rankled most among the defenders of Galen was Vesalius' claim that Galen had *cheated*, pretending to have dissected human bodies but in fact making do with animals. On the other hand, there were those who thought that Vesalius had made a bold new start and a confident assertion that medicine could progress without constant recourse to the ancients.

[55] For the authority of anatomical illustrations see Martin Kemp, ' "The mark of truth": looking and learning in some anatomical illustrations from the Renaissance and eighteenth century', in W. F. Bynum and Roy Porter, *Medicine and the Five Senses*, Cambridge (Cambridge University Press), 1993, pp. 85–121.

Vesalius himself claimed that by dissecting human bodies he was restoring the anatomy of Herophilus and Erasistratus (about which he could have known little). This looks like the Humanists' and Hellenists' search for the true old form of disciplines, the *prisca scientia* of the ancients, but it is not easy to include Vesalius in one or other of these categories. Certainly he eschewed medieval commentary and disputed questions, which had been standard components of anatomy texts even for the generation before him.[56] In attempting to dethrone Galen he did not turn away from Greek medicine and anatomy, but it was the Hellenists among his enemies who accused him of defiling the pure founts of Greek knowledge. He did not have sympathy with Arabic medicine but used Hebrew, in an age when religious sensitivities and a search for ever older sources of knowledge gave importance to the language. He was a man of the schools as a student and teacher, but he avoided the double-column, black-letter textual format, the hallmark of medical and legal texts designed for the school market. He used 'scholastic' in a pejorative way. His topic was a technical one, and manual, yet he gave his Latin the elevated tone and structure that most Hellenists sustained only in their self-regarding prefaces and dedications.[57]

In fact the *Fabrica* seems well designed for Vesalius' purposes, one of which was undoubtedly self-promotion. He addresses the emperor as a client and sounds like somebody looking for a patron and a retained position for himself. His message is about medicine, not just anatomy. His argument is that medicine should be (and in ancient times had been) a single discipline and that its practitioner should grow and collect herbs, make up medicines and perform surgery, rather than leaving these tasks to specialists. He claims to have done this, involving himself personally and manually in dissection in order to learn the anatomy that was an integral part of a complete medicine. Vesalius generates the image of the good anatomist handling the scalpel, demonstrating the parts to an audience and knowing (critically) the standard texts. This would have been far removed from the usual situation in which, according to Vesalius, an illiterate artisan would cut the body, an *ostensor* would point to the organs and a learned teacher would sit in a chair reading a text of Galen. As Vesalius says, this style of dissection had

[56] For example, Berengario da Carpi, *Commentaria*.
[57] A modern translation is therefore useful. See Andreas Vesalius, *On the Fabric of the Human Body. A Translation of De Humani Corporis Fabrica Libri Septem*, Books 1 and 2, trans. William Frank Richardson and John Burd Carman, San Francisco (Norman Publishing), 1998–. The standard biography of Vesalius is C. D. O'Malley, *Andreas Vesalius of Brussels 1514–1546*, Berkeley (University of California Press), 1965.

prevented any discrepancy between the appearance of the body and the words of the text becoming apparent. But then, such a thing was not the purpose of medieval dissections; and it is Vesalius' picture that has coloured many historical accounts.[58]

Dedications to potential patrons quickly became a feature of printed books. Medieval manuscripts customarily begin with the text itself, so that its first words serve to identify it, although there is occasionally some prefatory material, such as Alfred of Shareshill's address to Roger of Hereford in his commentary on the pseudo-Aristotelian *De Plantis* (late twelfth century).[59] Early printed books often have a 'title-page' addressing the potential reader directly and listing what the volume contains: *Lector, habes in hoc volumine*...But soon, between the reader and the text, appears the figure of the editor, who justifies the selections of a text and its preparation from the manuscripts and who in effect promotes the text.[60] As we saw, when authors began to publish works in their own lifetime then printed books could be effectively used for self-promotion.[61] Dedication to a potential patron could be reinforced by congratulatory verses about the author by a third party.[62]

MEDICAL ETHICS

We have seen that the Hippocratic ethical works were, in part, defences of the medicine of one group of doctors in rivalry with another. In the medieval

---

[58] For a novel view of the purposes of human dissection, see Andrew Cunningham, *The Anatomical Renaissance. The Resurrection of the Anatomical Projects of the Ancients*, Aldershot (Ashgate), 1997. For 'in-school' critics of ancient medicine it is worth noting Giovanni Argenterio (1513–72), who taught in Pisa from 1543 to 1555 – the dates of the two editions of Vesalius' *Fabrica* – attacked Galen, developed the 'whole substance' doctrine of disease and was called a Pyrrhonian sceptic for his view that medicine was not a true *scientia*. See Nancy Siraisi, 'Giovanni Argenterio: medical innovation, princely patronage, and academic controversy', in her *Medicine and the Italian Universities*, pp. 341, 346.

[59] See Nicolaus Damascenus, *De Plantis. Five Translations*, ed. H. J. Drossaart Lulofs and E. L. J. Poortman, Amsterdam (North-Holland), 1989.

[60] An example is the discussion of the merits of Arnau de Villanova and Gentile da Foligno in the biographical essay on Arnau written by Symphorien Champier and the editor of Arnau's *Opera omnia*. See Arnau de Villanova, *Opera Omnia*, Basel (Conrad Waldkirch), 1585. For a discussion of the role of the editor, see Arrizabalaga, 'The death of a medieval text', p. 190.

[61] See Arrizabalaga, 'The death of a medieval text', p. 187.

[62] A number of well-known figures in the history of medicine were successful (in the sense used in this book) in seeking and securing patronage. Leoniceno taught medicine and was physician to the dukes of Ferrara for over half a century. His pupil Giovanni Manardi was physician to the king of Hungary. Giovanni Matthioli was a doctor at the Hapsburg court and was able to employ a team of artists for an edition of Dioscorides. Its translation into Czech and German was sponsored by Emperor Ferdinand partly for reasons of prestige. Court physicians such as Johannes Crato von Crafftheim (at the imperial court in Vienna) acted as centres of correspondence and wielded considerable power. See Nutton, *Medicine at the Courts of Europe*, introduction, pp. 7, 9.

classroom, the internal ethic of the pupil putting his trust in the teacher and the medical tradition was similar. The pupil received his knowledge from the teacher, was promoted by him in exercises that made him too a potential teacher, and perhaps went on to teach. The Hippocratic and the scholastic defended the reputation of their kind. But in the Middle Ages this training did not extend beyond the school in which the pupil had been taught.[63] Gentile da Foligno and Berengario da Carpi wrote partly for the honour of their *studia*, in Perugia and Bologna, and it was normal in disputed questions to undermine the opinions of masters in other institutions. This caused little difficulty where the faculty or professional college was powerful and protected the interests of its members.

But the potential for discord was there. In particular, the separation of the teaching *studium* from the examining college in Italy caused problems. There was hard feeling when students left their *studium* to take their degrees (perhaps because it was cheaper) at another college. The college included practitioners who did not teach and who had interests different from the doctors who did teach. By the Renaissance some doctors recognised that disagreements between these kinds of Rational and Learned Doctors could lead to a loss of reputation for *all* university-trained physicians.[64] Some such professional clash seems to have been behind the *De Cautelis Medicorum* of Gabriele de Zerbi in Padua.[65] This is a book of medical ethics, addressed to rational and learned physicians as a whole. Probably it was prompted by Zerbi's experience of being contradicted publicly by other physicians whose authority he could not deny. They were 'collegiants', doctors from a college separate from the *studium* in Padua: perhaps they were members of the powerful college in Venice, the city that controlled Padua as part

[63] McVaugh points out that in the Crown of Aragon in the fourteenth century physicians hardly thought of themselves as a group, and competed at a personal level. In Barcelona they refused the opportunity to form a professional college. See Michael McVaugh, *Medicine before the Plague*, Cambridge (Cambridge University Press), 1993, p. 235.

[64] In London, the College of Physicians was modelled on the Italian professional colleges. Parliament agreed on the attributes of the ideal physician, particularly his ethics or deontology and his learning, subjects that constantly recur in this book: the physician should be 'p[ro]founde, sad and discrete, goudlie lerned and deplie studied in physyk'. Quoted by Harold Cook, 'Institutional structures and personal belief in the London College of Physicians', in Ole Grell and Andrew Cunningham, eds., *Religio Medici. Medicine and Religion in Seventeenth-Century England*, Aldershot (Scolar Press), 1996, pp. 91–114, at p. 92.

[65] Gabriele de Zerbi, *Opus perutile de Cautelis Medicorum, in Pillularium Omnibus Medicis Necessarium clarissimi doctoris magistri Panthaleonis*, Lyons (Antonius Blanchard), 1528. See also Roger French, 'The medical ethics of Gabriele de Zerbi', in Andrew Wear, Johanna Geyer-Kordesch and Roger French, *Doctors and Ethics: the Earlier Historical Setting of Medical Ethics*, Amsterdam (Rodopi), 1993, pp. 72–97. For a slightly different interpretation, see David E. J. Linden, 'Gabriele Zerbi's *De Cautelis Medicorum* and the tradition of medical prudence', *Bulletin of the History of Medicine*, 73 (1999) 19–37.

of the Veneto.[66] Zerbi saw that the vulgar and the plebians, ever ready to poke fun at the learned pomposity of doctors, could cause immense damage to the reputation of all properly trained physicians by showing that, since they disagreed in their learning, it could not be trusted. Central, then, to Zerbi's ethics was the need never to air disagreements with other doctors in public.

This was medical ethics in the sense we have met before, rules designed at least as much for the benefit of the doctors as of the patient. The doctor should live in a big house, partly so that everyone knew where it was and partly because it suited his status. The doctor should not play games, go shopping, cultivate land or join in politics, each of which would detract from his image as a man totally immersed in medicine. He should, of course, devote himself to reading, partly because learned medicine was the best and it would be unethical with regard to the patient to practise anything else,[67] and partly because learning impressed the patient. The doctors were often direct about their self-interest, and it was a commonplace that the fee they extracted from a patient in pain was greater than that received when he was returning to health.[68] The doctors also knew that expensive remedies acted more surely than cheap ones: princes expected to pay a great deal, leaving common cures to the common people. This belief was no doubt encouraged by the doctors, especially if they worked closely with the apothecaries, but it was not wholly cynical. The doctor believed that his treatment would be more effective if he had the trust of the patient: in the doctors' terms this was a question of asserting their authority over the patient and securing his obedience. In all these ways the doctor was moulding the expectations of the patient into forms the doctor could reasonably hope to meet: it was by this (and not by any modern criterion) that his success was measured.

The ethics of a medical man such as Clementi Clementini (a near-contemporary of Zerbi) were partly the result of a recognition that Hippocratic ethics could apply to all those who had become learned in the

---

[66] Sometimes the colleges, such as that in Milan, restricted entry exclusively to those of local origin. See Ann G. Carmichael, 'Epidemics and state medicine in fifteenth-century Milan', in French et al., *Medicine from the Black Death to the French Disease*, p. 222.

[67] See Luis García-Ballester, 'Medical ethics in transition in the Latin medicine of the thirteenth and fourteenth centuries: new perspectives on the physician–patient relationship and the doctor's fee', in Wear et al., *Medical Ethics*, pp. 38–71.

[68] This was also a criticism of the doctors which was made at least since the time of John of Salisbury. *Dum dolet accipe* he said of the doctor's attitude to his fee. See C. I. I. Webb, ed., *Ioannis Saresberiensis Episcopi Carnotensis Policrati sive de nugis curialium et vestigiis philosophorum*, 2 vols., Oxford (Clarendon Press), 1929; vol. 1, p. 168. On the taking of fees see also Carole Rawcliffe, 'The profits of practice: the wealth and social status of medical men in later medieval England', *Bulletin of the Society for the Social History of Medicine*, 37 (1985) 27–30.

medical tradition. The ethical works began to appear in the old medical textbook, the *Articella*, and Renaissance editions of the Hippocratic works sometimes begin with them, as though they were the deontological imperatives for the whole of medicine.[69] This is perhaps why Clementini dwells on prognosis, the attractions and dangers of which had been well known since Western doctors began to read the 'glorious' Hippocrates.[70] Do not make more prognostications than necessary, says Clementini, because the outcome of diseases, like that of wars, is uncertain. If the case looks hopeless, do not tell the patient (it would be a self-fulfilling prophecy) but take the assistants to one side. In any case make your prognostications gloomier than the case warrants, to avoid blame if the patient dies and to reap the rewards of money and glory if he recovers.[71] Prognostication, concludes Clementini, is made on the basis of learning and experience, but learning – especially philosophy – has also the quite different function of enabling the physician to stand out from and even control the ignorant crowd. The rewards of medical experience are also twofold. It should be gained, says Clementini, from charitable practice among the poor: this will make you pleasing in the eyes of God (who will reward you in his own way), and constant charitable practice will make you a better doctor, which will increase your reputation, which will multiply your fees.[72]

MEDICINE AND RELIGION

The Reformation changed many attitudes to authority, including the European learned tradition. This was notably the case in natural philosophy, and consequently had an effect upon the theory of medicine. Aristotle was, once again, central. We have seen that in the thirteenth century Aristotle's physical works could in different circumstances be used to both promote and suppress heresy – different perceptions of authority. After Aquinas' masterly synthesis of natural philosophy and Christianity, the church's guidance was intellectual as well as spiritual. But the reformers disliked the fact that this guidance was provided only by priests and they began to question its content. Aristotle, after all, had considered that the world was eternal and did not have a Creator; philosophy began to look rather pagan. At the reforming university of Wittenberg Jakob Milich tried to construct part of an arts course using Pliny's *Natural History* in place

[69] See chapter 1, above.   [70] See chapter 3, above.
[71] For the physician's reason for not telling the truth in his prognosis, see Winfried Schleiner, *Medical Ethics in the Renaissance*, Washington, DC (Georgetown University Press), 1995, esp. p. 30.
[72] Clementi Clementini, *Clementia medicinae . . . noviter in lucem aedita*, Rome (J. Mazzochius), 1512.

of Aristotle's *Meteorology*.[73] While Luther rejected Aristotle, reformers like Melanchthon used him constructively in discussing topics such as the human soul. Indeed, the use of Aristotle in the newer German universities began with the medical faculties, where Vesalius' *Fabrica* was part of a new look at human anatomy.[74] More generally, Protestants often held that Aristotle's philosophy was useful, but, like the rest of Catholic knowledge, needed reforming.[75]

An important consequence of the Reformation with respect to medical discussions was the new attention paid to the soul and the body. The soul was, of course, the immortal soul of Christian teaching, and the body, its terrestrial home, was often seen as the image, or temple, of God. To return to Philip Melanchthon (1497–1560) in Wittenberg, we see that he turned to the anatomy of Vesalius and had anatomical figures printed for his students.[76] This meant that anatomy was now taught in the arts course and not in conjunction with the higher faculty of medicine. Potentially at least, it reached far more students; and in removing the connection with medicine it reinforced the autonomy that anatomists had looked for. As an arts course subject in a reformed curriculum, anatomy reached as far as St Andrews, Glasgow and, by the early seventeenth century, Aberdeen, where they used the up-to-date textbook of Bauhin.[77] These circumstances played their part in ensuring that anatomy survived the crisis in the theory of medicine, as we shall see.

In extreme cases the Protestant attitude led to complete rejection of the learned tradition. It is well known that Paracelsus thought that he could learn more medicine by travelling and observing than from any library, and that the books of Hippocrates and Galen should be burned.[78] The Rational and Learned Doctors of the universities saw how disastrous this would be for their kind of medicine, so they prevented him from getting a teaching position and burned *his* books. Paracelsus held that medicine was a gift

---

[73] See *Commentarii in librum secundum Historiae mundi C. Plinii conscripta a Iacobo Milichio*, The Hague (Petrus Brubacchius), 1535. This work represents Milich's lectures at Wittenberg. The text and its editions are also discussed by Bruce Eastwood, 'Plinian astronomy in the Middle Ages and Renaissance', in French and Greenaway, *Science in the Early Roman Empire*, pp. 197–235, at p. 218.

[74] Lohr, 'Metaphysics', p. 621. See also chapter 6, below.

[75] This view is summarised in the work of the later teacher of logic in Leiden, Adriaan Heereboord, who had considerable influence in contemporary Cambridge. See his *Ermeneia* [Ερμηνεια] *Logica: seu Explicatio tum per Notas tum per Exempla Synopsis Logicae Burgersdicianae… accedit ejusdem Auctoris Praxis Logica*, Leiden (David à Lodensteyn and Severyn Matthysz), 1650.

[76] See Vivian Nutton, 'Wittenberg anatomy', in Ole Peter Grell and Andrew Cunningham, eds., *Medicine and the Reformation*, London (Routledge), 1993, pp. 11–32.

[77] See Roger French, *Anatomical Education in a Scottish University, 1620. An Annotated translation of the Lecture Notes of John Moir*, Edinburgh (MacInnes and Whytt), 1974.

[78] See Copenhaver, 'Astrology and magic', p. 290.

from God, and that doctors were born, not made. God sent diseases, but also cures; and it was the true doctor who could recognise from signs the abundant natural remedies that God had provided so that the poor and unlettered could help themselves. The *scientia* of medicine was not to be acquired from authority, but existed in the natural objects themselves as much as in the mind of the doctor. Like many Protestants, Paracelsus was suspicious of the priestly monopoly of knowledge, and published much of his medical thought in the vernacular, as others were translating the Bible. As a champion of medicine for the people, he argued that any doctor accepting a retained position – the Rational and Learned Doctor's preferred mode of practice – was betraying his obligations to use medicine for the common good.[79] In short, Paracelsus was a figure outside the universities and standard academic medical training; he and his many metal-based remedies proved attractive to medical men in a similar position, and they became a group that grew in power and came to rival university doctors.

There are other aspects of Renaissance medicine that can be related to the change of attitude to authority and religion. When the arguments over Vesalius and his attitude to Galen had died down a change came over anatomy. To some extent there was a return to a study of function, which had not played a large part in Vesalius' morphological studies. But there was also the loss of the classicism of Vesalius, who had answered Galen in Galenic terms. Before Vesalius it was possible to write a professional anatomy in the schools, as Zerbi did, or an aggressively Hellenist anatomy, as Benedetti did, but later in the century references to ancient founts of knowledge often included the hermetic. In a period of new religious sensibilities the human body was now the image of God, or His temple. This was not Galen's demiurge, but the Christian God as Creator. Anatomists worked literally in anatomy theatres but also in the theatre of creation, a stage on which the 'properties' revealed the working of God in Creation. In more general terms, the Hellenists, in attempting to restore a *prisca scientia* by returning to pre- or non-Christian Greek writings, could be seen as more pagan than Western Christian.[80]

Like the anatomists, the natural historians used the term 'theatre' in a similar way. A surprisingly large number of them were Protestant or had reformist backgrounds. It was for them a religious duty to explore the world

[79] See Charles Webster, 'Paracelsus: medicine as popular protest', in Grell and Cunningham, eds., *Medicine and the Reformation*, pp. 57–77, at p. 66.

[80] Perhaps, having lost their own church and state, the new Greek state they called for involved the disestablishment of the Western church. See Geanakoplos, *'Sibling' Byzantine and Western Cultures*, p. 248.

that God had made, whose stamp was on all natural objects. This was seeing for oneself rather than accepting the authority of another, reading the book of nature alongside the book of revealed knowledge. Systematic knowledge of the world's plants and animals related directly to medical knowledge but it was not itself learned and rational in the senses in which we are using the terms. It was up to the elite doctor to bring it into his domain, to medicalise it.

In contrast to the reformers, the Catholics reaffirmed the validity of their learned tradition. It is well known that the Jesuits, particularly of Coimbra, studied Aristotle's natural philosophy with a new passion and vigour, but there were also movements that related more directly to medicine. It is equally well known that Paracelsus was given by Catholics the insulting title of *Luther medicorum*, and to Bellarmine the whole of the reform movement was a plague. Medical men were particularly worrying to the Inquisition because Padua was tolerant of Protestant students, providing they kept quiet. Medical men were also used to discussing things across a wide range of disciplines, which reminds us of their long education, with its disputations, maturity and their ability to perform many functions for the rich and powerful. University physicians were, after all, learned; and they had the freedom to visit and talk to patients. In Venice in 1568, the Inquisition brought to light a full Protestant conventicle which met in apothecaries' and barbers' shops.[81]

THE FRENCH DISEASE

A century and a half after the plague arrived in Europe there came another epidemic. It started in 1495, when Charles VIII of France led an army into Italy to besiege Naples and Ferdinand and Isabella sent a Spanish army to protect the city. This new epidemic was like no other that Europe had seen before. The French called it the Italian or Neapolitan Disease. In England the disease was popularly known as the Pox. But in educated circles throughout Europe, the phenomenon was widely referred to as the 'French Disease' (*morbus gallicus*). Unlike the plague, which came in successive waves and killed its victims quickly, the French Disease lingered painfully in its sufferers and made them hideously disfigured. As with the plague, the empirics took their opportunity and sold specifics and secret remedies. The doctors complained, but this time their claim to be practising

[81] Richard Palmer, 'Physicians and the Inquisition in sixteenth-century Venice', in Grell and Cunningham, eds., *Medicine and the Reformation*, pp. 118–33, at pp. 118, 120, 121.

a superior kind of medicine fell on some unwilling ears. We have noticed that Paracelsus denied the validity of traditional medicine, and Ulrich von Hutten, an angry and literate sufferer of the French Disease, bitterly complained of the doctors' inability to cure him.[82]

There was, in other words, a threat to the authority of the Rational and Learned Doctor. This went hand in hand with other changes in society. We have seen that the doctor's preferred form of practice was to be retained in a household to guide regimen and study the idiosyncrasies that led his patients into this or that disorder.[83] But epidemics came quickly to large numbers and seemed to be the same in all, and the doctors were not certain what to do. When towns signed contracts with physicians it was the result of a feeling of responsibility for the health of the population; the situation owed something to a revival of Roman Law and Aristotelian political thought.[84] The doctor was expressly required to remain in town during epidemics, but it was clear that there was little he could do in the face of the French Disease. It was religious charity that built hospitals, often called, significantly enough, the *incurabili*.[85] It was the city authorities who organised quarantine or turned people from the gates.[86] There was, in fact, a *civic* notion of disease, which, in however small a way, detracted from the authority of the learned doctor.

This is no place for a potted history of the hospital,[87] primarily because it was late in his history that the Rational and Learned Doctor learned to take advantage of them. But hospitals are of interest here because they were medical centres that were partly in lay control and they helped to weaken the authority of the doctor. Elite university doctors knew from early on that

---

[82] Ulrich von Hutten, *De guaiaci medicina et morbo gallico Liber unus*, Mainz (J. Scheffer), 1519.

[83] In the 1540s John Caius, the Italian-educated English humanist physician, welcomed the fact that the English gentry and the court were using doctors properly, by retaining them; in other words, the doctors had successfully established this expectation in the minds of their well-to-do patients. See Nutton's introduction to Vivian Nutton, ed., *Medicine at the Courts of Europe, 1500–1837*, London (Routledge), 1990, p. 3. As Nutton points out, once established as a retained physician, the learned and rational doctor had less need to publish. If he did, it was appropriate that he wrote on the diseases particular to courts. See Werner Friedrich Kümmel, '*De Morbis Aulicis:* on diseases found at court' in Nutton, ed., *Medicine at the Courts of Europe*, pp. 15–48.

[84] See García-Ballester, 'Medical ethics in transition', p. 50.

[85] See Arrizabalaga et al., *The Great Pox.* On the ethics of charity and medical skill see also Chiara Crisciani, 'Valeurs éthiques et savoir médical entre le XIVe et le XIVe siècle', *History and Philosophy of the Life Sciences*, 5 (1983) 33–52.

[86] Milan was in the forefront of such civic actions. See Carmichael, 'Epidemics and state medicine in fifteenth-century Milan'.

[87] The hospital has recently become a focus of interest to historians, with a growing literature, though no attempt will be made to cover it here. For an introduction to the earlier Western history of the topic see John Henderson, *Piety and Charity in late Medieval Florence*, Oxford (Clarendon Press), 1994.

Haly Abbas had recommended doctors to visit (Islamic) hospitals, learn
about cases and diseases and talk to other doctors; and the Hospitaller
knights built refuges where medical care was available.[88] By the end of
the thirteenth century there were hospitals with doctors in Marseilles and
Siena.[89] To a certain extent the doctors were medicalising the hospital
(as they medicalised empirical remedies); and the new duties of recording
the causes of death[90] called for methods of medical rationalisation not so
appropriate for the retained or visiting doctor. Perhaps it was when the
big Italian hospitals became associated with a wider civic pride[91] that the
elite doctor saw the advantages of working in them. Even royal physicians
did so.

To return to the French Disease, and in particular the specialist hospitals
that were founded to treat it, the problem for the doctors was that, like
the plague, it did not have a proper name. Some of them felt that real
names, given to diseases by the ancients, in some way expressed the essence
of the disease. More generally, the absence of a name prevented the disease
from being located in the medical literature. Like the plague too, it could
not be 'capitulated' to the appropriate chapter of Avicenna's *Canon*. The
Hellenists, who ignored this text, could not believe that the disease had not
existed in antiquity, or had not been adequately described by the ancients.
They consequently searched through Hippocrates and Galen, blaming the
barbarity of the Middle Ages for the loss of the name and description
of the disease. At the very least they needed to know what *kind* of disease it was, so that the medical theory of complexion and the appropriate
therapy of evacuation could be used. Again the doctors disagreed, and the
Arabists, the Hellenists and the 'establishment' school doctors had radically
different ideas and aired them in disputations in the universities and in the
courts of the great. Some said it was indeed a new disease, brought by sailors
from the New World, where its natural remedy was also to be found in the
form of 'holy wood' or guaiac. In Germany, the Fuggers, who had control
of the guaiac trade, contrived to promote its use in medical texts. Others
said that the only treatment was mercury, which made the patients sweat

---

[88] For the Hospitallers see Jessalynn Bird, 'Medicine for body and soul: Jacques de Vitry's sermons to
   Hospitallers and their charges', in Peter Biller and Joseph Ziegler, eds., *Religion and Medicine in the
   Middle Ages*, University of York (York Medieval Press), 2001, pp. 91–108 and the texts that follow.
   For hospitals in Byzantium see David Bennet, 'Medical practice and manuscripts in Byzantium', in
   Peregrine Horden and Emilie Savage-Smith, eds., *The Year 1000. Medical Practice at the end of the
   first Millennium* [*Social History of Medicine*, 13 (2000)], pp. 279–291, at p. 288.

[89] See Agrimi and Crisciani, 'Charity and aid in medieval Christian civilization', pp. 188, 191.

[90] Carmichael, 'Epidemics and state medicine in fifteenth-century Milan', p. 226.

[91] See Agrimi and Crisciani, 'Charity and aid in medieval Christian civilization', p. 190.

a great deal. The fact that the disease also seemed to be God's punishment for blasphemy did not prevent a German inspection team from going to Spain to study the guaiac method.[92]

The doctors were aware of their failure to agree and of the damage to their reputation. Some even admitted that the empirics might by chance have hit on a successful treatment. But this was a preliminary to doing what the doctors did very well: they *medicalised* things. An empirical remedy was drawn into the apparatus of theory and the doctors claimed that only they could administer it properly, by considering the age, sex, disposition and habits of the patient; only they could determine the quantities that made the remedies effective but not dangerous.

At the heart of the matter was the difference between the theory of medicine and its actual practice. Although 'theory' and 'practice' had been separate categories since late Alexandria,[93] and had become institutionally separate in Bologna in the first half of the fourteenth century, most writings on practice were on what we might call the theory of practice. Manual practice was taught by example and experience and accordingly left fewer records. In considering this difference it becomes clear that one of the main reasons for writing a medical text was to promote the author. Even surgical texts, which we might expect to be severely practical, were written partly for status.[94] Sometimes the operations described had not been undertaken or observed by the author, and in some cases they seem to have been reconstructions of operations described by the ancients. Theoretical texts reflected well on the author and his university, and often contained matter that explicitly concerned the intellect or imagination only, without any possible application to practice.[95]

---

[92] See Arrizabalaga et al., *The Great Pox*, p. 100.

[93] See Andrew Cunningham, 'The theory/practice division of medicine: two late-Alexandrian legacies', in Teizo Ogawa, ed., *History of Traditional Medicine* (Proceedings of the 1st and 2nd International Symposia on the Comparative History of Medicine – East and West), Osaka, 1986, pp. 303–24. According to Jacquart, 'Medical scholasticism', the division was made in Paris in the late thirteenth century, before Bologna.

[94] See Siraisi, *Medieval and Early Renaissance Medicine*, p. 162. See also chapter 4, above.

[95] Gentile's plague tract was written for the students and for the glory of Perugia; and his exercises on quantification are in part purely intellectual. See Roger French, *Canonical Medicine. Gentile da Foligno and Scholasticism*, Leiden (Brill), 2001, ch. 6, and chapter 4 above.

PART III

The Crisis

CHAPTER 6

The crisis of theory

*All the order of teaching is troubled and the doctrine of Physick is endeavrd
and learned altogether preposterously and confusedly, without any certain
method.*[1]

With these words Jacobus de Back reported the confusion in the schools
at the collapse of traditional natural philosophy. He had taken his MD in
Franeker in 1616, when medicine and natural philosophy were still sisters,
as they had been throughout the Latin tradition.[2] But by the 1630s not
only were philosophers seeing a battle between Aristotelianism and the
mechanical philosophy, but within medicine some of the major doctrines
of Hippocrates and Galen had been shown to be wrong. De Back felt
the pull of old loyalties and declared that he still belonged to the ancient
physicians; but clearly they were going to need another re-evaluation to
show that they still had authority in a changed society.

How had this crisis come about? Rather than retell a traditional story of
a revolution in natural philosophy, let us look at its relation to medicine
from the point of view of the Rational and Learned Doctor, who still wanted
to be successful.

---

[1] *The Anatomical Exercises of Dr William Harvey... with the Preface of Zachariah Wood... to which
is added Dr James De Back, His Discourse on the heart...* London, 1653; the English translation is of de Back's original discourse of 1648. For a view of the economic and political crisis
in medicine in London, see Charles Webster, 'William Harvey and the crisis of medicine in
Jacobean England', in Jerome J. Bylebyl, ed., *William Harvey and his Age. The Professional and Social
context of the Discovery of the circulation*, Baltimore (The Johns Hopkins University Press), 1979,
pp. 1–27.
[2] Scholastics such as Pietro d'Abano used the phrase, derived from the well-known commentary on
De Sectis by John of Alexandria (as we saw in chapter 3): *philosophia et medicine duae sorores sunt.*
It was a famous dictum of the medieval doctor: see Cornelius O'Boyle, 'Discussions on the nature
of medicine at the university of Paris, ca. 1300', in John van Engen, ed., *Learning Institutionalized. Teaching in the Medieval University*, Notre Dame, Indiana (University of Notre Dame Press),
2000, pp. 197–227. It is part of the rational and learned doctor's message about the nature of his
medicine.

EPIDEMICS CHANGE MEDICINE

The two great epidemics, the plague and the French Disease, left marks on European medicine.[3] While the Learned and Rational Doctors struggled to get to grips with these new and unknown, or at least improperly labelled diseases, laymen took practical measures such as quarantine and isolation of the affected, and built hospitals to contain them. The theory of medicine centred on the individual and his constitution and circumstances (the naturals and non-naturals). Epidemics reversed this. The disease was now a person. Its approach could be charted, from city to city, and when it arrived it killed or maimed a large proportion of the population, and did so largely in the same way, irrespective of individual differences. As an entity, it went from one person to another. Like an unwelcome visitor, the person of the plague went away and returned at intervals. The person of the French Disease was an unwanted guest who stayed too long; so long in fact that many doctors of the sixteenth century thought that it was growing old and feeble and would shortly die.[4]

CONTAGION

The theory of complexion could not adequately explain these epidemics. A central issue was contagion. It was clear – especially to the layman[5] – that both epidemics spread from person to person. For religious reasons, this perception was not possible in Arabic medicine, which still had great authority in the medicine of the schools.[6] That epidemics could be transmitted by clothes or merchandise added to the difficulties of explaining them on the basis of the traditional elementary qualities, which were part of the individual's environment and acted directly on him. To pursue our image of the French Disease as a person, some doctors began to think that

---

[3] Some measure of this is the huge quantity of medical literature generated by the plague and the almost equally large number of treatises on the French Disease. This led in our period to attempts to collect and publish all the relevant literature, to try to capture the 'natural history' of the disease as a *thing*. See Jean Astruc, *De Morbis Venereis libri sex*, Paris (Widow of P. du Mesnil for G. Cavelier), 1736.

[4] Jon Arrizabalaga, John Henderson and Roger French, *The Great Pox. The French Disease in Renaissance Europe*, New Haven (Yale University Press), 1997, esp. ch. 10.

[5] On the lay reaction to epidemics see Sheldon Watts, *Epidemics and History. Disease, Power and Imperialism*, New Haven (Yale University Press), 1997.

[6] But see Lawrence I. Conrad, 'A ninth-century Muslim scholar's discussion of contagion', in Lawrence I. Conrad and Dominik Wujastyk, eds., *Contagion. Perspectives from Pre-Modern Societies*, Aldershot (Ashgate), 2000, pp. 163–77. See also in the same volume Vivian Nutton, 'Did the Greeks have a word for it?', pp. 137–62 and François-Olivier Touati, 'Contagion and leprosy: myth, ideas and evolution in medieval minds and societies', pp. 179–201.

it had a material basis, the matter of disease. Postmortem dissection had been practised since the thirteenth century to discover causes of death, and the dissector relied on a knowledge of the normal body in order to identify what was pathological; but in the sixteenth century those who dissected victims of the French Disease were generally looking for an intrusive substance. Some found a white or viscous matter close to the bones, where so much pain had been felt (some called it *virus*, 'slime').[7]

The wide and rapid spread of both epidemics was explained in some quarters as part of God's punishment.[8] Perhaps He had used secondary causes, such as corruption of the air from celestial sources that were open to astrological interpretation. But then it was disputed whether air, as an element, was capable of being corrupted. Astrology too was coming under question in the early sixteenth century by influential scholars who objected on humanist and Hellenist grounds to its determinism and implications for human and divine free will.[9] It is to similar sources that we must turn to follow the story of how medicine changed over the sixteenth century.

PLATONIC MEDICINE

It is partly a story of neo-Platonism. This was not the neo-Platonism of Pico and Ficino, neither of whom lived into the sixteenth century, but a medical neo-Platonism that seems especially suited to deal with the problem of contagion. Common to both kinds, however, was a deliberately pious (rather than traditionally philosophical) concept of a down-flow of divine power and doctrines of cosmic sympathies, whereby earthly things responded to celestial forces. From the middle to the end of the sixteenth century and across many fields writings began to appear in a new genre. The central word was 'subtlety'. Subtlety provided an explanation of the world that was an increasingly attractive alternative to the traditional and largely Aristotelian world-view of the schools. In fact it contributed a great deal to the ultimate collapse of that system, a collapse that precipitated the crisis in the theory of medicine with which this chapter is concerned. We shall see how the doctors, who had relied on this philosophy for their theory, and on their theory for their reputation as being rational and learned, coped with the crisis.

---

[7] Astruc, *De Morbis Venereis*, cites several sixteenth-century authors who use the term *virus*.
[8] An example is the physician to Philip, Elector to the Palatinate, Conrad Schellig (fl. 1496) who, at his request, drew up a *consilium* against the pox: *In pustulas malas Morbum quem Malum de Francia vulgus appelat... Salubre Consilium*, Heidelberg, 1495–6.
[9] See Giovanni Pico della Mirandola in chapter 5, above.

'Subtlety' was used to denote natural powers of things that did not work in an obvious way. Sometimes these powers were unknowable and thus 'occult' at the same time as being natural. Sometimes they were cosmic sympathies or the action of God; but in general the term was used in conscious opposition to what now became known as the 'manifest qualities', the elementary qualities of traditional natural philosophy. These now looked coarse in operation and there were many things they could not explain. What caused the magnet to attract iron? What travelled from the electric eel up through the net or spear of the fisherman and stupefied his arm? Why were some plants so antipathetic to others that they would never grow together? In medicine, the amount of substance – and therefore the qualities it could bear – that passed from a mad dog or a poisonous animal to the human body was small, out of all proportion to the effect it had, and a mechanism involving manifest qualities seemed out of the question. Girolamo Cardano (1501–76) not only wrote on subtlety, but believed that of the four manifest qualities two, cold and dry, were merely opposites of the other two and did not act on their own.[10]

Traditional natural philosophy could not work on such a basis and those who sought subtlety had to find other foundations. Some did with confidence. In Paris, Jean Fernel (1506/7–58)[11] knew that the learned physician's claim to superiority over the apothecary (and therefore his reputation) lay in his knowledge of causes. Traditional doctors had used the same arguments for the same purposes, but Fernel is not referring to Aristotelian causes. In a prefatory letter he addresses his king with an optimism about Renaissance society that justified a break with the past: printed books, the compass, the discovery of the New World, all seemed to make the world of the ancients narrow and limited. For these reasons the old philosophers should not be slavishly followed; in any case, they were pagan.[12]

---

[10] On Cardano see Nancy Siraisi, *The Clock and the Mirror. Girolamo Cardano and Renaissance Medicine*, Princeton (Princeton University Press), 1997, pp. 6, 7, 119 and 159 (which deals with Fernel and Cardano). It can be argued that another form of 'subtlety' was represented by the strange and wonderful things seen in the course of a long practice, that is, medical events not covered by the canons of Galenic medicine and its natural philosophy. Possibly new diseases came into this category. On personal experience, especially the *mirabilia* of Antonio Beniveni and Cardano, see also Siraisi, ' "Remarkable disease", "remarkable cures", and personal experience in Renaissance medical texts', in her *Medicine and the Italian Universities, 1250–1600*, Leiden (Brill), 2001.

[11] On the date of Fernel's birth, see the still useful biography by Sir Charles Sherrington, *The Endeavour of Jean Fernel. With a List of the Editions of his Writings*, Cambridge (Cambridge University Press), 1946, p. 136.

[12] Fernel deals with subtlety in his *De Abditis Rerum Causis*. The two books with this title are in the collected works: I have used the edition of Geneva, 1643, the *Universa Medicina*, published by P. Chouët.

In practice, Fernel relies on a Renaissance interpretation of the alternative ancient philosophy, Platonism. This does not mean he has forgotten what he said to the king, for his neo-Platonism is not very closely related to what Plato wrote. In the first place, it could be made pious in a Christian kind of way. It was also a culture of a self-perceived elite, like that of the earlier Hellenists. Fernel expresses himself in the form of a Platonic dialogue, and the new natural philosophy is discussed by the speakers in a sodality, a characteristically Renaissance gathering of like-minded people.[13] Their ideal philosophy is mathematically demonstrative, a very non-Aristotelian ideal.

The subtlety that Fernel invoked in his medical writing to explain contagion was the doctrine of 'whole substance' action. This was a concept used by Galen to explain how certain medicines, and poisons, acted on the body, perhaps in an unknown way, by virtue of their completeness as natural objects. It was a mode of action that did not depend on the manifest qualities and it was where Galen, as a medical man, departed from Aristotelian principles. Fernel turned the principle round and argued that contagion acted on the whole substance of the body in a way that could not necessarily be understood. This was the nub: the manifest qualities were observable to the sense and open to reason, while Fernel's 'subtle' or 'occult' actions were not necessarily rational in the same way. The stories of the electric eel and the magnet come from Galen, as examples of 'whole substance' action, and it was natural for Fernel to turn to them in discussing contagion.

Fernel was not prepared to abandon traditional natural philosophy and still less the theory of medicine. Medicines still worked by manifest qualities, and diseases were categorised in a Galenic way according to the similar and organic parts. To reject such things and rely wholly on irrational and unknowable causes would have been to lose one of the learned doctors' principal claims to be superior to more empirical practitioners, and, as we have seen, Fernel was aware of this. In dealing with the treatment of the *lues venerea* (Fernel naturally did not call it 'the French Disease') he accordingly deals with the manifest qualities of the guaiac wood in an orthodox way, and one of the purposes of doing so was to show that although this was a remedy discovered empirically, only the Rational and Learned Doctor could understand its action and construct a proper course of treatment.

A major reason behind the unknowability of subtle actions for Fernel was that they were God's action. The laws of nature had been laid down directly by God, they produced a general sympathy between natural things

---

[13] For example, Martin Pollich of Mellerstadt, who annotated Mondino and disputed bitterly with Simon Pistoris in Leipzig about the nature of the French Disease, belonged to the *Sodalitas Literaria Rhenana* of the humanist Conrad Celtis (1459–1508). See Arrizabalaga et al., *The Great Pox*. p. 94.

and they were good. Diseases too were natural and divine in this way, like magnetism and the action of rhubarb in purging bile: inexplicable perhaps, or inexpressible in words, but universally acknowledged.[14] To deny the divinity of these things, says Fernel, is to lack faith.[15]

The links between epidemics, contagion, subtlety and neo-Platonism are demonstrated also by Fernel's countryman and commentator Jean Riolan (the Elder, c. 1538–1605).[16] He thought Fernel was too extreme, for example in his 'metaphysical' description of the diseases of the similar parts, but his account of contemporary neo-Platonic medicine is as revealing as Fernel's use of it. Riolan too held that there were diseases of 'whole substance' which did not act by manifest qualities but by a poisonous quality. He preferred to call them 'diseases of form' because they attacked the 'formal principles', *formalia principia*, of life. The model is epidemics, spread by poisonous contagion. When he declares that the ancients did not know of these, he reminds us of the European experience of epidemics of the previous two centuries or so. One feature of the plague and the French Disease that came to have considerable intellectual impact on European medicine was the widespread idea that they were *new* diseases and that ancient medicine was not necessarily able to cope with them. Like Fernel, Riolan is confident that the medicine of his time is progressing (like all the arts, from rude beginnings) and that this newly recognised kind of disease counts as a discovery which will be improved upon. But Riolan cannot bring himself to say that the ancients did not know of these diseases. He adopts the common strategy of claiming that the knowledge was there, if hidden or incomplete. Clearly, the ancients described and distinguished epidemics, endemics, pestilences, contagions and poisonous diseases and other 'diseases of form' (Riolan does not say they knew the French Disease) but remained in ignorance of the causes, believing all diseases to be *intemperies*, disordered complexion.[17]

---

[14] For Fernel's reliance on the senses when faced with the inexplicable, see Laurence Brockliss, 'Seeing and believing: contrasting attitudes towards observational autonomy among French Galenists in the first half of the seventeenth century', in W. F. Bynum and Roy Porter, *Medicine and the Five Senses*, Cambridge (Cambridge University Press), 1993, pp. 60–84.

[15] For a comparison of Fernel and Cardano on these matters, see Siraisi, *The Clock and the Mirror*, p. 159.

[16] See his *Opera cum Physica, tum Medica*, Frankfurt (D. Zacharias Palthenius), 1611, which contains (ch. 9) his commentary on Fernel's *De Abditis Rerum Causis*; and his *Praelectiones in Libros Fernelii Physiologicos, et de Abditis Rerum Caussis*, Paris (Hadrian Perier), 1601.

[17] Riolan, *Opera*, p. 95, even claims to have found in Hippocrates and Alexander of Aphrodisias words that correspond to his own notion of a poisonous effluvium, *virus*, that was responsible for contagion. They were 'not ignorant' of the poisonous quality that endangers life, but their knowledge of it was not *dioti* – in Riolan's time it was fashionable to use this Greek term in place of the medieval Latin *propter quid*, 'reasoned knowledge'; its opposite was *quia*, simple knowledge of fact.

Neo-Platonic medicine provided an alternative to traditional medical theory and is very much part of the story of the decline of traditional natural philosophy. Riolan finds it particularly appropriate in dealing with contagion, the issue at the centre of the 'new' diseases. He insists that all diseases are either manifest or occult. The manifest are traditional Galenic diseases where the senses and reason follow the actions of the manifest qualities, and Riolan has no need to abandon this authority in his learned and rational medicine. Occult diseases are, in general, poisonous; they work by the mechanisms Riolan has already described, and they relate mainly to the 'new' diseases and contagion. In explaining contagion Riolan invokes the new rationality. Contagion is twofold, he says. One kind is formal, potential and qualitative. These are Aristotelian terms, not out of place in traditional theory: they are *physical* attributes. Physical contact is by transmission of quality and does not need contiguous surfaces: the magnet attracts iron at a distance; the peony placed on a patient's neck affects but does not touch the brain. The second kind of contact in contagion is 'corporeal, actual and quantitative': these are *mathematical*.[18] This kind of contact is when the surfaces of the two things touch, as a craftsman works his materials. It is also a link to neo-Platonic medicine, for it reflects the importance of mathematics in the Platonic world-view. While the Aristotelians did not give much importance to mathematics, the neo-Platonists talked of mathematical demonstration and 'mathematical forms': all the medical men educated in the schools of the Platonists, says Riolan, prefer mathematical to physical (that is, Aristotelian) forms in being freer from matter and closer to the metaphysical.

Neo-Platonic medicine as described by Riolan shared some features with the earlier neo-Platonism of Ficino and others, particularly the influence of the heavens. Riolan agreed with them that there was something 'transnatural' in diseases which involved celestial power and opened up a new kind of rationality. Ultimately, it was God and the Intelligences who sent first principles to matter in which a potentiality had been prepared by secondary causes. The sun, for example, does not send souls to bodies[19] but excites souls to appear in prepared matter. The medium carries the message, not the result; semen is inanimate but prepares for an animated foetus. This is part of subtlety, and Riolan interprets the story of the electric eel to explain why the fisherman's net (or spear) does not become stupefied like his arm because its matter is not capable of stupefaction: it is the 'unaltered medium'. In Riolan's account of neo-Platonic medicine there are

---

[18] Riolan, *Opera*, p. 102.   [19] That is, unlike the Arabic *dator formarum*. Ibid., p. 102.

the celestial correspondences that appeared in the writings of the fifteenth-century neo-Platonists. Categories of earthly things have a sort of celestial archetype, 'a certain First', which gives power to them.[20] In this way numbers, although expressed in artificial figures, are potent. So are words, both spoken and written; Riolan uses the terms of old systems of allegory, in which words surround the inner message.[21] In the same way appropriate artificial shapes will form alliances with the descending powers. It followed that the neo-Platonist doctors of Riolan's day believed that diseases could be treated with amulets, accompanied by appropriate words.[22] Riolan says that the Peripatetics derided this, claiming that the practice was a series of tricks by imposters, superstitiously believing in ceremonial magic. Riolan observes that the theologians too were opposed to the use of amulets, because their effect was achieved by the work of *cacodemones*, perhaps those demons with special knowledge of natural things.[23] Clearly, neo-Platonic doctors were using an alternative natural philosophy to enhance the reputation of the intellectual component of their medicine.

SUBTLETY AND SEEDS

Experience with epidemics that led to a perception of disease as a 'person', an invasive entity, called into being another kind of explanation of contagion. This was that the disease had seeds, which could pass from one person to another. They could also lie dormant in clothes and merchandise, becoming viable on contact with a new victim; a clear indication of experience gained from the transmission of disease along trade routes.

Like other kinds of subtlety, the idea of seeds of disease could be used without abandoning the doctrine of manifest qualities, because it was a 'special case' argument, limited to the rapid spread and cross-infection of epidemics. But, again like other forms of subtlety, in the cases where it applied, it was radically different from Aristotelian natural philosophy, and helped to loosen its grip. Sometimes the seeds were seen as atoms, and the promulgators of this view took authority from the poem of Lucretius, rediscovered as recently as the previous century. Ancient atomism claimed that the world was composed of atoms moving without purpose in a void, and was rejected by Aristotle precisely because of the absence of purpose.

---

[20] Ibid., p. 105.   [21] Ibid., p. 104: *volucria*.

[22] The men who used amulets in tertian fevers were called *circulatores*. Ibid., p. 106.

[23] Riolan (ibid., p. 105) does not enlarge on the similarities between prayer and incantations. Words to stop the flow of blood included *Sanguis mane in te sicut Christus ferit in se; Sanguis mane, in tua vena, sicut Christus in sua poena; Sanguis mane fixus, sicut Christus fuit crucifixus.*

For him the irreducible components of the world were the four elements, but atoms were a quite different kind of irreducibility, for they were the smallest possible units of existence, incapable of subdivision. For the Latin humanists Lucretius was an attractive figure, for he wrote in verse, and pulled philosophy into the Humanists' arena; as a Latin writer he could be used in defence of the *Res Latina*.

Fracastoro's *Syphilis* (1531) illustrates this. It identifies the poet as a man who although medically trained in the schools was distant from them and their Aristotelian natural philosophy. Fracastoro declares himself as a Humanist by choosing to write in verse, and the setting of his topic is that of the ancients, with their pantheon and uncreated, eternal world. The title gave the name to the French Disease that we still use, which is a measure of the popularity of Fracastoro's work. Later, he wrote separately on sympathy, as a form of subtlety, and on contagion, both giving a philosophical justification for the poem. It is a world-view very different from the Aristotelianism of the schools, and closer to the neo-Platonism of Fernel. The whole world sympathises: the needle of the compass has a sympathy to the pole, angry bulls become calm when tied to fig trees, adamant is softened only with goat's blood. Like Fernel, Fracastoro celebrates the modern miracle of the compass, unknown to the ancients, and is anxious to see the world explained in a new way. But Fracastoro's sympathies are not purposeful actions or expressions of a natural appetite, for matter is passive; nor is it directed by something that does have a purpose or final cause.

'Final cause', of course, is Aristotelian language, and Fracastoro often uses the terms of traditional natural philosophy, sometimes investing them with new meanings, but often allowing them to stand. It is as if Aristotelian natural philosophy had penetrated too deep to be removed at a stroke. This residual Aristotelianism was often too condensed to reflect accurately what Aristotle had said, and it was sometimes these debased doctrines that came to be criticised most. An example is 'nature abhors a vacuum', which implies a conscious choice on the part of nature, where 'nature' is, perhaps, a rational demiurge. Fracastoro was well enough read to know that such an idea was not Aristotelian, and he has standard arguments against the existence of a vacuum. Indeed, the topic is central, for the final cause of universal sympathy was that a vacuum should not exist. But Fracastoro cannot give an answer to the question of what it is that resists the separation of two contiguous sympathising surfaces in circumstances where a vacuum would form.

Applying his first principles to contagion, Fracastoro explains that it is a special kind of sympathy, mediated by particles, the smallest possible parts into which a body can be divided. These are seeds of the disease, to be identified with the white matter found close to the nerves and joints in postmortems. The particles are partly Lucretian atoms and partly medieval 'species': images of objects radiating off their surfaces and impinging on our senses.

In the case of Daniel Sennert (1572–1637), the great medical teacher in the Protestant university of Wittenberg, consideration of contagion led to a reformulation of natural philosophy. In 1607 he began to teach on 'occult' diseases and poisons, where the amount of the infective agent or poison was so small that it could not act by the four primary or manifest qualities. Sennert claimed to be within the medical and philosophical traditions (it was his enemies, he said, who were neoterics and hence spoke in paradoxes) and he spent most of his working life within a university, yet it is clear that traditional Aristotelianism and Galenism were no longer satisfactory. Contagion, primarily of the French Disease and the plague,[24] led Sennert into the whole business of subtleties – the action of the magnet, the electric eel, the poison of a rabid dog and of noxious animals, the action of rhubarb in purging, 'whole substance' action, sympathies and atoms. Although he does not deny the traditional actions of the manifest qualities, he says that in *physica* (he means natural philosophy, not medicine) nothing is more damnable than the attempt to derive all causes from the elementary qualities.[25] He saw describing the subtle qualities as a new research exercise,[26] begun by Fernel, Cardano, Fracastoro, J. C. Scaliger, Thomas Erastus and others. Sennert was writing at a very Protestant university in troubled and sensitive religious times. It is clear that one of the advantages of departing from the manifest qualities of Aristotle into the realm of subtle qualities was that some 'occult' qualities, that is, unknown or unknowable, could be attributed directly to the action of God, whose activity was so plainly absent from Aristotle's natural philosophy.[27]

FORCES OF CONSERVATISM AND CHANGE

Historians normally like to tell a story that seems to be going somewhere, where the signposts are significant changes in people's beliefs and behaviour.

---

[24] Daniel Sennert, *Opera Omnia in tres tomos distincta: Operum Tomus I [-III]*, Paris (Societas), 1641, p. 1013.

[25] Ibid., p. 694.　　[26] Ibid., pp. 966, 967.

[27] On Thomas Erastus and the divine origin of some qualities, see Brian P. Copenhaver, 'Astrology and magic', in Quentin Skinner and Eckhard Kessler, eds., *The Cambridge History of Renaissance Philosophy*, Cambridge (Cambridge University Press), 1988, pp. 264–300, at p. 286.

But we also need to know why other people did not change. We have already seen that in their guild-like corporations, Learned and Rational Doctors were, in the sense we have identified, successful: they determined what the best medicine was and helped to shape the expectations of their contemporaries. For all the novelty and attacks on ancient belief by Renaissance figures, there were many more doctors who preferred to do and think in the same way as their predecessors in the Latin tradition of medicine. Hellenists and Humanists thus shared with their predecessors a desire to understand the ancients, but of course their method was different, to 'listen' to the ancients in another way. An example here is Leonard Fuchs (1501–66), who explains that his purpose was to correct the mistakes of recent writers and restore the *prisca* medicine of the ancients. In his address he expects Hildric, Duke of Wirtemberg, to institute true religion, piety and learning, and he makes a strong argument for their linkage. 'Learning', of course, was especially his own vision of medicine.[28] Securing preferment from Hildric, Fuchs set out his ideal medicine in a work called *The Institutes*.[29] The work is designed for students, and he speaks of the danger of young minds being perverted by new ideas. Following Galen, he says that diseases are complexional or the result of bad structure or the solution of continuity. Subtle causes were not classical enough for Fuchs.[30]

To look ahead for a moment, it has been pointed out that the *Canon* of Avicenna remained on the statutes of some universities until the Enlightenment,[31] and the appearance of an edition of the work in Arabic in 1593 indicates that, to some, progress in medicine centred upon a tighter reading of the traditional sources.[32] Bolognese graduates in medicine swore until 1671 to be faithful to Galen and Aristotle,[33] and in 1652 even the violently neoteric Englishman Nicholas Culpeper felt no need to justify

---

[28] Leonhard Fuchs, *Paradoxorum Medicinae libri tres*, Basel (J. Bebellius), 1535.

[29] *Institutionum Medicinae ad Hippocratis, Galeni, aliorumque veterum scripta recte intelligenda mire utiles libri quinque*, Leiden (J. Faure for Thomas Guerinus), 1555. See especially the dedicatory letter. He was now a professor at Tübingen, apparently as a result of impressing Hildric.

[30] For Fuchs' *Institutes* I have used the Basel (Oporinus), 1583 edn, pp. 522, 793. Another example of a classicising physician is Laurent Joubert (1529–83), *Medicinae Practicae priores libri tres*, Geneva, 1572, who begins by saying that all diseases come from distemper or bad structure (and not, therefore, from occult qualities).

[31] See Nancy G Siraisi, *Avicenna in Renaissance Italy. The Canon and Medical Teaching in Italian Universities after 1500*, Princeton (Princeton University Press), 1987. There were at least sixty full or partial new editions of the *Canon* between 1500 and 1674 (Siraisi, p. 3).

[32] See Owsei Temkin, *Galenism. Rise and Fall of a Medical Philosophy*, Ithaca and London (Cornell University Press), 1973, p. 128; but according to Siraisi, *Avicenna*, pp. 14, 143, the effect on medical teaching was negligible.

[33] Temkin, *Galenism*, p. 168.

his translation of Galen's *Tegni* (now called the *Ars Parva*).[34] A hundred years after the Bolognese oaths were finally abandoned, graduation exercises in Oxford included the candidate giving six solemn lectures on works by Galen.[35] It is likely that these statutory prescriptions were vehicles for modern discussions, perhaps on how to interpret Hippocrates and Galen (on whom the Regius Professor had to lecture),[36] but their persistence indicates that in a corporation continuity meant stability.

We shall return to the persistence of Galenism in a later chapter; here we must return to the changes in natural philosophy that had direct repercussions on medicine. Two names well known in the history of philosophy concern us first: Bernadino Telesio (1509–88) and Francesco Patrizi da Cherso (1529–97). Telesio was opposed to both Galen and Aristotle, denying, for example, that the soul was the form of the body or that it was the result of the complexion of the body. His training was in philosophy and mathematics (in Padua) which gave him little 'classroom faith' in physical philosophy or medicine. He was a man of the schools only in the sense of setting up his own academy to teach his own philosophy.[37] Part of it was a scepticism about attaining a full knowledge of things, a knowledge that drew largely on sense experience. For him the active forces of the world were heat and cold, and all the parts of the universe were sentient. His *De Rerum Natura* (1565) was put on the Index in 1593 as heretically new (it was the year in which the first Arabic edition of Avicenna's *Canon* appeared in print).[38] Patrizi was even less a man of the schools, acting as secretary to the Venetian nobility and travelling widely. He adopted Platonism, developed a metaphysics of light and proposed in 1591 a new philosophy that he hoped would serve as an ideology for the Catholic Church and reunite Christendom.

---

[34] Indeed, it was the value of bringing Galen's theory to bear on practice that convinced Culpeper of the need for an English version. Culpeper is a microcosm of opposition to traditional medicine. He fulminates against the College of Physicians for its monopoly and its secretive use of Latin and against the Catholics for related practices in religion. He defends Paracelsus and astrology as the Book of Nature, and although rejecting the 'rusty old Authors' of traditional medicine, he presents the Galenic text 'as Primmer to learn Physick by', Galen's last epitome of all he wrote. Nicholas Culpeper, *Galens Art of Physick*, London (Peter Cole), 1652, the address to the reader.

[35] See *Parecbolae sive Excerpta e Corpore Statutorum Universitatis Oxoniensis*, Oxford (Clarendon Press), 1771, p. 54.

[36] *Parecbolae*, p. 18. The Oxford statutes also specify medical disputations. When the candidate lectured on Galen's *De Temperamentis, De Differentiis Febrium, De Usu Partium* or *De Locis Affectis* he gave (as in the Middle Ages) three days' notice by an announcement on the walls of All Souls and Oriel colleges.

[37] Temkin, *Galenism*, p. 145.

[38] See Paul F. Grendler, 'Printing and censorship', in Skinner and Kessler, eds., *Cambridge History of Renaissance Philosophy*, pp. 25–53, at p. 47.

For Patrizi, then, religion and philosophy were almost the same thing, or at least were mutually supportive. In a period of religious unrest it was necessary on all sides that this should be so, and Aristotle's natural philosophy did not always meet with approval. Certainly the Jesuits, such as those in Coimbra, developed a sophisticated and detailed Aristotelianism as part of reinforcing the traditional learned tradition of the church. On the other hand, some Protestants thought that for related reasons Aristotle needed reforming as the church had needed reforming. In Oxford at the end of the sixteenth century, Aristotle's natural philosophy was taught from handbooks in an abbreviated form that in fact made criticism easier; it was also rather defensive.[39]

It is useful to look at the relationship between medicine and philosophy from a third point of view, that of the theologian. While systematic theologies[40] of the mid-sixteenth century can draw readily on the synthesis between Galenic–Hippocratic medicine and Aristotelian natural philosophy that had been evolving since the thirteenth century, by the early seventeenth century it was clear from without that this synthesis could come apart. The relationship between natural philosophy, medicine and religion was close and also complex, and we should not over-emphasise the differences between the religious groups. Natural philosophy in the early seventeenth century remained Aristotelian in a Protestant university like Cambridge, but its textbooks are replete with references to Coimbran and other Jesuits.[41] Lutherans, more often than Calvinists, took readily to the 'book of nature' as a road to God, and from the example set by Melanchthon, Aristotle was studied in many Lutheran universities. Sometimes Lutheran theologians refused to pronounce on a matter that Luther had not dealt with, and turned it over to philosophy.[42] The study of the soul was an essential part of Melanchthon's programme, and he encouraged the use of the new anatomy of Vesalius in conjunction with it. The result

[39] For example, that of John Case, *Ancilla Philosophiae, seu Epitome in Octo Libris Physicorum Aristotelis*, Oxford (J. Barnesius), 1599. A similar textbook available in Cambridge was that of Johannes Magirus (d. 1596), a teacher of natural philosophy in Marburg. Both were opposed to Petrus Ramus, who had denied the Aristotelian doctrine that 'nature' was an internal principle of motion. See Magirus, *Physiologiae Peripateticae*, Wittenberg (Johannes Bernerus), 1609.

[40] For example, Hugo of Strassburg, *Compendium totius Theologicae Veritatis* (collated by Johannes de Combis), Venice, 1554.

[41] In general, Aristotelian scholarship was acceptable to the different Christian confessions. See Luce Giard, 'Remapping knowledge, reshaping institutions', in Stephen Pumphrey, Paolo Rossi and Maurice Slawinski, eds., *Science, Culture and Popular Belief in Renaissance Europe*, Manchester (Manchester University Press), 1991, pp. 19–47, at p. 43.

[42] When Sennert wanted reassurance on the question of whether animals had souls he wrote to a number of German theology faculties, some of which replied that it was a matter of philosophy only, for Luther had not pronounced on the topic. See Daniel Sennert, *Opera Omnia*, pp. 1–18.

in some universities was the teaching of anatomy in the arts course, where students began their training in the truths of their religion.[43]

This complex situation is illustrated by the systematic and Calvinist *De Veritate Religionis Christianae* of Philippe de Mornay, published in Leiden in the early seventeenth century.[44] It is directed expressly at the 'atheists, Epicureans, heathens, Jews and Muslims'. Often these are literary categories, as in the case of Renaissance medical men who had reinvented Galen's enemies as their own (as we saw). But here they are part of de Mornay's real world: there is a new as well as an old Aristotle and Plato; there are Pythagoreans and Academics. They are the *pseudophysici*, who lie about the names of natural things and talk too much about Nature, calling themselves her Disciples, Interpreters, Disquisitors or Dissectors, each to his own sect. These are the new natural philosophers, and de Mornay's major complaint is about the modern Epicureans, who deny the providence and jurisdiction of God. That the atoms moved without purpose in their void had been as offensive to Aristotle as it was to the church, and de Mornay contradicts it with an assertion that God is the governor of everything and 'does nothing in vain', a phrase with Galenic and Aristotelian overtones. But de Mornay's God is not Galen's demiurge or Aristotle's natural purpose, which both rearrange extant matter, but a Creator *ex nihilo*. He knows that 'nothing comes out of nothing' is an axiom of the schools that condenses an Aristotelian argument, and he knows too that to attack it excites resentment in the schools.

Another difficult Aristotelian doctrine was the eternity of the world. By the early seventeenth century this was increasingly seen as a heathen belief – *ethnicus* – and was a criticism of Aristotle at least as strong as it had been in the early thirteenth century. De Mornay attacks it with the argument that the human arts (especially medicine) have a history, demonstrating growth from rude beginnings early in the history of the world.[45] As in the opinion of other Renaissance figures we have met, excellence was the modern result of development, not the full recovery of ancient opinion. The model for de Mornay was perhaps church doctrine, which began to take perfect form only with the birth of Christ: like so many others in defence or justification of a modern novelty or perfection, de Mornay argues that the doctrine of the Trinity was known, but imperfectly, to the old philosophers.[46] His

---

[43] See chapter 5, above.

[44] I have used the edition published in Leiden in 1605 by Andreas Cloucquius.

[45] De Mornay, *Veritate*, pp. 121, 133. Clearly, if religious truths have had a development to reach a perfection, whether Jesuit or Calvinist, defending such positions lends urgency to a theory of development.

[46] Ibid., p. 79.

words have a Renaissance confidence and the new piety of the time. Like Fernel and Riolan, he talks of the magnetic compass as a modern perfection which in his time made possible the circumnavigation of the globe.[47] His piety leads us in another direction that is important for us. The newly explorable globe and the New World are now open to be civilised in the forward progress of all the arts (from old humble origins). The barbarity of Canada, Patagonia, Brazil and Greenland will be replaced by the civilisation we know. But this is not a divided Christendom: de Mornay does not set Calvinists, Lutherans or Catholics against each other and insists that what is common to the heathen and the Jew (and by implication all Christians) is that nature is the same to them and provides a common philosophy and common principles.[48] This is nature as an expression of God as the *rector* of the world and is, in fact, the 'nature' of Natural Law.

We should pause here to reflect on the changes in the relationship between medicine, philosophy and religion. The older Humanists, Hellenists and the searchers after the ancient wisdom of Hermes were, in some sense, looking for a golden age of knowledge to which they could again give birth in a Renaissance, just as the older scholastics had hoped to repair prelapsarian knowledge. But we have now seen a number of examples where the new knowledge and arts of the sixteenth and seventeenth centuries reduced the lustre of the ancient world. In whatever fields the modern world was superior to the ancient, its story was one of development from ruder beginnings. Progress became desirable and history became progressive. While Humanist and Hellenist histories of medicine often stopped with Galen, those written in and beyond the seventeenth century (such as that of Leclerc in 1699) often sought to justify modern medicine.

A progressive view of history was perhaps sharpened by religious sensibilities. First, in the seventeenth century, perhaps in line with a piety of neo-Platonic[49] or Paracelsian origins, the old medical authors began to look pagan. Both Aristotle and Galen looked 'heathen' especially to chemists.[50] Second, the Reformation had made both Catholics and Protestants aware of the superiority of their own form of religion. Quite expressly, the learned tradition of the Catholic church was marked by progress, built up by the church over the centuries. Quite as clearly to Protestants, the Reformation was progress away from decadence. We have seen that medicine could never be totally separated from religion; it is significant that the quotation with which this chapter began is an English translation from the

---

[47] Ibid., p. 4 of preface (not paginated).   [48] Ibid., p. 4 of the preface.
[49] See also Siraisi, *Clock and Mirror*, p. 159.   [50] Temkin, *Galenism*, pp. 164, 167.

Latin text of a Dutchman. In political, educational and religious terms there was some sympathy between Interregnum England and the United Provinces, and the controversy over the circulation of the blood was most vigorous and most favourable in both places. Progressive history has seen the intellectual changes of the seventeenth century as new beginnings, but we have to remember that this is a selective view, centring on England. Leclerc records that in his day there were many Galenic physicians, and we shall see in the next chapter that perfectly traditional texts, and new attempts to rehabilitate Hippocrates, were produced well into the eighteenth century.

BACONIAN EXPERIMENTAL PHILOSOPHY

We have now glanced at a number of challenges to traditional philosophy, from medical men or others whose criticisms helped to lessen the bond between medicine and philosophy. By far the two most important figures in this respect were Francis Bacon (1561–1626) and René Descartes (1596–1650) who were both used extensively by doctors who had to face the collapse of traditional natural philosophy. Bacon was a lawyer (he became solicitor-general in 1607 and lord chancellor in 1618) and represented a professional grouping separate from the theologians, philosophers and medical men. His chief complaint against traditional natural philosophy was that it did not reveal the truth of the natural world, and had no means of doing so. His answer to the problem was to work out a method that *would* lead to the truth. He did not construct a system that would replace that of Aristotle but made suggestions about procedure that were widely read.

This is no place to go into the details of Bacon's proposals for natural philosophy.[51] Its salient points were firstly that the method was collaborative. No single mind could hope to gather enough information. Perhaps his model was legal, for his attention was given to assaying 'witness' reports of the natural world. The method was inductive and experimental, quite the opposite of traditional natural philosophy. Whether or not medicine was also a model, doctors could see in the inductive method a reflection of their enduring concern with the rival claims of observation and reason in medicine. Likewise, the medical experiment – especially vivisection – had a long history, extending back through Vesalius to Galen and Herophilus. Learned doctors also knew the rationalist Galen's appreciation of empirical

---

[51] For Bacon, see Stephen Gaukroger, *Francis Bacon and the Transformation of Early-Modern Philosophy*, Cambridge (Cambridge University Press), 2001.

observation and of Aristotle's collected *historiae* and recognised at least the principles of Bacon's programme.

It was a programme designed to replace not only Aristotle's natural philosophy, but the logic that introduced and supported it. Aristotle's logical works were collectively known as the *Organon*, the 'instrument' of rational thought. Bacon's *Novum Organum* of 1620 was to supply the rational method that was complementary to such works as the *Advancement of Learning* (1605) and its bigger Latin version, the *De Dignitate et Augmentis Scientiarum* of 1623. Together, these were ways of generating knowledge – we would call it research – and it was to be useful knowledge, for practical ends. Again, the medical men, who all agreed that medicine was a practical and useful business, however much it was also a theoretical *scientia*, recognised the link between intellectual procedures and principles, and practical application.[52] Although in contradistinction to traditional natural philosophy, Bacon's method was to generate practical and truer knowledge of the natural world, yet he saw that the old philosophy had a social function almost independent of its content, or truth-value: as long as everyone agreed with it, it contributed to the stability of society.

CARTESIAN MECHANISM

Descartes' attack on traditional natural philosophy was fundamentally different from that of Bacon. Again (because this is not a history of philosophy), space does not permit a detailed analysis of it and we can note only those parts that related more or less directly to medicine.[53] Descartes was educated badly by the Jesuits: that is, they did not convince him of the things that Jesuits usually did convince people of. In pulling down the house of knowledge and starting again, Descartes could not at first even believe in the existence of himself or of God. This scandalised later theologians (which had a direct effect on his attempts to promote his philosophy). Arguing that a falsity cannot be imposed upon a sceptic, he proved himself to exist (*dubito ergo sum* would be a better rendering of the traditional phrase) and then that God existed. Because God was not a deceiver, argued Descartes, any clear and simple idea that Descartes entertained must be

---

[52] Medical men would not, however, agree that Hippocrates, still widely respected as the Father of Medicine, was a 'quack' offering 'a few sophisms sheltered from correction by their curt ambiguity': Bacon's rejection of the ancients was complete. See Gaukroger, *Francis Bacon*, pp. 106–7.

[53] In general see G. A. Lindeboom, *Descartes and Medicine*, Amsterdam (Rodopi), 1979. On Descartes' search for medical knowledge (announced as his final task at the end of the *Discourse on Method*), see his *Oeuvres*, ed. C. Adam and P. Tannery, Paris, 1896–1913, vol 3, pp. 443, 456–7, 459, 462.

true. His clear and simple ideas about the natural world were mainly that it consisted of particles in motion. They were all in contact (there was no void) and so the doctrine was not strictly atomism, although it could not be wholly untouched by the contemporary interest in Lucretius. Together, atoms constituted matter, which God had created as extended unthinking substance; God had also created motion, and thirdly, the soul, which was unextended thinking substance.

The term 'soul' had none of the intellectual baggage of *anima*, no connotations of Greek philosophy that included the powers of nutrition, motion, growth, generation and so on.[54] All these faculties were accounted for *mechanically*, by the motion of the particles. This had two important consequences for medicine. The first was that because all motion was by impact or pressure of particles there could be no power of attraction. Galenic medicine had made much of the power of hollow organs to attract, retain, digest and expel, linking these powers to the three kinds of fibres that made up hollow organs and faculties of the soul that controlled these organs. Attraction also looked impossible to the new philosophers because it appeared to be action at a distance, without any means of exercising itself. In this respect Descartes' doctrine was also radically different from the different kinds of neo-Platonism we have glanced at, for the neo-Platonic world was full of sympathies, antipathies and macro–microcosmic relationships across distances and explained by the sentience of the parts or a flow of *spiritus*. The 'neo-Platonic' magnet or compass needle sympathised with iron or the pole and was celebrated for the fact, as well as for being an example of the superiority of modern inventions (as we saw with Fernel and others). The medical man knew of sympathies in the body, one of which was explained by the doctrine of 'community of origin' where two parts felt each other's pain by reason of an embryonic connection, lost in the adult body. In contrast, the 'mechanical' or 'corpuscular' magnet demanded an explanation in terms of a flow of strangely shaped corpuscles.

The second consequence of the mechanical philosophy, particularly that of Descartes, for medicine was that because the particles moved mechanically by contact, there was no *purpose* in nature. To be sure, God had designed the world rationally, but so that it ran like a machine. This cut directly

---

[54] The theologians, long since accommodated to traditional medical-philosophical accounts of the heart's action, were indignant at the loss of the traditional faculties of the soul in the heart. One of them was Libert Froidment (1587–1653), to whom Descartes had sent a review copy of the *Discourse on Method*. Froidment replied with a traditional account of the soul (Fromondus, *Philosophiae Christianae de Anima libri quatuor*, Louvain (Hieronymus Nempaeus), 1649) and was not wholly opposed to the notion of circulation of the blood.

through the complex system of medical causality in which the 'similar' parts of the body had an 'action' and the organs a purpose and a use, all subsumed under the purpose of enabling the animal to live and live well. Secondly, the mechanical philosophy also destroyed Aristotle's 'nature', the purposeful actions of the animal to fulfil its potentiality and achieve its full adult form. Thirdly, it did nothing to reinforce the Galenic and Platonic notion of a rational and providential demiurge. Lastly, it ran counter to what was an apparently Aristotelian dictum that 'nature abhors a vacuum'. We have seen that Aristotle had a number of reasons for saying that no such thing as a vacuum existed, but this dictum is a late compression and alteration of what he had said. Renaissance engineers thought that water followed the rising piston in what we would call a suction pump *in order* to stop the formation of a vacuum; this is what nature abhorred, and the purposefulness of the action seemed like local sentience acting in an appropriate way to prevent it. The new philosophers could not agree with this, nor accept that 'suction' in a suction pump or medical cupping glass or syringe was a kind of attraction, and rival theories were constructed to explain how it was all done by particles.

WILLIAM HARVEY (1578–1657)

The discovery of the circulation

Harvey was as rational and learned as any doctor of the time. Yet, if we adhere to the programme and terms adopted in this book, he was also a failure. People thought him mad and his practice fell away. A peer wrote to his daughter warning her that it was a mistake to have a physician with too much imagination. His opponents reasonably pointed out that the doctrine of circulation would destroy not only the theory of medicine but also the major therapeutic technique of selective blood-letting. They considered that traditional theory and practice had served them well enough and that change was destructive. In our terms the medicine they professed and practised had evolved expectations on the part of patients that the doctor had helped to form and was largely able to meet. It need hardly be added that Harvey's failure is not a question of his clinical effectiveness, about which we can form no idea.[55]

---

[55] See Jerome J. Bylebyl, ed., *William Harvey and his Age. The Professional and Social Context of the Circulation*, Baltimore (The Johns Hopkins University Press), 1979.

While there is not the space here to tell Harvey's story in detail, there are nevertheless things we must note because the discovery of the circulation was a major factor in the loss of traditional theory and the consequent difficulties of the doctors. It is something of a paradox that Harvey was a traditionalist and a great admirer of the ancients, especially Aristotle, at a time when they were coming increasingly under attack and when his own work was eagerly adopted by the opponents of Aristotelianism. Harvey made the acquaintance of late Renaissance Aristotelianism in Cambridge. In Padua, where he took his medical degree in 1602, Aristotle was treated differently. Harvey's teacher, Fabricius of Aquapendente, was interested in Aristotle's works on animals. He reconstructed what he took to be Aristotle's method and applied it to organs and organ-systems of animals with the purpose of generating new knowledge about them.[56]

Returning to England, Harvey became a fellow of the College of Physicians. The college had a monopoly of the practice of internal medicine in London, and the qualifying procedures for candidates for membership were strict: essentially, an examination in Galenism. The college also expected its members to know the works of Hippocrates, and to be able to conduct a dissection of the human body. Harvey was elected to the Lumleian lectureship in anatomy and gave his first lecture in 1616. The endowment of the lectureship was intended for a cycle of lectures for medical and surgical purposes, which were to be given partly in English – but Harvey's lectures were in Latin and not surgical. His anatomy was, in fact, philosophical: when justifying or explaining their business, anatomists commonly gave a short list of the purposes of anatomy, on which its use to medicine generally came third or fourth. In first place was either the religious purpose of demonstrating the work of the Creator, or the uses to philosophy.

Harvey's philosophy was that of Aristotle and Fabricius, together with the experimental method of the medical tradition through from Galen to the Italian anatomist Realdo Colombo (1516–59). When he came to deal with the heart, Harvey found some terminological confusion in the work of Colombo, which he decided to clarify by experimental vivisections of animals. It was a question of identifying correctly the diastolic and systolic phases of the heart's motion, when it is expanding and when it is

---

[56] See A. R. Cunningham, 'Fabricius and the "Aristotle project" in anatomical teaching and research at Padua', in A. Wear, R. K. French and I. M. Lonie, *The Medical Renaissance of the Sixteenth Century*, Cambridge (Cambridge University Press), 1985, pp. 195–222; on Padua in general see J. J. Bylebyl, 'The school of Padua: humanistic medicine in the sixteenth century', in Charles Webster, ed., *Health, Medicine and Mortality in the Sixteenth Century*, Cambridge (Cambridge University Press), 1979, pp. 335–70.

contracting. Galen had argued that the heart expanded forcibly, sucking blood out of the vena cava, and that the aorta then expanded forcibly, sucking blood from the relaxing heart and making the arterial pulse. But in the living animal, Harvey could not see expansion and contraction, only a forcible elevation of the heart followed by a relaxation. He decided on theoretical grounds that the forcible elevation of the heart was its 'proper' motion, the one most directly concerned with its function; and experimentally (by puncturing an artery) he showed that the elevation of the heart was a forcible *contraction* that expelled blood into the passive arteries, making the pulse.

Harvey was proud of his discovery of the forceful systole, which he saw as correcting an error that had been part of the medical tradition since before Galen, and he taught it in the lectures. Naturally, in a Galenic institution he found opposition and was compelled to carry out further vivisections to provide additional evidence. To make the case for an active systole he emphasised the force and amount of the blood emerging from the heart. He made a modest estimate of the difference in volume between a relaxed and a contracted ventricle, which corresponded with the amount of blood ejected at every beat. But when he added up the amounts of blood emerging over an hour or a whole day from a heart beating about 70 times a minute he saw that it was impossibly large. Such a quantity of arterial blood could not be absorbed by the body, as Galen said it was, nor could the venous blood entering the heart from the liver be produced in sufficient quantity from food, as Galenic theory maintained. It was a moment of crisis. Harvey's new doctrine of forceful systole seemed at risk, yet his demonstrations seemed incontrovertible. Then he remembered the recent discovery of valves in the veins, the purpose of which seemed to be to slow down the centrifugal flow of blood to prevent it from accumulating in the legs. But Harvey and Colombo had already decided that valves such as those in the heart imposed a unidirectional flow and did not allow a partial leakage in the reverse direction (as Galen claimed of the valves of the heart): if the valves in the veins were real valves, they controlled the centripetal flow of blood, from the tissues back to the heart.

Institutional Galenism

Harvey made his discovery of the circulation in about 1618 and taught it in the anatomy lectures for about nine years before publishing *De Motu Cordis* in 1628. In that time he disputed the thesis with his colleagues in the manner of a university, with the president of the College of Physicians

acting as *praeses*, the adjudicating master. The book itself is also formally
structured as an academic exercise in a way that would meet the expectations
of an educated readership across Europe.[57] The new doctrines and the
book met with a very mixed reception. The college was justifiably nervous
that it would be seen as endorsing the book, and took steps to distance
itself from it. Parigiano, who was a member of the Venetian College of
Physicians, and an outspoken opponent of Harvey, did indeed regard the
book as expressing the London College's opinion, and was sarcastic about
what could be seen and heard in London but not in Venice. The London
College was concerned that so great a novelty would destroy the image
of learned Galenism with which they maintained their reputation. They
were already in conflict with doctors who professed a chemical medicine
and who resented the monopoly of the college, and they disliked men who
talked in terms of the particles and mechanism of nature.

In other words, for a long time the college wore a Galenic mask for
professional purposes. Harvey, like Bacon, saw that the old philosophy,
however wrong, at least generated unity of belief. In a similar way, Harvey,
as censor of the college, examined candidates on their Galenism even after
he had discovered the circulation. He saw that his opponent in Paris, the
great anatomist Jean Riolan (the Younger), also maintained a Galenism for
reasons connected to the professional reputation of the Paris faculty.[58] It
seems likely that in Montpellier they also maintained a face of corporate
Galenism until at least 1650, when Lazarus Riverius was called on to resign
for teaching the circulation.[59]

---

[57] For the view that the book was written in two halves, the first before he had made the discovery, see
Jerome J. Bylebyl, 'The growth of Harvey's *De Motu Cordis*', *Bulletin of the History of Medicine*, 47
(1973) 427–70. But the formal nature of an academic exercise meant that the discovery was presented
in its proper place; likewise Harvey's treatise on animal motion deals with the necessary preliminaries
before mentioning 'muscle', about half way through. For an extended discussion of the point and its
associated secondary literature, see Roger French, *William Harvey's Natural Philosophy*, Cambridge
(Cambridge University Press), 1994, ch. 5.

[58] As Harvey said, Riolan could be seen as speaking not personally, but officially: 'It was doubtless
fitting for the Dean of the College of Paris to keep Galen's medicine in good repair . . . lest (as
he says) the precepts and dogmata of the physicians be disturbed, and lest the pathology which
has obtained for so many years, with the agreement of the physicians . . . be corrupted.' Harvey to
Schlegel, 1651: Harvey, *The Circulation of the Blood and other Writings*, trans. Kenneth J. Franklin,
London (Dent: Everyman's Library), 1963, p. 185. See also Harold Cook, 'Institutional structures and
personal belief in the London College of Physicians', in Ole Grell and Andrew Cunningham, eds.,
Religio Medici. Medicine and Religion in Seventeenth-Century England, Aldershot (Scolar Press), 1996,
pp. 91–114.

[59] See William Richard Lefanu, 'Jean Martet, a French follower of Harvey', in E. Ashworth Under-
wood, ed., *Science, Medicine and History. Essays on the Evolution of Scientific Thought and Medical
Practice written in honour of Charles Singer*, 2 vols., Oxford (Oxford University Press), 1953, vol. 2,
pp. 33–40.

CONTROVERSIES

If we look forward for a moment and outline the fortunes of Harvey's doctrines of the forceful systole and the circulation of the blood in the period before he died, there are obvious signs of a division of opinion along religious lines. About two dozen men were concerned enough to express their approval in print. Almost all of them were from northern Europe and most often Protestant. Robert Fludd, Thomas Bartholin, Johannes Walaeus and his student Roger Drake, Jacobus de Back, George Ent, Albert Kyper, Anton Vesling, Herman Conring and Olaus Rudbeck are some of the better known names; Descartes and Henricus Regius (whom we shall meet later) are exceptions in the sense that their radical philosophy could not readily be given a religious position. In Louvain, the Catholic Vobiscus Fortunatus Plemp (1601–71) changed his mind, at first rejecting the circulation and then becoming its defender. At first he was a stout defender of Arabic and Latin medicine, translating parts of the *Canon*. He regarded the Hippocratic works as equivalent to the Bible in containing revealed knowledge; Avicenna is the Aquinas of medicine, bringing order to earlier diffuse works (of Galen and Augustine). He called his textbook the 'foundations' of medicine;[60] yet in its second edition he supported Harvey. What had happened was that he had read Harvey properly and disengaged the doctrine of circulation from Cartesian mechanism, a much more offensive novelty. This exposed Harvey's experiments as persuasive.

Harvey's opponents were generally from the south and most often seem to have been Catholic. Only about ten of them wrote opinions significant enough for us to make judgements about. The most voluble were Parigiano and Riolan, whom we have met. Parigiano the Venetian brought his religion to bear directly on his medicine and regarded Harvey with distaste. His anatomy began with the brain of man as the seat of the Christian immortal soul, which generated the body. The perfection of the body was a reflection of the glory of God. Parigiano could therefore see no point whatsoever in descending with Harvey into the realms of vile, disgusting and imperfect animals which poisoned the senses and intellect and were at such a great distance from man's almost divine perfection. Harvey's Aristotle project and experiments were of no importance.[61] In contrast, Marco Aurelio Severino,

---

[60] V. F. Plemp, *Fundamenta Medicinae*, Louvain (Hieronymus Nempaeus), 1654 (first edition before 1644).
[61] William Harvey, *De Motu Cordis et Sanguinis in Animalibus, Anatomica Exercitatio. Cum Refutation-ibus Aemylii Romani, Philosophi, ac Medici Veneti et Jacobi Primirosii in Londonensi Collegio doctoris*, Leiden (Ioannes Maire), 1639.

an Italian with Reformist tendencies, not only agreed with Harvey but set forth a whole new philosophy – zootomia – based on dissection and experiment.[62]

In Catholic eyes there was a clear connection between the new heresy of the reformers and novelties in medicine and philosophy. What the heresy was attempting to destroy was the learned tradition of the church. Because of the authority of the church this tradition had extended to all learning, including that of medicine and philosophy, that is, what we are calling in this book the Latin medical tradition. We have seen that the Counter-Reformation came to stress the learned tradition in the sixteenth century, and here it is useful to glance at a figure who counted for a good deal in the seventeenth. It is Robert Bellarmine, a Jesuit, member of the Inquisition and friend of Galileo. As a theologian he was a controversialist; for example, he disputed with James I of England on the subject of the divine right of kings (which, it was generally held in England and France, could enable the Royal Touch to cure scrophula). In rebutting the theologies of Luther, Calvin and Zwingli, Bellarmine gives force to the learned tradition: revelation is the written word of God, tradition the unwritten. Tradition is God's word expressed by the apostles and, notably, by the church. The latter 'ecclesiastical tradition', says Bellarmine, has the same force as decrees and constitutions of the church. Thus the humanly written tradition has divine authority, the point uppermost in Bellarmine's mind when directing this argument against the Protestants who thought that the revealed knowledge of the Bible was enough.[63] The authority of the tradition went back ultimately to the transfer of Roman power to the church;[64] it gained its greatest philosophical strength from the Aristotelianism of Aquinas. For Bellarmine, even the councils of the church have the four Aristotelian causes.[65]

There is a sense in which Bellarmine sees that the Protestants had replaced 'tradition' with 'nature' as a second book in which God's words might be read. He devotes little space to 'nature'. Indeed, the first question in 'naturals', he says, is whether faith is needed to recognise a natural truth. Is not the human mind so damaged by sin as to be unable by natural forces alone to recognise any natural, mechanical truth?[66] He allows that natural cognition, which is also theoretical or 'mechanical' in belonging

---

[62] The story of the reaction to Harvey's doctrines across Europe is given in French, *William Harvey's Natural Philosophy* and need not be repeated here.

[63] *Roberti Bellarmini Politiani S.R.E. Cardinalis Solida Christianae Fidei Demonstratio*, Antwerp (Martinus Nutius), 1611, p. 24. The volume was put together by Baldvinus Iunius from various controversies.

[64] Ibid., p. 143.   [65] Ibid., p. 156.   [66] Ibid., p. 782.

to the lowest level of human activity, is akin to the productive arts. At the intermediate level is moral cognition and at the highest, supernatural, supplied only by revelation. While some Protestants saw the hand of God in the fabric of the human body as clearly as Caesar's face appeared on coins, or felt themselves in a theatre of creation where God was so close that it was almost possible to reach out and touch him, it remained a major question for Bellarmine whether the light of reason, without the special help of grace, could prove the existence and singleness of God.

Bellarmine's book was assembled from his arguments in controversies. Topics such as the perfection of Christ and his descent into hell were controversies, and the term passed readily into other disciplines. In medicine by the seventeenth century there were controversies that at least potentially weakened the traditional system from within. One such concerned whether venous blood passed through the interventricular septum of the heart and became arterial, as Galen had claimed. This particular controversy had been created by Realdo Colombo and Michael Servetus in the previous century. They had thought that the septum was not pervious and that blood instead went through the lungs from right to left ventricle. Servetus thought that it was in the lungs that the divine spirit entered the blood, but Calvin had him burned, along with his book, and the subsequent controversy centred on Colombo. Before Harvey there was a controversy about the lacteals,[67] and the controversy over the circulation ended in Harvey's favour largely when an interesting new controversy – on the lymphatic vessels[68] – eclipsed it. In some sense a controversy replaced the disputed question as a device for generating knowledge. Contenders often published series of pamphlets of increasing bitterness in a way that was not possible in the Middle Ages, and medical controversies often involved experiments. Controversies naturally appeared in medical topics where there were religious or philosophical differences between the parties. These differences were an aspect of the collapse of the Latin tradition, of which we are concerned with the philosophical and hence medical component.

Controversies also reveal a new aspect of the universities in the seventeenth century. While medical students were generally there to obtain professional qualifications, the same was not true of all arts students. It has

[67] The problem of the lacteal vessels, described by Gaspare Aselli in 1622, was that they seemed to be involved in the process of converting food into blood, yet contained only a milky liquid and did not share the function of the portal vein, which was thought to convey chyle from the intestines to the liver (where blood was made).

[68] The lymphatics were described by Olaus Rudbeck, who had been born in the year Harvey published *De Motu Cordis*. See Sten Lindroth, 'Harvey, Descartes and the young Olaus Rudbeck', *Journal of the History of Medicine and Allied Sciences*, 12 (1957) 209–19.

often been pointed out that the new prosperous middle classes in England, for example, might send their sons to Oxford and Cambridge as finishing schools; and in a later chapter we shall look at gentlemanly education in the Italian universities. It was not always necessary for such men in England to obtain the degree from the university, and they could enter into what was essentially a private contract with their college tutor. These students included those sometimes called the *virtuosi* at the time of the 'scientific revolution' and, not needing to adhere to university statutes, they could take up experimental and mechanical philosophy with enthusiasm, thus weakening traditional philosophy. In medicine, students were fascinated by the novelties in controversies and their teachers felt obliged to resolve such questions. They might do so by experiment, followed by disputation and even the construction of a textbook.

MECHANISM AND CIRCULATION

The controversies over the circulation of the blood and Cartesian mechanism became closely related in a paradoxical way. Descartes read Harvey's book in about 1630 and decided that Harvey's doctrine of the circulation was the ideal vehicle for his own mechanism, – from the single motion of the circulation of blood he could derive, by particle-to-particle impulsion, all the other motions of the body. Aware that he might be attacked like Galileo, Descartes tended to be circumspect in expressing his notions of mechanism, but in his *Discourse on Method* he was unusually confident and forthright about the motion of the heart and blood. It was a centre-piece of his mechanism and he said that if his account were not true, the whole of his philosophy would fail. It was paradoxical, then, that Harvey's doctrine should be carried to many readers on the back of Descartes' new philosophy, which was entirely foreign to Harvey, that staunch admirer of Aristotle.

But Descartes disagreed with Harvey in one important respect. Descartes could not allow that the heart contracted forcibly – Harvey's first discovery – because it implied that the parts of the heart were *attracting* one another, illicit in the new philosophy. He proposed therefore that blood entering the heart drop by drop was vapourised by the heat of the heart and expanded, forcing its way across the valves before condensing in the aorta. Again, many people first met the idea of the circulation in this form and treated it as a part of the new mechanical philosophy. We can form some idea of their response because Descartes sent out review copies of the *Discourse* and engaged in correspondence with his reviewers. Some rejected mechanism entirely, arguing that the soul played its traditional role in moving the heart.[69] Others argued that the heat of the heart was entirely insufficient to vapourise the blood. Others made vivisectional experiments, showing that pieces of a living heart contracted in circumstances that made inflation impossible. Descartes was driven to make experiments himself and modified the doctrine of inflation, which became something closer to an intestinal fermentation.

Descartes had ambitions. He had constructed a new philosophy of nature and wanted to become the New Philosopher to replace Aristotle. Like Bacon, he saw that this natural philosophy had to be supported by a new form of rationality in the same way as Aristotle's natural philosophy rested on the logical works that the student met earlier in the arts course. Descartes also saw that arts-course philosophy in its turn supported medicine. His own philosophy could not, of course, support traditional medicine with its Galenic and Aristotelian theory, and Descartes began to construct a mechanical medicine on his own principles. It seems that he was constructing a package of academic subjects of the same curricular 'shape' as the traditional philosophy and medicine that he was trying to displace.

This is suggested too by the fact that Descartes chose a medical man in his bid to insert his own philosophy into the universities. This man was Henricus Regius in Utrecht, who had written to Descartes expressing admiration of the new philosophy, and the mechanism they used was the disputation. As in the Middle Ages this consisted of the promulgation and defence of a thesis, but contemporary discussions about the nature of university disputations indicate that arguments drawn from sensory observation were considered valid.[70] Indeed, some university masters engaged in the controversy over the circulation of the blood by defending theses they had developed in formal disputations and verified by vivisection. Descartes was not a university teacher and needed Regius to propose the theses. Normally Descartes made the suggestion, Regius drew up a formal thesis for Descartes' approval and the thesis was accordingly offered for disputation. Sometimes Descartes would listen from a concealed room. The Utrecht theologians were not at all happy that there should be in their university these echoes of a philosophy that had begun with a doubt as to the existence of God. Then Regius went too far. His topic was the Cartesian

---

[69] As we have seen, an example is Libert Froidmont, a teacher of Plemp. See also Descartes, *Oeuvres*, ed. Adam and Tannery, vol. 1, p. 399 (Plemp to Descartes).

[70] See Adriaan Heerebord, *Ermeneia* [Ἑρμηνεία] *Logica: seu Explicatio tum per Notas tum per Exempla Synopsis Logicae Burgersdicianae . . . accedit ejusdem Auctoris Praxis Logica*, Leiden (David à Lodensteyn and Severyn Matthysz), 1650.

distinction between soul as unextended thinking substance and matter as extended non-thinking substance. The thesis he tried to sustain was that man was a being in which matter – the body – and soul were united 'accidentally' rather than essentially. Moreover, this time Regius had not sought Descartes' approval. Descartes was horrified, the theologians were scandalised and the students rioted. The university banned philosophical novelties and ordered that Aristotle should be the basis of all philosophical disputation: above all, Aristotle was safe.

CHAPTER 7

Resolutions

INTRODUCTION

Few histories of medicine are without an evolutionary approach. Histories adopting this approach are not now generally 'whiggish', but they invariably give much attention to signposts indicating the direction of the road and bearing legends such as 'mechanism' or 'circulation'. Many of these directional milestones are clustered in England and the United Provinces of Holland, and, even in the seventeenth century, medical mechanism could be seen by a major figure in Paris as so much modern Dutch nonsense.[1] But as we have seen, Learned and Rational Doctors were successful in the familiar territory of traditional natural philosophy where they did not need signposts or milestones. This was mostly the case in Catholic countries such as Italy and Spain,[2] and we have glanced at some probable religious reasons for this. In Spain in particular, the universities were happy to do without the new doctrines from England and Holland, and viewed with suspicion the instrument of their dissemination, the *tertulia*, which were private associations. In 1700 the rector of the University of Seville wrote to his counterpart in Osuna urging the destruction of a *tertulia*. These organisations co-operated, he said, with the object of destroying the Aristotelianism and Galenism of the schools.[3] There were also political and economic circumstances that seem to bear on the matter. The economic centre of gravity of Europe was moving north. Spain was finding it difficult to sustain its colonial empire, which had grown so rapidly in the early sixteenth century, almost as if the conquerors of South America were the descendants of the

---

[1] See J. Riolan (the Younger), *Opuscula Anatomica Nova. Quae nunc primum in lucem prodeunt. Instauratio magna Physicae et Medicinae per Novam Doctrinam de Motu Circulatorio in Sanguinis in Corde*, London (M. Flesher), 1649, p. 49.

[2] On the position of the new philosophy in Spain, see W. G. L. Randles, *The Unmaking of the Medieval Christian Cosmos, 1500–1760. From Solid Heavens to Boundless Æther*, Aldershot (Ashgate), 1999, p. 168.

[3] Much of his rhetoric was directed against the new Royal Society of Medicine in Seville. Randles, *Christian Cosmos*, p. 204.

re-conquerors of Muslim Spain. Italy was slowly losing its economic dominance. But a century or more later it was England, now increasingly prosperous, that was colonising North America; and at the same time Holland, having released itself from Spanish rule, was becoming a rich maritime trading nation, also with overseas possessions. Leiden supplanted Padua as the premier medical school of Europe and it taught medicine of a new kind, gathered from the novelties – mechanism, chemistry and circulation among them – that were seen as actual or potential heresies further south.

THE CRISIS IN PHILOSOPHY

It was in the north that the doctors faced the crisis of the collapse of natural philosophy. Even in the universities Aristotle ultimately lost his position as The Philosopher, and his moral and natural philosophy was replaced by the disciplines of natural law (see below). The law of nature and nations was cultivated by Protestants because they had rejected Canon Law, and the 'customary law' of the north differed widely from Civil Law; moreover, the 'law of nations' was useful in commerce with nation states of differing natures. The law of nature could be accommodated to some form of mechanism,[4] but since it was all, ultimately, the law of God, this was not contentious.

Indeed, it was the divinity of nature that made natural philosophy possible. The broad spread of scepticism, often called Pyrrhonism, which extended from Gassendi to Boyle, denied explanations of nature that rested on the intellectual 'system' of a single man, whether Aristotle or Descartes.[5] Experimental observations, especially when repeated in front of witnesses, could be relied on, but inferences drawn from them were limited to 'probable knowledge': there was no demonstrable knowledge, nothing *propter quid*. Yet no one could deny that the natural world was God's handiwork, or that God was rational and beneficent. This is what made the study of natural things attractive and instructive: the rationality of any philosophy of nature lay in the natural world itself.

---

[4] See, for example, Martin Heinrich Otto, *Elementa Iuris Naturae et Gentium una cum Delineatione Iuris Positivi Universalis*, Halle, 1738. Natural actions in man are those that occur mechanically from the structure and force given to the body by God. Halle was the Pietist university of Friedrich Hoffmann (see below) where Christian Wolf wrote an *Institutiones* of natural law in 1750. See his *Jus Gentium Methodo Scientifica Pertractum*, 2 vols., Oxford (Clarendon Press), 1934.

[5] As observed by J-B. Pittion, 'Scepticism and medicine in the Renaissance', in Richard H. Popkin and Charles B. Schmitt, eds., *Scepticism from the Renaissance to Enlightenment*, Weisbaden (O. Harrassowitz), 1987, pp. 103–32, at p. 105, medicine had its own internal history of scepticism, drawn largely from Sextus Empiricus, which became popular again in the late sixteenth century.

The doctors were compelled to consider what they had indignantly rejected for centuries, namely that medicine was an empirical art, not a rational *scientia*. It was argued by Nathaniel Highmore that 'demonstration', the traditional mark of a 'science', belonged only to geometry and was impossible in medicine. Highmore was English and was attacking James Primrose, Harvey's opponent, whose 'system' was the traditional Aristotelian/Galenic synthesis. Highmore uses the language of the experimenters, saying that knowledge is only probable.[6] In France, Pierre Gassendi asserted that the whole business of medicine was conjectural, even the circulation of the blood.[7] In Holland the professor of medicine at Leiden (where there had been troubles similar to those at Utrecht over the Cartesian system) was Albert Kyper, who declared that medicine was not part of reasoned knowledge, but an art, depending on experience and observation. Now, while the practitioner had lost the support of traditional natural philosophy in telling a good story to his patients, a teacher stood to lose much more. If medicine really was an art of experience and observation, it could hardly be taught in a classroom, with words and the usual formal devices of exposition. Kyper had no wish to remove medicine from the universities and make himself and his kind redundant, and he struggled to come to terms with the implications of his belief. Indeed, he wrote a textbook to show that medicine was an autonomous art, separate from the systems of Descartes and Aristotle.[8] His purpose was to guide his students out of the crisis of philosophy, to steer, in his words, between Scylla and Charybdis. Traditional medical learning was a hindrance, not a help, and one of his aphorisms was that 'a learned doctor is a bad practitioner'.[9] This was, of course, exactly the opposite of what university doctors had been claiming since the Middle Ages, and is a sure sign of the crisis of the middle of the seventeenth century. There were other reasons for the crisis being felt so sharply in Holland, for as Kyper explains in his dedication, having thrown off the yoke of Spanish and Catholic rule, now is the time to cultivate true religion and true knowledge.

---

[6] Nathaniel Highmore, *Corporis Humani Disquisitio Anatomica*, The Hague (Samuel Broun), 1651, p. 149: *Ars Medica non est demonstrationibus ornata . . . nobis sufficiat ex probabili ratiocinari*. See also Steven Shapin and Simon Schaffer, *Leviathan and the Air-Pump: Hobbes, Boyle, and the Experimental Life*, Princeton (Princeton University Press), 1985.

[7] Pierre Gassendi, *Discours Sceptique sur la passage du Chyle & sur le Mouvement du Coeur*, Leiden (Jean Maire), 1648, p. 56. Gassendi did not put his name on the title-page, giving only the initials S. S., but the identity of the author was known for example to Jean Riolan, *Notationes in tractum clarissimi D. D. Petri Gassendi . . . de Circulatione Sanguinis*, Paris, n.d.

[8] Albert Kyper, *Institutiones Medicae, ad Hypothesin de Circulari Sanguinis Motu compositae. Subiungitur ejusdem Transsumpta Medica, quibus continentur Medicinae Fundamenta*, Amsterdam (Joannes Janssonius), 1654.

[9] *Doctus theoreticus est infelix practicus*. See the address to the reader in the *Transsumpta*.

The Rational and Learned Doctor faced other problems in the middle and second half of the seventeenth century. As the towns and their money economies expanded there was more opportunity for middle-class patients to seek out other kinds of medical practitioner, out of reach of the professional colleges. The London College of Physicians remained comparatively small, a strategy that worked to the advantage of the fellows in previous centuries, but which now diminished their power.[10] Apothecaries and surgeons had professional groupings which grew in power. In 1704 the House of Lords decided that an apothecary could practise internal medicine, thereby challenging the college's old monopoly. As in Paris, the college maintained the professional face of Galenism while Galen was falling rapidly from favour elsewhere. In England, royal patronage of the college ended abruptly with the Interregnum, and its regulatory power dropped off 'precipitously'.[11] Indeed, it was difficult to regulate medicine when it could not be said with certainty what its principles were. In 1678, for example, the favourite of the viceroy of Naples was killed by a chemical remedy administered by a Galenist. When the viceroy asked the profession for guidance, he was told that medicine was so confused that regulation was impossible. It was without rational principles and was not a *scientia*.[12]

CREATING A NEW ORTHODOXY

Kyper chose to call his book the *Institutes of Medicine*, a title often used when a particular form of medicine was to be presented in attempting to lay down a new orthodoxy.[13] What Kyper did was to grasp a few principles which seemed still to be true in natural philosophy and 'bring them over' into medicine. This was precisely the strategy of the medieval doctors who had declared that medicine was an extension of natural philosophy and that the doctor began where the philosopher finished. It will be recalled

[10] On the earlier history of the college, see Sir George Clark, *A History of the Royal College of Physicians of London*, vol. 1, Oxford (Clarendon Press for the College), 1964.

[11] For an introduction to the topic, see Toby Gelfand, 'The history of the medical profession', in W. F. Bynum and Roy Porter, eds., *Companion Encyclopedia of the History of Medicine*, 2 vols., London (Routledge), 1993; vol. 2, pp. 1119–50, at p. 1126.

[12] See Nancy Struever, 'Lionardo di Capoa's *Parere* (1681): a legal opinion on the use of Aristotle in medicine', in Constance Blackwell and Sachiko Kusukawa, eds., *Philosophy in the Sixteenth and Seventeenth Centuries. Conversations with Aristotle*, Aldershot (Ashgate), 1999, pp. 322–66, at p. 322. Di Capoa, like others in uncertain times, wrote a short history of medicine, complaining how the fall of philosophy had brought down medicine too.

[13] A new orthodoxy could, of course, be a reassertion of an old one, as in the *Institutes* of the Hellenist Fuchs (see chapter 6) and the anatomical *Institutes* of Vesalius' teacher Guinter of Andernacht: *Institutionum Anatomicarum secundum Galeni Sententiam, ad Candidatos Medicinae*, Paris (Simon Colinaeus), 1536.

that part of the programme was that such philosophical axioms could not and should not be questioned by the medical man. Kyper was in a difficult position because the old philosophy was discredited and the new was not widespread, detailed or consistent among its proponents. He preferred to speak of *physica* rather than *philosophia*, no doubt to avoid connotations of 'systems'. One of his axioms was the circulation of the blood. Another was that repeated sensory observation can add up to a universal statement of truth. Part of his strategy was to use some of the terms of Aristotle's philosophy, which although discredited as a system, still retained some force of meaning for educated men. Thus, efficient causality seemed explicable, while final causality was impossible. Like Boyle, he saw that nature had an underlying rationality because it was God's creation: in the absence of a philosophical system, this gave coherence and order to the world, even to a sceptic. Kyper is largely traditional on the powers of the soul in the body, and, while siding with the moderns in giving attention to the solid parts of the body rather than the humours, his account of details such as the *humidum radicale* are medieval. He stoutly defends the validity and durability of medical healing procedures despite the changes in theory. While the medievals had discussed the difference between knowledge *propter quid* (largely demonstrated knowledge derived from something else) and knowledge *quia* (simple knowledge of a thing), Kyper uses the more fashionable *to dioti* and *to oti*, giving the dignity of erudition, and his approval, to simple experiential knowledge. This enables him to say that the theory of medicine, with all its faults, is an attempt to understand the human body in general, while the practical art of medicine is a study of particulars in individuals.[14]

THE PHYSICIAN'S LEARNING

There were two areas of traditional medical learning that survived, in a diminished form, the crisis of medical theory. The first was knowledge of the powers of natural substances. This was the most widespread form of medical learning, and even in the days of high theory doctors were always anxious to learn of new substances or new properties. One of the reasons why Philip II of Spain sent a doctor to South America in the first half of the sixteenth century was to explore the new drugs of the New World, and colonial doctors in North America also examined Indian medicine.[15] Indeed, by

---

[14] The *Transsumpta* are separately paginated: this is his Prolegomena, p. 3.
[15] See, for example, Jean de Léry, *History of a Voyage to the Land of Brazil*, trans. Janet Whatley, Berkeley (University of California Press), 1990.

the middle of the seventeenth century so populous were the Americas, with their European culture and medicine, that the northern European crisis in philosophy now seems somewhat parochial. What the knowledge of the powers of substances had lost was the theoretical apparatus, the intension and remission of qualities, the doctrine of change of substantial form in the 'fermentation' of compounds and the mathematics of dosage.

The second survival of the crisis was anatomy.[16] This relied upon sensory observation, experience and experiment, so it suited the sceptical temper of the experimenters and did not necessarily lead to a theoretical system of medicine. Indeed, 'anatomy' in the experimental sense became something of a slogan for the new philosophers, for example for those of the Royal Society. What anatomy lost in the process was the hierarchy of action, use and utility of the similar and compound parts, the final causality that had determined true knowledge of a part, and the faculties of the vital and sensitive aspects of the soul (in particular the faculty of attraction). In short, anatomy became morphological, with an increasing interest in fine structure. In this form, without its theory, anatomy came to be more closely associated with surgery, particularly where taught in private schools outside the universities. But academic anatomy also drew support from the microscope, which revealed structure at an unexpected level. While gross anatomy was sometimes called 'simple' anatomy, it extended not only to fine structure – including fibres – but to 'vital anatomy', chemistry.[17]

EMPIRICISM

We have seen that a number of men thought that medicine was, or should be, after all, an empirical art, not a theoretical *scientia*. This would have made them empirics, the kind of practitioner that the university-trained doctor had denigrated for centuries. But there were ways out. One could, like Kyper, grasp some of the few certainties left in philosophy and rebuild medicine from them, in a rather traditional way. Another escape route was to return to Hippocrates, the Father of Medicine. He had been (by mutual agreement) without many of the sciences and arts that later and weaker medical minds needed to understand the great medical wisdom that underlay Hippocratic texts such as the *Aphorisms* and *Prognosis*. But it was also generally agreed that Hippocrates, although patient, observational and

---

[16] Medical educators saw anatomy not merely as a survivor of the crisis but as an area of growth, particularly when identified with microscopic studies. See J. Antonius Vulpius, *Opuscula Philosophica*, 3rd edn, Padua, 1744, p. 208.

[17] Struever, 'Di Capoa', p. 331.

even experimental, was not an empiric. Many doctors of the seventeenth century and later could call themselves Hippocratics without the odium of empiricism. Indeed, Hippocratic texts remained popular down to the nineteenth century, in contrast to the declining publication of theoretical Galenic texts.

It was possible to be a non-empirical Hippocratic by deciding that what had made Hippocrates great was his *method*. This is what was believed by Thomas Sydenham (1624–89), who was sometimes known as the 'English Hippocrates' and who eschewed theory.[18] He held that the proper method of medicine was twofold: collecting a 'history' of diseases and establishing a method of cure. Hippocrates is the only ancient author he mentions in his preface[19] and it is clear that in part his inspiration comes from the Hippocratic case-histories and the circumstances of the patient given in *Airs, Waters and Places*. But Sydenham is more explicit – he declared that a 'history' of a disease is also what was set out by Francis Bacon in the method of gathering natural histories. Bacon was a useful resource for those caught up in the crisis of theoretical medicine, for he had set out a detailed and influential procedure for discovery while the old theory and, institutionally at least, the old philosophy was intact. Sydenham's quotation from Bacon explains how a true natural history is without fables, philology, disputes or quotations, matters not fit for the 'institutes of philosophy' – that is, in fact, a proposal for a new orthodoxy. What a true Hippocratic–Baconian history would reveal, said Sydenham in essence, was the identity of disease. As he himself put it, diseases ought to be reduced to certain kinds, in the same way as botanists treat plants. This heralds an important change in medicine. We have seen that the preferred kind of practice of the Rational and Learned Doctor was contractual or retained service over a period of time to a community or an individual. We also saw that epidemics like the Black Death and French Disease did not suit this kind of practice at all and that, as a result, diseases acquired a weightier ontology. Sydenham is now saying not only that diseases are things, but that they have similarities and differences that enable them to be classified in the manner of physical objects. He stresses that this classification should be done in the Baconian way, for previous classifications had been made only to support hypotheses

---

[18] Sydenham is generally associated with his friend John Locke and sensory epistemology. See also W. F. Bynum and Roy Porter, eds., *Medicine and the Five Senses*, Cambridge (Cambridge University Press), 1993, introduction. There is a biography by Kenneth Dewhurst, *Dr Thomas Sydenham (1624–1689). His Life and Original Writings*, Berkeley (University of California Press), 1966.

[19] Thomas Sydenham, *The entire Works of Dr Thomas Sydenham, newly made English from the Originals*, ed. John Swan, London (Edward Cave), 1742, preface.

(he is perhaps thinking of types of tumour named after the predominant vitiated humour).

Sydenham believed (with Bacon) that by building up a history from repeated observations, constant symptoms could be distinguished from accidental and (with Hippocrates) that histories are to be correlated with the seasons, for some diseases follow the seasons by a 'secret tendency of nature'. Histories also gave indications of cure, largely by trial and error.[20] This is consistent with Sydenham's belief that no deeper cause than the most immediate is discoverable; and it is also consistent with the language of the experimenters about 'matters of fact' (rather than of theory) and 'probable knowledge'. Sydenham was aware of Boyle's beliefs.[21]

Sydenham's distrust of theory was shared by his friend, the philosopher John Locke, who also practised medicine. Both drew from seventeenth-century scepticism but lived to see a new assertiveness about theory as an answer to the crisis of traditional natural philosophy. 'Theories, that are for the most part but a sort of waking Dreams... I wonder, that after the Pattern Dr Sydenham has set them of a better Way, Men should return again to that Romance Way of Physick'.[22]

Probably Sydenham's ontological concept of disease was related to the nature of his practice. Perhaps for political reasons (he was a Parliamentarian who practised medicine after the Restoration) his work was mainly among the poor. He had to see many of them to make up his income, and they suffered much from epidemic fevers. It was the opposite of being retained and the individual meant less than the disease; possibly too he had greater freedom to experiment with his remedies.

DENIAL

The changes in philosophy were viewed differently across Europe. In Paris the great anatomist Riolan fiercely defended Galen, as his predecessors had done. It was he who had tetchily remarked that mechanism was a newfangled Dutch invention. Ultimately he was compelled to agree – because by now most learned men had agreed – on the changes in medicine, but he tried to claw back his reputation by claiming their discovery for himself. Indeed, he claimed that he was about to reformulate natural philosophy itself

---

[20] He thought that Hippocrates' rules for removing diseases were given in the *Aphorisms* and *Prognosis*.

[21] See Andrew Cunningham, 'Thomas Sydenham: epidemics, experiment and the "Good Old Cause"', in Roger French and Andrew Wear, eds., *The Medical Revolution of the Seventeenth Century*, Cambridge (Cambridge University Press), 1989, pp. 164–90, at p. 180.

[22] See Kenneth Dewhurst, *John Locke (1632–1704) Physician and Philosopher. A Medical Biography*, London (Wellcome), 1963, p. 310.

in a Grand Instauration. But he was by now an old man and it amounted to little; and it fell on deaf ears.

At the other end of France, in common with most Mediterranean countries, the new philosophy looked distant and heretical. Montpellier had for centuries been a famous medical school and men could go there to be trained in rational and learned medicine of the traditional sort. It worked for them as it had done before: in the terms we are using they were successful. In the 1650s the dean of the regius professors there was Lazarus Riverius (1589–1655), who found it desirable to restate traditional medicine in an *Institutes*, a term whose circumstances we have met before. This had a long publishing history: it first appeared in print in 1640 and new editions were brought out regularly until 1737 when the final edition appeared in the form of Riverius' collected works.[23] The appearance of so many editions implies a good market for the book and many readers, but little more can be read into this in terms of historical significance if the editions contain nothing new. (Sir) Thomas Browne went to Riverius' lectures in Montpellier in 1630,[24] when the Latin tradition of medicine had hardly been challenged; Riverius kept it alive for over a century. By the 1650s Riverius was well aware of the changes in philosophy and medicine in other parts of Europe, but for him scepticism and its implications counted for nothing. He asserted that medicine was indeed a *scientia*, capable of demonstration. His was no Hellenist or Humanist revival of ancient learning but a continuation of the medieval tradition. He takes up the medieval question of whether medicine is an art or science and argues on both sides, as a scholastic would. Yes, in being directed to a practical goal, medicine is a productive art; yet on the other hand, it has principles, axioms and demonstrations, founded on nature herself. When he says that these principles are more certain even than those of natural philosophy (*physica*) itself, which are derived from a faith in senses, it is likely that he was thinking of contemporary natural philosophy further north, where its practitioners were refusing to elaborate 'systems' out of sensory experience. For Riverius, medicine was a separate and older discipline than this, with a superior means of demonstration and with its own noble subject, the human body. Unlike the arts, medicine was *learned* and was to be acquired by much reading and the *institutio* of the doctors, a phrase that encapsulates the authority of the medical tradition and which

[23] Lazarus Riverius, *Opera Medica Universa*, Geneva, 1737. Riverius is said to have accepted the circulation of the blood by 1650.
[24] See Charles W. Bodemer, 'Materialistic and Neoplatonic influences in embryology' in Allen G. Debus, ed., *Medicine in Seventeenth Century England. A Symposium held at UCLA in Honor of C. D. O'Malley*, Berkeley (University of California Press), 1974, pp. 183–235, at p. 199.

was built into the title of his book. He uses 'demonstration' not only in its Aristotelian sense but also in a geometrical way (by contrast, the English empiricists thought that the term 'demonstration' could be used only in a geometrical sense): like medicine, geometry was certain knowledge and was only secondarily practical, in measuring the earth.

In its long life Riverius' book came to be presented in a different way. After Riverius' death in 1655, Daniel Horstius contributed an address in 1668. The edition of 1737 contains editorial matter designed to temper the eagerness of Riverius' Galenism, which by now looked medieval, at least in Enlightenment Geneva. By then it needed explaining why Riverius had used Aristotle's discussion in the *Metaphysics* about the relationships between the disciplines to argue that medicine was a full *scientia*. It needed explaining why Riverius built up the content of his medicine in the traditional and compositive way from the four elements, their qualities, complexions, humours and the seven 'naturals'. It certainly needed explaining why Riverius resurrected the huge debate of the late Middle Ages about the perfect balance of qualities in complexion and the highly mathematical distinction between *ad pondus* and *ad justitiam* complexions. Riverius was not being simply medieval, for he dismisses (in the manner of the schools) the attacks on the theory of elementary qualities made by Telesio and Cardano, significant enemies of Aristotelian natural philosophy. There can be little doubt that Riverius' very complete Galenism was a reply to such attacks.

Later editions of Riverius' book contain two significant editorial insertions. One is a little tract on medical deontology written by the emperor's physician.[25] It comes with the approvals of a theologian and a medical man and is expressly designed to inform the Catholic doctor of his medical and religious duties. It gives the attributes of the good physician and the disciplines with which he must be familiar. Of these, philosophy is by far the most important, and it may be that this tract was thought suitable for Riverius' text, because its philosophy is as traditional as Riverius' Galenism. The cause seems to have been the same, that is, that the northern crisis in philosophy and its effect on medicine could be avoided by denying it. Medical principles, says the emperor's doctor, are the *arcana* of philosophy; philosophy 'is the uterine sister of medicine, offering a light to it. Without it medicine is more like a bloodless corpse than a living body, a branch torn from a tree.'[26] This relationship between philosophy and medicine had been an axiom since the early Middle Ages, but the reference to the

---

[25] F. C. Weinhart, *Medicus Officiosus*, without date or place; separately paginated.
[26] 'Philosophia medicinae soror germana & uterina est, facem et praeferens.' *Medicus Officiosus*, p. 3.

damage done to medicine by the absence of philosophy applies to the crisis of the late seventeenth century. Medicine without philosophy becomes enervated, all discussion recedes from truth, axioms are impossible to prove, proofs are offered that prove nothing, monstrous novelties appear, the parts of medicine lose their order and the result is a bad method of cure. The Good Doctor, whose medicine is *rationalis*, must be a student in the arena of theory before becoming an athlete in practice.

Again we may suppose that the publisher saw a market for the late editions of Riverius' work on a traditional medicine supported upon a traditional philosophy. But perhaps he wanted to hedge his bets with a second editorial addition that addressed once more the old question of whether medicine was an art or a science. But the answer is new, with arguments drawn from writers of the late seventeenth century: Marcello Malpighi, Lorenzo Bellini and even Friedrich Hoffmann. Now are given the views of Boyle on the importance of the senses and the dangers of intellectual systems. 'Demonstration' now carries a Baconian as well as other meanings. The purpose is not to deny the traditionalism of Riverius or the truths of traditional philosophy, for we hear of Aristotle's discussion of the relationship between the productive arts and the intellectual sciences, and there is a very rationalist discussion of 'demonstration' and 'utility', partly in connection with the first aphorism, always a nexus when such things are discussed. No, the overall purpose is once more to escape the medical consequences of the fragmentation of philosophy: medicine as an art cannot be damaged by changes in philosophical fashion. The author provides in explanation the image of a man faced with a burning house: when you are trying to put out the flames with water there is little point in asking whether they consist of Democritean atoms or Aristotelian substantial forms.

THE LONDON COLLEGE OF PHYSICIANS AND THOMAS WILLIS

Institutional Galenism is well illustrated by the London College of Physicians. It had been founded in the sixteenth century by Henry VIII on a suggestion of John Caius and was inspired by the Italian professional colleges. Its task was to control the practice of physic, and by the time of Charles I it had begun to look to parliament like a royal monopoly. The City of London was growing in size and power and in 1630 it gave formal recognition to the Apothecaries' Company, which four years later directly refused to be controlled by the College of Physicians. As a royal foundation the college lost more of its power in the Civil War and Interregnum, and at the Restoration its new charter was less favourable than the old. These were local English circumstances, on which much has been written and the story does not need to be repeated here.[27] But they coincided with the story of the 'scientific revolution' in which many contemporaries saw the importance of what was happening in England. One of these was the formation of groups of like-minded philosophers culminating in the Royal Society. The members shared a belief in a philosophy which was variously mechanical, corpuscular, experimental or anatomical, and they pursued research topics that arose from Harvey's work and that of Continental mechanists such as Giovanni Borelli and Malpighi.

The College of Physicians, in contrast, had a professional need to be Galenic, the measure of the authority and effectiveness of university medicine since the Middle Ages: the statutes of 1647, for example, betray no departure from Galenic–Hippocratic ideals.[28] But the college felt acutely the intellectual rivalry of the Royal Society and the professional rivalry of the Apothecaries' Company and the Society of Chemical Physicians, both growing in power. The college remained small at a time when London was growing rapidly, and to offset criticism in 1664 it admitted a large number of honorary fellows, a new category of membership. In a bald statement of professional 'ethics' it told them exactly what to do to promote and defend the reputation of the college.[29] But it was of little use. When the plague came in the following year, most of the physicians left town, leaving the medical market free to the apothecaries, and the following year the Fire of London burned down the college building and it had no funds to rebuild.

The college could no longer defend a Galenic medicine and turned to mechanism in about 1680. The members had defended themselves against the criticism of the chemists by claiming that they had already adopted a number of chemical remedies (which did not necessarily conflict with Galenic theory). They had also answered Boyle's criticism of their traditional theory by claiming that the *practice* of traditional medicine worked better than any medicine based on the new philosophy. The argument for effectiveness had always been part of the Rational and Learned Doctors'

[27] See in the first instance Theodore M. Brown, *The Mechanical Philosophy and the 'Animal Oeconomy'. A Study in the Development of English Physiology in the Seventeenth and early Eighteenth Century*, New York (Arno Press), 1981. Brown's introduction to Domenico Bertoloni Meli, ed., *Malpighi: Anatomist and Physician*, Florence (L. S. Olschki), 1997, sums up the changes in the field and its literature.

[28] Brown, *Mechanical Philosophy*, p. 138.

[29] As in earlier schemes of medical ethics, the honorary fellows were forbidden to converse with 'empirics' or enemies of the college, but to work for the 'honour and advantage of the College'. Above all, the new fellows were not to publicly argue with any licensed physician, that is, of the rational and learned elite, a point of medical ethics for centuries. See Brown, *Mechanical Philosophy*, p. 144.

armoury, but now it was time to link it to the new philosophy. This was done largely in the way set out by Thomas Willis (1620–75). Willis showed the physicians that they could maintain a largely traditional practice of medicine by constructing mechanical reasons for it. This was another way of resolving the crisis: restore some of the dignity to practical medicine and show that now the reasons for its success are better known. Willis' 'rational pharmaceutics' thus have a *mechanical* rationality in which his learning draws strength from contemporary philosophy.[30] His 'mechanism' is a solidist one, with much attention given to fibres (which can, for example, provoke vomiting when irritated).[31] He finds it necessary to defend medicine, reminding the reader that it should be among the most noble of the sciences. But, in mathematics and mechanics, experiment, experience or chance lead more readily to causes than in medicine. Medicine was first handled by empirics, he says, and then stolen by mountebanks and the little old ladies (who so constantly plagued the Rational and Learned Doctor). The result was that it became a mysterious rite, an inexplicable matter in which no reasoning could be found.[32] 'Mountebank' here is a rendering in English of *agyrta*, apparently a term recorded only in British seventeenth-century sources, so it is a very specific insult for those who practised the wrong kind of medicine or criticised the right kind. His language gets stronger. The 'literate cynics' who criticise medicine are no doubt the philosophical sceptics who refused to admit systems and causes, and the *vilissimi quique e plebis faece* are the literal equivalent of those neoterics whom (Aubrey tells us) Harvey called 'shitt-breeches'.[33] It clearly reflects the disputes between the Galenists and the mechanists, between the mechanists themselves, and between the chemists and everyone else. 'Pseudochemists', Willis calls them. The official pharmacopoeia of the college was the battleground with the apothecaries, who finally refused to follow it: Willis is moving in a highly charged political atmosphere. In principle, Willis' 'mechanical' account of the actions of *materia medica* is taken in conjunction with anatomy, a surviving part of traditional medicine, and he gives an account of the major regions of the body where the remedies act. In practice this means that he categorises medicine in the conventional way as purges, vomits, diuretics

[30] Thomas Willis, *Pharmaceutice Rationalis sive Diatriba de Medicamentorum Operationibus in Humano Corpore*, The Hague (Arnout Leers), 1675. Leers was part of the English–Dutch connection, specialising in English medical works and publishing four of the seven editions of Harvey in Holland.
[31] Willis, *Pharmaceutice Rationalis*, p. 46.
[32] '*Ars tamen medendi licet primo ab Empiricis tradita, & ab Agyrtis quibusque & mulierculis passim arrepta, usque tamen quasi mysterii ritu, in cuius rationes minime inquirere fas esset, inexplicata permansit.*' The preface to the reader.
[33] See Geoffrey Keynes, *The Life of William Harvey*, Oxford (Clarendon Press), 1978, p. 434.

and so on. Discussion of *how* they act mechanically is not a major part of Willis' treatment. The context of Willis' projected programme of giving new philosophical muscle to fairly conventional medical therapy was the attempt by officials of the college and iatromechanical authors 'to rebuild the physicians' decaying income, power and prestige'.[34]

Willis' career illustrates a number of themes of this book. He was born into a family of the middling sort, the class who supplied the bulk of learned and rational physicians, for gentry did not become doctors[35] (although we shall see that doctors tried to become gentry). His lifetime saw the crisis in traditional natural philosophy and the attempts by the physicians to resolve it. His medical education was, like Sydenham's, interrupted by the English Civil War and he may have had less than six month's formal training; he certainly developed a taste for chemical explanations. He also lived at a time of great competition in the medical marketplace. While the earlier professional colleges and faculties had exercised some form of *numerus clausus* to protect the status and market share of the learned physician, it seems that medical qualifications were easier to come by in Willis' time. Many French universities had two levels of the same medical degree, the lower being pretty much a purchase made by foreigners who would not practise within the faculties' jurisdiction. Aberdeen frankly sold its degrees on the recommendation of two established practitioners.[36] Some of these foreign degrees could be traded-in for an Oxford or Cambridge degree and so make possible a membership of the London College for candidates with a less than rigorous medical education. Moreover, the king or bishops could confer the degree of MD.[37] Competition meant that not even fellowship of the London College always led to success: Nathanial Hodges, for example, an Oxford-educated fellow in Willis' time, died in a debtors' prison.[38] Other things were needed to secure a practice and make money. In the rapidly changing economic and social conditions of seventeenth-century London, physicians found that attention to dress and manners could be

---

[34] Brown, *Mechanical Philosophy*, p. 124. Willis still has spirits and humours, although of a new kind. His listing of the formulae for remedies connects to the pharmacopoeia and looks rather traditional, including mithradatium (p. 257) and the theriac of Andromachus (p. 167). Theriac and mithradatium remained in the Edinburgh Dispensatory until 1756 and their last vestige did not disappear from the Paris Codex until 1908. See David L. Cowen, 'Expunctum est mithradatium', in his *Pharmacopoeias and Related Literature in Britain and America, 1618–1847*, Aldershot (Ashgate), 2001, item III.

[35] On Willis and Boyle see Kenneth Dewhurst, *Thomas Willis's Oxford Lectures*, Oxford (Sandford Publications), 1980.

[36] See Roger French, 'Medical teaching in Aberdeen: from the foundation of the university to the middle of the seventeenth century', *History of Universities*, 3 (1983) 127–57.

[37] Harold J. Cook, *The Regulation of Medical Practice in London under the Stuarts, 1607–1704*, PhD dissertation University of Michigan, 1981, p. 32.

[38] Ibid., p. 43.

useful. Appointment to a hospital or a faculty had a certain cachet and for the physician (even without an MD) who made it to court respect was inevitable. Curing a famous figure often led to a secure word-of-mouth reputation, and securing a wealthy patron was just as good (John Locke left Oxford without taking his medical degree to work for Lord Ashley).[39] These were not, however, the sort of opportunities that presented themselves to many doctors. Rather, they would be obliged to sit in fashionable coffee-houses or visit the local market 'casting Waters', that is, inspecting urine samples.[40] Willis himself was a 'piss prophet' in Abingdon market, where he travelled from his rooms in Christ Church, Oxford, on a shared horse on Mondays. In 1646 he was a bachelor, not a doctor of medicine (and may have counted his army service as university terms). His patients were largely poor countryfolk until a series of epidemics struck Oxford in 1658. He capitalised on this by writing a largely chemical theoretical tract on fevers.[41] Like Harvey, he married wisely, and into Royalist circles, and was rewarded at the Restoration by being made Sedleian Professor of Natural Philosophy and by being given the degree of MD at the insistence of Charles II. The Sedleian chair was first occupied in 1620, when traditional natural philosophy was still undisturbed, and the statutes of 1636 governing it specify that the Aristotelian *libri naturales* were to be lectured upon in an entirely traditional way. Willis, however, gave lectures that centred on medical topics in the chemical manner.[42] But still Aristotle represented continuity and authority and with Charles II enjoyed a triumphant and even divine Restoration (especially at Willis' college, Christ Church).[43] Outside the university, in contrast, Willis' kind of medicine made him very rich and famous. Of all these devices to secure a reputation perhaps the most effective was to write a book. This was certainly Richard Mead's advice: 'Should you have an itching to make your name known by writing a book, choose one that will be business and money-making, like fevers, smallpox; address it to a great man or get your fellow doctors who agree to commend each others' books by letters.'[44]

THE ITALIAN COLLEGES AND GENTLEMANLY MEDICINE

Medical men at the universities of Paris and Montpellier had their own academic reasons for resisting the new philosophy; in Italy learned medical men had additional professional reasons for wishing to retain Galenic

[39] Ibid., pp. 34, 35.   [40] Dewhurst, *Willis's Oxford Lectures*, p. 9.
[41] *Diatribae duae Medico-Philosophicae*, London (Thomas Roycroft), 1659.
[42] His later *De Anima Brutorum* is partly an expansion of these lectures.
[43] Dewhurst, *Willis's Oxford Lectures*, p. 39.   [44] Cook, *Regulation*, p. 35.

medicine. Through the sixteenth century the medical colleges had been extending their power over the old guilds, which often included apothecaries and surgeons. The *protomedicato* and the colleges were able to extend monopolistic control of internal medicine, including licensing and examination. The physicians, separated from the apothecaries and surgeons, were assimilated into the upper classes. While the guilds had an open policy on matriculation, the colleges operated a *numerus clausus* which made them literally more exclusive, each member with a greater share of the monopoly. Cities and universities both had medical colleges and were jealous of their privileges, refusing to admit the theoretically universal degree of master from other universities and cities. The Milanese College was initially open only to the local patricians[45] and that in Bologna was restricted to Bolognese citizens. Inevitably medical dynasties grew and ramified through both kinds of college and the faculty. The college of Pavia in 1667 obtained a privilege from the emperor that made all its members Counts Palatine, and the social standing of some physicians was so great that they did not practise medicine. Moreover, the older physicians had greater power and all in all these 'ancients' adhered closely to Galen and Avicenna. The 'moderns' lectured illicitly and formed their own academies but did not defeat the ancients until the middle of the eighteenth century.[46]

When university statutes continued into the eighteenth century to specify the texts of Aristotle and Galen they were often taken as a framework into which to fit another kind of discussion. Our example here is Johannes Vulpius, a teacher of arts in that famous home of Aristotelianism and medicine, Padua. His academic oration on *physica* of c. 1727 gives a picture of a manner of discussing these things in what was still a Counter-Reformation climate (the permission to publish explains that the book contains nothing against the Catholic faith).[47] The tone of the whole is one of studied elegance, and Vulpius sometimes provides a Greek version of his Latin. This is classical education, with instruction in proper language as important as the subject matter of philosophy and medicine. It is also a liberal education, of the kind that many doctors in the eighteenth century undertook to make themselves gentlemen. It was an obvious strategy to adopt,

[45] See Ann G. Carmichael, 'Epidemics and state medicine in fifteenth-century Milan', in Roger French, Jon Arrizabalaga, Andrew Cunningham and Luis García-Ballester, eds., *Medicine from the Black Death to the French Disease*, Aldershot (Ashgate), 1998, pp. 221–47, at p. 222.

[46] See David Gentilcore, 'The organisation of medical practice in Malpighi's Italy', in Bertoloni Meli, ed., *Malpighi*, 75–110.

[47] Vulpius, *Opuscula Philosophica*; the first scholion on Aristotle carries the date 1727 (p. 73).

for a rich medical market was provided by the newly prosperous urban middle classes, who concerned themselves with civility and gentility; in Prussia there were 'galant' doctors and patients. When disputes occurred between English practitioners the most serious crime was to break the gentlemanly code.[48] It was a question of behaviour, not clinical success or failure, and the doctor's reputation was his success. For Vulpius there were, of course, practical advantages in having a knowledge of nature, for it enabled one to lead the good and blessed life; and understanding the nature of the body helped the physician to apply effective remedies in cases of illness.[49]

Vulpius taught *physica* by order of the Venetian Senate and the 'triumvirate of letters'. *Physica* was a new name for natural philosophy, and its purpose, 'as of old', was to explain Aristotle's works: Vulpius had to give lectures on *De Caelo et Mundo* and on *De Generatione et Corruptione* with the traditional purpose of preparing students for medicine, law or theology.[50] Indeed, *physica* is a close sister, in the old way, of medicine, and the physician begins where the philosopher finished.[51] But in spite of all these traditional features, Vulpius uses the statutes as a framework to discuss all manner of philosophical and medical subjects. He writes as a historian reporting at a distance from his subject. There is no urgency to discover the physical truth in the disputes between the Cartesians and the Newtonians, or whether there is a vacuum or not. He prefers Newton and John Keill, seen as geometers, to Descartes, the past 'dictator' of philosophy, and he defends Galen against the attacks of ignorant little men of weak character.[52] The overall educational purpose is to teach the young gentlemen to understand enough about the body and the natural world (which God had constructed as its dwelling place) for them to live in peace within it, in accordance with divine order.

Clearly, the doctor could gain status by placing himself in the genteel classes. But if Italian Galenists were also striving after gentility, then the search for this new social status cannot, in itself, be interpreted as a strategy for escaping from the collapse of philosophy (although that remains a possibility in the northern countries). It seems rather that new urban prosperity helped to generate a 'polite' or 'genteel' Enlightenment in the early eighteenth century and that doctors such as George Cheyne

---

[48] See David Harley, 'Honour and property: the structure of professional disputes in eighteenth-century English medicine', in Andrew Cunningham and Roger French, eds., *The Medical Enlightenment of the Eighteenth Century*, Cambridge (Cambridge University Press), 1990, pp. 138–64.

[49] Vulpius, *Opuscula*, p. 22.   [50] Ibid., p. 24.

[51] Ibid., p. 97. He gives particular attention to the role of anatomy.

[52] Ibid., p. 197.

(1673–1743) practised an appropriate medicine. He saw that a rigid and complex Newtonianism was beyond the intellectual taste and abilities of his fashionable patients at Bath and elsewhere.[53] A rising Bristol surgeon spoke of an 'imposing exterior' of the physician: 'He moved in a measured step and affected a meditating abstraction of countenance with a pomposity of diction and manner which served to keep the vulgar at a respectable distance – The doctor's Peruke alone was enough in itself to command respect.'[54] In Italy for the sake of dignity the physician was obliged to keep a carriage; he wore a fur-lined gown, velvet cap, black gloves and a gold ring.[55] As we have seen, these were the items to which he had become entitled at graduation and they remained symbols of his profession through the seventeenth century.[56] In 1696 Prospero Mandioso published a 'theatre' of biographies of papal physicians, showing that they were men of good learning and good families. Like most contemporary assessments, clinical excellence was not a big criterion of the good doctor.[57] From the days of Melchior Adam's collection of biographies of German doctors,[58] gentlemanly behaviour, cultural achievement and contacts were more tangible attributes.[59] Adam's collection was paralleled by the publication in Amsterdam of Zacutus Lusitanus' *De Medicorum Principum Historia libri sex* by Henricus Laurentius in 1629. Lusitanus was a sixteenth-century Portuguese *converso* and this gives us information on the European network of such minorities.[60] Adam's and Zacuto's works are examples of a genre of medical literature that came to include medical histories and

---

[53] See Akihito Suzuki, 'Anti-Lockean enlightenment? Mind and body in early eighteenth-century English medicine', in Roy Porter, ed., *Medicine in the Enlightenment*, Amsterdam (Rodopi), 1995 (The Wellcome Institute Series in the History of Medicine), pp. 336–59, at p. 330.

[54] Quoted by Mary E. Fissell, *Patients, Power, and the Poor in Eighteenth-Century Bristol*, Cambridge (Cambridge University Press), 1991, p. 62.

[55] See David Gentilcore, 'The organisation of medical practice in Malpighi's Italy', in Bertoloni Meli, ed., *Malpighi*, pp. 75–110, at p. 78.

[56] The guilded stirrups and horse-blanket were otherwise used only by princes and prelates.

[57] Richard Palmer, 'Medicine at the papal court in the sixteenth century', in Vivian Nutton, ed., *Medicine at the Courts of Europe, 1500–1837*, London (Routledge), 1990, pp. 47–78, at p. 49.

[58] I am grateful to Nancy Siraisi for drawing my attention to Adam's *Vitae Germanorum Medicorum*, Heidelberg (J. Rosa), 1620.

[59] Collections of biographies of the famous, often made to glorify a particular city, were made in the Middle Ages. While of course *patients* chose their doctors on the basis of their clinical reputations, what interested the biographers was not the low-level and mundane business of medical practice but the intellectual achievements of the biographee in medical theory and philosophy. See Nancy Siraisi, 'The physician's task: medical reputations in humanist collective biographies', in her *Medicine and the Italian Universities 1250–1600*, Leiden (Brill), 2001, pp. 157–83.

[60] See Luis García-Ballester, 'The Inquisition and minority medical practitioners in counter-reformation Spain. Judaizing and Morisco practitioners, 1560–1610', in Ole Peter Grell and Andrew Cunningham, eds., *Medicine and the Reformation*, London (Routledge), 1993, pp. 156–91, at p. 166.

bio-bibliographies of the seventeenth and eighteenth centuries. Patrons, towns and universities sought out doctors with wide erudition: the learned and gentlemanly physician was, above all, an educated man and could turn his hands to many things for an important master. Physicians educated at King's College, Cambridge in the Middle Ages went abroad to further their education, apparently to qualify them for careers in something other than medicine.[61] Harvey went on foreign embassies for his king; and some of his contemporaries were essentially Protestant secret agents.[62] In the smaller German courts physicians took on a range of jobs such as administration and ambassadorial activity; many had studied mathematics and could make astrological forecasts and oversaw building and engineering.[63] The important thing was that the learned and gentlemanly doctor had been educated in a university approved of by his patron, whether Catholic or Protestant.

Many of these things lead back to the question asked in the Introduction: in what senses could a doctor be called *successful?* In what way did he meet or even create the expectations of society? Proud chroniclers writing about their Italian cities often included the names of the great and the good. Thus Filippo Matteo eulogised Florence and its early medical men including Taddeo, Dino, Turisanus and Tommaso del Garbo. Filippo points to intellectual excellence in interpreting old and developing new texts by which rich and famous patients are attracted; the superiority of intellect over practice in Filippo's view, such a frequent topic within medicine, emphasises the point made at the beginning of this book that clinical criteria can hardly, if ever, be used to measure medical practice.[64]

Another example is Bartolomeo Fazio of Genoa (d. 1547) who wrote a collective biography in which he said of medicine, 'For what is higher than the investigation and the knowledge of the cause of those very things by which the whole of nature is contained?'[65] Nothing could better express what has, in this book, been called the Good Story by which the Rational and Learned Doctor in the Latin tradition related the patient's symptoms

---

[61] I am grateful to Peter Jones, Librarian of King's College, for this information.

[62] Hugh Trevor-Roper, 'The court physician and Paracelsianism', in Nutton, *Courts*, pp. 79–94. For example, Theodore de Mayerne was a secret agent. He bought a castle and used it as a listening post for Protestant Europe (p. 92).

[63] See Bruce T. Moran, 'Prince-practitioning and the direction of medical roles at the German court: Maurice of Hesse-Kassel and his physicians', in Nutton, *Courts*, pp. 95–116.

[64] See Nancy Siraisi, '*The Physician's task*: medical reputations in humanist collective biographies', in her *Medicine and the Italian Universities*, pp. 157–83.

[65] Quoted by Nancy Siraisi, '*The Physician's task*', p. 176.

and disease, with their Galenic physical reasons, to the very basis of the Aristotelian world-view. The ancient superiority of intellect – soon to be dismissed as a 'system' – is also very notable.

THE END OF THE LATIN TRADITION

It is notable that the gentlemanly physician continued to read his sources in Latin and even in Greek. As late as the nineteenth century the big editions of Galen and Hippocrates by Kühn and Littré appeared in Greek, with Latin and French versions respectively standing opposite. But the working doctor who published for status or preferment increasingly turned to his vernacular language. This was the end of the Latin tradition which has been a theme of this book and it is worthwhile glancing at it in a little more detail as the story draws to a close.

Latin had been in common use throughout Europe because it was the learned language of the undivided church. It was the medium in which Aristotle, Hippocrates and Galen were read. It became the language of philosophy and of the theory of medicine. Its technical terms carried a wide range of connotations that the Rational and Learned Physician knew well. But, with the crisis of traditional philosophy, the continued use of the old terms could be confusing, for they related to a network of meanings in a discredited 'system' and many authors seem to have opted to express themselves in the vernacular. In Harvey's time writing in Latin was a way of securing a Europe-wide readership, which is what Harvey was aiming at. In his notes for his anatomy lectures he sometimes used English: the point was that the general principles of his Aristotelian natural philosophy could be expressed with the full authority of formal Latin, but when he wanted an arresting image or analogy to convince and stay in the mind of his audience, he used English. Harvey's opponents, Primrose and Riolan, used Latin for its authority in its reasoning and learning, and in contemporary terms their arguments were extensive and powerful. Newton too addressed a European audience in Latin; his was high philosophy and needed a formal language despite (like Harvey's) containing radical novelties. But Boyle and sceptics such as Gassendi, both distrusting past 'systems' of natural philosophy, made extensive use of their vernaculars; Descartes, with a new system designed to replace the old, broke with the old by using French. Experimental observations, such as Harvey's sensory images, were best expressed in English without any philosophical baggage. Medical teaching in the newer universities such as Edinburgh was often in the vernacular from the early eighteenth century, although to reach an international studentship Latin was necessary (as in Boerhaave's Leiden). Writers of reference works such as Haller (see chapter 8) also used Latin for related reasons.

CHEMISTRY AND MEDICINE

Chemical medicine cannot form a direct part of this story because its practitioners were not learned and rational in the senses we have adopted[66] (and because it has attracted a good share of historical attention).[67] The interest of chemical medicine for us is that it was a real challenge – professional and intellectual – to traditional medicine at a time when its theory had faltered; it was part of the crisis and for some, a resolution. The chemists sought their inspiration from Paracelsus and the Hermetic tradition, where Hermes was thought to be contemporary with Moses or Abraham. This was not only a 'dignity of age' device, but a claim of piety where the ancient Greek philosophers were expressly seen as pagan. In making the world, they believed, God had created powerful natural substances recognisable by signs to the Godly physician. While Paracelsus had rejected all of Greek medical theory, the chemists of the seventeenth century rejected the claims of contemporaries that geometry (and anatomy) had the force of demonstration; they preferred some form of numerology (and a system of celestial, sympathetic anatomy).

As an attack on an established tradition, chemical medicine was often preached by Protestants.[68] In Galenic Paris, it was bitterly attacked in the early seventeenth century by the Galenic Riolans, father and son, but Montpellier was much more tolerant. The second stage in the growth of chemical medicine is attributable to the work of Jean Baptiste van Helmont (1577–1644), whose doctrines were an effective challenge not only to traditional medicine but to the new mechanical philosophy. An indignant church defended its own by locking him up for a while.[69] But prudent

---

[66] Where it was supported by the princely patron of a university, it almost became rational and learned. See Trevor-Roper, 'The court physician'. While Paracelsus never got or wanted patronage, his followers shed the revolutionary image and were sometimes supported by princes. The duke of Neuburg had a Paracelsian as his court physician before 1545. By 1570 Latin Paracelsianism was becoming respectable, and Maurice of Hesse, patron of Marburg university, appointed a Paracelsian, Johan Hartmann (1568–1631). This was the beginning of *chemiatria* as an academic discipline.

[67] See in particular the works of Allen G. Debus, especially *The French Paracelsians. The Chemical Challenge to Medical and Scientific Tradition in Early Modern France*, Cambridge (Cambridge University Press), 1991; and 'Paracelsianism and the diffusion of the chemical philosophy in early modern Europe', in Ole Grell, ed., *Paracelsus. The Man and his Reputation. His Ideas and their Transformation*, Leiden (Brill), 1998, pp. 225–44.

[68] In France, by the Huguenots. When Henry of Navarre assumed control of Paris in 1593 the chemists were favoured. See Debus, *The French Paracelsians*, p. 48.

[69] Debus, *The French Paracelsians*, p. 106.

doctors of the traditional kind could accommodate some chemistry. It was entirely possible within the structure of Galenic and Hippocratic medical theory to search out new drugs, justified perhaps by the theoretical claim than modern man was weaker than the ancients and needed stronger remedies. A powerful incentive in the Spanish explorations of the Indies was the desire to find new medicines.[70] In particular, attention was given to metals, which did not feature in the old category of simples: mercury was used for the French Disease and there were constant squabbles over the uses and dangers of antimony.

Broadly speaking, the chemists discussed actions in liquids: fermentations, acids reacting with alkalis, and intestinal motion in general. Distillation was central, for it seemed to be a way of extracting the essence of a medicine from the grossness of its matter. The notion of purification in this often had Reformist overtones, nowhere more so than with the Rosicrucians, for whom the alembic was a parable for the whole world. While doctors of the traditional and mechanist persuasion could adopt a number of spagyrical remedies from the chemists, they often saw chemical medicine as a new 'system', on offer from the chemists only as a whole. When Georgio Baglivi was attacked by Jacob Le Mort, the Leiden teacher of chemistry, a commentator observed that the tyranny of chemistry was that it had lovers but no friends.[71] Consequently even doctors who were prepared to accept a good deal from the chemists, such as Antoine Deidier in Montpellier, thought that the whole chemical package was 'vulgar'.[72] Hoffmann thought it was grandiloquent but medically useless.[73]

Perhaps the most pronounced form of medical chemistry was that of van Helmont and it was conspicuous in England, where traditional natural philosophy had failed so signally. Helmontians sought a new and not mechanical natural philosophy on which to build a new medicine. In 1665 Marchamont Nedham, like Noah Biggs before him, spoke of tearing down the old building of medicine and beginning again from different and deeper foundations, knowing that nothing new could be grafted on to old beginnings.[74] The identities of philosophy and medicine had changed, but

---

[70] See, for example, Robert Fludd, *Clavis Philosophiae et Alchymiae Fluddianae*, Frankfurt (Guilhelmus Fitzerus), 1633.

[71] 'It considers itself to be despised when no longer adored; it has slaves but no listeners': the anonymous writer of the preface to Georgius Baglivi, *Opera Omnia Medico-Practica, et Anatomica*, 15th edn, Venice, 1723.

[72] Antonius Deidier, *Institutiones Medicae Theoricae, Physiologiam et Pathologicam Complectens*, Paris (Carolus-Mauritius d'Houry), 1731, p. 7. These are the *novatores Chymici*, p. 3.

[73] See the preface (1728) to volume 1 of the collected works: Friedrich Hoffmann, *Opera Omnia Physico-Medica*, vol. 1, Geneva (The Brothers De Tournes), 1748.

[74] See Andrew Wear, *Knowledge and Practice in English Medicine, 1550–1680*, Cambridge (Cambridge University Press), 2000, p. 363.

the argument was the same as it had been since the Middle Ages: 'Natural Philosophy is the Basis or the main Fundamental of Medicine: for where Philosophy ends, there Medicine is to be enterprised'.[75]

The Baconian Instauration

By the end of the seventeenth century there were, then, a number of ways of resolving the crisis of the fragmentation of traditional philosophy. But one general question remained in medicine: what weight was to be given to ancient opinion? On the one hand, many held that the old authors were still authorities. Moreover, however convincing personal observation was, it was a particular, not a universal, and it had to be communicated to others. If it was experimental, then others would need the apparatus or need to do the vivisection. Scepticism in any case forbade the assembly of observations to make an argument that dealt with causes.

The problem of ancient authority and the collapse of traditional medical theory is exemplified by Giorgio Baglivi (1668–1707). He is an important figure in our story and begins a new chapter within it, one in which physicians began to construct a new theory of medicine. His book, published near the end of the seventeenth century, had gone through fifteen editions by 1723: clearly he had found a huge market and his doctrines were influential. We must look at it in a little more detail, but in short his story is one of a man who found medical theory chaotic and turned instead to practice. He could in this way retain Hippocrates as the Father of Medicine, while rejecting much Greek theory. He decided that his practical medicine would be a question of studying diseases as entities in a Baconian way, compiling 'histories' of them over a long period of time (for the art is long and life is short). The aim of this method was to produce aphorisms, modelled on the Hippocratic, but which Baglivi held were capable of giving the causes of disease, as many of the old rational systems did. Baglivi was not hampered

---

[75] Noah Biggs (1651), quoted by Wear, *Knowledge and Practice*, p. 364. In England the instauration of a new chemical medicine was conditioned by the Civil War, and it is not the present purpose to go over ground that has attracted so much historical attention. Important are Charles Webster's *The Great Instauration. Science, Medicine and Reform, 1626–1660*, London (Duckworth), 1975; and the works of Allen Debus, particularly his *English Paracelsians*, London (Oldbourne), 1965. The topic and its literature are usefully reviewed in Wear, *Knowledge and Practice*, esp. chs. 8 and 9. The chemists took advantage of the plague of 1665 in London, which killed about a fifth of the population: they saw it as a trial of their own Godly medicine against the atheistical (i.e. philosophical) medicine of the Galenists. See Ole Grell, 'Plague, prayer and physic', in Grell and Cunningham, eds., *Religio Medici*, pp. 204–27, at p. 204.

by scepticism, which had been an intellectual guarantee against systems for Boyle. Indeed, 'descent' into scepticism was now seen as a fault, for scepticism was now 'Pyrrhonianism', which limited the intellect and was moreover pagan: for Baglivi as for Boyle it was the Christian God as Creator who ultimately assured the rationality and coherence of nature.

Writing in 1696, he tells the reader of his studies in Naples, his travels along the Dalmatian coast and his attention to practical medicine in a number of Italian universities. Nothing was agreed as to the principles of medicine among the men who taught him. Many of his contemporaries had abandoned the pristine (*prisca*) wisdom of medicine and left it a shaky structure. There were rumours of great novelties; in some universities they were so much opposed to the ancient authors that they said it belittled the human mind to read the works of Galen. In others the theories of the ancients were anxiously and religiously observed and new discoveries were constantly attacked. Often, in the uncertainty, practice was reduced to purging, bleeding and vesication. In all universities Baglivi found contention, ill will and imprudence among the medical men. Worst of all, Hippocates himself, *medicinam Parentem suam, et magistram*, was defamed as uncertain and fraudulent, both privately and publicly.

Faced with an almost infinite variety of opinion, confused and uncertain, what was he to do? The first thing was to recall that the ultimate purpose of medicine was practical. The disputes of his training were matters of words, the fallacies of 'explodable vanities of systems', things that did not direct his actions when he decided to visit Italian hospitals to make notes of diseases. Like many others, he decided in the face of uncertainty to be led by the light of reason and experience. But, of course, it was to be reason and experience of a particular kind, historically local. It was, in short, a method that was both Christian and Baconian. Baglivi's 'Christian philosopher' was the man who saw God as the Creator of the world and nature as expressions of His will. No philosophical scepticism could deny this, and, as with Boyle, it provided the rationality and coherence of the natural world. In his preface, Baglivi addresses the pope and prays to *Deus Optimus Maximus* that reason and experience will in this way bring peace to the warring doctors of the Christian Republic.[76] Baglivi saw the parallel between the fractious medical men of his day and the arguing philosophers described by Bacon: Baglivi's programme amounted to a Medical Instauration.[77] Its *Organon*, a method of acquiring useful knowledge, was to be personal observation over a long

---

[76] '*sed solo praeeunte Rationis, et Experientiae lumine*'. Georgii Baglivi, *Opera Omnia Medico-Practica, et Anatomica*, 15th edn, Venice, 1723; Baglivi's preface.

[77] Baglivi, *Opera*, p. 78.

period. Baglivi is emphatic that this should be done simply, even simple mindedly, thus avoiding all distractions of theory or systems. Here Baglivi is most explicitly Baconian: the collection of observations is a 'history' (*historia*) of disease, and Baglivi quotes the passage that seemed to have a particular attraction for medical men, in which Bacon writes that in the construction of a natural history it serves no purpose to include stories, citations of the authors, antiquities, controversies, superstitions, ornaments or etymologies; and above all, says Bacon, include no systems. Use plain language, says Baglivi, and omit no detail, however slight. The doctor during this process, he adds, is a witness, not a judge; a *historographus* who needs no other *scientia* or reading to help him in compiling his history. The history is composed of a rich and fertile 'forest' of particulars: Baglivi uses the Baconian term *sylva*.[78]

Putting the history together could take years. Baglivi wanted the doctor to look out for diseases as an entity, so that by noting every day the vehemence, circumstances and outcome of the disease, the history became chronological as well as simply descriptive. Baglivi thought that a doctor practising this method might collect 1,000–2,000 observations on a single disease, like colic. The doctor was to note also the effect of remedies and the time and place of observation. When he was told too to make a note of the 'constitution' of the year it reveals that Baglivi had in mind some causal connection between the weather and the disease that owed something to Sydenham and something to Hippocrates and which was connected to attempts elsewhere to use the barometer medically.

These simple observations are in themselves useless, says Baglivi: they are like letters of the alphabet which have to be arranged in significant groupings. Baglivi is entering the second stage of his *Organon*, arranging the observations under common headings and locations. With 2,000 observations on colic in his notebook, the doctor can now group them into the paired categories of constant and variable (Bacon's voice is audible) and diagnostic and prognostic. Baglivi's ideal doctor is now rising above the level of the empiric, and having arranged his observations, begins to digest them. It was, of course, a major problem for a doctor engaged in empirical observation to avoid being labelled an empiric, the traditional enemy of the Learned and Rational Doctor. The danger was greater when the doctor was unable to substantiate his medicine with an authoritative natural philosophy, and in supplying a method of procedure rather than an intellectual system, Baglivi was coming to the rescue of his colleagues.

[78] Baglivi, *Opera*, p. 111; p. 112 '*copiosa sylva*'.

The third stage of his Baconian programme was the digestion of the particulars. Arranging them had shown what was constant; what was not could be rejected as accidents. The doubts and cautions that had been entered in the notes while the history was being compiled could now be evaluated. Baglivi was aware that induction from particulars was imperfect in traditional logic, but he rests comfortably on the authority of Bacon in claiming it as a demonstration based on the senses which illuminates the mind and provides conclusions close to nature. Baglivi becomes rhetorical here, indicating the centrality of this point in his method, which is a kind of divine fire in the mind, illuminating the vast desert of particulars – signs, symptoms, causes – that lies below as we labour the mountain to the peak of nature; from here we can descend with tranquil mind and a serene view to medical practice. It is at the 'peak of nature' that the fourth stage of the programme is reached, the production of precepts or general axioms: Baglivi speaks of 'abstracting' or 'deducing' these from the digested particulars. Sometimes he calls them 'middle propositions', but he is principally concerned to show that they have the same standing and nature as traditional medical aphorisms.[79]

In this way Baglivi can defend Hippocrates by interpreting him, as almost everyone did, and strengthen his own novelty by enlisting Hippocrates on his side, which was also popular. But Baglivi makes bigger claims for his axioms, for they are not only aphoristic but can reveal *causes*, which the Hippocratic aphorisms do not. The causes underlie the appearances, provide signs and indicate remedies. Moreover, causes are part of *natural philosophy*: for all his denigration of other people's systems and philosophies, Baglivi admits to a philosophy which supplies the theory of medicine. It is, to be sure, a different natural philosophy, because it is true, and it is true, says Baglivi, because it is based on experiment and the truth of mathematics.[80] Baglivi prefers to use 'nature' rather than 'philosophy' so that he can speak of the laws of nature, being close to nature, at the peak of nature and drawing histories from nature. He claims that Hippocrates spoke with the voice of nature, not of man.[81] He also adopts the not uncommon motto that the physician is the servant of nature, but only by understanding her.[82] Nature

[79] Baglivi, *Opera*, pp. 109, 112.
[80] Baglivi approved of experiment as a form of observation, and argued that some philosophical systems had failed by being insufficiently grounded on experiments: the chemical philosophy, with its acids and alkalis, Gilbert's magnetical philosophy, Mayow's 'nitrous air' physiology. These too must have added to the general picture of uncertainty in natural philosophy. Baglivi, *Opera*, p. 107.
[81] Ibid., p. 1.
[82] The first book of his *De Praxi Medica* (the first numbered page of the volume) opens with '*Medicus naturae Minister, et Interpretes....*'.

was also part of Creation. Baglivi uses the term 'Christian philosopher' to imply that he saw that God was the Creator of nature and her laws, that God's rationality was now understood in those laws and that there was thus divine reason not to sink into scepticism.[83] Baglivi prayed that by the use of reason in this way the current battles between doctors in the Christian Republic would come to an end.[84]

It was here in the method, at the generation of Hippocratic-philosophical axioms, that Baglivi allowed the ideal doctor to undertake reading for the first time. He had been greatly insistent and very rhetorical that the doctor should in no way allow his mind to be distracted from the collection of particulars of the *historia* at the beginning of the method. Compiling a history, he said, was a science all of its own, not drawing its principles from elsewhere.[85] It was therefore very important to do this with a clear mind, far from the influence of disturbing books. In fact, Baglivi has a formal list of things that have hindered the development of a truly axiomatic medicine. These remind us again of the conflicts between the philosophers and the plight of the medical men without a solid theory. They also remind us of Baglivi's debt to Bacon, for these are Idols, falsities on which men have spent too much time in the past. Baglivi quotes Bacon's view that having despaired of finding truth, men fell into the habit of disputing rather than maintaining a strict enquiry.[86] Some of the Idols we have met, such as the propensity to construct systems and the refusal to make observation the beginning of medicine and to generate axioms in the proper way. In fact, most of Baglivi's Idols relate to the disrupted state of philosophy in his youth. The Idol of Deriding the Ancients represents Paracelsus and van Helmont, building their systems impertinently amid the ruins of the Galenic. The fourth is the Idol of Reading Preposterous Books. Baglivi is very severe here (for it was, of course, how people got wrong ideas). There are far too many books anyway, he says, so do not be greedy in reading: too many books are as bad as too much food. Indeed, never read a book until you have a method for doing so; never read a book until you have asked yourself 'Is it true?' Too much reading trains the memory instead of the reason, and takes up the time that should be devoted to experience. Learned

[83] One could read (in the appropriate books) what laws God had made for matter. Baglivi, *Opera*, p. 106.

[84] Ibid., p. 1.

[85] That is, it is not subalternated, a relationship we met in connection with medieval disciplines. Ibid., p. 9.

[86] Baglivi quotes Bacon as saying '*Postquam homines de veritate invenienda semel desperaverint, omnino omnia fiunt languidiora, ex quo fit ut deflectant potius ad amaenas disputationes, et rerum quasdam peragrationes, quam in severitate inquisitionis se sustineant.*' Ibid., p. 5.

doctors are therefore like spiders spinning webs from undigested thought, and Baglivi, like Kyper before him, argued that the learned doctor makes a bad practitioner. Too many different opinions drive a man mad or into Pyrrhonism (that is, late seventeenth-century philosophical scepticism).

Like other doctors who sought to bring order into a troubled medical world, Baglivi sketched out a little history of medicine, to show how things had gone wrong and to indicate how they might be put right.[87] It was appropriate for him (given his conception of aphorisms) to show that Greek medicine was good in practice despite the garrulity of the Greeks in theory. Left 'without light or leader' at the end of the Roman period, medicine was taken up and distorted by the Arabs, who made it disputatious, like quarrelsome children. From them medicine was received by the Latins like a wrecked ship creeping into harbour, and was slowly repaired by men like Fuchs (the *Institutes*) and Fernel. The heroes of the salvage operation were otherwise largely Italian, like most of Baglivi's heroes. But no sooner had some purity been restored to medical practice than new storms arose. The first was that of the chemists, whose three fundamental principles (salt, sulphur and mercury) did not allow for the proper constructions of histories of disease. Similarly bad for practice were the new philosophies: the Cartesian, atomistic, mechanical and physico-mechanical. Baglivi has reached the point where he entered the story, and he recalls again the troubled period of his youth, when for twenty-five years, unsupported by wildly different and highly philosophical theory, medical practice had nothing solid to rest on.[88] Even while writing, Baglivi saw that the principles of medical practice were wholly disturbed and that even the most skilled of practitioners disagreed and were uncertain. His rhetoric flows fast round the inane axioms, false generalities, diverse sects and preposterous rules of method, and we can see how his circumstances drove him to concentrate on practice and to a method that was both Baconian and Hippocratic.

The Newtonian Instauration

While the attraction of Bacon's work was that it presented a method of discovery in place of the 'system' of Aristotle, the case of Newton was

---

[87] It is notable that separate histories of medicine (and anatomy) begin to appear in the late seventeenth century, perhaps to give support to a tradition under attack. Baglivi's editor noted from Daniel le Clerc's history of medicine how far the chemical philosophy had 'infected' educated minds. Le Clerc's (1652–1728) history was published in 1696. See John C. Burnham, *How the Idea of Profession Changed the Writing of Medical History*, London (Wellcome Institute for the History of Medicine), 1998, p. ix.

[88] Baglivi, *Opera*, p. 77.

different. His authority was unquestionable: he was a 'stupendiously Great Man'.[89] He famously declared that he was not concerned with hypotheses – *hypotheses non fingo* – which was his own rejection of the causal systems of the past. The point was that he described the regularities of nature, nature's 'laws', without seeking causal explanations. In practice, however, his work became a new system, depending on Newton's name as an authority.[90] It was an opportunity for medical men to grasp a natural philosophy again to give strength to their theory and practice of medicine. The opportunity was taken first by Archibald Pitcairne (1652–1713) who had pupils and followers at Edinburgh, Leiden and Oxford. This group constructed a medical theory, which they called 'the principles of mathematical theoretical medicine', which they considered analogous to Newton's own work.[91] It was derived partly from the atomism of Newton's essay on the nature of acids and partly from the queries added to the 1706 edition of the *Opticks*. By the time the *Opticks* was revised again in 1717–18 Newton had begun also to think in terms of subtle fluids or 'ether',[92] and his medical followers had a wide range of explanations for physiological changes. They were even able to think, once more, in terms of attraction (between the Newtonian atoms) and subtleties, both of which had been strenuously denied by earlier mechanists.[93] Newtonian doctors agreed on some of the principles on which the theory of medicine was now built, but it is unlikely that they shared a complete understanding of all of Newton's philosophy, particularly its mathematical aspects. There is good evidence that one of the attractions of Newtonianism in medicine was that it gave the doctors authority in their efforts to form themselves into a professional body.[94]

Perhaps the main intellectual attraction of Newton's work was that it offered the certainty of mathematics. We can recall that earlier in the century the collapse of traditional natural philosophy had made some doctors declare that 'demonstration' had a place only in mathematics; what the Newtonian George Cheyne now proposed to do was to restore mathematical certainty to medicine. Writing on fevers he pointed out the sorry state of medicine as a *scientia* and proposed to reform it. The body was made,

---

[89] The description is that of George Cheyne: see Anita Guerrini, 'Isaac Newton, George Cheyne and the "Principia Medicinae" ', in French and Wear, eds., *Medical Revolution*, pp. 222–45, at p. 228.

[90] On the relationship between natural philosophy, religion and society, see also M. C. Jacob, *The Newtonians and the English Revolution, 1689–1720*, Hassocks, Sussex (Harvester Press), 1976.

[91] Guerrini, 'Isaac Newton', p. 222.

[92] See in general G. Cantor and J. Hodge, eds., *Conceptions of Ether: Studies in the History of Ether Theories, 1740–1900*, Cambridge (Cambridge University Press), 1981.

[93] However, Pitcairne and Cheyne were hesitant about attraction.

[94] Guerrini, 'Isaac Newton', p. 223.

after all, of fluids and vessels, all of which were quantifiable and amenable to physical and geometrical analysis. The steps to a reformed *Principia* of medicine included a more thorough knowledge of anatomy (the survivor of the old theory of medicine) and complete mechanical philosophy.

Another Scottish member of the circle of Newtonians centred on Pitcairne was John Keill (1671–1721), who had secured the post of deputy to the Sedleian professor of natural philosophy at Oxford. He was a medical man and his lectures, 'an introduction to the true physics', are full of Newtonian confidence that medicine is once more equipped with a philosophy of nature.[95] The point is made with force when Keill identifies the faults of sects of philosophers who have yet to embrace Newton: in our terms the result of the collapse of natural philosophy. His 'best way of philosophising' was to take what was valuable from each sect and dismiss the rest. From the Platonists he takes arithmetic and geometry, leaving them with their numerology and diagrams to explain essences of things. The *physici* that Keill describes are the descendants of the Aristotelians and he says that to the usual peripatetic array of manifest elementary qualities – matter, form, substance and so on – they add occult qualities and sympathies. This latter pair probably represent 'whole substance' action and the effect of poisons, in a medical context. Keill can salvage little from this philosophy and supposes that its purpose was not to discover causes but to invent and impose names on things and actions. This would certainly be an adequate description of the late school Aristotelianism that survived in the English universities down to the second half of the seventeenth century.[96] It did not set out to *explore* causes but used an ancient and wordy apparatus with manifold connections with other parts of intellectual life; certainly its treatment of causes was passive in comparison to that of the new natural philosophy.

Clearly the Aristotelians were the most objectionable kind of philosopher to Keill, but he also distances himself from the experimental philosophers. In their experiments, he says, they take notice only of the properties of a body and of actions that are perceptible to the senses. Keill argues that philosophy in this way has taken only small steps. That is, he saw the restraint that scepticism had imposed upon the imaginations of the experimenters, but also believed that from the true, Newtonian viewpoint, such restraint was no longer needed. (Keill also thought that some experimenters did draw

---

[95] John Keill, *Introductio ad Veram Physicam: seu Lectiones Physicae Habitae in Schola Naturalis Philosophiae Academiae Anno Domini 1700*. I have used the third edn, Oxford, 1725. It seems likely that *physica* was preferred to *philosophia* in being less related to 'system'.

[96] For example, Daniel Stahl, *Axiomata Philosophica*, Cambridge (Rogerius Daniel), 1645 (3rd edn).

up theories, and falsified the experiments to obtain proof.) The last sect mentioned by Keill are the *mechanici*. Although the mechanical philosophy is much celebrated in this age, says Keill, there is little of true mechanics in it. Its proponents talk of invisible particles, pores, shapes, pathways and battles between acids and alkalis. This is Cartesian mechanism with a dash of chemistry, explained on a basis of particles all obeying laws of mechanics. What is wrong with this system according to Keill is that it takes no account of the quantity and proportion of physical motion or the size, shape and powers of moving bodies. These, then, are what Newton added to the common mechanism of his day. The powers of bodies included attraction, a term Keill uses with confidence, although proscribed by earlier mechanists. He does so because it was simply a description of a motion that had intension and remission, that is, it could be measured. Keill also uses 'quality' and 'faculty' (terms taken from the peripatetic sect) in the same way: gravity is a measurable quality and not a statement about causes. Keill confirms the truth of his Newtonianism with a common device, a little history about how the truth became known. The father of the discipline was Archimedes, who left a monument to geometry and provided the basis of statics and mechanics. As in most such stories, the work of the Father was lost and then recovered by the Restorers, here Roger Bacon and Cardano. Galileo's Geometrical Key showed how to look for mechanical causes. Besides more recent heroes such as Torricelli, Pascal, Boyle, Wallis, Huygens, Halley and his predecessor as Savilian professor in Oxford, Gregory, Keill drew attention to the collaborative efforts of the Royal Societies of London and Paris. Of course, *vera physica* was finally revealed by Newton.

SOLIDISM

Microanatomy and mechanics

In traditional medicine disease had been caused by disturbances in the humours and their elementary qualities, but these had no place in the new views about nature. Stepping into the space left by the collapse of traditional theory, chemical physicians also talked of liquids and their intestinal movements and fermentations. But it also proved possible to fill the same space by constructing a theory based on the solids of the body. This had a number of sources. The first was anatomy, which had not been eclipsed as a discipline in the seventeenth century and which, towards the end of the century, tended towards fine anatomy with the increasing use of the microscope. The discovery of unexpected structure below the visible level seemed to support the doctrines of particulate mechanism; it certainly destroyed Aristotle's doctrine that the similar parts were homogeneous. Machines after all were solid, and some interesting ones in the seventeenth century were made to handle fluids: water and air. Machines were also rationally designed and so were a ready analogy of the created body. A number of men began to think that the body was indeed a hydraulic machine, a notion that could be seen as having a Newtonian basis. The idea could be used to tackle a problem arising from the discovery of the circulation of the blood: many medical men took the action of the heart to be one that gave the blood projectile motion: it 'threw' the blood into the arteries. Again, in the many experiments performed to confirm the circulation, an artery opened at some distance from the heart also seemed to emit blood in a projectile way. But was this projectile force great enough to throw the blood to the very ends of the arteries? Would it not soon be lost by the friction of the tortuous vessels?

In the absence of pathological humours and of nervous spirit, attention was increasingly given to the solids of the body in explanations of how it worked and how it went wrong. After all, it was the solids of the body that controlled the fluids. A thorough-going theory of solids could satisfy the physicians' need for a natural philosophy of the body, particularly when it had a direct application to pathology and treatment, for many who felt the loss of the old theory had re-emphasised the practical nature of treatment. There was another advantage. The basic unit of the solid parts seemed to be the fibre, for example in nerves and muscles, and the nature of muscular contraction was a problem to many who did not believe Descartes' theory of inflation. But it was a motion, and it took place in delimited structures: many thought that it could be explained *geometrically*. This was clear and intelligible and it allowed into medicine the only kind of demonstration, or proof, which was still possible. And, when the new theorists came to think of it, was it not true that Hippocrates himself had categorised the parts of the body into the Contained (the fluids), the Containing (solids) and the *impetum faciens* (that which gave motion)? Hippocrates could generally be relied on to have first recognised the beginnings of any new system that later writers elaborated, but this was a seminal distinction that served also another group of physicians in the eighteenth century, as we shall see.

Earlier we looked briefly at some of the figures who attacked traditional natural philosophy, such as Cardano and Descartes, but we have not touched upon that other hero of the 'scientific revolution', Galileo. Unlike Descartes, Galileo did not have half an eye on a new medicine, but his work had an important influence on the way some doctors thought. In the terms we are using here, Galileo helped to precipitate the crisis in philosophy, but he also provided some of the materials out of which a new theory could be built. The important figure here is Giovanni Alfonso Borelli (1608–79) whose early work on fevers was a sort of manifesto for the mechanist cause. Like Galileo he was a mathematician, and his best-known work (published after his death) sets out in geometrical form the gross mechanics of the motion of animals. Borelli's system was not totally mechanical (he believed in an essentially vital sentience in the beating heart)[97] but we are reminded again of the general awareness of the power of demonstration that geometry possessed in a post-Aristotelian intellectual world.

One of Borelli's students was Marcello Malpighi (1628–94), who developed a mechanical programme within microanatomy. One of the principal advantages of this was that it provided an explanation of glandular activity, namely secretion. There was a comparatively small group of men working on related areas, largely concerned with fibres: Nicholaus Steno on muscles, Bellini following Malpighi and, later, Giovanni Santorini, who broadly agreed that geometry and the level of the microscopic solid parts could explain the motions of the body.[98] In this respect it was a medical business, and these men might be seen as attempting to build a new medical theory. But it was, more directly, natural philosophy rather than medicine. Malpighi's microanatomy was clearly philosophical too in being extended to animals and plants.[99] Just as Riolan had complained that Harvey's doctrine of circulation was of no medical use whatsoever, so Giovanni Sbaraglia, Malpighi's opponent, argued that microanatomy and mechanism were irrelevant to the practice of medicine.[100] At best, he said, the new discoveries were philosophical, not medical; and probably *function* was not dictated by microstructure. Sbaraglia was in a powerful position in Bologna, teaching Galenic medicine, a member of the college and the holder of a chair of anatomy, options not open to Malpighi. Historians have not noticed

[97] See Roger French, 'Sauvages, Whytt and the motion of the heart: aspects of 18th century animism', *Clio Medica*, 7 (1972) 35–54.

[98] The notion of geometrical demonstration was strong in these authors. Steno argued that he was doing for muscles what astronomers did for the heavens, geographers for the earth and optical writers for the eyes. See *Steno on Muscles* [*Transactions of the American Philosophical Society*, 84, Part 1], Philadelphia (The American Philosophical Society), 1994. This is a collection of facsimile materials with translations. In building a system and impressing a patron (as Steno was doing) technical terminology was as important as it had been in the Middle Ages. Steno says that the geometry of muscles is . . . *ut mediae carnes parallelepipedum constituant, tendines vero oppositi duo prismata tetragona componant* (p. 94).

[99] See Domenico Bertoloni Meli, 'The new anatomy of Marcello Malpighi', in Bertoloni Meli, ed., *Marcello Malpighi*, pp. 23–62.

[100] See Marta Cavazza, 'The uselessness of anatomy: Mini and Sbaraglia versus Malpighi', in Bertoloni Meli, ed., *Marcello Malpighi*, pp. 120–45.

him until recently because (like Primrose in Harvey's case) he was in the shadow of an innovator. The neoterics themselves, like the Hellenists of the fifteenth and sixteenth centuries, formed a self-supporting minority clique, but, outside their rhetoric, we can see that the bulk of physicians were conservative, well enough satisfied with traditional medicine. Not even the neoterics could assume that there was anyone in Spain or Portugal who agreed with them. In practising medicine Malpighi himself used traditional remedies that had been used for centuries before and would be for a century to come. The same may be said of Bellini, for whom evacuation remained central.[101] Even in England the university faculties continued to learn, teach and practise conventional medicine throughout the seventeenth century.[102]

In short, the Italian exercises in mechanism and microanatomy from Borelli to Santorini can be seen as a new and partly mathematical escape from the scepticism about 'systems' of the later seventeenth century. But it is important to remember that the new Galilean philosophers were in a minority and were made to feel it. Borelli's influence was felt in the Accademia del Cimento, where, however, the superior academic power of the Galenists and Aristotelians emerged by 1670.[103] The majority was not silent, and Michele Lipari's *Triumph of the Galenists* helped to drive Malpighi back to Bologna from Messina.[104] The new philosophers claimed the principle of 'the freedom to philosophise' and called their philosophy the 'free philosophy': Malpighi uses the phrase *libera Philosophia*.[105] It was also called 'Democritean', which historians generally take to mean 'atomic'.[106] But more often it was used to invoke Democritus *physicus*, whom we met in chapter 1 as the dissecting investigator of the secrets of animals. This vision of Democritus had several advantages in the seventeenth century: Democritus was even more ancient than Aristotle, a venerable to whom veneration could still be given; what was known of his philosophy did not constitute a system and so did not attract scepticism; his dissections could be seen as anatomical experiments, which survived the crisis in philosophy and were a major item on the agenda of the new philosophers; he was traditionally

---

[101] See Anita Guerrini, 'The varieties of mechanical medicine', in Bertoloni Meli, ed., *Marcello Malpighi*, pp. 111–28, at p. 123.

[102] See Andrew Wear, 'Medical practice in late seventeenth- and early eighteenth-century England: continuity and union', in French and Wear, eds., *Medical Revolution of the Seventeenth Century*, p. 300.

[103] Susana Gómez López, 'Marcello Malpighi and Atomism', in Bertoloni Meli, ed., *Marcello Malpighi*, pp. 175–89, at p. 177.

[104] See Rosario Moscheo, 'The "Galenistarum Triumphus" by Michele Lipari (1665) : a real edition, not merely a bibliographical illusion', in Bertoloni Meli, ed., *Marcello Malpighi*, pp. 313–15.

[105] See Gómez López, 'Atomism', p. 175.

[106] See Charles Schmitt and Charles Webster, 'Harvey and M. A. Severino. A neglected medical relationship', *Bulletin of the History of Medicine*, 45 (1971) 49–75.

linked to medicine by way of the figure of Hippocrates, still the Father of Medicine; just as Hippocrates was variously mechanised or rationalised, so could the 'philosophy' of Democritus be adapted to new versions of the truth. The story of Democritus *physicus* was well known in the seventeenth century, and Thomas Bartholin, for example, refers to it approvingly in his *Anatomia* (1651)[107] and Boyle called Harvey the 'English Democritus' (clearly not a reference to atomism).[108] Walter Charleton called the College of Physicians 'Solomon's house' and its anatomically minded fellows 'sones of Democritus'; Marco Severino made the whole of his new discipline of 'zootomy' – the cutting of animals – Democritean.[109] Sometimes it was the 'wells' or 'springs' of Democritus that could now be drawn upon for new discoveries, and George Ent told Harvey that medical men wondered how it was that the circulation had been hidden in the well of Democritus.[110] When Gassendi used the same phrase for the new philosophy he may have been thinking of atoms but his main message was that Democritus' philosophy provided an escape from scepticism.[111] Above all, of course, it provided an escape from Aristotelianism, the enemies of which revelled in the legend that Aristotle had burned the books of Democritus so that his own philosophy would go unchallenged.[112]

We can turn to Baglivi again as an example of some of these trends in a solidist interpretation of the body. By the time he came to write on moving fibres he had moved to a teaching position in the school of the theory of medicine.[113] He wanted to go beyond Baconian *historia* and the aphorisms they produce to develop a theory of medicine to use in conjunction with his practice. It was to be geometrical because, essentially, God is a geometer and all created things obey the rules (and because in geometry alone do human beings have the power of demonstation).[114] And because it is geometrical it is not 'speculative' theory like those of the past, which were mere ostentations

---

[107] See Roger French, *William Harvey's Natural Philosophy*, Cambridge (Cambridge University Press), 1994, p. 168.

[108] See R. A. Hunter and I. Macalpine, 'William Harvey and Robert Boyle', *Notes and Records of the Royal Society*, 13 (1958) 114–127, at p. 118.

[109] Marcus Aurelius Severinus [Severino], *Zootomia Democritaea; id est Anatome generalis totius Animantium Opificii*, Nuremberg (Literis Endterianis), 1645.

[110] G. Ent, *Apologia pro Circulatione Sanguinis: qua respondetur Aemilio Parisano Medico Veneto*, London (Guilhelmus Hope), 1641. See the dedication to Harvey.

[111] Gassendi published anonymously, under the initials S. S.: *Discours Sceptique sur la passage du Chyle et sur le Mouvement du Coeur*, Leiden (Jean Maire), 1648, p. 148.

[112] The idea was indignantly rejected by Hermann Conring, *Introductio in Naturalem Philosophiam et Naturalium Institutionum liber 1*, Helmstadt, 1638 (thesis VII).

[113] *Specimen Quatuor Librorum de Fibra Motrice, et Morbosa.* It is included in the *Opera*.

[114] '*Qui communis salutis, Hominumque utilitatis erit cupidus; de Theorica Medicina ex Geometriae legibus judicabit*': Baglivi's preface.

of vanity.[115] He again gives his story of his youth in the schools amid such ostentations of opposed vanities. They drove him to the practice of medicine and to the writings of Hippocrates, which he claims to have committed to memory.[116] He was now impressed with the effectiveness of Hippocratic physical treatment of the solid parts – the frictions, incisions, exercises, vellications and so on. If diseases were located in the solid parts, that would explain the oriental treatment of moxibustion and acupuncture.

In the 1690s in Bologna and Rome, Baglivi began to look for signs of damage to the solid parts while performing postmortem examinations. In hospitals he met cases where head wounds had left the membranes of the brain exposed, and he knew that if they were touched tremors or convulsions followed.[117] It seemed to him that the *dura mater* as a membrane was composed of fibres that reached to all parts of the body. Indeed, he held that the *dura mater* was the controlling centre of the body, sending mechanical motions – contraction, relaxation, vibration and the like – along the fibres; such motions could, in principle, be expressed geometrically. He was geometrical in his mode of expression, introducing some experiments in a series of numbered passages called corollaries and postulates.[118] The experiments were in some sense too geometrical. Believing that the pulsation of the membranes of the brain caused the beating of the heart, he was able to quantify the force of the blood by measuring the height to which it spurted when he opened an artery.[119] Performing the experiment with two dogs, he argued that the blood emerged in its 'arc' more forcibly in the dog whose *dura mater* was simultaneously stimulated. These are experiments to prove, in some 'geometrical' way, his theory of the mechanical dominance of the *dura* and *pia mater*.

But he also did experiments of a more Baconian nature. Most of these were concerned with introducing foreign substances below the surface of the membranes surrounding the spinal cord, taken as extensions of the membranes of the brain. The point was to do many experiments, vary the injected fluids and carefully compile a list of the similarities and differences in constructing a sort of *historia*. He experimented with cats, dogs, pigs and cattle. He generalised about the results when the injected substance came into the class of acids or aromatic spirits. Spirit of wine injected into a dog made it tremble violently *sed cum hilaritate*.[120] Many other experiments

[115] 'etiamsi partes quasdam alias, et speculativas Medinae [sic] divisiones ignoret, que sunt propemodum ostentationes vanitatis, non peritiei in medendo': ibid.
[116] Hippocrates was the Oracle of Medicine, the Dux, Magister and Auspex.
[117] Baglivi, *Fibra Motrice*, p. 169.   [118] Ibid., p. 190.
[119] 'idest quantum velocitatis momentum.'   [120] Baglivi, *Fibra Motrice*, p. 183.

involved injecting substances into the veins of the animal and waiting, Bacon-like, for the 'accidents' of the experiment. Baglivi argued forcibly that there should be a great collaborative effort to make a systematic study; and to encourage others to do the experiments he spoke of the 'incredible joy' to be experienced when realising that the generalised accidents of experiments with acids included the tremors of the experimental animal, its wailings, the swelling of its stomach, its stupors, paralysis and incontinence.

CONCLUSION

We have seen that in those places where traditional natural philosophy came under attack and collapsed, the Rational and Learned Doctor lost the Good Story he could tell to patients, pupils and the law-makers. There were various solutions to the problem. He could claim a superior and practical method, untainted by systems. He could construct a new story, perhaps stressing the role of experience as superior to a theoretical system. He could defend the old philosophy. He could adopt a new philosophy. He could invoke the rationality of the Creator to avoid scepticism and bring extra piety into his medicine. He could medicalise parts of the chemical and mechanical philosophies. He could become a learned gentleman and focus upon a particular social class for his services; he could even frame his medicine in response to his patient's demands rather than working to produce suitable expectations in his patient. All went hand in hand with religious, institutional and economic changes.

As elsewhere in this book, this chapter has not sought to give a systematic account of the evolution of medicine or to give a magisterial view of the secondary literature, which so often seems to point in that direction. Examples of the strategies employed to escape the crisis are given as attempts to achieve medical 'success' in the terms set out in the Introduction.[121]

---

[121] Two modern views on the changing nature of historical studies of medicine may be usefully consulted: Ludmilla Jordanova, 'The social construction of medical knowledge', *Social History of Medicine*, 8 (1995) 361–81, and Burnham, *Idea of Profession*.

CHAPTER 8

Enlightenment, systems and science

INTRODUCTION

The scientific revolution of the seventeenth century has long been a centre of interest for historians of science. Traditionally, a major topic within it was astronomy, the ideal science on account of its being objective, intellectual, based on the senses, uncontaminated with contemporary unscientific things and pointing firmly to the future. This image – and the name 'scientific revolution' itself – are now seen to be constructions of recent historians, but the name has stuck and we are still invited to see science in the seventeenth century and celebrate its earliest exponents.[1]

But to many observers at the time, the new doctrines were a pernicious heresy spread by men who had betrayed the old traditions of learning and piety. The new doctrines were also a minority opinion, promulgated by a handful of people limited largely to two European countries, England and Holland. Elsewhere, the men with the greatest vocational need for philosophy were the physicians, whose use of it is the subject of this book. When and if they finally absorbed the new doctrines, it was not until well into the eighteenth century, which makes a European 'scientific revolution' a thing of the Enlightenment.

It is only recently that the role of medicine in these changes has begun to be appreciated. There are several things we should note. First, as we have seen, the doctors had a practical use for natural philosophy and treated it as professional knowledge. Second, medicine had, since the Middle Ages, given attention to the roles of experience and reason. Experience was not only the 'short life' of the first of the Hippocratic *Aphorisms*, it was the experimental procedure of Galen and the Renaissance anatomists such as Zerbi, Berengario, Vesalius, Colombo and Harvey. We have seen that 'anatomy' survived the crisis in theory because it was a semi-autonomous

---

[1] Removing medicine and the biological disciplines from 'science' makes it more justifiable to talk of a scientific revolution in the 'hard' sciences.

discipline based on experience which could supply medical theory but which was not an expression of an essential theory of its own. Anatomy had always been a study of action as well as morphology and it was the natural word to use for all kinds of experiments on living and dead animals by new and old philosophers. When groups of like-minded men, such as those that preceded the Royal Society, were formalised, 'anatomy' was included among their interests and purposes. It went hand-in-hand with experiment. Third, medical botany also survived the crisis, and for similar reasons: it was not theoretical, but practical, it was a useful specialism and it depended partly on sensory observation. The fourth thing we need to note about medicine and the scientific revolution was that doctors figured large in efforts to retain the old philosophy or, where this was impossible, to install a new one in its place. Physicians *needed* a philosophy.

Let us take one or two examples to illustrate these general remarks. We have seen that Aristotle represented stability in the universities of the United Provinces and it was the same in the German states for a long time. There, the universities were the centre of intellectual life and were under the control of powerful patrons. Catholic patrons had given their universities over to the Jesuits by 1622, but as in the Protestant universities, Aristotle and disputation were the tools of the educators. Altdorf was a 'progressive' university, but was rebuked by its patron as late as 1678 for departing from Aristotle. New universities such as Rinteln (founded in 1671) started their lives with Aristotle. France, too, was philosophically 'conservative' up to about 1620 and teachers did not know much of what was happening elsewhere. After the assassination of Henri IV in 1610 the Counter-Reformation climate led to the pronouncement in 1624 of the death penalty for departure from the ancient and approved authors. Reaction to the novelties of Fernel was a new Aristotelianism.[2]

In Spain and Portugal the Jesuits did much to retain the medical and philosophical status quo. The climate was Counter-Reformation: the death penalty had been introduced in Spain in 1558 for importing foreign books and the number of Spaniards going to unsuitable universities dropped dramatically (just as in Protestant England in the 1580s and 1590s there was official discouragement of travel to Catholic universities).[3] In the 1680s

---

[2] See L. W. Brockliss, 'The scientific revolution in France', in Roy Porter and Mikuláš Teich, eds., *The Scientific Revolution in National Context*, Cambridge (Cambridge University Press), 1992, pp. 55–89, at pp. 57, 59.

[3] See Harold Cook, 'Institutional structures and personal belief in the London College of Physicians', in Ole Grell and Andrew Cunningham, eds., *Religio Medici. Medicine and Religion in Seventeenth-Century England*, Aldershot (Scolar Press), 1996, pp. 91–114, at p. 96.

Juan de Cabriada was attempting to persuade the Galenists of Madrid to accept that the blood circulated. In the next century there were attempts in Portugal to depose Aristotle as The Philosopher: the agents were converted Jews who had turned to medicine and had studied abroad. Progress was slow, aided mostly by an 'enlightened' despotic government and the expulsion of the Jesuits in 1759; they were expelled from Spain eight years later, amid plans to replace Galen with Boerhaave.[4] In other words, by the time the new medicine – mechanical in its philosophy – became acceptable in the Peninsula, it was well into the Enlightenment. The new medicine involved reorganised bedside teaching, botany and anatomy theatres and it was resisted mostly by the university faculties, which perhaps resented it as a northern import; the professor of practical medicine in Padua (in 1727) complained that the northerners did not recognise earlier Italian contributions such as the microscope and thermometer.[5] In Spain the *medicina Galénica-Arábica* was still strong in 1768 and it was not until 1771 that the university of Salamanca adopted the ideas of Albrecht von Haller, Herman Boerhaave and his commentator Gerard van Swieten. It may have helped that van Swieten was Catholic, although it is also the case that many Lutherans and Calvinists resisted the new medicine. But it seems to be the case that the lack of new medical books and the Inquisition's distaste for medical works of Protestant origin helped to defend the old medicine. Lack of learned journals with book reviews also seems to have played a part. Another factor was relative prosperity. The Spanish economic decline is typified by Toledo, the population of which in 1650 was a third of what it had been in 1590, its industries undermined by cheap imports from the north; where there was greater prosperity, the new medicine was adopted more readily.[6]

The Jews were an important element in the Iberian story. They had been expelled very much earlier, but some elected to be baptised and maintain at least an outward appearance of Christianity. These *conversos* were often viewed with suspicion by the Christians, who thought that knowledge of medicine and drugs in a Jew would be dangerous; professional medical colleges drew up regulations about blood purity to exclude Jews. Yet Jews could rise to the heights of medicine, as they had in the Middle Ages:

---

[4] See David Goodman, 'The scientific revolution in Spain and Portugal', in Porter and Teich, eds., *Scientific Revolution*, pp. 158–177, at pp. 164, 172, 174.

[5] See Jonathan Israel, 'Counter-Reformation, economic decline, and the delayed impact of the medical revolution in Catholic Europe, 1550–1750', in Ole Peter Grell, Andrew Cunningham and Jon Arrizabalaga, eds., *Health Care and Poor Relief in Counter-Reformation Europe*, London (Routledge), 1999, pp. 40–55.

[6] Ibid., pp. 43, 46.

they were successful doctors. There were also more of them in relation to the size of the *converso* population; in the 1570s a local Inquisition had to seek permission to use the skilled advice of a *converso* doctor because they could not find an Old Christian physician. Perhaps Jewish physicians were successful because they were thought to have strange powers derived from their history; and, perhaps because they were numerous and successful, Old Christians avoided medicine to avoid suspicion of being Jewish. At all events, Jews were not subject to the pressures on philosophy generated by the Reformation and its reaction. Sometimes they were prevented by their elders from studying traditional philosophy until they were mature enough to resist its charms (but they were allowed to study medicine) and had no cultural need to preserve Aristotle.

Thus the attempts by *converso* physicians to introduce new philosophy and the expulsion of the Jesuits merge the 'scientific revolution' with the 'Enlightenment'. This 'age of reason' has been characterised as a period when men talked rationally about the Deity rather than promoting confessional differences. It has also been argued that it was a period in which European culture was 'de-Christianised'. In philosophy, confidence in human rationality recovered after the severe attack of Pyrrhonism of the previous century. In practice, and particularly in medicine, Newton's physics, for all its distance from 'hypotheses', became a new system. There were perhaps few medical men who fully understood Newtonian physics, which did not in any case relate as directly to medicine as traditional natural philosophy had done. Its great attraction was that it was mathematical, for mathematics always seemed to retain the promise of certain, demonstrated, knowledge.

EIRENICAL MEDICINE

Another way of dealing with the difficulties in medicine that resulted from the breakdown of traditional natural philosophy was to attempt a compromise, a synthesis of the important features of different kinds of medical theory. This too could offer a new system in the age of reason. While the Baconians thought they had a superior method in eschewing theory, not everyone wanted to go this far. There were still chairs of theory and practice in the universities, and teachers generally found that they had to give an all-round account of medicine from first principles. Teachers are necessarily rationalists, for no collection of curious observations would make a good university medical course. But what should those first principles be? As the Edinburgh medical men (see below) and authors like Baglivi pointed out, there were so many on offer, from the new elements of the chemists to species of mechanism that owed more to particles than to mechanics. One answer was to reach some sort of middle position, to emphasise what was common to all kinds of theory. It has already been noted that in troubled times a new stand could be made with the genre of medical literature called the *Institutes*. It will be instructive to look at two such constructions, those of Antoine Deidier and Herman Boerhaave.

Deidier (who died in 1746) was an adviser to the French king, a Fellow of the Royal Society of London and Regius Professor of Medicine at Montpellier, where in the previous century Riverius had attempted to halt the tide of novelty with his own Galenic *Institutiones* of 1640. This was no longer possible by the 1730s, but Didier was unwilling to leave the old authors completely, even Galen. His aim is eirenic, attempting to reconcile differences by emphasising similarities. Often he uses Galenic categories to cover chemical or mechanical explanations. It is Galenic to say that the human body is healthy, ill or neutral,[7] but the terms do not preclude being ill in an up-to-date way. The division of medicine into physiology, pathology, semiotics, hygiene and therapy is Galenic, but that does not prevent a superimposed and post-Galenic division of these five into theory and practice. Likewise the Galenic labels of the naturals, non-naturals and contra-naturals can be attached to categories more recent than Galen.

Deidier's broad strategy is to present traditional medicine as one of the alternatives available in the 1730s, when after all, Riverius' *Institutes* were still in print. Sometimes he is hesitant about ancient authority, and often is surprisingly detailed on doctrines elaborated in the Middle Ages. The two go together, for Deidier is in practice offering disputed questions, the presentation of which in the Middle Ages involved stating as fully as possible the arguments and opinions for and against the *dubium* before making a resolution. Deidier does not always come to a resolution and his *Institutes* in part takes on the nature of a review of the literature. Thus he gives a Galenic (and even pre-Galenic) account of the elements, their qualities and the complexions, and goes on to say that the new chemists[8] have radically changed things with the assumption that there are five elements – water, air, salt, sulphur and spirit. But the chemists still derive complexions in the old way from mixtures of the elements. 'Spirit' is also a term that has not wholly lost its traditional connotations, although the chemists (as Deidier

---

[7] The doctrine is found is the *Ars Parva*, the more modern title of the medieval *Tegni*.

[8] *'novatores Chymici'*. Antonius Deidier, *Institutiones Medicae Theoricae, Physiologiam et Pathologicam Complectens*, Paris (Carolus–Mauritius d'Houry), 1731, p. 3. Deidier had been professor of chemistry at Montpellier in 1697.

says) derive it from the fermentation of the blood. The chemists also had humours, separated from the blood by glands. 'They have changed only the names', says Deidier.

Moreover, the context of Deidier's presentation of these doctrines is the division of the body into solids and liquids. There is a hint of the Hippocratic contained–containing–*impetum faciens* division and a clear reference to the modern discussion of the hydraulics of the bodily machine. His proem ends characteristically: health is a [Hippocratic] balance between individual [Galenic] humours circulating [in a Harveian way] through their own [rather Newtonian] vessels. He begins the main body of the text in a characteristic way, too. The Galenic category of 'physiology' is divided into two smaller and more recent categories of humours and solids. He wants to *explain* ancient medicine by use of the modern tools of observation and anatomy. He also wants to explain what the chemists believe (but they are 'vulgar' here and he treats them with scepticism).[9]

Some of Deidier's exposition surely reflects the long tradition of medicine in Montpellier. From Arnau of Vilanova to Riverius and perhaps beyond, learned doctors in Montpellier were among the foremost of school doctors and Deidier may well be drawing from them. Discussing humours first, he makes fine distinctions which look more at home in the world of Arnau or Gentile. He has humours that nourish and others that are expelled. He has *ros* and *cambium*, terms for bodily fluids that look distinctly old fashioned for the Enlightenment. He distinguishes 'innate' from 'inflowing' spirits, concepts central to the huge discussion of complexion theory of Gentile, about four centuries earlier. Deidier is reviewing the literature, this time historically, for it was in the last century, he says, that *solertissimus* Harvey showed that it was the same blood that circulated and that separate humours could not exist in the traditional way. This made Deidier look with some favour at the chemists' assertion that the various fluids of the body, like lymph or saliva, were not carried round with the blood, but generated from it by fermentation and separated in the glands.[10] His scholastic distinctions between the seven different kinds of lymph enables him to explain the ancient separation of spermatic and sanguineous tissues of the body (which depended on their embryological origin).

Deidier's personal interpretations are at the physico-chemical level, in a framework of the solids of the body. There are no traditional spirits, for the solids control the flow of fluids, and suffocation has physical causes rather than chemical (the lack of nitrous particles of the air). Fine structure

[9] Deidier, *Institutiones*, p. 7.   [10] Ibid., p. 15.

was important for him and he subscribed to the theory that all parts of the future animal were present in the egg, even before fertilisation.[11]

The *Institutes* of Boerhaave (1669–1738) were quite different.[12] He taught at a medical school that was comparatively new, without a long tradition of teaching. He learned medicine there without even going to lectures. Instead, he began a course of self-instruction by reading through the medical authorities in chronological order. There was no reason for him to doubt that Hippocrates was the Father of Medicine, and it will come as no surprise to us that Boerhaave read in to Hippocrates all that he found best in modern medicine. Thus Hippocrates was the first 'dogmatic' physician. The term is generally interchangeable with 'rationalist', and Boerhaave attributes to Hippocrates a knowledge of what had gone on in medicine before him: the first doctors were Assyrians, Babylonians, Chaldeans and the Magi, who moved to Egypt and from there to Greece, especially its islands (and in particular, Cos, the home of Hippocrates). There, medicine developed by systematic comparison of remembered diseases and remedies, set down in tables on the walls of the temples; analogical reasoning provided prognosis. The perfection that Hippocrates brought to this medicine was in Boerhaave's view spoiled by Galen. Not only did Galen bring in Aristotelian principles but he made medicine a lucrative trade, profitable but servile. In their turn, the Arabs made it more subtle but no less damnable: for Boerhaave the history of medicine was a simple story of the Hellenists' recovery of early Greek medicine, on to which the moderns grafted scions from related disciplines of anatomy, botany and chemistry. It is among these disciplines and their practitioners that Boerhaave's *Institutes* was intended to be eirenical. He was immensely successful, teaching and influencing more medical men across Europe than anyone else. What mattered for a doctor's reputation now was whether he had sat at the feet of Boerhaave. Boerhaave's medical system represented, above all, stability in a confused world. In the words of a contemporary, Boerhaave did more services to medicine 'than all his Predecessors in the whole World put together; by digesting a huge Heap of Jargon and indigested Stuff into an intelligible, regular, and rational System'.[13] Boerhaave read his medical sources as he read the theological, holding that the purest opinions were

[11] Ibid., pp. 141, 152.

[12] Herman Boerhaave, *Institutiones Medicae in Usus Annuae Exercitationis Domesticos Digestae*, Leiden (Boutesteniana), 1727. On Boerhaave in general see G. A. Lindeboom, *Herman Boerhaave. The Man and his Work*, London (Methuen), 1968.

[13] Quoted by Andrew Cunningham, 'Medicine to calm the mind. Boerhaave's medical system, and why it was adopted in Edinburgh', in Andrew Cunningham and Roger French, eds., *The Medical Enlightenment of the Eighteenth Century*, Cambridge (Cambridge University Press), 1990, pp. 40–66, at p. 41.

the oldest and that the subsequent corruption had resulted in the medical controversies (the Heap of Jargon) of his time. His history of medicine jumps from Hippocrates to Sydenham (the 'English Hippocrates') whom Boerhaave saw as one of his own predecessors in putting matters right. Another predecessor was Boyle, whose religious eirenicism had led him to emphasise those things held in common by all Christians rather than the differences that had provoked such disastrous clashes in the seventeenth century. Boerhaave also had a high regard for Bacon, Harvey and Newton, and although neither Harvey nor Newton had much time for the views of Bacon, Boerhaave made them mutually consistent and all heirs of Hippocrates. Only by following the Father of Medicine could medical 'sectarianism'[14] be avoided; of course, hidden in the words of the Father were indications of experiments conducted in a way recognisable to the seventeenth-century mind, and suggestions of an underlying philosophy of atoms, vacuum and gravity that had finally been assembled by Newton. Hippocrates had been a mechanist and a solidist, for the body was divided into Contained and Containing. It is notable that Hippocrates had not been a chemist of the Paracelsian or Helmontian type, for Boerhaave could only extend the peace of his eirenicism to chemistry after it had been purged of its errors.

NOSOLOGY

In the rationalism of the Enlightenment not many doctors cared to claim, as the sceptics had done in the middle of the seventeenth century, that medicine was a mere empirical art. But it was clear enough to many of them that the troubled state of medical theory had had damaging effects on medical practice, and that practice had been ignored in the battles between the theorists. So it seemed to Johannes de Gorter (1689–1762), the ordinary professor at Harderwijk. Like Baglivi, de Gorter complained (in his inaugural oration of 1726) that the uncertainties of theory had not prepared him for practice. He proposed to put the matter right by a method of arranging and indexing aphorisms, ready for use in practice. This method followed two models. First, the aphorisms were to be classified in the way that botanists classified plants. Part of the botanists' interest in plants had always been medical, and knowledge of the medicinal properties of plants was a kind of medical knowledge which, like anatomy, had not been damaged by the collapse of traditional natural philosphy. The development of

[14] Cunningham, 'Boerhaave's medical system', p. 50.

botanical gardens is a well-known feature of early modern medicine (botany was one of the several chairs that Boerhaave came to hold) and by the end of the seventeenth century a great deal of thought was being given to how plants should be grouped.

The second model (again like Baglivi's) was Bacon. De Gorter suggests that the aphorisms are drawn from observation and set down without theory: this comprises a *sylva*, or nursery, and it deals with causes, effects, symptoms and indications of cure. Each aphorism is to be numbered and key words to be underlined and indexed. Alphabetic order of the index allows for additions, and the result is a series of genera of diseases subdivided into classes. Twenty-four years of experience modified de Gorter's method. It was no longer an attempt at a botanical classification of disease entities, but a mode of access in a practical way to diseases seen somewhat more traditionally as disturbed function. The ontological concept of disease was, however, taken up in several quarters. François Boissier de Sauvages (1706–67) had been (from 1722) a student of Deidier and Jean Astruc at Montpellier: Astruc was the more mechanical of the two, and Sauvages adopted a Newtonian version of mechanism. In 1730 he was in Paris, beginning to think that diseases could be categorised like plants. Boerhaave told him it would be a difficult business, but he pressed ahead with his project, which ultimately helped him to his chair at Montpellier. A new rational system was clearly a step on the career ladder.

It seems likely that treating diseases as entities and grouping them by their similarities was encouraged by the destruction of the elaborate and causal pathological theory of Galen.[15] Modern mechanism could supply various accounts of how the body worked, but it had little impact on pathology. Some doctors thought in terms of the traditional Galenic humours, some wrote of humours based on the five chemical elements and many agreed with Baglivi that diseases were seated in the solids of the body. An 'ontological' disease was one taken out of its theoretical framework and observed in a Baconian way (in Sauvages' case, from Baglivi's example). Sauvages denied that disease was 'disordered function' in Galen's terms, for that implied a context of causality that was no longer acceptable. Nor was there meaning in the Galenic categories of 'non-natural' and 'contra-natural', for all diseases are natural in being nature's attempt to rid the body of something noxious.

---

[15] Likewise the 'quiddity' or ontological status of diseases as seen by Helmontians was made possible by the removal of diseases from the Galenic theoretical apparatus (and by attributing them to the *archeus* of the body). See Andrew Wear, *Knowledge and Practice in English Medicine, 1550–1680*, Cambridge (Cambridge University Press), 2000, p. 370.

ONTOLOGY OF DISEASE

It has been a theme of this book that the doctor's perception of disease changed radically from the Middle Ages to the Enlightenment. The medieval view of disease as something that occurred in individuals and was identifiable only after long observation was changed by experience of two major epidemics. Instead, disease came to be viewed as a thing that moved indiscriminately from place to place and person to person. This did not fit in well with traditional causal medicine, and when the old theoretical system of causes disappeared physicians felt free to arrange diseases as botanists classified plants. The ultimate ontological view of disease came in the nineteenth century, and when medical scientists discovered germs, the disease was identified with the pathogen, the infective organism. This story is quite outside the range of this book, but it had a number of important effects. The doctor demonstrated more clearly than before that he could cure some diseases – he had *clinical* success. This gave him authority, including retrospective medical judgements: many early historians of medicine were doctors and they projected a modern search for pathogens upon old experiences of diseases, symptoms and so on.

Let us take an example. 'Tuberculosis' is a modern category of disease, identified by means of recognising, in a laboratory, the tubercle bacillus. It is often said that the disease was known to the Romantics and Victorians as 'consumption', which was a wasting disease that 'consumed' the body, and from which we cannot exclude other wasting diseases. It is even more difficult to identify twentieth-century tuberculosis and nineteenth-century consumption with seventeenth- and eighteenth-century scrophula, as some historians have tried to do. Scrophula existed in France and in Britain, and the surgeon to Charles II, Richard Wiseman, gave a detailed description of its symptoms, including *struma*, swellings in the neck, encysted tumours through the body, swollen lips and protruding eyes.[16] Scrophula was also known as the King's Evil because it was held to be curable, even after medicine had failed, by the touch of a king. But the king had to be of the true line, ordained and sanctified by God: indeed, touching for the Evil strengthened the position of the king and his supporters and was part of the attempts of the Old Pretender (who touched in Edinburgh in 1715) and of Prince Charles Edward (who did likewise in Aberdeen in 1745) to regain the throne. The French kings also touched for the Evil until the Revolution, and we should not be surprised that people in both countries

---

[16] Richard Wiseman, *Severall Chirurgicall Treatises*, London (R. Royston), 1676.

flocked around their kings to be touched. As we have seen in other cases, proven clinical success was, and is, not the issue.

Scrophula did not exist in Holland, where there had been no monarchs since the Dutch ejected the Spanish. Boerhaave does not deal with the disease, nor does it seem to occur in van Swieten's vast commentary on his work.[17] *Struma* is there, and some of the other symptoms of English scrophula, but they are unrelated. There was scrophula in Scotland, and when the Aberdeen Infirmary was opened in 1742 there were pressing needs to identify it. The Infirmary was a charitable institution, run on a shoestring compared with the English voluntary hospitals, and it was intended as a hospital for acute cases, to achieve a rapid turnover of patients for efficient use of funds. Scrophula was chronic and therefore excluded; but to satisfy the lay managers of the hospital, the physician or surgeon had to *write down* his diagnosis before the patient was admitted. He generally took care not to use named diseases (which were so completely described in the medical literature) and restricted himself to symptoms: but even then he often failed to recognise a scrophulous symptom or distinguish it from a scorbutic.[18] In crypto-Jacobite Aberdeen it was possible to see scrophula; when a new Leiden-trained physician was appointed to the Infirmary the disease vanished from the records.[19]

This little digression illustrates a number of points. First, it is very difficult to trace back through time the identity of a modern disease. The name changes. The description is elusive: either everyone at the time knew what it was (plague, pox) and there was no need for description, or the description was one of appearances that were significant in an etiology entirely different from our own. Second, the physician's self-justification is put to the test when he has to commit himself baldly to laymen. Just as the practice of medicine was changed by the lay and civic response to epidemics, so now the practical and improving urges of the Enlightenment dominate any Good Story the doctor could tell. Third, towards the end of the period covered in this book, hospital records, which were compiled for reasons of administration and economy, give some sort of insight into the actual clinical success of the physician.

[17] Gerardus van Swieten, *Commentaria in Hermanni Boerhaave Aphorismos de Cognoscendis et Curandis Morbis*. I have used the edition of Würzburg, 12 vols., 1787. See also the *Lexicum Medicum Renovatum*, Leiden (Lutchmans), 1735, of Steven Blankaart (Blancardus) which identifies scrophula with struma, without any other symptoms.

[18] Because the hospital had only six beds, the descriptions of the patient's conditions are unusually detailed.

[19] The records are in the unpublished *sederunt* books, the minutes of the sitting committee of management.

THE ENLIGHTENED DOCTOR

Another way to steer medicine to a new strength in the absence of traditional natural philosophy was to forget seventeenth-century scepticism about systems and construct a world-view where medicine was again intimately bound up with natural philosophy. Our example here is Friedrich Hoffmann, the primary professor of medicine at the new university of Halle. Hoffmann is quite explicit that his purpose is to build up a 'rational system' – the very thing the sceptics avoided – and that it is to be used by the *rationalis et peritus Medicus*, our Rational and Learned Doctor. The Good Story that Hoffmann's doctor tells is an entirely confident one of a natural philosophy that is now certain and stable, an ideal foundation for the theory and practice of medicine. The main reason for this certainty and stability is that the mechanism that runs the world is nothing other than the laws that God has established for matter. In a strong sense, Hoffmann has taken Boyle's route away from scepticism by declaring that no one can deny God's rationality in the world, His 'system'. Like Baglivi, Hoffmann calls himself a Christian Philosopher.

Hoffmann was born in 1660 and was well aware of the medical and philosophical problems of the late seventeenth century. By the time he was seventy-eight and had published the seventh volume of his 'rational medicine' he had created a system that proved enormously popular. He speaks of editions in Italy, Belgium, Switzerland and Germany. The six folio volumes of his collected works, printed in Geneva in a new edition between 1748 and 1753 made him an authority second only to Boerhaave. It seems very likely that this success came about because once again he gave medicine a firm basis, not only in natural philosophy but in a kind of Christianity that was acceptable in any European country. Part of his rational medicine was directed to the countries of north-west Europe, where the climate was different from that of Spain and Italy, and where the religion was Protestant; at the same time, the *Riformatori* (the Catholic censor at the *studium* in Padua) could find in his works no threat to the Catholic faith, to princes or to behaviour.[20] This was the standard formula and it indicates that the Catholic church had little objection to medical or philosophical novelty (with the exception of Cartesianism, founded on

---

[20] Friedrich Hoffmann, *Opera Omnia Physico-Medica*, vol. 1, Geneva (The Brothers de Tournes), 1748. The *Riformatori's* permissions to print (p. xix) are of the usual form. Hoffmann's 'rational and learned doctor' appears in the address to the reader, p. xvii. He has his eye on medical conditions in Denmark and Sweden: p. xxvi.

a doubt about the existence of God). What was important was stability, social and political.

Hoffmann's strategy was to develop a largely natural theology that locked as firmly into his medicine as into his natural philosophy. That this was an escape route is indicated by the title he gave to the preface to the whole of his collected works: 'The Different State and Condition of Medicine and Doctors'. He bewailed the fact that despite the dignity of medicine and the nobility of the human body, medicine was practised by the *plebs* and the vulgar. He meant, of course, people with whom he disagreed, whose learning was of the wrong kind. But much worse than wrongly learned doctors were those men, often doctors themselves, who even denied that medicine was *rational*. These were the men who held, like Albertus Kyper and Nathaniel Highmore, that medicine was simply an art and that theory means bad practice. Hoffmann, the great rational systematiser, thought that this was a monstrous calumny, and he argues energetically that no, medicine is not just a matter of labour, time and experience, and no, it is not a measure of a doctor's wisdom and skill that he has many patients. Better a doctor who can think well and straight about disease, even though he has only a few patients, than one who looks close to empiricism.[21] Hoffmann the rationalist believed that experience conformed to reason was *demonstrative*, in some sense providing certain knowledge. He makes a great deal of the principle of the Freedom of Philosophising, the greatest ornament and duty of the human mind. Nothing could be further from the scepticism of the previous century.

To escape the grandiloquent but medically useless systems of the modern chemists, Cartesians and others, Hoffmann turned to God. God as the Creator of everything was the grand reason why medicine was entirely congruent with natural philosophy. Hoffmann was also escaping from the atheists of his time and place. There was a contemporary saying that the man who went to Halle came back either a Pietist or an atheist, and quite clearly in Hoffmann's Halle there were men who openly admitted their atheism. This is arrogance of mind and blindness of heart, said Hoffmann, who believed that every person had in their heart a natural vestige of the idea of God, which ought to be developed, but which could be suppressed.

Hoffmann was also escaping from men who thought that natural philosophy, which he here calls *physica rationalis* or *experimentalis*, was mere curiosity (a charge levelled at others by scholastic theologians since the

---

[21] Hoffmann, Preface, p. xxxii.

Middle Ages). Indeed, says Hoffmann, it was precisely because nobody practised natural philosophy in the universities that misunderstandings often emerged between theologians and teachers of rational medicine. It looks rather as though Hoffmann himself had been involved in disputes with theologians and he consequently thought that theologians would be better if they modelled themselves on doctors.[22] 'Theology' was in this case simply the medicine of the soul and so had many parallels with the medicine of the body. Both could be theoretical and practical, for the theoretical theologian was one who defended his faith against others and his practice was pastoral care of the individual. In doing so, Hoffmann argued, he should take into account the variable nature of the individual and his circumstances, just as the doctor varied his practice according to the particular needs of his patient. Doctors since the Middle Ages had recognised the parallel between a general purging, the invariable first step in treatment of specific diseases, and confession, which purges the soul. Hoffmann knew of the long and sacred history of confession, but as a Protestant he also believed that it had become one of the worst abuses of the church: '... but O Immortal God! What deplorable abuse arose from it!'[23] Again like the schoolmen, Hoffmann saw that the purpose of both medicine and theology was *salus*, both 'health' and 'salvation'. He thought his own method of practice of medicine could be applied to theology, giving rules for healing the soul.[24] Both disciplines had unshakeable foundations, said Hoffmann: the basis of medicine was the wonderful order and concatenation of the parts of the body and of the world – in a word, mechanism. And the rock on which theology was built was the revealed word of God. Again, it is God who, as the Author of revealed and natural knowledge, ensured that the system is unshakeable: Hoffmann says that the system produces only *necessary* effects (which the doctor can accordingly handle). He represents theology as being like medicine in being a matter of reason and experience, where the theologian learns from symptoms about the faults in a patient's soul and applies spiritual remedies in accordance with the needs of the individual. While the physician is the servant and not master of nature, says Hoffmann (exploring another well-known theme), the theologian is the servant of God; and both kinds of practitioner may lose the patient's body or soul through lack of reason or skill.

[22] See his *Dissertatio Theologico-Medica de Officio Boni Theologi ex Idea Boni Medici* in the first volume of the collected works.
[23] *Operum Omnium Physico-Medicorum Supplementum... Pars Prima*, Geneva (The Brothers de Tournes), 1749, p. 58.
[24] *Methodum sanandi animam, Supplementum... Pars Prima*, p. 57.

Clearly then, a rational awareness of God was the basis of Hoffmann's world-view. In his work on 'the best way of philosophising' he makes the connections very plain. Philosophy is God's greatest gift to man and has the purpose of making man more perfect and rational. Hoffmann's optimism about human improvement is not an abstract principle, but is partly based on recent achievements. He held that the ancients did not know how natural things worked and could not therefore prognosticate about them. He pointed in contrast to the heights reached at this time by astronomy, 'physico-mechanical' anatomy (the actions and uses of the parts) and chemistry, all parts of the *scientia* of natural things. He agreed with his correspondent Leibniz that one piece of *physica experimentalis* was more worth reading than a hundred of the usual kinds of metaphysics, ethics or logic.[25]

The general intellectual orientation of Hoffmann's natural theology was towards the English writers: William Derham, Matthew Hall, John Ray, Edward Stillingfleet (bishop of Worcester) and Robert Boyle. More specifically he draws on authors known to him personally, such as Philipp Jakob Spener, who Hoffmann says was one of the first theologians to discuss physical things. Spener, a Pietist, had helped to set up the university of Halle, founded by Frederick III of Brandenberg-Prussia and was undoubtedly influential in the intellectual tone of the place. Hoffmann's particular friend was Christian Wolff, who arrived in Halle in 1706 and whose natural theology appealed to Hoffmann, but who aroused the opposition of the Pietists in 1721. For Pietists did not necessarily believe that a rational demonstration of God from his works was possible or desirable. Brought up on the mystical works of Jacob Boehme and Johann Arndt, Pietists believed in the presence of God within themselves and some of them behaved with a great deal more religious enthusiasm than others thought seemly; Hoffmann thought that *enthusiasmus* was the result of a physical disorder of the brain. His own theology was as distant as possible from enthusiasm. He writes in numbered paragraphs, geometry-style, with scholia and notes. He proves the existence of God *a priori* and *a posteriori*, from first principles and from effects. It is the argument from design, where the design is a set of invariant and necessary rules of motion, *mechanismus*. God is simply the perfect mechanic.[26]

---

[25] *Exercitatio de Optima Philosophandi Ratione* in his *Operum Omnium Physico-Medicorum Supplementum ... Pars Prima*, Geneva (The Brothers de Tournes), 1749, p. 4; the letters to and from Leibniz begin at p. 49.

[26] *'Deus rectissime summus et perfectissimus mechanicus.'* p. 14.

STAHL

Hoffmann's natural theology, a serene and confident product of his old age, hid what was probably the biggest intellectual battle of his life. The picture that he tried to build up of a new certain system – based on the undeniability of the Creator and the physical truths of mechanical nature, and which he hoped would be accepted as supporting medicine as closely and as widely as traditional natural philosophy – was challenged on his very doorstep. Georg Ernst Stahl (1660–1734) was a fellow teacher of medicine in Halle and a fellow Pietist, but of a very different stamp. He dismissed mechanism entirely. For him the centre of the body, and its actions in life, health and disease, was the soul. It was the direct action of the soul that turned food into blood and supplied heat and motion to the body. The soul generally acted for the good of the body and, for example, produced the symptoms of fever in ejecting noxious matter from the body. But it did not necessarily use conscious reason, and certainly not mechanism in doing these things. Indeed, it could act entirely wilfully, even choosing to leave the body. Stahl's term was not 'mechanism' but 'organism', the holistic action and reaction of the soul-and-body. For him the ordered coherence of the body was due to the soul's 'tonic motion' that behaved wisely, for example in directing the flow of blood to a part where it was needed.[27] The very enthusiasm of the Pietists led to physical disorders that Stahl clinically judged to come from the soul.

In Stahl's system there was no distinction in kind between perception, reason and emotion. Since Descartes, mechanists had tended to see the soul in terms of its two great gifts to man, immortality and reason. At its extreme, this made animals, mortal and irrational, mere machines. Mechanism also ignored actions in the human body that involved perception, seemed to be guided for the good of the body, or were not conscious: 'unconscious perception' was a nonsense to a mechanist. But for Stahl sensory perceptions turned into physical reactions and into feelings, intuition, knowledge and thought.[28]

Stahl's doctrines had considerable appeal to radical Pietists, those who tangibly felt God within themselves as both a driving force and a guide. To us they represent yet another philosophy that could flourish in the absence

---

[27] See Joanna Geyer-Kordesch, 'Georg Ernst Stahl's radical Pietist medicine and its influence on the German Enlightenment', in Cunningham and French, eds., *Medical Enlightenment*, pp. 67–87, at p. 75.
[28] Ibid., p. 77.

of traditional natural philosophy; to his contemporaries Stahl seemed retrogressive, going back to the very Aristotelianism of traditional philosophy. Certainly Stahl's body-and-soul was teleological in acting for a purpose, one that it seemed could not be read into the laws of matter and mechanics. Hoffmann was deeply antagonistic, for it seemed to him that Stahl's doctrines were extremely 'enthusiastic' and a threat to the calm tranquility of body and soul that was the goal of medicine and theology. Most of his preface to the entire collection of his printed works is given over to a rejection of Stahl's doctrine, although Stahl is not named; Hoffmann devoted a separate exercise to explaining the difference between his own system of medicine and Stahl's.[29]

ANIMISM

We have seen that in the absence of Galen's theoretical etiology and pathology some physicians gave their attention to the practice of medicine and the nature of disease. This suited what the Enlightenment saw as 'improvement', and perhaps nosology gave to medicine a new intellectualism to replace the old. With the collapse of the Galenic system some doctors also began to think of the soul and disease. It was now a single soul (unlike the two souls of Willis, for example, in the previous century) but it was not simply reason, in the Cartesian manner. Nor was it a *tabula rasa* at birth.[30] Just as Stahl's soul acted unconsciously in ejecting noxious matter from the body (and thus producing disease), so for example the nosologist de Gorter came to think that the soul acted without the knowledge of reason. In particular, glandular secretion was inexplicable in mechanical or chemical terms and relied on 'distinct laws of life'.[31] This was in the 1730s, when a number of other physicians felt obliged to withdraw from the orthodoxy of mechanism. Like Stahl, the nosologist Sauvages thought that the soul acted independently of reason in expelling noxious matter from the body,

---

[29] Stahl has received some attention from historians, and it is not the intention here to repeat what is readily available. A recent essay on Stahl is Francesco Paolo de Ceglia, *Introduzione alla Fisiologia di Georg Ernst Stahl*, Lecce (Pensa Multimedia), 1999. On Hoffmann see also Roger French, 'Sickness and the soul: Stahl, Hoffmann and Sauvages on pathology', in Cunningham and French, eds., *Medical Enlightenment*, pp. 88–110.

[30] For George Cheyne's discussion of the matter see Akihito Suzuki, 'Anti-Lockean Enlightenment? Mind and body in early eighteenth-century English medicine', in Roy Porter, ed., *Medicine in the Enlightenment*, Amsterdam (Rodopi), 1995 (The Wellcome Institute Series in the History of Medicine), pp. 336–59, at p. 344. Hobbes and Locke were regarded as materialists and even atheists by many.

[31] Johannes de Gorter, *Oratio de Animi et Corporis Consensione Mirabili*, (1730), Frankfurt and Leipzig (Johannes Fridericus Jahn), 1749.

the process constituting disease. The problem of the motion of the heart was again central, as it had been for Froidmont and other opponents of Descartes in the previous century. The heart beat was the only motion in the body that was not subject, to some extent, to the will, or in other words, it was not subject to the rational soul. Even the mechanist Borelli had to assume that some unconscious perception of the soul was involved,[32] and Sauvages constructed a thorough-going animist physiology.[33]

When Hoffmann declared that life was nothing more than a continuation of all the mechanical processes of the body, primarily the circulation of the blood, he put his finger on a cardinal point of theory. Its corollary was that the soul was, in this life, simply conscious rationality. Almost certainly this was a complexion given to mechanism by Descartes through his strict distinction between the extended body and the non-extended thinking soul. Just as many of Descartes' contemporaries thought it was impious or too radical to deny the action of the soul in, for example, making the heart beat, so in the next century some medical men began to wonder whether mechanism could in fact explain all the appearances of life. The central question that arose among such men was: given that the body was mechanical, what moved the machine? Many mechanists had traced out pathways of motion in the body, and it was the need to trace all motion from a single source that made Descartes both adopt Harvey's doctrine of the circulation and change Harvey's notion of the heart beat.[34] But some systems of mechanism derived the pulse of the heart from the brain by way of a nerve-juice, which in turn was originally moved by the heart. The mechanical absurdity of this perpetual motion was clear to many. George Cheyne said that the arrangement was a 'plain *Circulation* of *Mechanical* Powers; *ie* a *Perpetuum Mobile*' and therefore impossible.[35]

We shall meet further answers to the question 'What moves the machine?' later on, and we must here look at figures who were still formulating it. One of the earliest was John Tabor (born 1667), whose book was approved by the censors and president of the London College of Physicians in 1711. What was in his mind was the still troubling fact of conflicting theories

---

[32] Giovanni Borelli, *De Motu Animalium*. I have used the edition of Leiden (Petrus vander Aa), 1685: part 2, p. 109.

[33] For the network of animists invoked by Sauvages, see Roger French, 'Sauvages, Whytt and the motion of the heart: aspects of eighteenth-century animism', *Clio Medica*, 7 (1972) 35–54.

[34] That is, Descartes denied active contraction of the heart because it meant that the parts of the heart were attracting each other, which was unthinkable in Descartes' mechanism. See Roger French, *William Harvey's Natural Philosophy*, Cambridge (Cambridge University Press), 1994, esp. ch. 8.

[35] George Cheyne, *Philosophical Principles of Natural Religion: containing the Elements of Natural Philosophy*, London (G. Strahan), 1705.

within medicine: the Hippocratic, the chemical and the mechanical.[36] Hippocrates, as always, is an approved special case. Tabor, like the mechanists, argued that the directing parts of the body were the solids; and his notion of the intestinal motion of the liquids may be an echo of the 'fermentation' of the chemists (of whom he broadly disapproved). But the solids are moved not by an inherent or God-given force, the *vis insita* of the mechanists and Haller, but by an *animated* agent. Tabor is not systematic in this doctrine (he was concerned after all with diseases and symptoms) but it is clear that the soul and the external and divine principle, which began and above all guided motion, was Tabor's response to the perceived inadequacies of chemistry and the mechanical structures of the body, to which it was separate and superior.[37] What moves the muscles? What guides the parts of the growing embryo to their right places? His mention of gravitation, subtle matter and God's control suggests that he had found some answers in Newton.[38] By the 1730s mechanism of some kind had pretty well become an orthodoxy of a kind and the time had passed when medical men were trying to avoid the problems of the fragmentation of traditional natural philosophy. The 'animists', those eager to give a place to the soul in their medical thinking, sought to modify aspects of mechanism rather than to overthrow it (with the exception of Stahl). Indeed, both animists and mechanists often tried to find common ground in a new, confident and enlightened system of medicine.

ROSETTI

We can take as an example Josephus Thomas Rosetti, whose work was pronounced safe for Catholics by the Paduan *Riformatori* in 1733.[39] Its title announces that it is a new system – no room for scepticism here – which is at once mechanical and Hippocratic. We have seen in the endless interpretations of Hippocrates, and especially of the *Aphorisms*, that it was useful to enlist the Father of Medicine as somehow covertly using the rudiments of a new form of medicine. It showed that the new system had the dignity of age, the authority of a great name and it revealed a truer Hippocrates. But this was becoming a strategy that worked perhaps only for Hippocrates, and we are looking at a period when mechanism as a new orthodoxy was

---

[36] John Tabor, *Exercitationes Medicae, quae tam Morborum quam Symptomatum in plerisque Morbis Rationem Illustrant*, London (Guilhelmus Johannes Innys), 1724, p. xv.

[37] Ibid., pp. 5–8.   [38] Ibid., pp. 14, 36, 50.

[39] J. T. Rosetti, *Systema Novum Mechanico Hippocraticum de Morbis Fluidorum, et Solidorum, ac de singulis ipsorum Curationibus. Opus Theorico-Practicum*, Venice (A. Bortoli), 1734.

eclipsing the Galenic system of medicine. Rosetti's language reflects the new Enlightenment confidence of the period, which embraced the principle that the ancients had no automatic rights to veneration. He points with pride to modern achievements, from Columbus' discovery of a new world unknown to the ancients, to the modern anatomists, chemists and mechanists. Good God! he exclaims, think of anatomy since Harvey, chemistry after Paracelsus and physical theory after Descartes![40] Not surprisingly, given that his system is self-consciously new, he has some disagreements, especially with the chemists, but his programme is one of reconciliation, not aggression; a defence of the moderns. Like Hoffmann, he champions the principle of Freedom of Philosophising, which is compromised, he says, by too great a veneration of the ancients. In pointing to the great differences between the ancient sects of philosophers (and particularly the medical sects described by Galen) Rosetti is reversing the Renaissance desire to recapture ancient life and announcing the superiority of the modern, more uniform, orthodoxy.

Yet Rosetti's denial of the ancients is far from complete. With what looks to us like some considerable irony, Rosetti has ancient authority for both denying and accepting ancient authority. With Seneca he notes how the words of one's (ancient) teachers stay in the mind. The very superiority of modern doctrine justifies giving them the name of Athena, the goddess of wisdom.[41] 'Plato is my friend, Socrates is my friend, but truth is a greater friend' is an Enlightenment aphorism only because of the authority of Plato and Socrates. It is with Plutarch that Rosetti finds that philosophy never stops and he learns from Seneca of much ancient philosophy that was later ignored. He concludes that some of the ancients were more sagacious and had a desire to know and perfect things, a thirst for truth that has come down to us after a long interval. These *veteres cordatiores* were a special category of ancients, to whom belief could be given.[42]

In short, Rosetti is making a special plea for Hippocrates. He has a special reason for doing so, but he has to prepare the ground for it by explaining in Enlightenment terms why Hippocrates is the exception. When he denies the four elements, he destroys the whole of Galenic theory, from elementary qualities, complexions and humours to the faculties and spirits.[43] Most of his readers would have agreed. They would also have agreed that doctrines in medical theory had to be supported by experiments and observations,

[40] Ibid., p. 3.
[41] '*Et O quam decora est recens haec doctrinarum Athenas, prisca longe nobilior.*' Ibid., p. 5.
[42] Plato is the only ancient besides Hippocrates to be said by Rosetti to be in the group. Ibid., p. 3.
[43] Ibid., pp. 5, 6.

for (he says) it is a vanity to philosophise without experience.[44] He means
partly the experiments in anatomy, chemistry and mechanics that he says
have proved the principles he has selected from these areas to build up his
system, which he claims will avoid dissent.[45] And partly he means medical
experience, as in the first aphorism, where 'life is short but the art is long'.
We have seen that the first aphorism was always at the cardinal point where
theory and practice met. It was the point at which the learned doctor could
justify doing such an empirical thing as collecting observations, the point
where a doctor could argue that medicine was simply an art and not a
science, and the point where a commentator could argue that the length of
the art meant that Hippocrates had some rational system in mind. Rosetti
opens his preface by firmly locating his own 'reasons and experience' in the
context of the 'danger' of the art, which suggests that he had the aphorism
in mind (it goes on to state the danger of experiment).[46] It is in the context
of this first aphorism too that Rosetti justifies his new departure. For all the
superiority of a broadly mechanistic medicine, on its own mechanics does
not explain the appearances of life and its rules make for bad practice. The
'Mechanical Light' has not yet illuminated medicine so that the *judgement
of the art is less difficult* or the *dangerous experiment is less dangerous*.[47]

In other words, Rosetti is saying that at least where medical practice is
concerned, the programme of mechanising medicine is not complete. In
these circumstances, 'we ask the Oracle of Cos'.[48] It is not just that we first
follow the vestiges of Hippocrates before selecting our own reasons from
proven experiments, nor merely avoid dissent under the safest opinion of
the Divine Old Man,[49] but that we go to a location in Hippocrates that now
has an enormous significance for Rosetti. This is where Hippocrates says
that the body consists of Containing Parts, the Contained, and the *impetum
faciens*. There were several reasons why this was important for Rosetti and
others. The first was that it was a new way of looking at the body that avoided
the categories of the discredited system of Galen, for example the distinction
between 'similar' and 'organic' parts (they are all organic, says Rosetti).[50]
The second was that the Containing Parts could readily be seen by the
mechanists as the solids of the body – the fibres, membranes, nerves and
bones – held together by mechanical forces (Rosetti has another Hippocratic
location for this). Correspondingly, the Contained Parts were the fluids

---

[44] Ibid., preface.   [45] Ibid., p. 7.
[46] *'Experimentis itaque, et rationibus firmiter inhaerendo (saepius namque Artis pericula inspeximus) opus
hoc nostrum construere sategimus, his, inquam, tutus Morborum ditiones lustrare tandem deliberavimus.'*
Ibid., preface p. 1.
[47] Ibid., p. 6.   [48] Ibid., p. 8.   [49] Ibid., pp. 6, 7.   [50] Ibid., p. 8.

whose motions were controlled by the solids in an equally mechanical way. But by far the most attractive feature of the doctrine for Rosetti was the *impetum faciens*, that which gave motion to the whole.

It was this that made Rosetti's Hippocratico-Mechanical medicine different. The *impetum faciens* was non-mechanical and made him dissatisfied with mechanism as a total account of the living body. He called it the 'enormon' and argued that activity was its essence. He saw that in dismissing spirits from the body the mechanists had lost a source of motion. Those (such as Santorini) who denied the existence of a nervous spirit replaced it simply by geometry, and Rosetti's complaint is against those who were satisfied with a mechanico-geometrical machine. But, he claimed, neither physics nor medicine can deny the enormic *energia* of the living machine, for without it there would be no animal or vital functions. Rosetti's enormon was not the soul, but rather the soul's minister.[51] Part of its role was that of the traditional spirits, the moving power of the body in the traditional but now discredited 'seven naturals', the components of the body from the elementary qualities upwards. Rosetti sometimes calls the enormon 'spirit', having identified the quite different material spirits of the chemists and having dismissed the traditional spirits. It is the *energeticus spiritus*, or simply an *energeticum* that performs the vital functions at the bidding of the mind (or soul).[52] Sometimes he slips into more usual medical usage and uses 'spirit' to mean that which is guided by the enormon. He is not clear whether the enormon is material or not. He says it cannot be located, at least with the microscope; it has the smallest possible extension and the greatest possible activity; it is also present as 'spiritual corpuscles' which have as properties *energia* and an elastic force of expansion and contraction, all of which are essentially vital. The enormon is also present in animal bodies, Rosetti says, where it possesses simple powers of judgement that are able to decide, in the *sensus communis*, whether the impressions of perceived objects are good or evil, and to act accordingly.[53] In man this power is present but is 'mere popular feeling', a democracy subject to the soul.[54] But there can be rebellion in the democracy and the enormon can subvert natural regimen or lead flesh against the soul. Stahl is not mentioned, but Rosetti appears to use some of his doctrines, particularly when he claims that disease is not caused (as most doctors think) by insensible

---

[51] Ibid., preface. See also p. 11 where the soul, *anima*, is quite distinct.
[52] '*Itaque de facto datur in homine hoc activissimum vitalis impetum seminium, et incrementum, quod divinus Senex Enormon, seu impetum facientem nuncupavit.*' Ibid., p. 11.
[53] In animals the enormon is clearly material and mortal.
[54] Animals have *arbitrium* and *animale Judicium*. Rosetti, *Sytema Novum*, p. 11.

matter entering the body and changing it in accordance with the matter's qualities. No, diseases are caused by the enormon in ejecting noxious matter.

WHAT MOVES THE MACHINE?

Rosetti's emphasis on the *power* of the enormon can serve to introduce a problem not recognised by the early mechanists. Descartes and others had traced out *pathways* of motion in the body but had given little thought to its *quantity*. Geometers such as Santorini similarly explained, by the use of diagrams, only what *directions* could be taken within a mobile fibre. Considerations of quantity were entered into by those who followed what looked like a Harveian programme of work. A spurting of blood from a punctured ventricle of the heart showed that blood was literally being thrown out of the heart, and the Latin terms used were often variants of the verb 'to throw'. The natural apparatus to use in understanding this was ballistics, a subject of great importance in the Renaissance. As we saw with Baglivi, when an artery distant from the heart was opened, the blood also emerged forcibly, as though it had been thrown, and Baglivi used the term 'arch' to describe, and measure, the trajectory of the blood.

It appeared, then, as though blood was being thrown into the arteries and reached the capillaries by projectile motion. But, particularly in the context of Newtonian hydraulics, a number of people began to see that a projectile motion would rapidly be lost by friction through the tortuosity and subdivisions of the arteries. Attempts to determine whether the force of the heart was enough to circulate the whole mass of blood constitute a recognisable research topic of the eighteenth century. Muscular motion also became a problem.[55] The question of the loss of projectile motion through arteries became a special case of a general argument about loss of motion in machines. Those with a grasp of mathematics could calculate what proportion of motion coming into a machine was lost by friction. Machines in the eighteenth century were, of course, devices for turning one kind of motion into another: mills, pulleys, levers, screws and so on did not generate motion. It was also clear to many more men than Cheyne that perpetual motion was impossible. Yet the body moved constantly. What moved it? If motion was constantly being lost by friction, what replaced it? There was a real threat to the orthodoxy of mechanism when a number of

---

[55] So did animal heat – a problem caused by the lack of Aristotelian innate heat.

medical men began to think that it might, after all, be the soul, something so essentially alive that it *generated* motion.

There were other problems with mechanism too. How could a machine reproduce itself? How could animal machines perceive? In attempting to answer the first of these questions some mechanists suggested that all the parts of future bodies were contained in the eggs of the present.

DOCTORS AND PATIENTS

To summarise to this point there were, over the first three or four decades of the eighteenth century, a variety of new rational systems of natural philosophy available to the medical man. But simply because of their number they could not be used in the same way as traditional natural philosophy by the Learned and Rational Doctor who wanted a Good Story to tell. Galenic texts competed for market niches with the most neoteric treatises. Animists argued with Newtonian mechanists, and almost all learned doctors agreed in attacking the chemists, whom they saw as building up a new world-view based on a new set of elements. The chemists seemed arrogant and doctrinaire, producing the worst kind of 'system'. Competition among doctors made Newtonianism a useful adjunct to the doctor's learning in the traditional way. The self-proclaimed Newtonian doctors were so successful that they attracted the criticism of Bernard Mandeville in 1711: 'those Braggadocio's, who...only make use of the Name of Mathematicks to impose upon the World for lucre'.[56]

Thus, while a doctor could attempt to give some intellectual respectability to his practice and even regain his authority, he could no longer rely on an educated patient or potential student sharing his world-view. Indeed, it has been argued that the patient now took a more active role in the doctor–patient relationship and helped to decide what he was suffering from.[57] As a customer and consumer his voice had a part to play in the generation of medical knowledge. He could choose between different systems or diseases in which the doctor offered to drum up business, or 'force a trade' as Smollett put it.[58] The story is told of an apothecary who had just

[56] Quoted by Anita Guerrini, 'Newtonianism, medicine and religion', in Grell and Cunningham, eds., *Religio Medici*, pp. 293–312, at p. 296.
[57] See N. D. Jewson, 'Medical knowledge and the patronage system in eighteenth-century England', *Sociology*, 8 (1974) 369–85.
[58] Quoted from Dewhurst, *Thomas Willis's Oxford Lectures*, Oxford (Sandford Publications), 1980, p. vii.

read a learned book of 1764 on nervous diseases and realised that he had a new advantage in the medical marketplace:

Before the publication of this book, people of fashion had not the least idea that they had nerves; but a fashionable apothecary of my acquaintance, having cast his eye over the book, and having often been puzzled by the enquiries of his patients concerning the nature and causes of their complaints, derived from thence a hint, by which he cut the gordian knot – '*Madam, you are nervous*'; the solution was quite satisfactory, the term became fashionable, and spleen, vapours and hyp, were forgotten.[59]

In 'customer-led' medicine the doctor lost some of the traditional power to secure the 'obedience' of his patient. Grand patients such as kings often disregarded their physicians' advice, and French royalty frequently brought in 'quacks' (like the Englishman Talbot with his quinine wine in 1679): the court changed its doctors quickly and at a whim.[60] Popes, too, often ignored their doctors' advice[61] and it may have become fashionable for the aristocracy to do likewise.

THE NEW NATURE

In some universities, mostly Protestant (our examples are Halle and Cambridge), the crisis in philosophy was met with the construction of a new discipline, the Law of Nature and Nations. The basic doctrine was that things, and people, acted according to their natures. These natures were God-given and could be understood by the use of human reason. One of the origins of the discipline had been developed in the seventeenth century by scholars such as Hugo Grotius, who sought ways of handling the different national legal systems (demanded, for example, by commerce). An antecedent might be seen in the Roman *ius gentium*, the mechanism that kept different systems together in the empire. Roman Law too had a doctrine of natural law that held that, for example, since it was in the

---

[59] Quoted from James Adair (1786, speaking of the 1760s) in Richard A. Hunter and Ida MacAlpine, ed., *Three Hundred Years of Psychiatry, 1535–1860: A History Presented in English Texts*, London (Oxford University Press), 1963, p. 501.

[60] See Laurence Brockliss, 'The literary image of the *Médicins du roi* in the literature of the grand siècle', in Vivian Nutton, ed., *Medicine at the Courts of Europe, 1500–1837*, London (Routledge), 1990, pp. 117–54.

[61] See Richard Palmer, 'Medicine at the papal court in the sixteenth century', in Nutton, ed., *Courts*, pp. 49–78, at p. 63. But, of course, to be a papal physician was to have great status; after the death of a pope, his physician would open the body in a 'ritual which confirmed their mastery of their profession', i.e. they could demonstrate the cause of death, for instance, from a bladder stone. Palmer, 'Papal court', p. 67.

nature of birds to fly, your pigeons remained yours only while they lived in your loft. The *ius gentium* was in a sense eirenical, and the Law of Nations studied the rights and duties of man, as a rational and created being, that arose from his God-given nature. This was quite different from local law and potentially could be applied to all men. The unity of the new discipline came from the belief in God as the universal Creator. Just as Boyle, for all the scepticism of the time, could see coherence in nature because it was creation, so in the Enlightenment, with a new confident reason, they looked at man as created everywhere the same.

In some sense the Law of Nature and Nations replaced the philosophy of Aristotle in the universities. Its reasonings on the rights and duties of man had the same curricular role as moral philosophy, with the advantage that it was more pious than Aristotle's. Like Aristotle's physical works, the Law of Nature explained how the world worked. And the overall purpose of the educators was the same: to have a system that was, above all, agreed upon. The religious basis of the new discipline was apparent too in another Enlightenment use of reason, natural theology. This sought to demonstrate the existence and attributes of God in a rational way; and this too was eirenical in cutting across the confessional differences that had caused so much trouble in Christendom in the previous century. In practice, the natural-theological reading of the 'book of nature' was most prevalent in – and was valuable for – English and Dutch society.[62] Catholics treated natural theology and natural law in a different way, beginning with God and reaching to the natures of men and things.

To a certain extent the Law of Nature could, for the medical man, act as the old natural philosophy had done in lending authority to his medicine. It was still difficult to agree precisely on which principles God had decided to create the world (where once everyone had agreed they were Aristotelian). But the Law of Nature allowed one to say that the forces and structure within the body were direct creations of God. This is exemplified in Halle, the university of Hoffmann and Stahl, by the little textbook of Martin Heinrich Otto.[63] His *Elements of the Law of Nature and Nations* is the second part of a larger work on divine law, which reminds us that the whole doctrine had a cogency based on God as Creator. It is this too that binds natural philosophy to medicine. Because it was God's law that explained how the

---

[62] See Harold J. Cook, 'The new philosophies in the Low Countries', in Porter and Teich, eds., *Scientific Revolution*, pp. 115–49, at p. 140.

[63] Martin Heinrich Otto, *Elementa Iuris Naturae et Gentium una cum Declineatione Iuris Positivi Universalis*, Halle, 1738.

physical world worked, as much as it was God's law that gave man his nature, there was a *necessity* about it. Causes preceded effects and effects always followed causes. Physical or natural changes in the human body, says Otto, are those over which man has no control, those which necessarily follow from the *mechanism alone* of the body.[64] It is not just that the philosophers have taken over the terminology of the doctors (here what Hoffmann called *mechanismus*) but that they shared the belief that in a world where Newton had, without framing hypotheses, shown how God made the world, events necessarily occurred according to the physical natures of things. Otto declares that life consists of actions and motions that are produced mechanically by the structure of the parts, making use of a force that was created with all matter.[65] This, says Otto, is an inherent force, a *vis insita* of the material parts. He decides that he is going to follow those who call this mechanical structure together with its innate force 'nature', so that by 'natural law' he here means almost exactly what the 'mechanist' doctors thought in their theoretical considerations of how the body worked. We have seen that the mechanists needed an innate force to explain the motions of the body; Hoffmann agreed with Leibniz that a totally inert body could never receive motion, or even exist. In arguing against the animists and their higher-than-mechanical source of bodily motion, the great Albrecht von Haller also identified a God-given *vis insita* that needed no further explanation.[66] Almost another guarantee that the actions of the body were mechanical in this sense was 'right reason', the reason that resided naturally in man as a gift of God: Otto implies that insofar as it is ultimately divine, reason will not deceive us.[67]

Another way to avoid being deceived by different religious confessions was to look to mathematics. We have seen that after the collapse of traditional natural philosophy, demonstration was reckoned possible only in mathematics. It seemed to Christian Wolff, who was born in 1679 and who as a Protestant lived among Catholics, that religious truths could not indeed be demonstrated except by mathematics, which was universally accepted. Like Stahl, Hoffmann and Otto, he became a professor at Halle and taught mathematics, natural philosophy, natural theology and natural law.[68]

---

[64] Ibid., pp. 10–13.   [65] Ibid., pp. 92–3.

[66] Albrecht von Haller, *Ad Roberti Whyttii nuperum Scriptum Apologia*, n.p., 1764, p. 27. See also his *Elementa Physiologiae Corporis Humani*, 8 vols., Lausanne (M. M. Bousquet and Associates), 1757–66, vol. 4, p. 183.

[67] Otto, *Elementa*, p. 8.

[68] See Christian Wolff, *Jus Gentium Methodo Scientifica Pertracta*, 2 vols., Oxford (Clarendon Press), 1934.

In Cambridge they read Samuel Pufendorf,[69] who was the first to teach the Law of Nature and Nations at Heidelberg in about 1662.[70] It is worthwhile too to glance at what was being taught in Glasgow and our example is Francis Hutcheson's *Synopsis of Metaphysics*.[71] Like the Law of Nature, this is an arts-course text which informed the prospective medical student about the nature of the world and determined what kind of philosophy was available if he wished to make his medicine philosophical. Like the other new 'natural' subjects, this was a replacement for the old philosophy. Hutcheson opens his treatment by explaining how the ancient division of philosophy into physical, moral and intellectual was now inappropriate and that the modern metaphysics includes 'ontology' and 'pneumatology'. The former embraces the study of being, of existence, of causes and effects and the Law of Nature, which describes the invariable manner in which matter is moved (the Newtonians are mentioned). Pneumatology is likewise an explicit replacement of ancient doctrine, and deals with the human soul, other spirits and God.[72] The soul, as some of the animists also said, is simple (without parts), active and not extended with the body (which is, in contrast, inert and divisible). It is the soul of religion as well as of the new philosophy: it is divine and separable. It is in some sense the soul that moves the machine (for all material bodies are passive), although we cannot feel or tell how it excites the nerves to the muscles; perhaps it does so by God's original design or present intervention. Thus the new philosophy is to be more pious than that of the pagan ancient philosophers. Indeed, the third part of metaphysics is about God and opens with natural theology. It is the argument from design and Hutcheson's authorities are a remarkably consistent group of authors, found also, for example, in Hoffmann: Stillingfleet, Ray and Derham; Hutcheson also calls on Cudworth and Cheyne.[73] The Cartesian proof of the existence of God and of clear and simple ideas is indignantly rejected.[74]

---

[69] Like other new disciplines and doctrines, including those within medicine, the Law of Nature and Nations created a history for itself, and its exponents wrote texts of the 'Institutes' kind. See, for example, Samuel Pufendorf, *De Officio Hominis et Civis juxta Legem Naturalem libri duo*, London (G. Thurlbourn & J. Woodyer), 1758, ed. Thomas Johnson, Fellow of Magdalene College, which was intended for the Cambridge market. It is prefaced by a history of natural law by Johannes Franciscus Buddeus, the theologian of Jena, who establishes its ancient Fathers. Pufendorf is here concerned with 'natural law' rather than the 'law of nature'. For the latter see, for example, his *Of the Law of Nature and Nations*, trans. B. Kennet, London (R. Sare), 1717.

[70] See Basil Willey, *The Eighteenth Century Background. Studies on the Idea of Nature in the Thought of the Period*, Harmondsworth (Penguin/Chatto & Windus), 1962, p. 21.

[71] Francis Hutcheson, *Synopsis Metaphysicae, Ontologian et Pneumatologian complectens*, 4th edn, Glasgow (printed by Robert and Andrew Foulis for the university), 1756.

[72] Ibid., p. 103.   [73] Ibid., p. 201.   [74] Ibid., p. 220.

Another new 'nature' discipline was natural history. The natural historians of the sixteenth and early seventeenth centuries were for the most
part men of Reformist tendencies. It was agreed that the book of nature
could be read alongside the scriptures to discover more about God. The
anatomists who felt themselves to be standing in a theatre of creation as
well as an anatomy theatre expressed the same viewpoint as the natural
historians who sought the invisible things of God in the visible. The view
prevailed into the 'scientific revolution' and the Enlightenment, and it became a fashion to establish cabinets of specimens. The subject was akin to
medicine in a number of ways: it suffered no more elaborate theory than
God's rationality; its practice was by sensory observation of particulars,
producing 'matters of fact'; the results could be set down systematically to
produce a 'history', which had echoes of what was admirable in Aristotle's
treatment of animals and stronger connotations of Bacon's *sylva* and the
use made of his method by doctors such as Baglivi; and the collection and
cultivation of plants was directly related to medicine. Thus natural history
not only generated the cabinets of Enlightened gentlemen but also physic
gardens, for example those in the universities set up to direct the values
of the young of the United Provinces.[75] Many collectors of natural-history
items were medically qualified, and doctors sometimes set up their own
museums.[76]

Although natural history and the religious or at least edifying reasons
for practising and teaching it were not uniquely Protestant, the principles
behind it could be strikingly different in Catholic countries. While the
students at the universities of the United Provinces understood the 'nature'
group of subjects in something like the way described above, generally called
'physico-theology', it was different in Paris. Though some formal Catholic
expositions of theology do not mention nature at all,[77] we can take as an
example one of those that does address 'natural and revealed' religion, that
of L. J. Hooke.[78] It deals with the principles of the subject and, although it
was in use past the middle of the eighteenth century, it is set out in scholastic
form for the benefit of his Parisian students. It is essentially a re-emphasis of
points of doctrine of the church's learned tradition. It tackles the question
of natural theology in a manner that would have looked to Protestants to

---

[75] Cook, 'The new philosophies', p. 119.

[76] See, for example, Paula Findlen, *Possessing Nature. Museums, Collecting and Scientific Culture in Early Modern Italy*, Berkeley (University of California Press), 1994, esp. ch. 6.

[77] See, for example, Rev. Patr. Thomas, ex Charmes, *Theologia Universa*, Venice, 1757. The argument is that theology is ultimately a question of revelation, and while absolutely necessary for the church as a whole, was not necessary for the faithful individual.

[78] L. J. Hooke, *Religionis Naturalis et Revelatae Principia*, vol. 1, Venice (Johannes Baptista Pasquali), 1763.

be the wrong way round. It *begins* with God and uses reason to show how the *nature* of man should interact with God. It is from a knowledge of God and his relationship to man that this natural religion turns to the attributes of man, and from there to the 'offices' flowing by natural necessity from man to God. Hooke calls the first of these, knowledge of the *nature* of God, 'natural theology'. The second, the nature of man, is 'moral philosophy', and the third, man's duties to God, is 'natural law'. None of these terms corresponds to those used in the Dutch or English natural theology or physico-theology, for example that of William Derham.[79] Perhaps this is an attempt to give Catholic values to a new Protestant discipline. This view is encouraged by the address from a third party to the readers, who singles out (from Hooke's text) Bayle, Hobbes and Spinoza as deserving of refutation. These were the traditional 'atheists' of the new philosophy from a religious viewpoint (Boerhaave had to give up ambitions of a church career when he thought someone had accused him of being a follower of Spinoza), and indeed Hooke's substantive arguments begin with refutations of atheism. Hooke's reasons for the existence of God (the first point to be established in a scholastic disputation) include, in third place, the physical. This is the Argument from Design, and few Protestants would have disagreed with it. But they would have perhaps been surprised that it features so large in Hooke's account mainly because its opposite (that there was no design, or purpose, in nature) was said to be the common feature of all forms of atheism. Hooke says that the opposite of atheism is 'theism' – by which he means, of course, proper church doctrine – which elevates the nature of man and *holds society together*.[80] Like Protestant educators, he saw the need for uniformity of belief.

PEER GROUP REVIEW

It has been argued through this book that the university-trained doctor used his rationality and learning in the interests of professional success.[81] He was promoting an image of himself and his kind that gave him authority and helped to guide the expectations of patients and others. In the Middle Ages 'his kind' were perhaps only the other doctors of his school or immediate knowledge, while by the Renaissance there came an awareness that

---

[79] Derham (1657–1735) gave the Boyle Lectures in 1711–12, the basis of his *Physico-Theology* of 1713. It went through twelve editions in half a century and it was read by Hoffmann, perhaps in German.

[80] Hooke, *Principia*, p. 4.

[81] When criticism was made of Enlightenment doctors it was about behaviour and lifestyle, not clinical failure. See Mary Lindemann, 'The Enlightenment encountered: the German *physicus* and his world, 1750–1820', in Porter, ed., *Medicine in the Enlightenment*, pp. 181–7, at p. 185.

all Learned and Rational Doctors should behave in the same way for mutual benefit. On top of this there were individual efforts for self-promotion. A good teacher might achieve fame by the subtlety of his theory in disputations, particularly if they were written down and circulated, such as the works of Pietro d'Abano and Plusquam Commentator. But circulation was slow. It took a very long time to copy out the millions of words in Gentile da Foligno's commentary on the *Canon*. Work by his contemporaries likewise circulated to Gentile slowly, and, as we saw, he could not be certain that he knew the detail of what they were teaching. Yet the works of these three authors remained famous enough to be printed early in the sixteenth century.

Printing, of course, made a difference. In the history of printing the first works to appear were those considered important and which had a market, largely ancient works. But not long into the sixteenth century authors could see their own works published in their lifetimes.[82] This meant that an author could go into print, perhaps at his own expense, to justify or defend himself. Small tracts could be produced cheaply and quickly and distributed in a directed way: pamphlet wars became possible. By means of dedications and addresses the author could seek to ingratiate himself with a powerful figure as a patron, perhaps with a view to seeking a retained position in a great household. As we saw, Vesalius addressed the emperor and became imperial physician, and Fuchs in a similar way became a ducal doctor. The title-page was a Renaissance invention, enabling the work to be quickly identified in a growing number of books. The editor was also a Renaissance figure, justifying the published text or the particular collection of texts in an anthology. Pamphlet wars could be turned to advantage by publishers who collected together those on a particular topic and published them as a collection. We have seen how 'controversies' in the seventeenth century could be presented in this way. We saw, too, how Descartes sent out review copies of the *Discourse on Method* to test the field for the reaction to his doctrines. Publishing a book became a recognised step in a career. For example, Richard Mead and George Cheyne became famous and employable Newtonians who found employment as a result of writing on Newtonian topics.[83]

---

[82] See Jon Arrizabalaga, 'The death of a medieval text: the *Articella* and the early press', in Roger French, Jon Arrizabalaga, Andrew Cunningham and Luis García-Ballester, eds., *Medicine from the Black Death to the French Disease*, Aldershot (Ashgate), 1998, pp. 184–220, at p. 187.

[83] See Anita Guerrini, 'Isaac Newton, George Cheyne and the "Principia Medicinae"', in Roger French and Andrew Wear, eds., *The Medical Revolution of the Seventeenth Century*, Cambridge (Cambridge University Press), pp. 222–45, 230.

But sometimes it seemed that there were too many books. We noticed above that Baglivi held that a doctor should not read a book unless it was relevant to his programme *and true*. But, there was no mechanism of critically evaluating books which had been produced with a great range of motives – from ideological agenda to personal attack. Booksellers produced long lists of medical books which not even the most assiduous doctor could afford the time to read or the money to buy. From the end of the seventeenth century attempts were made to simplify the problems. There appeared histories of medicine (and of anatomy) that were in part a guide to the literature. Critical bibliographies were compiled, such as the vast collections of Albrecht von Haller. Anatomy in particular attracted the attention of biographers and bibliographers.[84] There also appeared a new form of publication, brief papers in a serial journal, edited by a professional group.[85]

Our example here is the anonymous 'Society' set up in the 1730s by serious-minded medical men in Edinburgh, where there was now a medical school to rival that of Leiden and based on the medicine of Boerhaave. They were concerned with the large number of medical books, doubly impossible for a learned doctor to cope with because each book referred back to many others. Moreover, not all potential medical authors wanted to write a whole book and what they did write did not therefore appear in booksellers' lists. The Society accordingly proposed to publish a series of volumes containing short pieces: more authors and fewer books.[86]

The important feature of the Society's plans was that each piece of writing submitted for publication was subject to scrutiny by the members of the Society in an editorial capacity. This is why they are anonymous. They called themselves 'Collectors' (that is, of the written material) and they felt that their peer-group review of submissions would be prejudiced by external influence if their names were known. They had, of course, their own agenda, a kind of medicine of which they approved. This made the intimidatingly long publishers' lists of medical books an unsatisfactory guide to the medical literature: not only were they so vast but not all the books listed were based on the repeated 'Observation of Facts' on which alone axioms can be based

---

[84] See, for example, James Douglas, *Bibliographiae Anatomicae Specimen sive Catalogus Omnium pene Auctorum qui ab Hippocrate ad Harveum* . . . , 2nd edn, Leiden (n.p.), 1734; and Andreas O. Goelicke, *Introductio in Historiam Litterarium Anatomes*, Frankfurt (J. G. Conradus), 1738.

[85] The *Journal des Sçavants*, the organ of the Academie Royale des Sciences, carried reviews of scientific books from 1665.

[86] *Medical Essays and Observations, Revised and Published by a Society in Edinburgh*, vol. 1, 2nd edn, Edinburgh, 1737, was printed by T. and W. Ruddimans for W. Monro and W. Drummond and sold by named booksellers in Edinburgh, London, Dublin, Glasgow and Amsterdam.

for medical practice. In short, their medicine was to be a branch of the natural philosophy pioneered by Boyle and others, just as we saw in the case of Hoffmann. This is why the Collectors in the first volume address Sir Hans Sloane as the president of the Royal Society, a 'glorious Example given to the World' and a model for their own Society. Like others who wished to promote a certain kind of medicine, the Collectors give a brief history of medicine, explaining its honourable origins and the reasons for its recent (but correctable) confusion. The Collectors are very clear on what we have called the fragmentation of philosophy.

As we descend nearer to our own Time, some of these difficulties are indeed gradually removed, tho' it is to be regreted, that [in] the Succession of different Philosophies prevailing in the theory, has continued other difficulties in the Practice of Medicine.

These *Medical Essays and Observations* were intended to be like the Royal Society's *Philosophical Transactions* but narrower in range and specialising in matters relating to the British Isles, where the climate and mode of life differed from those parts of Europe where most medical texts and early records emanated. The method of peer-group review was held by the Collectors to be superior to previous but similar publications, the Berlin *Acta Medica*, which the Collectors thought was simply a publisher's enterprise, and the *Acta Wratislaviensia*, which they thought too local and German. The Paris Philosophical Society, the Imperial Academy in St Petersberg, and the Academia Naturae Curiosorum in Germany get better notices for their practice of peer-group review. The Edinburgh Society also intended to promote its own kind of medicine through book reviews and medical news of the formation of new societies and the making of new discoveries.

The *Medical Essays and Observations* are indeed like the Royal Society's journal in recording observations rather than elaborating theory. Contributors whose names were printed above pathological observations or surprising cures no doubt added to their reputations, but as observational and experimental doctors, not as Newtonian philosophers. When John Stevenson wrote on the nature of animal heat he introduced his piece with an apology, justifying it only in terms of practice.[87] Indeed, the Collectors had a rigid code of conduct to be observed by their contributors. Descriptions of simple drugs had to omit *a priori* arguments, 'which are liable to lead in Error'; all experiments are to be fully described, and no ingredient to be kept secret; 'In all Questions and Disputes relating to the Animal

---

[87] *Medical Essays*, vol. 5, part II, 1744, p. 806.

Oeconomy, Theory and Practice of Medicine, we desire all personal Reflections, and offensive Terms may be shunned'; case histories are to be related without any theoretical reasoning; unsuccessful cases are to be reported (if desired, anonymously) when they contain a lesson. The language of the essays was to be plain English. Although the Collectors admitted that they would themselves make more mistakes in English than in Latin, the overall aim was intelligibility, 'which is the principal Thing in a Work of this Kind, where Elegance of Stile cannot be expected, and Wit would be hurtful'. Plain language, detailed descriptions, and absence of personal bickering and of theoretical systems is a protocol of what is now *group* medicine with clear echoes of experimental philosophy, Bacon, Hippocratic aphorisms and case-histories. Learned doctors who published in the *Medical Essays* were thus subscribing to a particular kind of medicine, and where the influence of the Society was strong, as in the Edinburgh medical school, publication could lead to advancement.[88]

HALLER AND THE SOUL

Whereas Boerhaave was the most famous medical teacher of the Enlightenment, the Swiss baron Albrecht von Haller was the greatest medical scholar. He surveyed essentially all of the medical literature then available, and published compendious bio-bibliographies of those who had written in various medical specialties.[89] He was a member of at least ten European medical and philosophical societies and president of two of them. He critically evaluated the work of others in the light of his own mechanistic orthodoxy. His huge *Elementa Physiologiae* draws out this orthodoxy from a wide range of diverse material and remains an excellent guide to the issues and personalities of Enlightenment medical controversies.[90]

Haller also experimented assiduously. We can recall that the medical experiment had had an important place in European medicine since the anatomists of the Renaissance had revived those of Galen. They were 'anatomical' experiments in the wide sense of including function, and

---

[88] For example, the reputation of Robert Whytt was founded on his publication on lime-water as a cure for the stone in the *Medical Essays* of 1743. For further biographical and bibliographical details of the animists, see Roger French, *Robert Whytt, the Soul, and Medicine*, London (Wellcome), 1969.

[89] See, for example, his *Bibliotheca Anatomica*. I have used the edition of Zurich (n.p.), 1774–7. Medical botany was dealt with in his *Bibliotheca Botanica* (see the edition of Zürich (n.p.), 1771–2). The whole bibliographical exercise was intended to be a *Bibliotheca Medica*.

[90] Albrecht von Haller, *Elementa Physiologiae Corporis Humani*, Lausanne (M. M. Bousquet and Associates), 1757: the first volume begins with the circulation of the blood, fibres and vessels, the prime interests of early eighteenth-century physiology.

anatomy and experiments survived the crisis in philosophy and provided a means of arguing in disputes such as the circulation of the blood and the nature of respiration.[91] In the eighteenth century experimenters such as Stephen Hales worked on remaining problems of bloodflow within a background of Newtonian mechanism. Part of Haller's concern was with the topic of 'sensibility and irritability', the ability of the animal machine to react to external stimuli.[92] The animists argued that both aspects of this ability – perception and motion – could result *only* from the soul, for no machine could perceive or initiate its own motion. In Edinburgh Robert Whytt, for example, showed that a frog with its head removed would still remove its foot from an unpleasant stimulus such as a prick of a needle. Clearly, this was not a rational action, for even assuming that the frog had a rational soul, it would have been in the brain. Yet it was in some sense a purposeful action that had the effect of protecting a part of the animal. Whytt assumed that purpose, sentience and motion were not at all mechanical and owed their existence to the soul, which was coextensive with the body and bound by 'laws of union' with the parts, so that it could initiate motion only in the muscles and perceive only in the nerves. This perception was necessarily unconscious, a concept unintelligible to Haller and other mechanists for whom Cartesian dualism was part of their mental furniture. Whytt showed further that the movement of the frog's leg at the prick of a needle was lost when the spinal cord was destroyed: to him, this showed that the soul in the cord had the power of organising local muscular motions in response to a stimulus in a purposeful way.

Haller disagreed with all explanations that involved the soul as more, or less, than a rational and immortal entity. He equated Whytt with the more famous Stahl, who attributed all motion to the freely acting and sometimes capricious soul. Haller defended his position with a series of experiments in which he tested the various parts of the body for their capacity to show reaction to stimuli. He had engaged in a controversy with Whytt, who argued that the ability of a muscle to contract could never be attributed to any arrangement of mere matter, and to hold that it could was an

[91] The problems of respiration and the work of Boyle, Richard Lower, John Mayow and others is a very traditional part of 'scientific revolution' history and it is not the purpose of this book to repeat the familar. An excellent introduction to these post-Harveians is Robert Frank, *Harvey and the Oxford Physiologists. A Study of Scientific Ideas*, Berkeley (University of California Press), 1980; see also Frank's 'The image of Harvey in Commonwealth and Restoration England', in Jerome J. Bylebyl, ed., *William Harvey and his Age. The Professional and Social Context of the Discovery of the Circulation*, Baltimore (The Johns Hopkins University Press), 1979, pp. 103–43.

[92] Albrecht von Haller, *A Dissertation on the Sensible and Irritable Parts of Animals*, London (J. Nourse), 1755, reprinted with an introduction by Owsei Temkin, Baltimore (The Johns Hopkins University Press), 1936.

impious materialism and mechanism. Haller replied that the 'innate force' of the contracting muscle was a direct gift of God, just as Otto had said in discussing the law of nature. This is no place to follow the later history of the animist/mechanist dispute except to say that the extreme animist position did not survive the period in which religion came to play a lesser role in philosophy and medicine. It was also generally recognised that there were, after all, limits to what machinery could achieve and that there was something special about the matter of the living body. The result was a vitalism that argued, for example, that only living bodies could produce organic compounds.

MEDICAL SCIENCE?

It has been argued in this book that the doctor's clinical success in the past has largely been invisible and that his success has to be measured on another scale. Success was distinguished patients, fame as a teacher and a fat income. Contemporaries often judged their peers in a similar way, as Melchior Adam had measured distinguished German doctors by their cultural erudition and the company they kept. Experimenters could be successful in the generation of medical knowledge, as the anatomists showed, but although practical, their success was not clinical. But towards the end of this story clinical success edges forward. The bills of mortality gave some sort of quantitative knowledge of how populations fared. When Hans Sloane and Charles Maitland inoculated six condemned prisoners in 1721 they were performing a very direct experiment.[93] It was intended to lead towards a very practical clinical success, the eradication of smallpox. When James Jurin compiled statistics of the success of inoculation he was essentially measuring the *clinical* success of a new technique,[94] the kind of success that we have so often noted generally left little evidence. He worked from individual case-histories and so established a link between the most ancient of medical experience and description (the Hippocratic) and a statistical procedure made possible by the new opportunities for rapid communication between medical men. When James Lind undertook clinical trials of remedies for ship-borne scurvy, he was perhaps making

[93] See Adrian Wilson, 'The politics of medical improvement in early Hanoverian London', in Cunningham and French, eds., *Medical Enlightenment*, pp. 4–39, at p. 27.
[94] See Andrea A. Rusnock, 'The weight of evidence and the burden of authority: case histories, medical statistics and smallpox inoculation', in Porter, ed., *Medicine in the Enlightenment*, pp. 289–315. On quantification and statistics see also Roy Porter, 'The eighteenth century', in Lawrence I. Conrad, Michael Neve, Vivian Nutton, Roy Porter and Andrew Wear, *The Western Medical Tradition, 800 BC to AD 1800*, Cambridge (Cambridge University Press), 1995, pp. 371–475, at p. 376.

experiments in a modern sense.[95] Again, the aim was a very practical one, of preventing the loss to scurvy of more men in ships of the line than were lost in battle, at a time when the British sea-borne empire was growing rapidly. The aims were to banish named diseases – smallpox and scurvy – and the experiments were not led by theory but suggested by observation.

Like a ship at sea, the hospital provided something of an experimental situation. Whereas for the Arabs hospitals existed for medical purposes (Haly Abbas recommended doctors go there for experience), we have seen that in the Western tradition of medicine hospitals were places for the exercise of charity. Certainly monastic infirmaries did their best to treat ill people and even began to call in professional doctors. But, for much of the Renaissance, hospitals were refuges for the disadvantaged. Charity supported the 'incurables' in the sixteenth century.[96] But now also hospitals were being used for teaching, for example by Zerbi and da Monte.[97] By the time of Baglivi and Boerhaave hospitals were very much places of teaching and treating, although the voluntary hospitals in Britain were still institutions of charity and improvement in the eighteenth-century manner, with medical or surgical attendants.[98] Some of them (the example of Aberdeen is given above) preferred acute cases for a rapid turnover of patient numbers and efficient use of financial resources. The patients were generally the poor, without other resources. While the doctor often deferred to his genteel patients outside the hospital, inside he not only gained status by his charitable practice but exerted a degree of authority over his patients that allowed experimentation.[99] Dealing with large numbers in clinical trials, hospitals or ships is very different from the old doctors' preferred form of retained practice, another theme of this book. But the medical man who admitted a patient to an acute hospital was responsible to the board of governors for the expenditure of designated monies and sometimes had to write down his diagnosis. In practice, he avoided naming the disease with which the medical literature was full and described instead the symptoms. Often enough he was unable to tell the difference between chronic and

95 James Lind, *Treatise on Scurvy*, ed. C. P. Stewart and Douglas Guthrie, Edinburgh (The University Press), 1953. But there is a sense in which Lind's experiments are, like Galen's, a rhetorical refutation of the opinions of others and a defence of his own; the context was prevention rather than cure.

96 See Jon Arrizabalaga, John Henderson and Roger French, *The Great Pox. The French Disease in Renaissance Europe*, New Haven (Yale Univerity Press), 1997.

97 See David E. J. Linden, 'Gabriel Zerbi's *De Cautelis Medicorum* and the tradition of medical prudence', *Bulletin of the History of Medicine*, 73 (1999) 19–37.

98 Mary E. Fissell, *Patients, Power, and the Poor in Eighteenth-Century Bristol*, Cambridge (Cambridge University Press), 1991, pp. 73–4.

99 Historians of later medicine point to French hospital medicine as a major step in the development of medicine. This cannot be part of our story here.

acute symptoms.[100] His diagnostic prowess would be judged by the ensuing *clinical* history of the patient.

Was Haller practising science? Is he an appropriate figure with whom to end a book devoted to prescientific medicine? It would take another book (and another author) to make the case for the first appearance of medical science, but there are certain external features of what he was doing that may be significant. He proceeded by experiments, which were intended to be repeatable and therefore to have potentially many witnesses (we have noted the 'jury principle' in the case of anatomical experiments). He had a thorough knowledge of the medical literature, treated it critically, prepared bibliographical guides to it and treated it historically. He read and published in journals that operated a system of peer-group review. He belonged to societies devoted to the improvement of medicine and natural philosophy. He expected that new medical understanding would be of practical, clinical use, that is, additional control of nature. He wrote in a plain style, without the elegance, wit or personal remarks that the professional bodies objected to, the style, in fact that was part of Bacon's and Baglivi's protocol for the assembling of *historiae*. It was indeed 'historical' language, the descriptive style of the Hippocratic case-histories (and of the aphorisms). It is arguable even that there is a predecessor in Aristotle's remarks on the language proper for putting together *historiae* of animals and nature, for he rejects other styles of reporting and prefers that of the Greek historians, who reported without embellishment from as close as they could get to the primary sources. Possibly 'scientific' writing has some such pedigree.

---

[100] See Roger French, 'Surgery and scrophula', in C. Lawrence, ed., *Medical Theory, Surgical Practice: Studies in the History of Surgery*, London (Routledge), 1992.

Select bibliography

Abano, Pietro d', *Conciliator Controversiarum, quae inter Philosophos et Medicos Versantur*, Venice (Heirs of L. A. Giunta), 1565.

Agnellus of Ravenna, *Lectures on Galen's De Sectis*, Buffalo N.Y. (Dept. of Classics, State University of New York at Buffalo), 1981.

Agrimi, Jole, and Chiara Crisciani, *Les Consilia Médicaux*, Turnhout, Belgium (Brepols), 1994.

Alanus de Insulis, *De Arte seu Articulis Catholice Fidei*, in *Patrologiae Cursus Completus*, ed. J. P. Migne (Latin Series), vol. 210, Paris, 1855.

Albumasar, *Introductorium in Astronomiam Albumasaris Abalachi octos continens libros partiales*, Venice (Jacobus Pentius Leucens), 1506.

Amundsen, Darrel W., *Medicine, Society and Faith in the Ancient and Medieval Worlds*, Baltimore and London (The Johns Hopkins University Press), 1996.

Arnau of Vilanova, *Opera Omnia*, Basel (C. Waldkirch), 1585.

   Arnaldi de Villanova medici acutissimi Opera nuperrime revisa, Lyons (Scipio de Gabiano), n.d.

Arrizabalaga, Jon, John Henderson and Roger French, *The Great Pox. The French Disease in Renaissance Europe*, New Haven and London (Yale University Press), 1997.

Articella, ed. F. Argilagnes, Venice (H. Liechtenstein), 1483.

Back, Jacobus de, *The Anatomical Exercises of Dr William Harvey... with the preface of Zachariah Wood... to which is added Dr James de Back, His Discourse on the heart...*, London, 1653.

Baglivi, Georgius, *Opera Omnia Medico-Practica, et Anatomica*, 15th edn, Venice, 1723.

Bates, Don, ed., *Knowledge and the Scholarly Medical Traditions*, Cambridge (Cambridge University Press), 1995.

Beagon, Mary, *Roman Nature. The Thought of Pliny the Elder*, Oxford (Clarendon Press), 1992.

Beccaria, Augusto, *I Codici de Medicine del Periodo Presalernitano*, Rome (Storia e Letteratura), 1956.

Bellarmine, Robert, *Roberti Bellarmini Politiani S.R.E. Cardinalis Solida Christianae Fidei Demonstratio*, Antwerp, 1611.

Benson, Robert L., and Giles Constable, eds., *Renaissance and Renewal in the Twelfth Century*, Oxford (Clarendon Press), 1982.

Berengario da Carpi, Jacopo, *Carpi Commentaria cum amplissimis additionibus super Anatomia Mundini una cum textu eiusdem in pristinum et verum nitorem redacto*, Bologna (Hieronymus de Benedictus), 1521.

Biller, Peter, and Joseph Ziegler, eds., *Religion and Medicine in the Middle Ages*, The University of York (York Medieval Press), 2001.

Blackwell, Constance, and Sachiko Kusukawa, eds., *Philosophy in the Sixteenth and Seventeenth Centuries. Conversations with Aristotle*, Aldershot (Ashgate), 1999.

Boerhaave, Herman, *Institutiones Medicae in Usus Annuae Exercitationis Domesticos Digestae*, Leiden (Boutesteniana), 1727.

Brain, Peter, *Galen on Bloodletting. A Study of the Origins, Development and Validity of his Opinions, with a Translation of the Three Works*, Cambridge (Cambridge University Press), 1986.

Brown, Theodore, *The Mechanical Philosophy and the "Animal Oeconomy". A Study in the Development of English Physiology in the Seventeenth and early Eighteenth Century*, New York (Arno Press), 1981.

Burnett, Charles, *Aristotle in the Middle Ages (Rencontres de Philosophie Médiévale)*, Turnhout, Belgium (Brepols), 1995.

Burnett, Charles, and Danielle Jacquart, eds., *Constantine the African and 'Alī Ibn Al-'Abbās Al-Magūsī. The Pantegni and Related Texts*, Leiden (Brill), 1994.

Buttimer, Bro. Charles Henry, ed., *Hugonis de Sancto Victore Didascalicon. De Studio Legendi*, Washington DC (The Catholic University of America), 1939.

Bylebyl, Jerome J., ed., *William Harvey and his Age. The Professional and Social Context of the Discovery of the Circulation*, Baltimore (The Johns Hopkins University Press), 1979.

Bynum, W. F., and Roy Porter, eds., *Medicine and the Five Senses*, Cambridge (Cambridge University Press), 1993.

 eds., *Companion Encyclopedia of the History of Medicine*, 2 vols., London (Routledge), 1993.

Canfora, Luciano, *The Vanished Library*, London (Vintage), 1991.

Cantor, G., and M. J. Hodge, eds., *Conceptions of Ether: Studies in the History of Ether Theories, 1740–1900*, Cambridge (Cambridge University Press), 1981.

Case, John, *Ancilla Philosophiae, seu Epitome in Octo Libris Physicorum Aristotelis*, Oxford (J. Barnesius), 1599.

Cheyne, George, *Philosophical Principles of Natural Religion: Containing the Elements of Natural Philosophy*, London (George Strahan), 1705.

Clark, Sir George, *A History of the Royal College of Physicians of London*, vol. 1, Oxford (Clarendon Press), 1964.

Collenuccio, Pandolfo, *Pliniana Defensio Pandulfi Collennucii Pisaurensis Iuri-consulti adversus Nicolai Leoniceni Accusationem*, Ferrara (Andreas Belfortis), 1493.

Conrad, Lawrence I., and Dominik Wujastyk, eds., *Contagion. Perspectives from Pre-Modern Societies*, Aldershot (Ashgate), 2000.

Conrad, Lawrence I., Michael Neve, Vivian Nutton, Roy Porter and Andrew Wear, *The Western Medical Tradition, 800 BC to AD 1800*, Cambridge (Cambridge University Press), 1995.

Cook, Harold J., 'The Regulation of Medical Practice in London under the Stuarts, 1607–1704', PhD dissertation, University of Michigan, 1981.

Cornarius, Janus, ed. and trans., *Hippocratis Coi Medicorum longe Principis, Opera quae ad nos extant Omnia*, Basel, 1557.

Culpeper, Nicholas, *Galens Art of Physick*, London (Peter Cole), 1652.

Cunningham, Andrew, *The Anatomical Renaissance. The Resurrection of the Anatomical Projects of the Ancients*, Aldershot (Ashgate), 1997.

Cunningham, Andrew, and Roger French, eds., *The Medical Enlightenment of the Eighteenth Century*, Cambridge (Cambridge University Press), 1990.

Damascenus, Nicolaus, *De Plantis. Five Translations*, ed. H. J. Drossaart Lulofs and E. L. J. Poortman, Amsterdam (North-Holland), 1989.

Debus, Allen G., *The English Paracelsians*, London (Oldbourne), 1965.

　　ed., *Medicine in Seventeenth-Century England. A Symposium held at UCLA in Honor of C. D. O'Malley*, Berkeley (University of California Press), 1974.

　　The French Paracelsians. The Chemical Challenge to Medical and Scientific Tradition in Early Modern France, Cambridge (Cambridge University Press), 1991.

Deidier, Antonius, *Institutiones Medicae Theoricae, Physiologiam et Pathologicam Complectens*, Paris (Carolus-Mauritius d'Houry), 1731.

Denifle, H. and E. Chatelain, eds., *Chartularium Universitatis Parisiensis*, 4 vols., Paris (Brothers Delalain), 1889–97.

Dewhurst, Kenneth, *Dr Thomas Sydenham (1624–1689). His Life and Original Writings*, Berkeley (University of California Press), 1966.

　　Thomas Willis's Oxford Lectures, Oxford (Sandford Publications), 1980.

Douglas, James, *Bibliographiae Anatomicae Specimen sive Catalogus Omnium pene Auctorum qui ab Hippocrate ad Harveum . . .*, 2nd edn, Leiden, 1734.

Edelstein, Ludwig, *Ancient Medicine*, Baltimore (The Johns Hopkins University Press), 1967.

Efron, John M., *Medicine and the German Jews*, New Haven (Yale University Press), 2001.

Ent, George, *Apologia pro Circulatione Sanguinis: qua respondetur Aemilio Parisano Medico Veneto*, London (Guilhelmus Hope), 1641.

Evans, G. R., *The Language and Logic of the Bible*, Cambridge (Cambridge University Press), 1984.

Fernel, Jean, *Universa Medicina*, Geneva (P. Chouët), 1643.

Fissell, Mary E., *Patients, Power, and the Poor in Eighteenth-Century Bristol*, Cambridge (Cambridge University Press), 1991.

Frank, Robert, *Harvey and the Oxford Physiologists. A Study of Scientific Ideas*, Berkeley (University of California Press), 1980.

French, E. J., 'Adam of Buckfield and the Early Universities', PhD dissertation, University of London, 1998.

French, Roger, *Ancient Natural History: Histories of Nature*, London (Routledge), 1994.

William Harvey's Natural Philosophy, Cambridge (Cambridge University Press), 1994.

Canonical Medicine. Gentile da Foligno and Scholasticism, Leiden (Brill), 2001.

French, Roger, and Andrew Cunningham, *Before Science. The Invention of the Friars' Natural Philosophy*, Aldershot (Scolar Press), 1996.

French, Roger, and Frank Greenaway, eds., *Science in the Early Roman Empire: Pliny the Elder, his Sources and Influence*, London (Croom Helm), 1986.

French, Roger, and Andrew Wear, eds., *The Medical Revolution of the Seventeenth Century*, Cambridge (Cambridge University Press), 1989.

French, Roger, Jon Arrizabalaga, Andrew Cunningham and Luis García-Ballester, eds., *Medicine from the Black Death to the French Disease*, Aldershot (Ashgate), 1998.

Fuchs, Leonhard, *Institutionum Medicinae ad Hippocratis, Galeni, aliorumque veterum scripta recte intelligenda mire utiles libri quinque*, Lyons (J. Faure for Thomas Guerinus), 1555, Basel (Oporinus), 1583.

Paradoxorum Medicinae libri tres, Basel (Jo. Bebellius), 1535.

Galen, *Galeni Opera ex nona Iuntarum Editione*, Venice (Giunta), 1625.

Garbo, Tommaso and Dino del Garbo, *Expositio Jacobi supra Capitulum de Generatione Embrionis cum Questionibus eiusdem. Dinus supra eodem. Dinus supra librum Ypocratis de Natura Fetus*, Venice (Bonetus Locatellus for the heirs of Octavian Scot), 1518.

García-Ballester, Luis, Roger French, Jon Arrizabalaga and Andrew Cunningham, eds., *Practical Medicine from Salerno to the Black Death*, Cambridge (Cambridge University Press), 1994.

Gassendi, Pierre, *Discours Sceptique sur la passage du Chyle & sur le Mouvement du Coeur*, Leiden (J. Maire), 1648.

Geanakoplos, Deno John, *Greek Scholars in Venice*, Cambridge, Mass. (Harvard University Press), 1962.

Interaction of the 'Sibling' Byzantine and Western Cultures in the Middle Ages and Renaissance, 1300–1600, New Haven (Yale University Press), 1976.

Gentile da Foligno, *Tertius Can. Avic. cum amplissima Gentilis fulgi. expositione. Demum commentaria nuper addita videlicet Jacobi de Partibus super fen vi et xiii. Item Jo. Matthei de Gradi super fen cxxii quia Gentilis in eis defecit*. The commentaries are in two volumes, the second being *Secunda pars Gentilis super tertio Avic. cum supplementis Jacobi de Partibus parisiensis ac Joannis Matthei de Gradi mediolanensis ubi Gentilis vel breviter vel tacite pertransivit*, Venice (Heirs of O. Scotus), 1522.

Getz, Faye, *Medicine in the English Middle Ages*, Princeton (Princeton University Press), 1998.

Goelicke, Andreas O., *Introductio in Historiam Litterarium Anatomes*, Frankfurt (J. G. Conradus), 1738.

Grell, Ole, ed., *Paracelsus. The Man and his Reputation. His Ideas and their Transformation*, Leiden (Brill), 1998.

Grell, Ole, and Andrew Cunningham, eds., *Medicine and the Reformation*, London (Routledge), 1993.

eds., *Religio Medici. Medicine and Religion in Seventeenth-Century England*, Aldershot (Scolar Press), 1996.

Grell, Ole, Andrew Cunningham and Jon Arrizabalaga, *Health Care and Poor Relief in Counter-Reformation Europe*, London (Routledge), 1999.

Grmek, Mirko D., ed., *Western Medical Thought from Antiquity to the Middle Ages*, trans. A Shugaar, Cambridge, Mass. and London (Harvard University Press), 1998.

Haller, Albrecht von, *A Dissertation on the Sensible and Irritable Parts of Animals*, London (J. Nourse), 1755.

Elementa Physiologiae Corporis Humani, Lausanne (M. M. Bousquet and Associates), 1757.

Bibliotheca Anatomica, Zurich, 1774–7.

Haly Abbas, *Liber Totius Medicine Necessaria Continens*, Lyons (J. Myt), 1523.

Healy, John F., *Pliny the Elder on Science and Technology*, Oxford (Oxford University Press), 1999.

Henderson, John, *Piety and Charity in late Medieval Florence*, Oxford (Clarendon Press), 1994.

Highmore, Nathaniel, *Corporis Humani Disquisitio*, The Hague (Samuel Broun), 1651.

Hippocratis Coi Medicorum Omnium longe Principis, Opera, Basel (Cratander), 1526.

Hoffmann, Friedrich, *Opera Omnia Physico-Medica*, Geneva (Brothers de Tournes), 1748.

Operum Omnium Physico-Medicorum Supplementum...Pars Prima, Geneva (Brothers de Tournes), 1749.

Hooke, L. J., *Religionis Naturalis et Revelatae Principia*, vol. 1, Venice (Johannes Baptista Pasquali), 1763.

Horden, Peregrine, and Emilie Savage-Smith, eds., *The Year 1000. Medical Practice at the End of the First Millennium*, in *Social History of Medicine*, 13, 2000.

Hugo of Strassburg, *Compendium totius Theologicae Veritatis* (collated by Johannes de Combis), Venice, 1554.

Hunter, Richard A. and Ida MacAlpine, *Three Hundred Years of Psychiatry, 1535–1860: A History Presented in Selected English Texts*, London (Oxford University Press), 1963.

Hutcheson, Francis, *Synopsis Metaphysicae, Ontologian et Pneumatologian complectens*, 4th edn, Glasgow (printed by Robert and Andrew Foulis for the University), 1756.

Jacob, Margaret C., *The Newtonians and the English Revolution, 1689–1720*, Hassocks, Sussex (Harvester Press), 1976.

Jacobi, Klaus, ed., *Argumentationstheorie. Scholastische Forschungen zu den logischen und semantischen Regeln korrekten Folgerns*, Leiden (Brill), 1993.

Jacquart, Danielle, *La Science médicale Occidentale entre deux Renaissances (XIIe s.–XVe s.)*, Aldershot (Variorum), 1997.

Jaeger, Werner, *Aristotle. Fundamentals of the History of his Development*, 2nd edn, Oxford (Oxford University Press), 1962.

Jones, W. H. S., and E. T. Withington, eds., *Hippocrates* (vols. I–IV), London (Heinemann) and Cambridge, Mass. (Harvard University Press), 1923–31.

Jouanna, Jacques, *Hippocrates*, trans. M. B. DeBevoise, Baltimore (The Johns Hopkins University Press), 1999.

Joubert, Laurent, *Medicinae Practicae priores libri tres*, Geneva, 1572.

Keill, John, *Introductio ad Veram Physicam: seu Lectiones Physicae Habitae in Schola Naturalis Philosophiae Academiae Anno Domini 1700*, 3rd edn, Oxford, 1715.

Keynes, Geoffrey, *The Life of William Harvey*, Oxford (Clarendon Press), 1978.

Kraye, Jill, W. F. Ryan and C. B. Schmitt, eds., *Pseudo-Aristotle in the Middle Ages: the Theology and other texts*, London (Warburg Institute), 1986.

Kretzmann, Norman, Anthony Kenny and Jan Pinborg, eds., *The Cambridge History of Later Medieval Philosophy*, Cambridge (Cambridge University Press), 1990.

Kühn, C. G., *Galeni Opera Omnia*, 22 vols., Leipzig (C. Knobloch), 1821–33.

Kyper, Albertus, *Institutiones Medicae, ad Hypothesin de Circulari Sanguinis Motu compositae. Subiungitur ejusdem Transsumpta Medica, quibus continentur Medicinae Fundamenta*, Amsterdam (Johannes Janssonius), 1654.

Lasserre, François and Philippe Mudry, eds., *Formes de Pensée dans la Collection Hippocratique. Actes du IVᵉ Colloque International Hippocratique* (Lausanne, 21–26 septembre 1981), Geneva (Libraire Droz), 1983.

Lawn, Brian, *The Rise and Decline of the Scholastic 'Quaestio Disputata'*, Leiden (Brill), 1993.

Lawrence, Christopher, ed., *Medical Theory, Surgical Practice: Studies in the History of Surgery*, London (Routledge), 1992.

Leader, Damian Riehl, *A History of the University of Cambridge. Vol. 1: The University to 1546*, Cambridge (Cambridge University Press), 1988.

Leoniceno, Niccolo, *Opuscula*, Basel (A. Cratander & J. Bebellius), 1532.

Lindberg, David C., *Science in the Middle Ages*, Chicago (University of Chicago Press), 1978.

Lindeboom, G. A., *Herman Boerhaave. The Man and his Work*, London (Methuen), 1968.

Lloyd, G. E. R., ed., *Hippocratic Writings*, Harmondsworth (Pelican Classics), 1978.

Longrigg, James, *Greek Rational Medicine. Philosophy and Medicine from Alcmaeon to the Alexandrians*, London (Routledge), 1993.

Loudon, Irvine, ed., *Western Medicine. An Illustrated History*, Oxford (Oxford University Press), 1997.

MacKinney, Loren, *Early Medieval Medicine, with special reference to France and Chartres*, Baltimore (The Johns Hopkins University Press), 1937.

MacLeod, Roy, ed., *The Library of Alexandria. Centre of Learning in the Ancient World*, London and New York (I. B. Tauris), 2000.

Magirus, Johann, *Physiologiae Peripateticae*, Wittenberg (Johannes Bernerus), 1609.

Mahoney, Edward P., ed., *Philosophy and Humanism: Renaissance Essays in Honor of Paul Oskar Kristeller*, Leiden (Brill), 1976.

Maierù, Alfonso, *University Training in Medieval Europe*, Leiden (Brill), 1994.

Malagola, Carlo, ed., *Statuti delle Università e dei Collegio dello Studio Bolognese*, Bologna (N. Zanichelli), 1888.

Mardersteig, Giovanni, *The Remarkable Story of a Book made in Padua in 1477. Gentile da Foligno's commentary on Avicenna printed by Petrus Maufer*, London (Nattali & Maurice), 1967.

Martianus, Prosperus, *Magnus Hippocrates Cous Prosperi Martiani Medici Romani Notationibus Explicatus*, Padua, 1719.

May, Margaret T., *Galen on the Usefulness of the Parts of the Body*, 2 vols., Ithaca (Cornell University Press), 1968.

McVaugh, Michael, *Arnau de Vilanova Opera Medica Omnia. II Aphorismi de Gradibus*, Granada-Barcelona (University of Barcelona Press), 1975 and 1992.

  Medicine before the Plague. Practitioners and their Patients in the Crown of Aragon, 1285–1345, Cambridge (Cambridge University Press) 1993.

McVaugh, Michael and Nancy Siraisi, eds., *Renaissance Medical Learning. Evolution of a Tradition*, in *Osiris*, 2nd series, 6 (1990).

Milich, Jacob, *C Plinii Liber Secundus, de Mundi Historia cum Erudito Commentario V. Cl. Jacobi Milichii*, n.d., n.p.

Mirandola, Giovanni Pico della, *Disputationes adversus Astrologiam Divinatricem*, ed. Eugenio Garin, 2 vols., Florence (Vallechi), 1946–52.

Mornay, Philippe de, *De Veritate Religionis Christianae*, Leiden (Andreas Cloucquius), 1605.

North, J. D. and J. J. Roche, eds., *The Light of Nature: Essays in the History and Philosophy of Science Presented to A. C. Crombie*, Dordrecht (M. Nijhoff), 1985.

Nutton, Vivian, ed., *Galen on Prognosis*, Berlin (Corpus Medicorum Graecorum), 1979.

  ed., *Medicine at the Courts of Europe, 1500–1837*, London (Routledge), 1990.

O'Boyle, Cornelius, *The Art of Medicine. Medical Teaching at the University of Paris, 1250–1400*, Leiden (Brill), 1998.

O'Boyle, Cornelius, Roger French and Fernando Salmon, eds., *El Aprendizaje de la Medicina en el Mundo Medieval: las Fronteras de la Ensenanza Universitaria*, Granada, 2000 (*Dynamis*, 20, 2000).

O'Malley, Charles Donald, *Andreas Vesalius of Brussels 1514–1546*, Berkeley (University of California Press), 1964.

Otto, Martin Heinrich, *Elementa Iuris Naturae et Gentium una cum Delineatione Iuris Positivi Universalis*, Halle, 1738.

Ottosson, Per-Gunnar, *Scholastic Medicine and Philosophy. A Study of Commentaries on Galen's Tegni (c. 1300–1450)*, Uppsala (Bibliopolis), 1982.

Paniagua, Juan A, and Pedro Gil-Sotres, eds., *Arnaldi de Villanova Opera Medica Omnia. VI. 2. Commentum in quesdam Parabolas et alias Aphorismorum Series: Aphorismi Particulares, Aphorismi de Memoria, Aphorismi Extravagantes*, Barcelona (University of Barcelona Press), 1993.

Park, Katharine, *Doctors and Medicine in Early Renaissance Florence*, Princeton (Princeton University Press), 1985.

Paterson, Linda M., *The World of the Troubadours. Medieval Occitan Society, c. 1100–c. 1300*, Cambridge (Cambridge University Press), 1993.

Petrarca, Francesco, *Invective contra Medicum*, ed. P. G. Ricci, Rome (Storia e Letteratura), 1950.

Pliny the Elder, *Historia Naturalis*, 6 vols., ed. Carolus Mayhoff, Stuttgart (B. G. Teubner), 1967–70.

Popkin, Richard H., and Charles B. Schmitt, eds., *Scepticism from the Renaissance to Enlightenment*, Weisbaden (O. Harrassowitz), 1987.

Portal, M. *Histoire de l'Anatomie et de la Chirurgerie*, 6 vols., Paris (Fr. Didot), 1770.

Porter, Roy, ed., *Medicine in the Enlightenment*, Amsterdam (Rodopi), 1995 (The Wellcome Institute Series in the History of Medicine).

Porter, Roy, and Mikuláš Teich, eds., *The Scientific Revolution in National Context*, Cambridge (Cambridge University Press), 1992.

Pritchet, C. D., ed., *Iohannis Alexandrini Commentaria in Librum de Sectis Galeni*, Leiden (Brill), 1982.

Randles, W. G. L., *The Unmaking of the Medieval Christian Cosmos, 1500–1760. From Solid Heavens to Boundless Æther*, Aldershot (Ashgate), 1999.

Rashdall, Hastings, *The Universities of Europe in the Middle Ages*, ed. F. M. Powicke and A. B. Emden, 3 vols., Oxford (Oxford University Press), 1936.

Ridder-Symoens, Hilde de, ed., *A History of the University in Europe*. Vol. I: *Universities in the Middle Ages*, Cambridge (Cambridge University Press), 1992.

Riolan, Jean (the Younger), *Opuscula Anatomica Nova. Quae nunc primum in lucem prodeunt. Instauratio magna Physicae et Medicinae per Novam Doctrinam de Motu Circulatorio in Sanguinis in Corde*, London (M. Flesher), 1649.

Notationes in tractum clarissimi D. D. Petri Gassendi . . . de Circulatione Sanguinis, Paris, n.d.

Riolan, Jean (the Elder), *Opera cum Physica, tum Medica*, Frankfurt (D. Zacharias Palthenius), 1611.

Riverius, Lazarus, *Opera Medica Universa*, Geneva, 1737.

Rosetti, Josephus Thomas, *Systema Novum Mechanico Hippocraticum de Morbis Fluidorum, et Solidorum, ac de singulis ipsorum Curationibus. Opus Theorico-Practicum*, Venice (A. Bortoli), 1734.

Schellig, Conrad, *In pustulas malas Morbum quem Malum de Francia vulgus appelat . . . Salubre Consilium*, Heidelberg, 1495–6.

Schleiner, Winfried, *Medical Ethics in the Renaissance*, Washington D.C. (Georgetown University Press), 1995.

Sennert, Daniel, *Opera Omnia in tres tomos distincta: Operum Tomus I [–III]*, Paris (Societas), 1641.

Severinus, Marcus Aurelius, *Zootomia Democritaea; idest Anatome generalis totius Animantium Opificii*, Nuremberg (Literis Endterianis), 1645.

Shatzmiller, Joseph, *Jews, Medicine and Medieval Society*, Berkeley (University of California Press), 1994.

Sherrington, Sir Charles, *The Endeavour of Jean Fernel. With a List of the Editions of his Writings*, Cambridge (Cambridge University Press), 1946.

Siegel, Rudolph E., trans., *Galen on the Affected Parts*, Basel (S. Karger), 1976.

Singer, Charles, trans., *Galen on Anatomical Procedures*, London (Oxford University Press), 1956.

Siraisi, Nancy, *Taddeo Alderotti and his Pupils. Two Generations of Italian Medical Learning*, Princeton (Princeton University Press), 1981.

    Avicenna in Renaissance Italy. The Canon and Medical Teaching in Italian Universities after 1500, Princeton (Princeton University Press), 1987.

    Medieval and Early Renaissance Medicine. An Introduction to Knowledge and Practice, Chicago (University of Chicago Press), 1990.

    The Clock and the Mirror. Girolamo Cardano and Renaissance Medicine, Princeton (Princeton University Press), 1997.

    Medicine and the Italian Universities, 1250–1600, Leiden (Brill), 2001.

Skinner, Patricia, *Health and Medicine in Early Medieval Southern Italy*, Leiden (Brill), 1997.

Skinner, Quentin, and Eckhard Kessler, eds., *The Cambridge History of Renaissance Philosophy*, Cambridge (Cambridge University Press), 1988.

Smalley, B., *The Study of the Bible in the Middle Ages*, 3rd edn, Oxford (Clarendon Press), 1984.

Smith, Wesley, D., *The Hippocratic Tradition*, Ithaca and London (Cornell University Press), 1979.

Southern, R. W., *Scholastic Humanism and the Unification of Europe*, Vol. 1: *Foundations*, Oxford (Blackwell), 1995.

Spade, Paul Vincent, *Lies, Language and Logic in the Late Middle Ages*, London (Variorum Reprints), 1988.

Spencer, W. G., ed., *Celsus De Medicina*, London (Heinemann) and Cambridge, Mass. (Harvard University Press), 1971.

Spitz, Lewis W., *The Religious Renaissance of the German Humanists*, Cambridge, Mass. (Harvard University Press), 1963.

Strauss, Gerald, ed., *Pre-Reformation Germany*, New York (Macmillan), 1972.

Swan, John, *The Entire Works of Dr Thomas Sydenham, newly made English from the Originals*, London (Edward Cave), 1742.

Tabor, John, *Exercitationes Medicae, quae tam Morborum quam Symptomatum in plerisque Morbis Rationem Illustrant*, London (Guilhelmus Johannes Innys), 1724.

Taddeo Alderotti, *Thaddei Florentini Expositiones in arduum aphorismorum Ipocratis volumen. In divinum pronosticorum Ipocratis librum. In preclarum regiminis acutorum Ipocratis opus. In subtilissimum Ioannitii Isagogarum libellum*, Venice (A. Giunta), 1527.

Temkin, Owsei, *Galenism. Rise and Fall of a Medical Philosophy*, Ithaca and London (Cornell University Press), 1973.

    Hippocrates in a World of Pagans and Christians, Baltimore and London (The Johns Hopkins University Press), 1991.

Ullmann, Manfred, *Islamic Medicine*, Edinburgh (Edinburgh University Press), 1978.

Van Engen, John, ed., *Learning Institutionalized. Teaching in the Medieval University*, Notre Dame, Ind. (University of Notre Dame Press), 2000.

Vesalius, Andreas, *On the Fabric of the Human Body. A Translation of De Humani Corporis Fabrica Libri Septem. Book I. The Bones and Cartilages*, trans. William Frank Richardson and John Burd Carman, San Francisco (Norman Publishing), 1998.

Vincent of Beauvais, *Bibliotheca Mundi Speculum Quadruplex, Naturale, Doctrinale, Morale, Historiale*, 4 vols., Douai (Baltazar Bellerus), 1624.

Von Staden, Heinrich, *Herophilus. The Art of Medicine in Early Alexandria*, Cambridge (Cambridge University Press), 1989.

Vulpius, Johannes Antonius, *Opuscula Philosophica*, 3rd edn, Padua, 1744.

Watts, Sheldon, *Epidemics and History. Disease, Power and Imperialism*, New Haven (Yale University Press), 1997.

Wear, Andrew, *Knowledge and Practice in English Medicine, 1550–1680*, Cambridge (Cambridge University Press), 2000.

Wear, Andrew, Roger French and Iain Lonie, eds., *The Medical Renaissance of the Sixteenth Century*, Cambridge (Cambridge University Press), 1985.

Wear, Andrew, Johanna Geyer-Kordesch and Roger French, eds., *Doctors and Ethics: The Earlier Historical Setting of Professional Ethics*, Amsterdam (Rodopi), 1993.

Webb, Clement C. I., ed., *Ioannis Saresberiensis Episcopi Carnotensis Policrati sive de nugis curialium et vestigiis philosophorum*, 2 vols., Oxford (Clarendon Press), 1929.

Webster, Charles, *The Great Instauration. Science, Medicine and Reform 1626–1660*, London (Duckworth), 1975.

ed., *Health, Medicine and Mortality in the Sixteenth Century*, Cambridge (Cambridge University Press), 1979.

Willis, Thomas, *Pharmaceutice Rationalis sive Diatriba de Medicamentorum Operationibus in Humano Corpore*, The Hague (Arnout Leers), 1675.

Wolff, Christian, *Jus Gentium Methodo Scientifica Pertractum*, 2 vols., Oxford (Clarendon Press), 1934.

Zerbi, Gabriele de, *Liber Anathomie Corporis Humani et singulorum Membrorum illius*, Venice (B. Locatellus), 1502.

Opus perutile de Cautelis Medicorum, in *Pillularium Omnibus Medicis quam Necessarium clarissimi doctoris magistri Panthaleonis*, Lyons (Antonius Blanchard), 1528.

Ziegler, Joseph, *Medicine and Religion c. 1300. The Case of Arnau de Vilanova*, Oxford (Clarendon Press), 1998.

Index